From the myths and legends that fashioned the i
the diversity of literary performance in contemporary cities around the world,
literature and the city are inseparably entwined. The international team of
scholars in this volume offers a comprehensive, accessible survey of the literary
city, exploring the myriad cities that authors create and the genres in which cities
appear. Early chapters consider the literary legacies of historical and symbolic
cities from antiquity to the early modern period. Subsequent chapters consider
the importance of literature to the rise of the urban public sphere; the affective
experience of city life; the interplay of the urban landscape and memory; the form
of the literary city and its responsiveness to social, cultural, and technological
change; dystopian, nocturnal, pastoral, and sublime cities; cities shaped by
colonialism and postcolonialism; and the cities of economic, sexual, cultural, and
linguistic outsiders.

Kevin R. McNamara is Professor of Literature at the University of Houston–Clear
Lake. He is the author of *Urban Verbs: Arts and Discourses of American Cities*
(1996) and the editor of *The Cambridge Companion to the Literature of Los
Angeles* (2010). McNamara has published more than twenty articles primarily
on cities and urban culture in such journals as *Arizona Quarterly, Canadian
Review of American Studies, College Literature, Contemporary Literature,
Criticism, Interactions*, the *Journal of Urban History*, and *Prospects*. His work
has also been published in the *Encyclopedia of American Studies* ("The Idea of
the City"), *A Concise Companion to American Studies* ("Regionalism"), and
collections edited in the United States, Belgium, the Netherlands, and Turkey.

A complete list of books in the series is at the back of this book.

THE CAMBRIDGE
COMPANION TO

THE CITY IN LITERATURE

THE CAMBRIDGE
COMPANION TO

THE CITY IN LITERATURE

EDITED BY

KEVIN R. McNAMARA
University of Houston–Clear Lake

CAMBRIDGE
UNIVERSITY PRESS

CAMBRIDGE
UNIVERSITY PRESS

32 Avenue of the Americas, New York, NY 10013-2473, USA

Cambridge University Press is part of the University of Cambridge.

It furthers the University's mission by disseminating knowledge in the pursuit of
education, learning, and research at the highest international levels of excellence.

www.cambridge.org
Information on this title: www.cambridge.org/9781107609150

© Cambridge University Press 2014

First published 2014

Printed in the United States of America

A catalog record for this publication is available from the British Library.

Library of Congress Cataloging in Publication data
The Cambridge Companion to the City in Literature / edited by Kevin R. McNamara.
pages   cm. – (Cambridge companions to literature)
Includes bibliographical references and index.
ISBN 978-1-107-02803-6 (hardback) – ISBN 978-1-107-60915-0 (paperback)
1. Cities and towns in literature.   2. City and town life in literature.
3. Literature and society.   I. McNamara, Kevin R., 1958–
PN56.C55C36   2014
809'.93321732–dc23   2014002492

ISBN 978-1-107-02803-6 Hardback
ISBN 978-1-107-60915-0 Paperback

CONTENTS

CONTENTS

FIGURES

NOTES ON CONTRIBUTORS

ANTONIS BALASOPOULOS is Associate Professor of Comparative Literature and Cultural Studies in the Department of English Studies, University of Cyprus. He has published extensively on utopias and utopianism, political theory, Marxism, cinema, postcolonial studies, and American literature. His most recent publications have dealt with Giorgio Agamben and the concept of the state since Hegel; Plato, animality, and utopia; and Cormac McCarthy's *The Road*.

NICK BENTLEY is Senior Lecturer in English Literature at Keele University in the UK. His research interests are in post-1945 fiction and literary and cultural theory. He is author of *Radical Fictions: The English Novel in the 1950s* (2007), *Contemporary British Fiction* (2008), and *Martin Amis* (2013) and editor of *British Fiction of the 1990s* (2005). He has published journal articles and book chapters on Martin Amis, Julian Barnes, Doris Lessing, Colin MacInnes, Sam Selvon, Zadie Smith, and the representation of youth in 1950s fiction. He is currently researching youth subcultures in fiction and film.

STUART CULVER teaches English at the University of Utah. He has published widely on topics in American literature and culture, including studies of Henry James and L. Frank Baum.

LUC DE DROOGH is lecturer at University College, Ghent, Belgium. He teaches on social work, social work research and the history of social work, adult education, and community development. He has published several articles on social work (in Dutch) mainly on rights-based social work, the ethics of social work, and the history of social work. He is currently doing research on poor people's organizations and the citizenship of the poor.

CHRISTOPHE DEN TANDT teaches literatures in English and cultural theory at the Université Libre de Bruxelles. He is the author of *The Urban Sublime in American Literary Naturalism* (1998) and of articles on U.S. literature (classic realism, early twentieth-century naturalism), popular culture (music, crime fiction), and postmodernist theory. He is currently working on an essay about the theoretical groundings of contemporary realism.

JAMES R. GILES is Distinguished Professor Emeritus at Northern Illinois University, where he taught in the Department of English from 1970 to 2007. He is the author of nine books including *The Spaces of Violence* (2006), *Violence in the Contemporary American Novel* (2000), *The Naturalistic Inner-City Novel in America* (1995), and *Confronting the Horror: The Novels of Nelson Algren* (1989). He is also the co-editor, with Wanda G. Giles, of six volumes of the *Dictionary of Literary Biography*. In addition, he has published more than thirty articles or short stories in various journals. Most recently, he published essays in *The Oxford Handbook of American Literary Naturalism* (2011) and *A Companion to Twentieth-Century United States Fiction* (2010).

SETH GRAEBNER is Associate Professor of French at Washington University in Saint Louis and the author *of History's Place: Nostalgia and the City in Algerian Writing in French* (2007).

TIMOTHY GRAY is Professor of English at the College of Staten Island, City University of New York. He is the author of *Gary Snyder and the Pacific Rim: Creating Countercultural Community* (2006), *Urban Pastoral: Natural Currents in the New York School* (2010), and a book of poems, *Moonchild*. His current book project on Americana music is entitled *Reading Roots Rock Writing*.

CAROLINE HERBERT is Senior Lecturer in Postcolonial Literatures at Leeds Metropolitan University. Her research centers on contemporary South Asian literature, visual culture, and film, with a specific interest in narratives of urban modernity, secularism, and economic liberalization in India. She is currently completing a monograph that examines literary and visual representations of Bombay/Mumbai. She has published widely on South Asian literature in journals such as *Textual Practice, Journal of Commonwealth Literature*, and *Journal of Postcolonial Writing*, as well as in book collections. Caroline is editor of *Postcolonial Cities: South Asia*, a themed issue of *Moving Worlds: A Journal of Transcultural Writings* (2013), and co-editor with Claire Chambers of *Imagining Muslims in South Asia and the Diaspora: Secularism, Religion, Representations* (2014).

JEFF HICKS is a PhD candidate at the University of California, Riverside, whose research interests include science fiction and fantasy, dystopian literature, and cult film. He has published reviews in *Science Fiction Studies* and *Science Fiction Film and Television*, and he is the co-author of the *Oxford Bibliographies Online* entry for the film *Blade Runner*. He is currently researching the ways in which twentieth-century literature and film have responded to the explosion of urban populations and the geographic territory of urban areas.

BART KEUNEN is Professor of Comparative Literature at Ghent University, Belgium. He is co-director of the Ghent Urban Studies Team (GUST) and teaches graduate and postgraduate courses in European literary history, sociology of literature, and comparative literature. He publishes on topics concerning urban studies, genre criticism, literary historiography, and literary sociology in international journals and books. Book publications include *Time and Imagination: Chronotopes in Western Narrative Culture* (2011) and, with GUST, *The Urban Condition: Space, Community, and Self in the Contemporary Metropolis* (1999).

ROB LATHAM is Professor of English at the University of California, Riverside. A senior editor of the journal *Science Fiction Studies* since 1997, he is the author of *Consuming Youth: Vampires, Cyborgs, and the Culture of Consumption* (2002) and co-editor of *The Wesleyan Anthology of Science Fiction* (2010). He is currently editing *The Oxford Handbook of Science Fiction* and completing a book manuscript on New Wave science fiction of the 1960s and 1970s.

KEVIN R. MCNAMARA is Professor of Literature at the University of Houston–Clear Lake, and he has taught in Turkey and the Czech Republic. He is editor of *The Cambridge Companion to the Literature of Los Angeles* (2010) and author of *Urban Verbs: Arts and Discourses of American Cities* (1996) and other essays on cities, literature, and culture.

MALCOLM MILES is Professor of Cultural Theory and Chair of the Culture-Theory-Space research group in the School of Architecture, Design and Environment at the University of Plymouth (UK). He is author of *Herbert Marcuse: An Aesthetics of Liberation* (2011), *Cities and Cultures* (2007), and *Urban Avant-Gardes* (2004), and he has contributed to journals such as *The Journal of Architecture, Cultural Geographies*, and *Urban Studies*.

CATHERINE NESCI is Professor of French Literature and Comparative and Feminist Studies at the University of California, Santa Barbara, with doctoral training from the University of Paris-7. Her 2007 book, *Le Flâneur et les flâneuses. Les femmes et la ville à l'époque romantique* [The Flâneur and the Flâneuses: Women and the City in French Romanticism] provides a gendered rereading of flânerie through discussions of Walter Benjamin and panoramic literature, Balzac's urban novels, and various works by female writers in the 1830s and 1840s. She is currently expanding her reflection on flânerie through explorations of women journalists and journalistic and ethnographic reporting, from George Sand and Flora Tristan to Agnes Varda and Regine Robin. She is the president of the George Sand Association and associate editor of *Nineteenth-Century French Studies*.

KAREN NEWMAN is Owen Walker Professor of Humanities and Professor of Comparative Literature and English at Brown University. She has written widely on early modern English and continental letters and culture and on Shakespeare and Renaissance drama. Recent books include *Cultural Capitals: Early Modern London and Paris* (2007, paperback 2009) and *Essaying Shakespeare* (2009). She is currently working on the reception of Shakespeare in Europe and on early modern translation.

ALISON O'BYRNE is a lecturer in the Department of English and Related Literature and the Centre for Eighteenth Century Studies at the University of York. She has wide-ranging interests in representations of the city in the long eighteenth century, and she is currently completing a project on representations of urban pedestrianism in eighteenth- and early nineteenth-century London.

AZADE SEYHAN is Fairbank Professor in the Humanities, Professor of German and Comparative Literature, and Affiliated Professor of Philosophy at Bryn Mawr College. She is author of *Representation and Its Discontents: The Critical Legacy of German Romanticism* (1992), *Writing outside the Nation* (2001), and *Tales of Crossed Destinies: The Modern Turkish Novel in a Comparative Context* (2008). She has published widely on German idealism, Romantic theory and literary modernity, multilingual literatures of the United States and Germany, and exile and translation studies. She is working on a book tentatively titled *Exile in Translation*.

SUSAN STEPHENS is Sara Hart Professor in the Humanities and Professor of Classics at Stanford University. Her work includes *Ancient Greek Novels: The Fragments*, co-authored with Jack Winkler (1995); *Seeing Double: Intercultural Poetics in Ptolemaic Alexandria* (2003); and *Callimachus in Context: From Plato to Ovid* (2012), with Benjamin Acosta-Hughes. Her current work is on "geo-poetics," or the ways in which poets create collective identity for ancient spaces.

ARNOLD WEINSTEIN is the Edna and Richard Salomon Distinguished Professor and Professor of Comparative Literature at Brown University. His publications include *Vision and Response in Modern Fiction* (1974); *Fictions of the Self: 1550–1800* (1981); *The Fiction of Relationship* (1988); *Nobody's Home: Speech, Self and Place in American Fiction from Hawthorne to DeLillo* (1993); *A Scream Goes Through the House: What Literature Teaches Us About Life* (2003); *Recovering Your Story: Proust, Joyce, Woolf, Faulkner, Morrison* (2006); *Northern Arts: The Breakthrough of Scandinavian Literature and Art from Ibsen to Bergman* (2008); and *Morning, Noon and Night: Finding the Meaning of Life's Stages Through Books* (2011). He was also editor of *Infection and Contagion* (2003), a special issue of *Literature and Medicine*.

GREGORY WOODS is the author of *Articulate Flesh: Male Homo-Eroticism and Modern Poetry* (1987), *A History of Gay Literature: The Male Tradition* (1998), and several volumes of poetry. He has been Professor of Gay and Lesbian Studies at Nottingham Trent University, UK, since 1998.

ca. 2500 BCE	Myth of Inanna and Enki
ca. 2150–2000	*Epic of Gilgamesh*
Twelfth century	Fall of Troy
Eighth century	Homer, *Iliad*
Mid-seventh century	Royal Library of Ashurbanipal in Nineveh established
Sixth century	Institution of the City Dionysia, the urban part of the annual festival to honor Dionysus, which included theatrical performances
ca. 510	Roman Republic founded
ca. 508	Cleisthenes' reforms establish *demokratia* (rule by the people) in Athens
486	Addition of comedic drama to the City Dionysia
451	Pericles' citizenship law
404	Rule of the Thirty Tyrants in Athens
403	Civil war in Athens; restoration of democracy
399	Death of Socrates
ca. 380	Plato, *Republic*
ca. 360	Plato, *Timaeus*
ca. 350	Aristotle, *Politics*
ca. 340	Plato, *Laws*

332	Alexandria founded
Early third century	Library of Alexandria established
19	Virgil, *Aeneid*
70 CE	Sack of Jerusalem by Titus
Late first century	Petronius, *Satyricon*
410	Sack of Rome
426	Augustine of Hippo, *City of God*
476	Fall of Rome
ca. 940	Nasr al-Fārābī, *On the Perfect State*
ca. 1351	Boccaccio, *Decameron*
1381	Peasants' Rebellion (Wat Tyler's Revolt) in London
ca. 1390	Chaucer, *Canterbury Tales*
1456	François Villon, *Le petit testament*; *Le grand testament* follows in 1461
1516	Thomas More, *Utopia*
1532	Machiavelli, *The Prince*
1573	Isabella Whitney, *A Sweet Nosgay*
ca. 1598	William Shakespeare, *The Merchant of Venice*
1599	Thomas Dekker, *The Shoemaker's Holiday*
1602	Tommaso Campanella, *City of the Sun*
1604	*Relation aller Fürnemmen und gedenckwürdigen Historien*, the first printed and circulated newspaper, debuts in Strasbourg
1608	Thomas Middleton, *The Roaring Girl*
1619	Johann Valentin Andreæ, *Christianopolis*
1624	Francis Bacon, *New Atlantis*
1632	Donald Lupton, *London and the countrey carbonadoed* (a city guide)

1662	Blaise Pascal opens the world's first public omnibus line in Paris shortly before his death; its run is brief
1666	Great fire of London
1698–1700	Ned Ward, *The London Spy*
1711–12	Joseph Addison and Richard Steele, *The Spectator* (briefly revived by Addison in 1714)
1716	John Gay, *Trivia, or The Art of Walking the Streets of London*
1722	Daniel Defoe, *Moll Flanders*
1728	John Gay, *The Beggar's Opera*
1762–3	James Boswell in London, his journal is later published
1771	Tobias Smollett, *Humphry Clinker*
1774	Five-volume edition of *The Newgate Calendar* published, collecting earlier editions of the pamphlets; expanded editions are issued in 1824 and 1826
1778	Fanny Burney, *Evelina*
1800	*Journal des débats* publishes the first feuilleton in Paris; in 1836 the Parisian newspaper *La Presse* is the first to issue a feuilleton as a separate sheet
1802	William Wordsworth, "Lines Composed upon Westminster Bridge"
1807	First public street lighting with gas, Pall Mall, London
1820	Paris adopts gas lighting
1823	William Hazlitt, "Of Londoners and Country People"
1826	Public omnibus line introduced in Nantes, France, by Stanislaus Baudry, who opens lines in Paris in 1828; London and New York follow in 1829

1832	Horse-drawn streetcars debut in New York
1834	Rifā'a Rāfi'al-Ṭahṭāwī, *An Imam in Paris: Account of a Stay in France by an Egyptian Cleric*
1835	Honoré de Balzac, *Père Goriot*
1836	Charles Dickens, *Sketches By Boz*; other city writings include *Oliver Twist* (1838), *Hard Times* (1854), and *Our Mutual Friend* (1865)
1840	Edgar Allan Poe, "The Man of the Crowd"
1842–3	Eugène Sue, *The Mysteries of Paris*, serialized in *Journal de débats*
1845	Benjamin Disraeli, *Sybil, or the Two Nations*
	Friedrich Engels, *The Condition of the Working Class in England*
1848	Elizabeth Gaskell, *Mary Barton*; *North and South* follows in 1855
	Revolutions in cities throughout Europe
1849	Victor Hugo, *A Discourse on Misery*
	Bainbridge's, Newcastle upon Tyne (founded in 1838), begins to record revenue by department, thus becoming the first known department store; the Bon Marché in Paris (also founded in 1838) does the same ca. 1850
1851	Henry Mayhew, *London Labour and the London Poor*
	Napoleon III coup d'état, becomes emperor in 1852
	London Exposition, features the Crystal Palace
1852	Elisha Otis invents the safety elevator; Equitable Life Insurance Building (New York City) becomes the first office building with an elevator in 1870
1853	Baron Georges-Eugène Haussmann commences renovation of Paris, destroying the city's medieval core, creating grand boulevards and plazas

1856   Walt Whitman, "Crossing Brooklyn Ferry"

1861   Second edition of Charles Baudelaire's *The Flowers of Evil* published, includes "Parisian Tableaus"; his "The Painter of Modern Life" is published in 1863

1862   Victor Hugo, *Les Misérables*

1863   Jules Verne, *Paris in the Twentieth Century* (not published until 1994)

            Metropolitan Railway opens in London, first rapid transit system

1864   Fyodor Dostoevsky, *Notes from Underground*

1866   James McNeil Whistler begins his series of London Nocturne paintings

1871   Émile Zola, *The Fortune of the Rougons*, the first of the twenty-volume Rougon-Macquart series, including *Nana* (1880), *The Ladies' Paradise* (1883), *Germinal* (1885)

1871   Paris Commune

1873   First urban cable-car line opens in San Francisco

1874   James Thomson, *The City of Dreadful Night*

1878   First commercial telephone exchange opens in New Haven, Connecticut

1879   Newcastle upon Tyne (one lamp) and Cleveland (twelve lamps) become the first cities to use arc lamps for streetlighting; both are demonstration projects by inventors

1880   Werner von Siemens builds the first electric elevator

1881   Siemens opens the first electric tram line in Lichterfelde, Germany, a suburb of Berlin

1884   Samuel Barnett establishes Toynbee Hall in East London

1885   William Le Baron Jenney's Home Insurance Building (Chicago), a ten-story construction using structural steel, initiates the skyscraper age. Four years later, Daniel Burnham and John Root's Rand-McNally Building, also in Chicago, becomes the first all-steel-framed construction

Lionel Jeffries, *After London*

Carl Auer von Welsbach patents a gas mantle used in streetlighting

1886   Robert Louis Stevenson, *The Strange Case of Dr. Jekyll and Mr. Hyde*

Richmond Union Passenger Railway, the first tram system, opens in Richmond, Virginia

1887   'Alī Pāshā Mubārak, *New Plans for Egypt under the Khedive Tawfiq: Cairo and Other Cities*

Ferdinand Tönnies, *Gemeinschaft and Gesellschaft*

1888   Edward Bellamy, *Looking Backward, 2000–1887*

1888–91   Whitechapel ("Jack the Ripper") murders

1889   Jane Addams and Ellen Gates Starr establish Hull House in Chicago

Exposition Universelle in Paris, features the Eiffel Tower

1890   Ignatius Donnelly, *Caesar's Column*

William Dean Howells, *A Hazard of New Fortunes*

Pierre Loti, *Morocco*

Jacob Riis, *How the Other Half Lives*

1891   Oscar Wilde, *The Picture of Dorian Gray*

1893   Stephen Crane, *Maggie: A Girl of the Streets*

Émile Durkheim, *The Division of Labor in Society*

Bradford Peck, *The World a Department Store*

World's Columbian Exposition in Chicago; its Court of Honor, the "White City," becomes the model for City Beautiful planning

1894	Arthur Morrison, *Tales of Mean Streets*
1895	Gustave Le Bon, *The Crowd: A Study of the Popular Mind*
1898	Ebenezer Howard, *To-morrow: A Peaceful Path to Real Reform*, republished in 1902 as *Garden Cities of To-morrow*, effectively the manifesto of the Garden Cities Movement
1899	John Law (Margaret Harkness), *In Darkest London*
	Frank Norris: *McTeague, a Story of San Francisco*
1900	Theodore Dreiser, *Sister Carrie*
	Paris Metro opens
1901	Colette, *Pauline in Paris*
	Edward A. Ross, *Social Control: A Survey of the Foundations of Order*
1903	Jack London, *People of the Abyss*; publishes *The Iron Heel* in 1908
	Georg Simmel, "The Metropolis and Mental Life"
	Letchworth, first New Town (Garden City) established in England
1904	New York City subway opens
1905	Frederick Clemson Howe, *The City: The Hope of Democracy*
	Heliopolis section of Cairo built under the plan of Baron Édouard Louis Joseph Empain
1906	Mikhail Kuzmin, *Wings*
	Upton Sinclair, *The Jungle*
1907	Joseph Conrad, *The Secret Agent*
	Simon Nelson Patten, *The New Basis of Civilization*
1910	Jane Addams, *Twenty Years at Hull House*

1911   Ceremonial laying of foundation stone of New
        Delhi; designed by architects Sir Edwin Lutyens
        and Sir Herbert Baker, the city is christened New
        Delhi in 1927

1912   Thomas Mann, *Death in Venice*

1915   Dorothy Richardson, *Pointed Roofs*, first volume
        of the thirteen-novel sequence, *Pilgrimage*

        Patrick Geddes, *Cities in Evolution*, a key text
        of early regional planning influenced by Herbert
        Spencer's application of Darwin to the social
        sciences. Lewis Mumford will become Geddes's
        most influential disciple.

1916   Andrei Bely, *Petersburg*

1917   Abraham Cahan, *The Rise of David Levinsky*

1920   Edith Wharton, *The Age of Innocence*

1922   T. S. Eliot, *The Waste Land*

        James Joyce, *Ulysses*

1924   Bertolt Brecht, *Jungle of Cities*

        Yevgeny Zamyatin, *We*

1925   F. Scott Fitzgerald, *The Great Gatsby*

        John Dos Passos, *Manhattan Transfer*

        Le Corbusier, *Urbanisme* (translated as *The City of
        To-morrow and Its Planning* in 1929); followed by
        the Plan Obus for Algiers (1930), *The Radiant City*
        (1935), and *The Athens Charter* published for the
        Congrès internationaux d'architecture moderne
        (1943)

        Robert E. Park Ernest W. Burgess, and Roderick D.
        McKenzie, *The City: Suggestions for the Study of
        Human Nature in the Urban Environment*

        Virginia Woolf, *Mrs. Dalloway*; publishes "Street
        Haunting: A London Adventure" in 1930

1926   Louis Aragon, *Le Paysan de Paris*

Charlie Chaplin (dir.), *Modern Times*

John Henry Mackay, *The Hustler*

1927 Fritz Lang (dir.), *Metropolis*

1928 André Breton, *Nadja*

Claude McKay, *Home to Harlem*

King Vidor (dir.), *The Crowd*

Congrès internationaux d'architecture moderne (CIAM) founded

1929 Alfred Döblin, *Berlin Alexanderplatz*

Hugh Ferriss, *The Metropolis of Tomorrow*

Dziga Vertov (dir.), *Man with a Movie Camera*

1930 Hart Crane, *The Bridge*

Sigmund Freud, *Civilization and Its Discontents*

1934 Philip Roth, *Call It Sleep*

1935 Walter Benjamin, "Paris, Capital of the Nineteenth Century" (revised version, 1939; neither version published in Benjamin's lifetime)

1938 Louis Wirth, "Urbanism as a Way of Life"

1939 Christopher Isherwood, *Goodbye to Berlin*

1940 Federico García Lorca, *Poet in New York*

Richard Wright, *Native Son*

1940–1 London Blitz

1945 Dresden bombings and firestorm

Atomic bombs dropped on Hiroshima and Nagasaki

1946 Lion Feuchtwanger, *Venice (Texas) and Fourteen Other Stories*

Ahmet Hamdi Tanpınar, *Five Cities*

William Carlos Williams, *Paterson, Book One*; Books Two through Five appear in 1948, 1949, 1951, and 1958

1947	Naguib Mahfouz, *Midaq Alley*; *Cairo Trilogy* (*Palace Walk, Palace of Desire, Sugar Street*) follows in 1956–7
	Independence and partition of India and Pakistan
1948	Gore Vidal, *The City and the Pillar*
	Reunited National Party wins South African Election on a platform promising institution of an apartheid system
1949	George Orwell, *Brave New World*
1951	Yukio Mishima, *Forbidden Colors*
1952	Ralph Ellison, *Invisible Man*
1954	Driss Chraïbi, *The Simple Past*
1956	Guy Debord, "Theory of the Dérive"; *The Society of the Spectacle* follows in 1967
	Sam Seldon, *The Lonely Londoners*
	Kateb Yacine, *Nedjma*
1956–7	Battle of Algiers, part of the Algerian War of Independence (1954–62)
1961	Jane Jacobs, *The Death and Life of Great American Cities*
	Lewis Mumford, *The City in History: Its Origins, Its Transformations, and Its Prospects*
1962	Frantz Fanon, *The Wretched of the Earth*
1963	John Rechy, *City of Night*
1964	Frank O'Hara, *Lunch Poems*
1965	Claude Brown, *Manchild in the Promised Land*
	Thomas Pynchon, *The Crying of Lot 49*
1968	Paul Erlich, *The Population Bomb*
	Ahmadou Kourouma, *The Suns of Independence*

	Antiwar, antiracism, and antigovernment protests and civil unrest in many European and US cities
	Stonewall riots
1969	Doris Lessing, *The Four-Gated City*
1970	First Gay Pride marches held in Chicago, Los Angeles, New York, and San Francisco
1972	Thomas Disch, *334*
1973	Rita Mae Brown, *Rubyfruit Jungle*
	David Harvey, *Social Justice and the City* (rev. ed., 2009); books that follow include *The Urban Condition* (1989), *The Condition of Postmodernity: An Enquiry into the Origins of Cultural Change* (1989), and *Paris, Capital of Modernity* (2003)
1974	Henri Lefebvre, *The Production of Space*
1975	J. G. Ballard, *High-Rise*
1976	First "Reclaim the Night" march held in Brussels by participants in the International Tribunal on Crimes against Women
1977	Angela Carter, *The Passion of the New Eve*
1978	Andrew Holleran, *The Dancer from the Dance*
	Larry Kramer, *Faggots*
1979	Armistead Maupin, first volume of the *Tales of the City*
1982	Henri Lopes, *The Laughing Cry*
	Ridley Scott (dir.), *Blade Runner*
1982–9	Alan Moore and David Lloyd, *V for Vendetta*
1983	C. K. Williams, *Tar*
1984	Martin Amis, *Money: Suicide Note*, first volume of the London Trilogy (includes *London Fields* [1989] and *The Information* [1995])
	Michel de Certeau, *The Practice of Everyday Life*

William Gibson, *Neuromancer*

1985–6   Paul Auster, *New York Trilogy* (*City of Glass*, *Ghosts*, and *The Locked Room*)

1987   Michael Ondaatje, *In the Skin of a Lion*

1988   Neil Bartlett, *Who Was that Man?*

Kate Braverman, *Palm Latitudes*

Alan Hollinghurst, *The Swimming-Pool Library*

1989   Hanif Kureishi, *The Buddha of Suburbia*

1990   William Gibson and Bruce Sterling, *The Difference Engine*

Orhan Pamuk, *The Black Book*; publishes *Istanbul: Memories and the City* in 2003

1991   Bret Easton Ellis, *American Psycho*

Iain Sinclair, *Downriver*

1992   Emine Sevgi Özdamar, *Life Is a Caravanserai: Has Two Doors I Came in One I Went Out the Other*; followed by *The Bridge of the Golden Horn* (1998) and *The Courtyard in the Mirror* (2001)

1992–6   Siege of Sarajevo during the Bosnian War

1994   Nelson Mandela becomes president of South Africa

1996   Edward Soja, *Thirdspace: Journeys to Los Angeles and Other Real-and-Imagined Places*; *Postmetropolis: Critical Studies of Cities and Regions* follows in 2000

1997   Edmund White, *The Farewell Symphony*

1999   Roberto Bolaño, *Amulet*

Samuel R. Delany, *Times Square Red, Times Square Blue*

2000   Zadie Smith, *White Teeth*

2001	Hijacked passenger airplanes fly into the twin towers of the World Trade Center in New York City
2002	Kamila Shamsie, *Kartography*
2003	R. Raj Rao, *The Boyfriend*
2004	Chris Abani, *Graceland*
	Sarnath Banerjee, *Corridor*
2005	José Saramago, *Blindness*
2006	Tahar Ben Jelloun, *Leaving Tangier*
	Mike Davis, *Planet of Slums*
	Will Self, *The Book of Dave*
	Ed Roberson, *City Eclogue*
	Ivan Vladislavić, *Portrait with Keys: The City of Johannesburg Unlocked*
2009	China Miéville, *The City and the City*
2009–10	Haruki Murakami, *1Q84*
2011	Teju Cole, *Open City*
	First "Slutwalk" protest held in Toronto
	Occupy Wall Street, first encampment of the Occupy movement
2012	Lauren Groff, *Arcadia*
2013	Manil Suri, *The City of Devi*

KEVIN R. McNAMARA

Introduction

> [T]he city and the urban environment represent [humanity's] most
> consistent and, on the whole, [its] most successful attempt to remake
> the world [it] lives in more after [its] heart's desire. But if the city is
> the world which [humans] created, it is the world in which [they are]
> henceforth condemned to live.
>
> Robert E. Park, "The City as Social Laboratory" (1929)

The history of the city in literature is as lengthy and rich as the histories
of literature and cities themselves. The Royal Library of Ashurbanipal's
seventh-century BCE holdings are estimated at 25,000 volumes, a diverse
and multilingual collection of approximately 1,200 distinct texts comprising 200,000 verses.[1] Among them was the oldest surviving epic, *Gilgamesh*
(ca. 2150–2000 BCE), which opens with praise for the eponymous king who
"built the wall of Uruk-Haven / the wall of the sacred Eanna Temple, the holy
sanctuary / … which gleams like copper."[2] The still-earlier tale of Inanna and
Enki (ca. 2500 BCE) is a myth of urban succession in Sumer. Uruk replaced
Eridu as the principal city in southern Mesopotamia, the narrative tells us,
after the god Enki feted the goddess Inanna on her arrival in Eridu and,
while he afterward slumbered, she returned to Uruk with his drunken gift of
me, or divine decrees that comprise the foundations of civilization.[3]

As these examples begin to suggest, literary forms such as epic, myth,
drama, encomium, and eulogy have been building blocks of civil religion,
civic history, and collective identity for millennia. Homer's *Iliad* (eighth century BCE) recounts the destruction of the Anatolian city of Ilium (Troy)
by assembled Greek forces four centuries earlier. Greek drama was a form
of civic spectacle. Comedy frequently addressed topical matters. Tragedy
"mediat[ed] the old heroic ethos … to the democratic world of the *polis*
which provided its primary audience," Peter Burian argues; its staging of
dispute and dissent "*participate[d]* in democracy" by calling attention to
the "commitment to free expression" as a fundamental element of Athenian
civic ideology.[4] Greek philosophers deepened the discussion in practical and
speculative texts of political (affairs of the polis) philosophy. Eight centuries
after Homer, Troy's fall became the incident that set in motion the events
of *The Aeneid* (19 BCE), Virgil's epic of Rome. From legends of Aeneas's

I

journey and his association with the city's founding, Virgil wove this poem of the Trojan hero's voyage to Italy, his martial triumph, and the founding of the Roman lineage through his son Iulus. In thereby claiming for Rome the legacy of Greek civilization, and offering in the person of Aeneas a new model of heroic virtue based more firmly on civic duty than on individual honor, Virgil brought Troy into Roman culture as a symbolic city, a kind of city that, we shall see, has a long and significant history in city literature.

Many of these ancient texts are still consulted for what they tell us about cities and citizenship, even if the continuity between ancient and modern cities is a matter of some dispute. Raymond Williams argued in *Keywords* (1976) that the word *city* was used "to distinguish urban areas from rural areas" only from the sixteenth century, and that only in the early nineteenth century is "the city as a really distinctive order of settlement, implying a whole different way of life, ... fully established, with its modern implications."⁵ Yet while the scale, spatial extent, and material conditions of cities indeed changed profoundly with the Industrial Revolution's onset, neither the social and spatial changes wrought by industrialism nor the history of the word *city* erases the social, economic, and cultural continuities between ancient, early modern, and contemporary cities.

If modern cities are regarded as concentrators of diversity and proving grounds for rights and freedoms, Athens itself was "a vast city, a Mediterranean crossroads with an ethnically diverse population, including naturalized citizens with prominent political careers. And while Athens was less diverse culturally than a modern nation, it was in some ways *more* diverse socially and intellectually."⁶ Alexandria, as Susan Stephens observes in Chapter 2 of this volume, was by 200 BCE a megacity of 300,000 people – Egyptians, Greeks from many city-states, and a diasporic Jewish population, each group identified with a different quarter of the city.

The "functional specialization of man and his work," a hallmark of industrial production that "makes each man the more directly dependent upon the supplementary activities of all others,"⁷ is found in ancient cities. Lewis Mumford noted that in Egyptian civilization, "it was possible ... to spend an entire life in a fractional occupation." To bolster his assertion that "the worker was [already] a uniform replaceable part in a complex social machine," Mumford cited evidence as diverse as "The Satire on the Trades" (ca. 1900 BCE), second-millennium BCE records detailing the division of labor on expeditions to quarry stone for the pyramids, and Herodotus's fifth-century BCE observations on specialization in Egyptian medicine.⁸

The effects on cities of changing cultural, social, and economic conditions, and on the representation of cities by these same changes and developments in literary history, are addressed by this *Companion*'s chapters and account for their chronological arrangement. Rather than rehearse that history, this introduction offers an overview of the forms of the literary city we will encounter. Michel de Certeau's well-known distinction between the city as seen from above and without (a God's-eye view) and the fragmentary city seen and experienced at street level by an individual person is repeated in literature as a distinction between literary cities presented as totalities by narrators who look out (or down) on the urban scene, and the limited perspective of a character or characters in the streets.[9] The city-as-totality has three principal manifestations. Symbolic cities stand for ideals. They may be historical cities that have become emblematic of ideas, as Athens has come to stand for democracy through its repeated invocation as an ideal of democratic form, or fictional ideals like the utopias discussed in Chapter 1, or the city on a hill of Puritan and, later, American political rhetoric. Literary texts that map the social, economic, and cultural geographies and relations of actual cities, whether presented under their own names or pseudonymously, supply a second form of city-as-totality. The cities in realist novels (Stuart Culver's subject in Chapter 6) are the most obvious representatives of this mode. The category also includes historiographic metafiction, a term coined by Linda Hutcheon to name fictions that incorporate historical events and persons into narratives that function both as historical fictions and as a questioning of the possibility of accurate historical representation.[10] We encounter several such texts in Caroline Herbert's chapter on postcolonial cities. Occupying a position between these two forms are cities whose forms are systematically distorted to convey a particular mood or quality. The urban gothic, urban sublime, dystopian city, and certain modalities of the nocturnal and postmodern cities are principal exemplars.[11] The city focalized through a character's perception is necessarily a fragmentary and subjective experience of the city built from perceptions, emotions, and memories. While this mode never presents the city in its totality, Arnold Weinstein shows us in Chapter 10 that many modernist authors sought to render a more complete, but still subjective and non-totalizing, account of their cities by presenting the city from multiple, spatially dispersed perspectives.

Symbolic cities figure prominently throughout our first three chapters, which treat the cities of ancient and early modern literature. The critic Harry Berger, Jr., perceptively argued that the function of idealized worlds is not only to seduce with their promise of happiness, but also to expose their own shallowness and untenability, thus to return readers to their lives with a critically enhanced perspective on both the world they inhabit and their own desires.[12] In his discussion of ideal cities, Antonis Balasopoulos demonstrates that the Greeks knew this truth. They recognized the inevitable opposition between, on one hand, their "ontological and political investment" in a perfectly ordered, harmonious, and just city, and, on the other hand, the inescapable facts of heterogeneity and transmutability, the very things that make us human. So the "best" place (the *eu-topos*) is unsuited to us; it is *ou-topos* (no place), as Thomas More's punning title, *Utopia*, signals. Even as the ideals it embodies and the desire it excites tell us something fundamental about our condition (and inform so much of the literature of the city), the "best" city reminds us of why, as the pioneering urban sociologist Robert E. Park wrote, our actual cities are where we are "condemned" to live. The utopias of Renaissance writers, Balasopoulos goes on to show, were properly literary texts, fictive ethnographies that incorporate verbal play and ambiguity and therefore require interpretation.

The ancient cities of which Susan Stephens writes in Chapter 2 are more than historical cities. Athens, Alexandria, Rome, and Jerusalem – all continuously inhabited for millennia – are also proper names indelibly associated with civic forms. *Athens* and *Rome* have for centuries been shorthand for democratic and imperial civic orders. Alexandria and the earthly city of Jerusalem (as distinguished from Augustine of Hippo's heavenly Jerusalem) have a more contemporary interest, Alexandria as a city of many cultures from the time of the Ptolemies, and Jerusalem as the archetypal diasporic city associated with loss and memory. Her discussion combines attention to literary depictions of the four cities by ancient authors with a focus on what these cities, as symbols, mean today.

Karen Newman's ensuing discussion of medieval and early modern Europe's cultural capitals notes that the symbolic city remains important throughout these centuries. Not only do figurative cities such as the City of God and the city on a hill loom large, but those cultural capitals each laid claim to be the rightful inheritor of the virtues and powers the ancient cities symbolize in part through modes of spectacle, pageantry, and rhetoric adopted from ancients. Nonetheless, it is in these same years that the urban types and in-the-streets writing we that associate with modern city literature emerge, as she also shows, in authors such as François Villon, Isabella Whitney, and Nicolas Boileau.

The modern history of the literary city itself begins with an ideal – perhaps a myth – of urbanity that is Alison O'Byrne's subject in Chapter 4. The public sphere is that part of public life in which people come together to discuss, debate, and seek consensus about a range of social and cultural matters. In eighteenth-century London and other cities, the public sphere encompassed the theater, the periodical press, and the coffeehouses where the products of the theater and the press were assessed. The hero of London's public sphere, "Mr. Spectator," was the joint authorial persona of Joseph Addison and Richard Steele, whose six-day-a-week paper, *The Spectator*, published 555 issues from 1711–12; its tenth number boasted a circulation of 3,000 and a readership of 60,000, approximately 10 percent of the city's total population.[13] Whether Mr. Spectator's advice and behavior were descriptive or prescriptive is debated, O'Byrne explains. Either way, London was a city of renown for good or ill, the destination for a young man on the make who was set afloat in a sea of strangers, and (like other cultural capitals) the point of reference for the period's debates about the personal and political morality of trade and luxury. In this milieu, character was represented and performed in the course of daily activity; Londoners and visitors alike had to learn how to read its conventions and divine underlying intent. All the while, O'Byrne observes, a counter-literature of the period satirized these urban ways as so much confusion, deception, and pretense; many of the character types in these fictions are brought forward from ancient comedy.

From this period forward, we accumulate a rich literature devoted to the depiction of actual cities and the modes of life they support, a body of texts that exemplify architect Robert Venturi and planner Denise Scott Brown's axiom, "A city is a set of intertwined activities that form a pattern on the land."[14] The built landscape is the most basic of these patterns on the land. Its creative destruction – the reshaping of the landscape in pursuit of profits, surveillance, social control, or some other goal – is the ongoing result of social, political, and economic processes. Elements of design and ornament communicate values, and structures themselves support, solicit, and curtail modes of individual or collective behavior, as we realize when we imagine the disparate effects of creating a public park or a private shopping mall in the middle of a city.

Exploring the interplay of urban environments and human behavior is one of the things that city literature does best, whether in fictions that map social spaces and interactions, utopian and dystopian speculations, or all manner of reformist projects built on foundations of sentiment, sensationalism, "experiment,"[15] or social and political theory. Robert Park honored the literary history of the city in 1925 when he remarked sociologists' debt "to writers of fiction for our more intimate knowledge of urban life."[16] Yet to conclude that the worth even of urban realism inheres in its documentary record surely is to misvalue it. Some authors may strain for documentary fidelity, and later literary tourists may follow the peregrinations of fictional characters through a city's actual streets, but this reality-*effect* neither grants the text a documentary validity nor accurately identifies the primary function of the literary text.[17] We do better to regard literary city-texts as selectively composing – they may also deform and thereby defamiliarize – the known in order to stage the *process* of making sense of the city, whether it is perceived from above or within. City literature invites the reader to see the patterns out of which the city is constituted, or to experience the life of the city, and to do the work of making sense of it. At its best, the reading experience is a recursive process that tests the reader's own assumptions and conclusions about the ways of cities and their inhabitants.

City literature is, however, part of the documentary record of urban thought throughout history. What the geographer David Harvey remarks of Honoré de Balzac's Parisian novels and stories is true of city literature more broadly:

> [It] provide[s] innumerable acute observations on urban life (a documentary source, however dubious as a record of actual facts, of some importance). [It] record[s] much about [the] material world and the social processes (desires, motivations, activities, collusions, and coercions) that flowed around them. [It] explore[s] different ways in which to represent that world and help[s] shape the popular imagination as to what the city was and might be about... [It] help[s] make the city legible.[18]

By the late nineteenth century, indeed, many literary authors wrote with acute awareness of the developing social-science literature of cities that modeled the city as a structural or functional totality. In Chapter 6, Stuart Culver examines the interplay between social science and the novel. Selecting texts that go beyond mere exemplification of a theory, he shows the novels "experimentally" testing the theories' validity against characters' motives and behavior, and exposing the inability of theory to contain and to order the messiness of everyday life. His discussion covers the effects – both alienating and liberating – of replacing more intimate bonds of organic community with the instrumental relations of the *Gesellschaft* world; contract as the foundational principle of social interaction; imitation as a mode of social reproduction (often expressed through consumer activity); the tutelary role of the press, civic organizations, and other urban institutions as agents of social control; and the blasé affect that insulates city dwellers against the shocks and surprises of urban life.

One of the greatest challenges facing urban social theorists and reformers has been poverty and the situation of the working classes. Bart Keunen and Luc De Droogh tell us in their chapter on urban economic outsiders (Chapter 7) that those outsiders' narrative function in the literature of the city pivots on whether they are destined to become fully integrated into the social order that their expropriated labor supports or to challenge it. The outsiders' role is further conditioned by other dimensions of identity: native-born workers and immigrants, members of the dominant ethnic strain and racial or ethnic minorities; each group faces different obstacles to full integration and represents a different kind of threat to the existing order. Keunen and De Droogh identify four principal narrative positions that economic outsiders have occupied over the past two centuries: Romantic underdog, moral problem, oppositional social force, and alienated individual with only a vague sense of class identity. Each of these roles asks readers to adopt a different mode of cognitive and affective understanding, and each reveals a different fate for the outsiders and truth about the society so constituted.

The literature of European overseas colonization simplifies social relations into those of two antagonistic classes: the colonizer and the colonized subject. Narratives of amelioration and integration are inapplicable to colonized peoples, while under a racial caste system, status as alienated (or any other kind of) *individuals* is unavailable to the colonized person.[19] Dominance and submission mark everything about the colonial city, from its social relations, to its built landscape (even down to its materials and amenities), to its inhabitants' freedom of movement, as Seth Graebner shows in Chapter 14. The spatial patterns of native and settler quarters likewise express fundamentally different beliefs about human nature, collective life, and the purposes of cities. The experience of domination and dislocation weighs on the consciousness of colonial subjects, leaving resistance and revolt as the only *authentic* options. Post-independence, as Graebner observes and Caroline Herbert develops in relation to postcolonial cities in Chapter 15, the markers of segregation that have been designed into the urban landscape resist effacement. But as Herbert shows, for that very reason they can be enlisted in efforts, literary and otherwise, to work through the historical trauma of colonization and its legacies, and to voice once-silenced viewpoints. The weaving of suppressed or otherwise lost stories into "official" histories accounts for the complexly textured – and fissured – historiographic metafictions of the postcolonial city that are her subject.

Herbert also reminds us of the variety of colonial situations during the "colonial era" (the 1500s–1900s) and the complex geography of the postcolonial order when she discusses Michael Ondaatje's novel, *In the Skin of a Lion* (1987). Ondaatje is a naturalized Canadian citizen born in Sri Lanka, an island colonized by Portuguese, surrendered to the Dutch, and under British rule at the time of his birth. *Skin* is set in postindependence Toronto and features Nicholas Temelcoff, a laborer who migrates from post-Ottoman Macedonia. Macedonians had enjoyed limited autonomy under the Ottoman millet system,[20] whereas in Toronto – a settler city whose colonial elite remained in power after Canadian independence, and where ethnic outsiders were officially invisible and often deported when their labor was not needed – Telemcoff is in many ways a colonial subject. Thus, the Canadian and Macedonian situations differ from each other, and both differ markedly from contemporaneous European colonial projects in Africa and Asia.

The dismantling of the colonial order, ever more forced displacements and willing departures for new lands, and cheaper, faster transportation that makes periodic returns to the homeland possible for a larger number of migrants have globalized the populations of the world's major cities. The many kinds of compelled and voluntary movements call forth a taxonomy to classify the variety of intentions and durations of resettlement, and the imagined connections of migrants to their home and adoptive lands, which Azade Seyhan surveys in Chapter 16. Such mobility has not necessarily made refuge and resettlement easier, Seyhan reminds us in her discussion of people who inhabit cities but not nations, whether they do so as cosmopolitans moving among cities, migrants, diasporans, refugees, or something else. These urban denizens give a new layer of meaning to the old idea of the city as a congregation of strangers. They also make the city "strange" in the attempt to make it familiar, as they project images, memories, and idealizations of their homelands onto new urban landscapes in order to make them more livable. Focusing on two writers, Emine Sevgi Özdamar and Lion Feuchtwanger, and characters in Kate Braverman's novel, *Palm Latitudes*, Seyhan highlights the diversity of situations and some of the factors that determine migrants' fates as they live in the cognitive space between languages and cultures, attempt to translate not only words and customs but also memories and landscapes, and try to preserve some core of identity through their displacements. Özdamar embraces German in Berlin despite its having, for her, no childhood, while Feuchtwanger continued to write in German after being granted asylum and settling in Los Angeles for good in 1941. Both authors found that translation offers enrichment of thought and feeling as well as dilution. In stark contrast, Gloria, a character in *Palm Latitudes* (1988), is economically and racially marginal, and she remains linguistically and culturally estranged. Like so many migrants who find themselves confined to ghettos and interstitial zones and struggling with a new language and culture (and unlike expatriates, who are insulated from these problems by wealth or other forms of privilege), Gloria and her fate remind us how elusive and even illusory the "freedom of the city" remains.

In texts whose urban forms are designed to convey a mood, the city is subjected to a systematic distortion that emphasizes particular qualities, usually of a dark and sensational nature, even if the narrative offers its city as an accurate depiction of reality. The melodramatic novel of urban reform was initiated with *The Mysteries of Paris*, Eugène Sue's episodic story of an aristocratic hero, a righter of wrongs who first appeared in daily feuilletons in the Parisian *Journal de débats* during 1842–3. Sue's example was quickly followed by George W. M. Reynolds's *The Mysteries of London* (1844), *The Mysteries and Miseries of New York* (1849) by Ned Buntline (pseudonym of

Edward Judson), and George Foster's *New York by Gaslight* (1850). Earlier than the New York efforts, George Lippard's over-the-top urban gothic, *The Quaker City, or the Monks of Monk Hall* (1845), "exposed" debauchery and criminality among the Philadelphian elite who meet in the titular mansion for rituals of seduction, rape, and murder under the accommodating eye of its caretaker, Abijah K. Jones, familiarly known as Devil-Bug.

The cover of darkness is a staple of these novels. James R. Giles's chapter on "The Urban Nightspace" (Chapter 8) shows us a city riven with lawless, Dionysian energies. Confined to the city, Dionysus is diseased and distorted, manifest in ways that expose the city's sadistic unconscious. These texts of the diseased, nocturnal city nevertheless contribute to social cartography as they show social "extremes meet[ing] by way of the passions. Vice indissolubly welds the rich to the poor" through the cash nexus that reduces marginal individuals to commodities.[21] Giles crucially expands the domain of the Dionysian to include other subversive forces that traverse the night; he specifies the forces of revolution and reaction in Roberto Bolaño's *Amulet* (1999) and the various isolatos and confederations of the disinherited who traverse Thomas Pynchon's *The Crying of Lot 49* (1965). One thinks, too, of *The Secret Agent* (1907), Joseph Conrad's corrosively ironic novel of London's anarchist circles, whose title character keeps a "legitimate" business in pornographic postcards and other paper goods as a cover. In all of these cases, the urban nightworld is the milieu of what is repressed by the collective fantasy that passes for social reality. Thankfully, the nighttime city occasionally supplies a warm bedroom and human contact, as we see in a scene from Claude McKay's *Home to Harlem* (1928) and Frank O'Hara's poem, "Present" (1964).

Another Romantic modality, the sublime, was transposed to the city at the turn of the previous century to convey the perceptual and conceptual incomprehensibility of its spatial extent, social and ethnic fabric, and industrial and economic processes. Christophe Den Tandt shows in Chapter 9 that the urban sublime draws its organizing tropes from biology and physics (as did most contemporaneous social-science discourse), and it portrays a city in constant transformation, coursing with the current and currency (as power, the two are often conflated) that drive the industrial machinery and the urban economy. The human subject, meanwhile, is dissolved into the dark, bestial force of the crowd. Nathanael West memorably called on the urban sublime at the climax of *The Day of the Locust* (1939), when in the midst of a swarming crowd outside a movie theater, Tod Hackett at last is "able to think clearly" about his own vision of the urban sublime – his painting, "The Burning of Los Angeles." Yet as Den Tandt predicts, West's modernist take on the urban sublime exhibits revulsion toward a necropolitan city filled with "people who come to California to die," rather than teeming with forces of life, as the naturalists' city is.²² The urban sublime returns to life, Den Tandt observes at the chapter's close, in versions of the postmodern city that are taken up by Nick Bentley in Chapter 13.

In literary and especially popular fiction, sublime terror gave way to an unambiguously dystopian vision that, as Rob Latham and Jeff Hicks demonstrate in Chapter 10, emerges in response to the utopias of literature and urban planning as much as from fears of war and ecological crisis. Tropes of the sublime undergo significant twists, they show: as the city expands, personal space contracts. Life swarms through the city, but in the form of disease. Technological marvels that allow us to see at scales unimagined become an omnipresent surveillance apparatus that watches us. Technology loops backward in the subgenre (and design aesthetic) of steampunk; the future city and its denizens are imagined as stitched together out of nineteenth- and early twentieth-century industrial technologies. The authors follow the dystopian genre's literary history through magazines, graphic novels, comics, and *manga*, as well as conventional novelistic fiction.

Latham and Hicks note that a dystopian sensibility infects contemporary literary cities outside the genre. Bentley opens his chapter on the postmodern city with the iconic landscape of Ridley Scott's *Blade Runner* (1982) – sublime in its opening panorama of pyramidal skyscrapers and fire-belching refinery towers, dystopic in the cramped swarm at street level; recognizably Los Angeles, yet systematically distorted to represent the depredations of global neoliberalism. Bentley discusses three key modalities of the postmodern city of fiction, the first of which one might call the consumer sublime. This world of hyper-consumption might seem the very opposite of a dystopia because it promises that through the manipulation and combination of fashion's signs one may become one's desires. Yet the seemingly infinite options for outfitting an identity are, these texts remind us, actually a form of managed consciousness. What differentiates the modern dystopia from this postmodern urb, then, is simply the replacement of the pure seriality of the man who is but a number with the illusion of freedom created by a spectacular array of types and taste cultures. Actual creativity seems reserved for those who engage with what Bentley calls "the play of traces" – a sublime excess of signification – and recycle urban leftovers into genuinely expressive forms. A second mode of postmodern city fiction that he discusses shares this interest in signs that refer to no stable, underlying reality. In such novels as Orhan Pamuk's *The Black Book* (1990) and Paul Auster's *New York Trilogy* (1985–6), the city is an unreadable, often self-referential, palimpsest whose patterns, meanings, and connections are invented rather than discovered; metaphorically or literally, it is often the site of two or more cities. The third mode that Bentley treats – psychogeographic novels – we will discuss momentarily.

The possibility of making one's own city out of what is given reintroduces human agency into the equation and reminds us that all is not as grim and gritty as the trajectory from the sublime to the dystopian implies. The twentieth-century avant-garde was not one thing, but as Malcolm Miles shows us in Chapter 11, for many of the avant-gardes, the city was the principal site of intervention against the institutions of western bourgeois culture, especially the fine arts and the museum. The various avant-gardes shared a number of interests that centered on strategies of "liberating" the city from the repressive forces of cultural history while taking art into the streets and incorporating (without aestheticizing) industrial technology. In addition to these avant-garde "interruptions," Miles discusses avant-garde and modernist "ambivalences" toward the city and, under the heading of "rebuilding," the work of avant-gardes and urban planners to remake the city for the second machine age in the wake of the century's European wars.[23]

The avant-gardes, denizens of the translated city, people who engage "the play of traces," and, in fact, all people who explore cities show us that the mobility that ties the city together is a property of the ambulatory consciousness that brings into constellation the city's disparate spaces and their histories, classes, and cultures; it is not the class mobility cherished by theorists of liberal individualism. As experiential records of actual individuals, these cognitive and affective geographies are documentary sources. As literature, these "cities of feeling," in Willa Cather's phrase,[24] serve a representative function: they stand for human experience, or at least the experience of a specific group (e. g., women, workers, minorities), and they invite readers to an empathic experience of the city from that standpoint. The expectation of mobility in city literature renders the absence or curtailment of mobility – a theme of much minority, colonial, and postcolonial literature – all the more stark.

If "[t]he city lives by remembering," as Ralph Waldo Emerson proclaimed,[25] then the authors of city texts are memory's agents. Weinstein argues in Chapter 10 that the modernist author captures experience in forms that articulate the city's spatial and temporal joints while respecting its anarchic energy. The subjective life that fills the void of alienation and social atomization plays across the city, thickening and texturing sensation with memory, while formal innovations convey the jagged breaks in thought and perception. The use of multiple, dispersed, and limited centers of consciousness may be modernist city literature's most important formal innovation: it expands the reader's fields of vision and vicarious experience, it offers a more complex accounting of the city, and yet it resolutely refuses to offer readers the city in its totality. Weinstein demonstrates that what holds these mobile texts together is not an achieved spatial unity but a temporal vision sensitive to the informing power of the historical and mythic pasts on the seeming chaos and confusion of contemporary history, as T. S. Eliot said of James Joyce's great Dublin novel, *Ulysses*. History is experienced in these novels as *force* – an array of forces, some making the world over and others burdening the solitary consciousness.

The predominant mode of urban mobility across all genres and periods is pedestrian. One sort of walker seeks contemplative solitude and evocative prospects, as does his country-walking counterpart, and may animate the city's mineral landscape through the alchemy of organic metaphors. This is one version of urban pastoral, the subject of Timothy Gray's and my concluding chapter. A mood, not a genre, urban pastoral is characterized by attitudes and orientations transposed from the world of pastoral to the city; they include temporary, contemplative withdrawal, desire for communion with others, and engagement with the aesthetic and affective properties of the landscape. As we shall also see, for some urban shepherds the city's sensory richness renders it a field of desire while for others a sense of history and loss suffuses the scene, yielding the material for a pastoral of ruins.

The flâneur, whom Catherine Nesci discusses in Chapter 5, is the most famous of urban walkers, the passionate spectator installed amidst the urban crowd. Charles Baudelaire is the flâneur par excellence, distinguished by his facility for registering the shock of the new at a time of urban upheaval: the Revolution of 1848, the sacrifice of the city's medieval core to Baron Haussmann's design for the Second Empire capital city, the transformation of nocturnal sociality by gaslit streets and the arcades in whose interior streets shops displayed their wares to passersby, and the steady influx from the provinces of people like the poet himself. As the "hero" of modern life, the flâneur is "at home" in the crowd; as artist, he distills the fugitive beauty from the roiling scene. Baudelaire makes this claim on occasion, notably in the prose poem "Crowds" (posthumously published in 1869), but as Nesci shows, much of his poetry belies that comfort and confidence. It is structured on a dialectic of communion and alienation, passion and estrangement; the incognito gaze is often undone by the poet-speaker's recognition of himself in the vanquished figures of the margins and the shadows. Thus, she explains, what endures in Baudelaire is the assault on identity as much as its creation. Each image is a record of consciousness shot through with loss if only because the depths of memory and subjectivity are threatened by the ephemerality of the urban scene that is his proper milieu.

The modernist flâneur is always more or less entangled in his or her own subjectivity – even Frank O'Hara's affably detached consciousness circles loss as it ambles the noontime streets, as Nesci remarks. In contrast, the Situationist who undertakes a *dérive* (drift) through the city brackets subjectivity and conscious choice in favor of "rapid passage through varied ambiances," guided by an unreflective, "playful-constructive behavior."[26] Like the contemporaneous American Beats, Situationist drifters were on the road. But unlike the Beats, who were rooted in Whitmanian romanticism and crossed the United States by car, Situationists searched on foot for interstitial survivals of an alternative to the social order of industrial labor and consumer spectacle. They were critics/provocateurs whose urban roving yielded psychogeographies that articulate these residual and alternative sites within the city. (Today's drifter may be aided by smartphone apps that facilitate getting constructively lost.) Malcolm Miles discusses the Situationists' interruptions of the urban order in Chapter 11; Nick Bentley considers the literary uses of psychogeography by Peter Ackroyd, Will Self, and Iain Sinclair in Chapter 13.

Anonymity is a given and even an enabling condition for urban strollers. It plays a more strategic and important role in the gay and lesbian city and its literary portrayals, which are Gregory Woods's subject in Chapter 17. While the city of gay literature is often a field of desire animated by a mobile protagonist – "the city means abundance," Woods says at the outset – the risk of exposure and physical violence has meant that the gay and lesbian city is invisible to anyone uninitiated in the codes that signal sexual identity or unable to spot public amenities that are sites for cruising and bars and clubs that cannot afford to give themselves away to casual passersby. And yet, as Samuel R. Delany argued in his memoir of porn theaters/essay on urbanism, *Times Square Red, Times Square Blue* (1999), this world of mobility and cross-class, cross-race contact – all of which are evident in the texts that Woods discusses – and the sense of community that arises not only despite but through contingent sexual and social couplings, enacts a powerful ideal of democratic urbanity, albeit one that retains a masculinist bias common in the discourse. Woods's chapter also looks to gay literature's own "symbolic city," Alexandria (in part the legacy of Constantine Cavafy's writing); the literature of the AIDS crisis; a historical literature in which a city's gay past is imaginatively projected onto its present; and gay literature from outside the west, including texts that "speak back," as he says, to "the erotic Orientalism of western literatures."

A chapter on women and the city was commissioned for the volume, but it never arrived. Women are by no means absent from the volume; the chapters and suggestions for further reading provide guidance for the reader. Nevertheless, a chapter devoted to women writers and representations of women's experiences of the city would have been an important counterpoint to a literary city whose default perspective has historically been male.

It might have considered further the possibility of the flâneuse (the female flâneur) that Catherine Nesci raises in Chapter 5; urban domesticity; the experience of shopping and the late nineteenth-century department store as a female space; the work of pioneer urban reformers such as Jane Addams, Ellen Gates Starr, and Lillian Wald; narratives of sexual danger and freedom; literature by and about immigrant, minority, and working-class women around the globe; or critiques of the gendering of urban space.

That chapter alone would not have exhausted our subject. Some topics engaged in passing in one or more chapters might well have received chapters of their own (e. g., the periodical press, the city in time of war and terror, urban domesticity), but this volume's charter set strict limits on the verbal space it could annex. Like any city guide, this *Companion* succeeds if it equips readers to become productively lost exploring on their own. Before leaving readers free to wander the chapters, the editor wishes to express his sincere thanks to the authors of these splendid essays for their expertise and commitment to the project. Special thanks to Antonis Balasopoulos, Caroline Herbert, and Gregory Woods – three distinguished scholars who graciously adopted chapters orphaned late in the process and produced fine work against unreasonable deadlines. Finally, I wish to express my gratitude to C. K. Williams for graciously allowing Timothy Gray and me to quote at length his poem, "From My Window," in Chapter 18.

NOTES

1 Gerald E. Max, "Ancient Near East," in Wayne A. Wiegand and Donald G. Davis, Jr., eds., *Encyclopedia of Library History* (New York: Garland, 1994), pp. 27–8. The majority of the collection appears to have been state documents.
2 *Gilgamesh*, trans. Maureen Gallery Kovacs (Stanford, CA: Stanford University Press, 1989), p. 3.
3 Samuel Noah Kramer, "Inanna and Enki: The Transfer of the Arts of Civilization from Eridu to Erech," *Sumerian Mythology: A Study of Spiritual and Literary Achievement in the Third Millennium B.C.* (Philadelphia: University of Pennsylvania Press, 1997), pp. 64–8.
4 Peter Burian, "Athenian tragedy as democratic discourse," in D. M. Carter, ed., *Why Athens: A Reappraisal of Democratic Politics* (Oxford: Oxford University Press, 2011), p. 98.
5 Raymond Williams, *Keywords: A Vocabulary of Culture and Society* (New York: Oxford University Press, 1976), pp. 46, 47.
6 Josiah Ober, "Learning from Athens: Success by Design," *Boston Review* 31.2 (2006), 17.
7 Georg Simmel, "The Metropolis and Mental Life" (1903), *The Sociology of George Simmel*, ed. and trans. Kurt Wolff (New York: Free Press, 1950), p. 409.
8 Lewis Mumford, *The City in History: Its Origins, Its Transformations, and Its Prospects* (New York: Harcourt, 1961), pp. 104, 104, 103–4.

9 Michel de Certeau, *The Practice of Everyday Life*, trans. Steven F. Rendall (Berkeley: University of California Press, 1984), pp. 91–6, 118–22.

10 Linda Hutcheon, *A Poetics of Postmodernism: History, Theory, Fiction* (London: Routledge, 1988), pp. 105–23.

11 I classify dystopian cities here rather than with symbolic cities because their form is extrapolated from patterns of historical development, whereas classical and early modern utopias (the subject of Chapter 1) are alternatives to historical cities. The utopian genre changed in the nineteenth century with ideal cities imagined as arising from the implementation of theories from the social sciences or urban planning; however, these texts lack the verbal play and interpretative challenges that Balasopoulos argues define Renaissance utopias.

12 Harry Berger, Jr., "The Renaissance Imagination: Second World and Green World" (1965), *Second World and Green World: Studies in Renaissance Fiction-Making* (Berkeley: University of California Press, 1990), pp. 33–6.

13 *Spectator* 10 (March 12, 1711), Joseph Addison and Richard Steele, *The Spectator*, ed. Donald F. Bond, 5 vols. (Oxford: Clarendon Press, 1965), vol. 1, p. 44.

14 Robert Venturi, Denise Scott Brown, and Steven Izenour, *Learning from Las Vegas: The Forgotten Symbolism of Architectural Form*, rev. ed. (Cambridge, MA: MIT Press, 1977), p. 76.

15 Émile Zola defined the experimental novelist in 1880 as someone who sought "to know what such a passion, acting in such a surrounding and under such circumstances, would produce from the point of view of an individual and of society," knowledge that would allow the "construct[ion of] a practical sociology ... [that] will be a help to political and economical sciences." (Zola, "The Experimental Novel," *The Experimental Novel and Other Essays*, trans. Belle M. Sherman [New York: Cassell, 1893], pp. 9, 26.)

16 Robert E. Park, "The City: Suggestions for the Investigation of Human Behavior in the Urban Environment," in Park, Ernest W. Burgess, and Roderick D. McKenzie, *The City* (Chicago: University of Chicago Press, 1967), p. 3. Park challenged the discipline to produce "a more searching and disinterested study than even Émile Zola has given us in his 'experimental' novels" (ibid.).

17 Taking the dissolution of the fiction/fact boundary one step further, Orhan Pamuk opened in Istanbul a museum filled with objects associated with Kemal and Füsun, the protagonists of his 2008 novel, *The Museum of Innocence*.

18 David Harvey, "The Cartographic Imagination: Balzac in Paris," in Vinay Dharwadker, ed., *Cosmopolitan Geographies: New Locations in Literature and Culture* (New York: Routledge, 2001), p. 65.

19 *Race* would have been the operative term in intra-European colonization as well; in the social science of a century ago, the continent was occupied by distinct races of Saxons, Celts, Nordics, Northern and Southern Italian races, various Slavic races, etc. It goes without saying that colonization and its literature are not a modern invention. The ancient Greeks even developed a literary genre to commemorate the establishment of colonies; see Carol Dougherty, *The Poetics of Colonization: From City to Text in Ancient Greece* (New York: Oxford University Press, 1993).

20 The millet system allotted certain forms of autonomy to confessional, not ethnic, groups. Macedonians were grouped with other Orthodox Christians.

21 Honoré de Balzac, *A Harlot High and Low*, quoted in Julie Abraham, *Metropolitan Lovers: The Homosexuality of Cities* (Minneapolis: University of Minnesota Press, 2009), p. 14.

22 Nathanael West, *The Day of Locust* (New York: Signet, 1983), pp. 200, 201.

23 Anyone interested in the architectural avant-gardes should consult Manfredo Tafuri, *The Sphere and the Labyrinth: Avant-Gardes and Architecture from Piranesi to the 1970s*, trans. Pellegrino d'Acierno and Robert Connolly (Cambridge, MA: MIT Press, 1990).

24 Willa Cather, *Lucy Gayheart* (1935; New York: Vintage, 1995), p. 20.

25 Ralph Waldo Emerson, *Journals*, 10 vols., ed. Edward Waldo Emerson and Waldo Emerson Forbes (Boston: Houghton, 1910–14), vol. 8, p. 419.

26 Guy Debord, "Theory of the Dérive" (1956), in Ken Knabb, ed. and trans., *Situationist International Anthology*, rev. ed. (Berkeley, CA: Bureau of Public Secrets, 2007), p. 62. See Simon Sadler, *The Situationist City* (Cambridge, MA: MIT Press, 1998), pp. 76–103.

I

ANTONIS BALASOPOULOS

Celestial Cities and Rationalist Utopias

> "I understand," he said. "You mean the city that we have built by
> narrating, the one that lies in words – for I do not think it exists
> anywhere on earth."
>
> Plato, *Republic* (ca. 380 BCE)

What is a city? The question is foundational in a double sense: it is a
question about the origins of social and political life, and it is also a question that haunts the very beginnings of the western tradition of thinking
about the nature and goals of collective life. It is also, perhaps by virtue of
being authentically foundational, an obscure question. "Who says," Martin
Heidegger asks, "that the Greeks, because they 'lived' in the πόλις [polis],
were also in the clear as to the essence of the πόλις?"[1] His skepticism is borne
out by the philosophical record of the classical city-state. The third book
of Aristotle's *Politics* (ca. 350 BCE) begins by stating that the question of
government type (*politeia*) can be addressed only on the grounds of a prior
examination of the question of what the polis is, only to add: "At present,
this is a disputed question."[2] This fact was already attested to at the level
of language usage in classical Greek, in which *polis* could mean "country,"
or "territory," or "country, as dependent on and called after its city,"[3] but it
could also designate the citizenry as a whole, the political and military state,
or the rights of citizenship.

The term's semantic instability is not simply a matter of everyday use. As
Greek philosophy extensively engages with the city, it exposes itself to conceptual incoherence and aporia. Aristotle, for instance, answers the question
by defining the city as a "multitude of citizens," but then immediately falls
into the problem of "difference of opinion," since the definition of the citizen
is already conditioned by the definition of the city and thus inevitably "often
disputed."[4] One cannot define the citizen simply as the inhabitant of a polis
because the polis is also inhabited by noncitizens (immigrants and slaves), as
well as old men, children, and women, none of whom are deemed as citizens
in the full sense. Even the very parameters of citizenship can change after
a revolution. Moreover, non-democratic political regimes cannot be said to
govern the *demos*. In short, the attempt to define the city in terms of citizenship merely exposes the impossibility of answering the original question.

This is why Heidegger is right to remark that for the Greeks, the question "what is a/the city?" can be answered only by affirming that the polis "is and remains what is properly worthy of question."[5] To the extent that with the Greeks the city becomes a question of *foundation* (of politics, citizenship, collective history, culture, everyday life, etc.), it is a properly abyssal one: *polis* is a name for the *indeterminate* ensemble of relationships between territory, its conversion into built environment, a population that is mutable and mobile in both a physical and a constitutional sense, and the religious, mythological, political, and juridical forms that bind this population into a threatened and precarious unity. This indeterminacy affirms itself by the proliferation of negatives whenever the city is at question. In Plato's early dialogues, "the [true] city is not a market, nor an army, nor a court of law," Jean François Pradeau remarks.[6] Similarly, for Aristotle's *Politics*, the city – which, strictly speaking, is neither the state nor the society – cannot be adequately defined in terms of a stable relation between population and territory (the two may be separated, as in the cases of immigration and foreign wars), spatial enclosure (a nation [*ethnos*] may also be walled), population stability (inhabitants are born and die), or constitution (which political turmoil changes). Philosophy registers what language already indicates: the city is not one thing or another because it is *no one thing*, however much the ideal of unchanging unity can be said to have haunted Greek political thought: "It is however obvious, that the more the city develops into One, the more it ceases to be a city," Aristotle wrote, "for the city is by nature the multitude... [E]ven if it were possible to unify the city, it should not be done; for that would instead undo the city."[7]

Unity, Division, and the Classical Polis

The fundamental parameters of Greek (and, to a large extent, of medieval and early modern) attempts to think the ideal city – the city Plato's Glaukon describes as not existing anywhere on earth – thus consist of both an ontological and political investment in absolute unity and unchanging stability and a coming to terms with the *impossibility* of realizing this desire. But this tension between the city conceived in terms of Being and the city conceived in terms of Becoming provides the only available form of an imaginary (and *imaginative*) resolution of the contradiction: in the ideal city, the ontological-political ideal of unity can be deployed as the foundation of a discourse that presupposes the necessary failure of actual cities to achieve that ideal. The ideal city is therefore a virtuous *antitype*, a city whose imaginative foundation presupposes an operation whereby the empirical features of an existing city are negated, inverted, or recombined in new forms.

Pradeau demonstrates that the temporal trajectory from the *Republic* to the *Timaeus* and *Critias* and finally to the *Laws* (given existing estimations as to the dates of composition) can be understood in terms of the ideal city's increasing concretization. Although the *Republic* is vitally concerned with engendering the unity of the polis, the means for thinking its unity reside not in any concerted engagement with civic space but in a strategic comparison between the city and the soul. The three kinds of social groups in the ideal city – the laboring and professional classes, the military auxiliaries, and the political Guardians – are neatly mapped onto the three modalities of the soul: desire, spiritedness, and reason. Since these modalities are capacities of a *single* soul, however, the social groups no longer designate discrete classes; they are functional capacities of a single entity. Philosophy thus procures the ideal city by making "justice" identical to the "harmony" that emerges when "one is made out of many,"[8] but at the cost of rendering the city immaterial, its harmonious unity "devoid of any physical dimension."[9] This city's principles of constitution lack any juridico-political specificity other than that conveyed by the strict respect for functional divisions and differentiations between persons differently equipped and an educational regime designed to ensure the proper training of the men who guard the city against external enemies and internal strife.

The *Timaeus* (ca. 360 BCE) begins with an explicit reference to the *Republic*. Appraising the view of "the ideal state [*politeia*] and its citizens"[10] that he had supposedly set forth on the previous day, Socrates notes with chagrin that although virtuous, the polis he has described also seems to him "motionless," like animals that are either alive but are seen at rest or are merely "painted" representations. He will therefore request an account of the ideal city "engaging in transactions with other states [*poleis*], waging war successfully and showing in the process all the qualities one would expect from its system of education and training."[11] Two of Socrates' interlocutors declare their willingness to satisfy his request. Timaeus presents a cosmological account that links the heavens and the earth, Being and Becoming, the creation of the world and the composition of the human body and soul. Critias transfers the end product of Timaeus's account – the human being – to the city of Athens as he has heard that it existed in antediluvian times, when it was at war with the now vanished city-state of Atlantis.

This division of labor is also a division between accounts of cosmic order and the city's physical order, or macrocosm and microcosm. While the *Republic* contented itself with gesturing at the translatability of the "fixed and immutable realities" of a higher sphere onto the "clean canvas" of the ideal city as still life,[12] the ambition of conjoining the *Timaeus* to the *Critias* concerns the construction of a political physiology and a physiological architecture that will model the lower on the higher spheres by seeking to connect metaphysics and politics, cosmos and polis. Several of the geometrical and architectural elements that appear in the description of Atlantis are thus allegorically prefigured in the cosmology and physiology of the *Timaeus*. While the *Timaeus*'s description of the divine making of the body translates anatomy into geography by referring to the neck as a "kind of isthmus and boundary" between the divine element contained in the head and the mortal realm of the breast, the account of the *Critias* translates geography back into anatomy by depicting the foundation of the perfectly spherical capital of Atlantis as the result of Poseidon's act of impregnating Cleito and enclosing the territory where she lives "with concentric rings of sea and land."[13] Similarly, in his discussion of the creation of the digestive and respiratory systems, Timaeus refers to the veins as a "system of conduits, like water gardens" and to the network of nerves as an "irrigation system," features that reappear in the *Critias* 's description of the overwhelmingly aquatic city of Atlantis.[14]

Yet while an "isthmus" of sorts connects the scales at which the dialogues proceed, the other side of their division of labor is the engagement with division itself – opposition between and within Athens and Atlantis, between the primary elements of earth and water, and, finally, within the connective tissue of analogy and metaphor. While the neck is described as a protective boundary in the *Timaeus*, in the *Critias* the canals Poseidon's descendants dug unravel the protective boundaries he has fashioned, exposing the city to the tumultuous world of maritime trade and to the familiarly Athenian temptations of empire. And while the *Timaeus* renders the sphere a replicable emblem of divine perfection, the *Critias* allows geometrical reason to collapse into incoherence as the spherical shape of the capital's center jars with the square shape of the individual districts and the rectangular shape of the plain that surrounds the capital. The result is a strangely jumbled anticipation of the urban utopias of the Renaissance, themselves deeply influenced by Platonic and Neoplatonic thought. Although the *Timaeus-Critias* is the first significant attempt to think the ideal city as something that can mediate between oneness and multiplicity, timeless immobility and material becoming, it is also a failure because the city that is concretely fleshed out in terms of built space is precisely the unbalanced, incoherent city.[15]

If the depiction of Magnesia in the *Laws* (ca. 340 BCE) moves Plato beyond the impasse marked by the unfinished *Critias* (where the spatially and temporally mobile city – Atlantis – is also the city wrecked by internal disorder), it does so by transforming *division* itself into an instance of a "passion for regulation,"[16] a means of rationally ordering the city. Magnesia is providentially a "new city" where there is therefore sufficient opportunity to obtain distributive effects – a balanced distribution of allotments, census classes, and different kinds of powers and jurisdictions to different segments of the population – that will prevent internal strife, the principal evil of civic life. The harmonization of law, territory, and population necessary for the prevention of dispute and faction will accordingly be grounded in the opportune properties of the number 5,040, which is the number of inalienable allotments of land postulated by the Athenian Stranger (one of the dialogue's interlocutors). As he explains, its outstanding divisibility – it has 59 divisors, excluding itself – is an eminent feature of its political suitability as a number. The initial population can be divided into four classes according to strictly set income criteria, yielding 1,260 allotments for each class. The wider territory [*chōra*] and the city, on the other hand, are to be divided into twelve qualitatively equal parts, as many as the months of the year and the Olympian Gods to whom each part will be permanently connected, while each of the 5,040 allotments shall be divided into two halves, one located in the city and one in the surrounding country. Nor is this all: evoking Pythagorian mathematics, Hippodamean urban planning, and Cleisthenian reforms (and perhaps anticipating something of Charles Fourier's "enumerative obsession"), the excited Athenian notes that the twelve segments of the city and its territory admit of "a multitude of further divisions." Hence, there will be a council of 360 members, divided into four groups of ninety for each class; three priests must be elected from a group of nine, which must itself be derived by dividing the twelve "tribes" of the city into three groups of four and having each of them vote thrice;[17] five "rural commissioners and captains of the watch" are to be selected in rotation from each of the twelve tribes so that they may in turn select twelve young men each, with the total of sixty guards to be conducted clockwise from district to district on a monthly basis, and counterclockwise after the completion of the first year.[18] Politically deployed, number is transformed to what Nicole Loraux might call a "bond of division": it splits the polis into a multiplicity of interchangeable, movable segments that can be recombined into a bewildering multiplicity of "brotherhoods, wards and parishes" – so many forms of bringing together civic bodies that are otherwise separated by geography, income, tribal belonging, or gender.[19] Division, sufficiently multiplied, becomes an engine for generating forms of *association* – safeguards against the permanent threat of *stasis*.

In attempting to reconcile a mathematical understanding of division with the social question of association, the *Laws* also necessarily involves an attempt to neutralize the contradictions between the constituents of stasis: immobility and movement. In fact, Magnesia is intended as the antitype of those already established (and faulty) cities where both evolutionary movement (*kinein*) and orderly immobility (*akinēton*) have become equally impossible. The movement of citizen bodies (from section to section, or from urban to rural dwellings) is to be regulated by the fixed laws of number, but from another perspective, number, despite its declared sacrality, is exposed to "the distortions and dissymmetries [that] the real imposes" because available land is not likely to be isotropic.[20] The twelve sections and the individual land shares cannot be perfectly equal: the capital city can be built only approximately in the center of the territory; the council of 360 delegates presupposes a division of the population by fourteen rather than twelve, generating a division that clashes with the duodecimal division into tribes; and the number of the magistrates or guardians of the laws, whom Pradeau considers "the most important figures in the city," is thirty-seven, which represents *no* possible division based on the number of allotments, but derives from a different order of calculation.[21] And of course, the existence of 5,040 allotments does not equal a stable population of 5,040 citizens, not only because of the problems posed by unequal fertility rates, but also because Magnesia will necessarily include slaves – emblems of the limits to equality – whose unspecified number haunts the formal beauty of Platonic calculations like a dangerous supplement. Indeed, if one is to concede that in Plato's political arithmetic the number "serves the same function as the law," one has to also concede that its instabilities and imperfections are to be taken as signs of the limits to the sovereign power of law itself.[22] Magnesia, after all, is only a "second-best" city, less ideal than possible; its constitution and its electoral system will both be mixed, for equality itself is divided between quantitative and qualitative possibilities. Although the utopian impetus of the *Laws* is inextricable from its proliferation of strategies of regulation and control, to the point where virtually the entire citizen population is involved in its own surveillance, it is also the case that its plan is unlikely to be fully realized because real citizens are not made "out of wax."[23] The city imagined by the *Laws* – a circle whose innermost ring is the sacred Acropolis, followed by the urban center, the suburbs and the country, and from whose center radiate the twelve lines that divide the territory – is certainly a model city, but the Athenian knows that models deprived of plasticity and adjustability to circumstance are just inanimate effigies.

Between Philosophy and Religion: The Medieval Virtuous City

The circumstances that occasioned Augustine of Hippo's vast *City of God* (426) – the sacking of Rome and the disintegration of the Roman empire – may suggest the state of severe political crisis, war, and internal disarray under which Plato undertook his project. However, the juxtaposition of political and social realms that characterized Greek culture had been replaced by their conflation into one and subordination to the realm of the sacred. As a result, the ideal city is no longer the experimental site in which the desire for a normative reorganization of political life seeks its spatial expression. The corresponding city in Judeo-Christian culture is marked by its vast conceptual distance from empirically existent cities.

Presupposing the specifically Christian dichotomy between temporal and spiritual realms, the *City of God* organizes itself as a grand religious narrative of the origins and destinies of two irreconcilable cities – less empirical entities than allegorical types into which "the many and very great nations throughout the world" can be retrospectively reduced.[24] Their designation in the text varies; pairings include the city of flesh and the city of spirit, the city of man and the city of God, and the earthly and the heavenly Jerusalem. The preservation of a stable opposition between positive and negative poles by no means entails that we are dealing with so many versions of the *same* binary. Augustine notes that only Cain, founder of the sinful city of man, built a city at all; Abel, "as though he were merely a pilgrim on earth, built none." The opposition between the worldly city and the city of God is thus supplemented by a second – effectively Neoplatonist – opposition between the true "eternal City," existing only in heaven, and its wayfaring "shadow," cast on earth as its typological anticipation.[25] Although it is marked by imperfection, this "shadow of the heavenly city" is by no means reducible to the "visible appearance of the earthly city,"[26] nor is it free like "that Jerusalem which is above" because it exists "in bondage to symbolic purpose."[27] Despite St. Augustine's constant deployment of the binary opposition as the ground of exposition, the operative terms of the *City of God* are thus three rather than two: to the ungodly and pagan city of the world (to which the classical philosophers of the polis are consigned) one must add both the worldly copy of the heavenly city and its celestial prototype and fulfillment.

The reasons for this lapse in rhetorical symmetry lie in the fact that *City of God* has a practical political purpose. Arguing against those who saw Christianity as responsible for the fall of Rome, it defends the viability *in this world* of a civic virtue that is compatible with Christian ethics. This argument is anticipated in Augustine's insistence that prophetic writings are not reducible to references to earthly and heavenly Jerusalems, but include a third class that references "both simultaneously."[28] It is taken up systematically only in later chapters, when the author attributes internal conflict to the chaotic nature of the city of worldly desires, as in Rome, which was plunged into violence and war because the lack of a "mutual recognition of rights" among its citizens deprived it of justice – the only foundation of a real commonwealth. At the same time, Augustine concedes, the conception of peace in the heavenly city's earthly manifestation – the "ordered harmony of authority and obedience between citizens" – is compatible with civil law and not harmed by its achievements.[29] Provided that religious duty is not compromised, in other words, the congregation of God's elect (the incipiently global community that really constitutes the *civitas Dei*) may acquiesce to worldly authority. The conceit of "dual citizenship" in the temporal and spiritual kingdoms safeguards submission to the hierarchical order of early feudal society and protects it from the insurrectionary potential of literal millennialism.

Although it is no more specific about the spatial composition or the political, economic, and juridical institutions of the model city than are the overwhelmingly allegorical Christian medieval texts, Abū Nasr al-Fārābī's *On the Perfect State* (ca. 940) is far more attuned to the rational core of classical Greek thought on the subject and therefore conversant with the secularist and voluntaristic conception of collective happiness that one finds in the early modern utopias produced by human effort. Al-Fārābī's treatise, the first work of a distinctly Islamic tradition of reflecting on civic virtue, is certainly indebted to the Neoplatonists' fusion of Platonic and Aristotelian philosophy. The structural logic of the *Timaeus* and *Critias*, for instance, is closely emulated by the structure of *On the Perfect State*. At the same time, al-Fārābī's religious metaphysics is firmly grounded in the Aristotelian unmoved mover, while his politics often strongly evoke the *Republic*, and his extensive engagement with relations among entities in the static celestial and changing sublunary worlds is Aristotelian and Neoplatonic at once.

This philosophically and culturally hybrid framework mediates experimentally between the hierarchical conception of cosmos and state vital to the corporate fictions of feudal society and the defense of the autonomy and supremacy of reason that would later challenge monarchical ideology in the rationalist utopias. Hence al-Fārābī elevates the "Active Intellect" (the quasi-divine principle that allows intelligibles to be grasped by "the intellect in actuality") to supreme status among the entities of the sublunary world, and makes "theoretical reason" the supreme and sovereign instance of the rational faculty.[30] Religious prophecy, even if it is the "highest rank of perfection"[31] attained by the faculty of representation, is far inferior to philosophical reason because the philosopher (who is closest to a God perceived in terms of pure contemplation) knows that symbols are imperfect approximations of truth.

Thus, although al-Fārābī shares Augustine's criticism of classical philosophy's pagan roots, the optimal organization of political life is not subordinated to religion or cosmologically derived determinism. While the virtuous city is functionally differentiated into classes, and its health and peace depend on the cooperation of its inferior organs with the "ruling organ" of a Platonically conceived "imam," the "dispositions and habits" of the city's denizens "are not natural but voluntary."[32] Collective felicity thus presupposes the intentional and rational human effort of each citizen, in stark contrast to what a properly destinarian conception like Augustine's would likely posit. Paradoxically, al-Fārābī's yoking of philosophical rationality to the questions posited by practical, material life yields something of an *anti-utopian* venture in the sense that its feasibility depends on the sharp rejection of the ancients' "pernicious" belief that what actually exists in this world is somehow unnatural, and that one's task is "voluntarily to direct one's aim and action towards bringing this existence to an end so that the other existence which is the natural perfection emerges."[33]

Islands of Reason: Renaissance Utopias

We have refrained from calling the ideal or nearly ideal polities of classical and medieval writers' *utopias* not only because the term's derivation from Thomas More's 1516 work would make it anachronistic. More importantly, the seminal pre-Reformation texts of the utopian genre to which we now turn exhibit traits that distinguish them from the broader tradition of the "ideal city" or "perfect moral commonwealth." Four epochal features structure our discussion of More's *Utopia*, Tommaso Campanella's *City of the Sun* (1602), Johann Valentin Andreæ's *Christianopolis* (1619), and Francis Bacon's *New Atlantis* (1624).

First, Renaissance utopias subordinate both philosophy and religion to the hybrid and elusive form of discourse that we call *literature*. Whereas dialogue, argumentative exposition, and pseudo-historical or Scriptural fable were the dominant modes through which the classical and medieval traditions grasped their object, Renaissance utopias tend to be structured around the discursive dichotomy between narrative and description, as they are incarnated in travel narrative and fictional cultural ethnography. As Louis Marin has shown, this duality of textual modes introduces a tension specific to the early modern transformation of earlier traditions. Narrative represents the empirically "realistic" persistence of contingency, conflict, and change that marks our world, while description tends to spatialize and freeze time into an eternal, unchanging present, wherein social life becomes effectively achronic, devoid of historical pertinence.[34] One would be correct to see in this tension a new way of posing the problem that the old antinomy of Being and Becoming presents to all efforts to imagine the ideal polity. However, the tendency of narrative to challenge, displace, or disfigure the seeming coherence and wholeness of a descriptive image is no longer a matter for explicit philosophical or religious contemplation; rather, it is a *textual* issue that pertains to literary interpretation. Narrative inscribes utopian space within the order of a possible yet contingent encounter between the known world and an unknown other world, and hence *connects* a "here" to a "there." At the same time, description *separates* the two, both to the extent that it highlights the radical differences between them and in the more profound sense that it seeks to ground such differences in the ontological difference between perfect and imperfect, coherent and incoherent, static and unstable worlds.

Second, Renaissance utopias imagine the utopian polity not simply as an insular and fortified state, but also as a concrete *model* of the possibilities and benefits promised by the rational reorganization of space and population. A confluence of scientific, technological, practical, and social factors underlies the hegemony of socially reformative architectonics in the Renaissance. The rediscovery and popularization (via Leon Battista Alberti) of Vitruvius's *De Architectura* in early fifteenth-century Italy had laid the technical foundations for the ambition to reconstruct existing cities or to found new ones according to principles of ideal symmetry and regularity: Filarete's (Antonio di Pietro Averlino) architectural plan for the ideal city of Sforzinda appeared in the second half of the same century, followed by the geometrically determined city plans of Leonardo da Vinci, Albrecht Dürer, Vincenzo Scamozzi, Johann Christian Schickhardt, and others. Filippo Brunelleschi's discovery of perspective, also in the early fifteenth century, meant that city space would be conceived by painters in terms of an isotropic, homogenous, and totalizable entity, as is the case with the late fifteenth-century triptych of ideal cityscapes attributed to Piero della Fransesca. Technological factors such as the gradual improvement of surveying and drawing instruments and the greater availability of paper reinforced the rise of architectural planning as an autonomous and ambitious discipline, while the need to solve problems of sanitation and to improve urban fortifications to cope with technological developments in warfare gave the proliferation of "ideal city" plans a rather practical edge. Finally, the canonization of a genre of ideal-city planning that Renaissance utopias exploit emerges from changes in the class structure of late medieval Europe. Beginning in Italy and spreading to the rest of Europe in the wake of the rise of merchants and the gradual emergence of capitalist relations of production, we find "the decline of the communal government and the concentration of power in the hands of seigneurial families"[35] keen to enhance their status by serving as patrons of ambitious architects and city planners and as promulgators of civic pride.

Indeed, the fundamental features of early modern urbanism and the utopian fictions that incorporate its discourse in their descriptions – the objectification of the city as image, its conceptual extraction from the ad-hoc world of everyday practices and needs, its mathematical and geometrical formalism, its reconstruction in terms of homogeneous, continuous, and extensible space – parallel transformations in the social order that belie apparent continuities with the literature of the ideal city in earlier epochs. As Leonard Goldstein demonstrates, the features that accompany the rise of early modern perspective owe much to the increasingly quantified and abstract nature of labor as process and to the alienation of humans from the given, natural world, which accompanied the slow rise of capitalism and necessitated the destruction of the persistently hierarchical, qualitatively differentiated cosmos of the classical period and the Middle Ages.[36] Between history and utopia, of course, an inversion emerges: in More, Campanella, or Andreæ, and to some extent in Bacon as well, the concept of the city as a "delocalized and reproducible" model is not depicted as the *product* of social processes.[37] Rather, it seems to govern and to regulate these processes, whether by safeguarding social uniformity and equality or educating citizens in the polity's scientific and ideological principles. More chooses uniformity, postulating fifty-four square-shaped, virtually identically laid-out, and equidistant cities and abolishing the city's privileges vis-à-vis the country. Campanella's architectural mnemotechnics, where the painted inner and outer walls of the circular city's seven circuits serve as constant instructors into every field of knowledge, and Andreæ's huge network of scientific, political, and economic institutions, and their models, samples, or pictorial representations exemplify the pedagogical solution. Even Francis Bacon's Bensalem betrays signs of a close interdependence between rational city planning and social engineering; if the street our narrator sees while visiting with one of the Fathers of the scientific center of Salomon's House is "wonderfully well kept," and the house windows lining it are well spaced, it is also the case that the inhabitants appear ordered according to a spontaneous and inbred quasi-military discipline, "as if they had been placed."[38]

Third, the positivistic character of Renaissance utopian urbanism is belied by a greater or lesser measure of conscious and deliberate textual ambiguity and paradox generated by the fact that Renaissance utopian texts place their rationally designed and disciplined island polities literally *nowhere*: More's island is supposed to lie somewhere in between the Old and the New Worlds, but it is not placed on the map when Hythlodaeus's circular itinerary from Portugal to America, Ceylon, Calcutta, and back is first mentioned; in the playful correspondence of More's humanist circle, it is proclaimed a neglected, or unfortunately overheard, question. Andreæ's island of Capharsalama is discovered by the ship of "Fantasy" sailing in the "Academic Ocean" and positioned at once specifically and impossibly.[39] The City of the Sun is simply somewhere vaguely around the legendary island of Taprobane (Sri Lanka). Bacon's narrator arrives in Bensalem only after a journey south is interrupted by winds that possibly led his ship to an unspecified northern locale. Textual features such as litotes and oxymoronic toponyms and proper names reinforce the effect: they generate an interpretive contract according to which the "good place" (*eu-topos*) is also an inexistent, anticipatory, perhaps unrealizable place (*ou-topos*).

Finally, the Renaissance ideal city distinguishes itself from its predecessors because it is grasped in terms of a concern with the organization of both production (agricultural, artisanal, artistic, and scientific) *and* consumption. Unlike the classical ideal city, in which the endorsement of a functional division of labor does not imply the possibility of changing the mode of production or transforming its corresponding modes of distribution and consumption, or the medieval city, which remains largely a spiritual and even allegorical abstraction effectively without any material economy, early modern utopias manifest extensive interest in either the equitable distribution of goods and the burdens of labor (More, Campanella, and Andreæ emphasize universal and compulsory employment) or the prospect for radical scientific improvements in productivity (which Bacon hints at but fails to develop). Inevitably, the Renaissance ideal city is inextricably linked to a new conception of class, which reflects the momentous upheavals that marked the transition from late feudal society. No longer a neutral census datum or a natural effect of cosmic hierarchy, class is a conflict-bearing threat to be managed and neutralized or else masked and repressed: More cannot abolish beggary, vagrancy, and idleness without also abolishing private property, while Campanella's and Andreæ's quasi-secularized monastic communities strive to contain the deleterious effects of the division of labor by similarly abolishing private ownership and the circulation of money, but they cannot altogether undo the abiding division between mental and manual labor. Although Bacon appears to eschew questions of social relations altogether, his "attempt to figure transformed forces of [early capitalist] production cannot," in Christopher Kendrick's estimation, "keep from betraying an allegory of new social relations" modeled on "possessive corporatism" and the "state joint-stock guild."[40]

In a sense, the duality we have seen haunting the figure of the ideal city – first in the ontological-political guise of oneness and multiplicity, unity and division; then in the religious form of sacred and profane, celestial and earthly – remains a determining factor in its properly utopian incarnation in the Renaissance. By the early seventeenth century, however, it has become not merely a formal or a conceptual symptom, but also the mark of a productive and generative tension between decaying and emerging social relations, between the autocracy of the imagination and its self-effacingly egalitarian aspirations, between the fixity of the state form and the destabilizing dynamism of new relations and forces of production. The imagined city becomes properly "utopian" by being transformed to the simultaneously concrete and uninhabitable image – the spectral projection – of a gaze suspended between a world collapsing and a world not fully graspable.

NOTES

1 Martin Heidegger, *Hölderlin's Hymn "The Ister,"* trans. William McNeill and Julia Davis (Bloomington: Indiana University Press, 1996), p. 80.

2 Aristotle, *Politics*, trans. Benjamin Jowett, in The Politics *and the Constitution of Athens*, ed. Stephen Everson (Cambridge: Cambridge University Press, 1996), p. 61.

3 On the complex and often ambiguous semantic relations between *chōra, topos, meros, polis*, and *astū*, see Jean-François Pradeau, "Être quelque part, occuper une place. ΤΟΠΟΣ et ΧΩΡΑ dans le *Timée*," *Les Etudes Philosophiques* 3 (1995), 376; and Anissa Castel-Bouchouchi, "L' espace civique: le plan de la cité des *Lois*," *Revue Philosophique* 125 (2000), 24–5, 33–4.

4 Aristotle, *Politics*, book 3, chap. 1, 1275a; author's translation.

5 Heidegger, *Hölderlin's Hymn "The Ister,"* p. 85.

6 Jean-François Pradeau, *Plato and the City: A New Introduction to Plato's Political Thought*, trans. Janet Lloyd (Exeter, UK: University of Exeter Press, 2002), p. 5.

7 Aristotle, *Politics*, book 2, chap. 2, 1261a; author's translation.

8 Plato, *Republic*, trans. Desmond Lee (London: Penguin, 1983), p. 153, translation modified by the author.

9 Pradeau, *Plato and the City*, p. 69.

10 Plato, *Timaeus*, in Timaeus *and* Critias, trans. Desmond Lee (Harmondsworth, UK: Penguin, 1977), p. 29.

11 Ibid., p. 31; translation modified by the author. The "painted city" is also the city of the Athenian painters, a city in which the tumultuous realities of political activity have been suspended.

12 Plato, *Republic*, pp. 223, 224.

13 Plato, *Timaeus*, p. 97; Plato, *Critias*, in Timaeus *and* Critias, p. 136. As an adjective, "capital" means "of the head" (Latin *caput*). The capital city is the "head city." The Timaeus *and* Critias are marked by a very similar co-implication of metaphysics, anatomy, politics, and urban planning when it comes to the multifold registers in which the figure of the sphere signifies.

14 Plato, *Timaeus*, p. 106.

15 On the failure of the *Critias'* attempt to satisfy Socrates' request, see Nicole Loraux, *The Divided City: On Memory and Forgetting in Ancient Athens*, trans. Corinne Pache and Jeff Fort (New York: Zone Books, 2006), p. 50.

16 Pierre Vidal-Naquet, *Politics Ancient and Modern*, trans. Janet Lloyd (Cambridge: Polity Press, 1995), p. 9.

17 Plato, *The Laws*, trans. A. E. Taylor, in *Plato: The Collected Dialogues*, ed. Edith Hamilton and Huntington Cairns (Princeton, NJ: Princeton University Press, 1991), pp. 1330, 1339.

18 Ibid., p. 1339.

19 Loraux, *The Divided City*, p. 93; the concept is analyzed on p. 96; Plato, *Laws*, p. 1330.

20 Castel-Bouchouchi, "L'espace civique," p. 33 (author's translation).

21 Pradeau, *Plato and the City*, p. 153.

22 Ibid., p. 159. The unspecified number of slaves disfigures the seeming perfection of numerical calculation not simply for formal and abstract reasons but also because it affects several aspects of political life. Normally, the size of a city's army and civic police would have to correspond to that of its slaves, as slavery entails risks of insurrection. Furthermore, slaves make the free population prone to idleness, corruption of civic morals, acquisitive temptations, and tyranny. This may be why the Athenian fails to mention their number, and why the discussion of Kallipolis – the ideal city in the *Republic* – attempts to gloss over the presence of slaves altogether.

23 Plato, *Laws*, pp. 1324, 1330, translation modified.

24 Saint Augustine, *City of God*, trans. Gerard G. Walsh, Demetrius B. Zema, Grace Monahan, and Daniel J. Honan (New York: Doubleday, 1958), p. 295.

25 Ibid., pp. 325.

26 Ibid., p. 326.

27 Ibid., p. 325.

28 Ibid., p. 381.

29 Ibid., pp. 469, 456.

30 Abū Nasr al-Fārābī, *On the Perfect State*, trans. Richard Walzer (Chicago: Great Books of the Islamic World, 1998), pp. 199–203, 209.

31 Ibid., p. 225.

32 Ibid., pp. 231, 233.

33 Ibid., pp. 317, 323.

34 Louis Marin, *Utopics: Spatial Play*, trans. Robert A. Vollrath (Atlantic Highlands, NJ: Humanities Press, 1984), pp. 33–60.

35 Ruth Eaton, *Ideal Cities: Utopianism and the (Un)Built Environment* (New York: Thames & Hudson, 2002), p. 50.

36 See Leonard Goldstein, *The Social and Cultural Roots of Linear Perspective* (Minneapolis: MEP Publications, 1988), pp. 63–87, 135–6.

37 Françoise Choay, *The Rule and the Model: On the Theory and Architecture of Urbanism* (Cambridge, MA: MIT Press, 1997), p. 139.

38 Francis Bacon, *New Atlantis*, in Susan Bruce, ed., *Three Early Modern Utopias* (Oxford: Oxford University Press, 1999), p. 176.

39 Johann Valentine Andreæ, *Christianopolis*, trans. Edward H. Thompson (Dordrecht, Netherlands: Kluwer Academic Publishers, 1999), pp. 155–6.

40 Christopher Kendrick, *Utopia, Carnival and Commonwealth in Renaissance England* (Toronto: University of Toronto Press, 2004), pp. 295, 302, 317.

2

SUSAN STEPHENS

The City in the Literature of Antiquity

Ancient cities were physical spaces: many of them have long been abandoned; others exist as palimpsests overwritten by more recent inhabitants. Ancient cities were also imagined spaces with histories and personalities bestowed on them by those who dwelt in them or wrote about them from a distant place or time. Because of the literature that was produced in and about them, four ancient cities have dominated the intellectual traditions in which this collection is conceived: Athens, Alexandria, Rome, and Jerusalem. Today their very names stimulate a set of predictable responses: Athens is coextensive with the "glory that was Greece" – the cradle of democracy, the birthplace of philosophy and tragic drama. Rome is the city of grandeur, where imperial power rose and fell, the center of a vast empire – and a synonym for decadence. In contrast, Alexandria was a city on the margins, neither fully Greek nor Egyptian, despite its location at the Mediterranean edge of the Nile. Alexandria was home to the western world's first great library, but it was also notorious for the incestuous marriages of its rulers, the most famous of whom was Cleopatra. Jerusalem is at once the capital of Judaea, the hereditary Jewish state, and its sacred city, as well as the spiritual center of western Christendom.

What makes these cities stand out, apart from continuous occupation, is their interconnection in a narrative of rise and decline, sharply delineated by specific dates and events. Athens' heyday was between the sixth and fourth centuries BCE. When it lost its empire and its political autonomy in the wake of Alexander's conquest of the eastern Mediterranean (333–23 BCE), the power and importance of Alexandria emerged under the Macedonian line of the Ptolemies. Alexandria reigned as first city of the Mediterranean from the third through first centuries BCE; then, in the wake of the battle of Actium waged between the warring Roman factions of Octavian (later Augustus, the first Roman emperor) and Marc Antony, the city fell to Octavian to become part of the Roman empire. Rome ruled supreme for five centuries, until overrun by Visigoths, first in 410 CE and finally falling in 476 CE. Jerusalem functions as a space of absence and of longing; its history is one of diaspora and loss for Jews, but its entry into western consciousness stems from its appropriation by Christians. The location of the death and resurrection of Jesus Christ, it becomes the spiritual capital of Christendom.

However much historians push back against this received wisdom, it continues to inform the popular as well as the scholarly imagination – it was, after all, Edward Gibbon who told us the seductive tale of the "decline and fall of the Roman Empire." The controlling trope of Gibbon's narrative was rooted in antiquity itself. The so-called father of historical writing, Herodotus thought in terms of growth and decline, claiming that the impetus for his work was to memorialize the rise and fall of power, that what was great was now inferior, and the reverse. Later, Romans writing about their own history saw their dominance as not just military but as divinely intended victories over those who lacked their stern moral principles. This belief is most boldly expressed by Virgil in the *Aeneid* (19 BCE), when Aeneas encounters his dead father, Anchises, in the underworld; he predicts the future glory of his descendants:

> Others, I believe, shall beat out breathing bronze more smoothly and coax a living aspect from marble, plead cases better, and trace with a pointer heaven's motions and predict the rising of stars. You, Roman, take care to rule the world – these are your arts – to impose the peace, to spare the conquered and to crush the proud.[1]

In what follows we shall first consider how the images of these cities were constructed by writers resident within them, then we shall look at the ways in which our modern views have been shaped by later writers principally of the Greco-Roman past.

Athens

The enduring symbol of Athens is the Parthenon. Although it was vividly painted in antiquity, the monument now stands on its hill rising above the city in a blaze of white marble, with pure and elegant lines, a shimmering tribute to the *idea* of the classical: all things in proportion, "nothing in excess." The image of Athens itself has been constructed to coincide with this idea. In his history, Thucydides includes a lyric encomium of Athens, supposedly spoken by Pericles, the great Athenian statesman of the fifth century BCE, as a funeral oration. In it he delineates the exceptionalism of the city, the uniqueness of its democratic institutions, its attachment to culture and intellectual inquiry:

> I say that the city is an education for Greece, and that the individual Athenian on his own seems to adapt himself to the most varied circumstances with

versatility and grace. This is not a boast of the moment, but a matter of fact, illustrated by the power that the city has acquired by means of these qualities.[2]

Thucydides introduces another claim that helped to create the memory of Athens, namely that the superior valor and virtue of its citizens saved all of Greece from the tyrant's yoke when Athens staved off the far larger, more powerful Persian empire first at the battle of Marathon in 490 BCE, then ten years later at Salamis. The theme of democratic Athens defeating tyranny was reinforced in the public venue of tragedy, an art form that seems to have been invented in Athens and grew to maturity in its soil. Aeschylus in the *Persians* stages the defeat of Persian Darius for his *hubris* in attacking Greece, while Theseus, the mythical founder of the Athenian democracy, often figured in tragedies as a wise statesman (e. g., Sophocles' *Oedipus at Colonus* and Euripides' *Suppliants*). In the fourth century BCE, orators such as Isocrates in his *Panegyricus* and Demosthenes in his *On the Crown* are complicit in the myth of decline as they continuously urged the Athens of their day rise to the level of their ancestors who had defended Greece against threats from external powers and excoriated them for failing to do so.

The city itself is a central topic of comedy, which, like tragedy, is closely associated with Athens; both were performed annually at a number of civic festivals. In comedies, the failures of the civic processes were often subject to scathing abuse, but the openness of the criticisms and the freedom to critique reinforces the image of Athens as a uniquely democratic state. For example, Aristophanes, in his *Lysistrata*, stages the women of Athens uniting with other Greek women to put an end to the Peloponnesian war by the simple expedient of holding a sex strike until the men sign a peace treaty. At the center of the play, Lysistrata uses her woman's knowledge of weaving to advise the city:

> First it's necessary [to cleanse the city] just like a fleece; putting it in a bath wash out the dung, then stretching it on a couch get rid of the chaff and pluck out the thorns. Those who clump themselves together for government positions, squeeze and pluck off their heads. Next card the wool into a basket of unity and goodwill, mixing in everyone... Take each portion and wind into the center, joining them together in one large spindle. From this finally weave together a strong cloak for the people.[3]

The valor and worth of Athens continued as a theme even in Plato. When Socrates is condemned to death by an Athenian court for corrupting the youth and not believing in the city's gods, some of his friends urge him to go into exile rather than accept the verdict to drink hemlock. In the dialogue known as the *Crito*, Socrates refuses, arguing that he owes a duty to the laws that have nurtured him for seventy years. He then ventriloquizes the personified Laws of Athens:

> "Are you so wise that you have forgotten that your country is more precious and more to be revered and is holier and in higher esteem among the gods and among men of understanding than your mother and your father and all your ancestors, and that you ought to show to her more reverence and obedience and humility when she is angry than to your father, and ought either to convince her by persuasion or to do whatever she commands, and to suffer, if she commands you to suffer, in silence..."
>
> What shall we reply to this, Crito, that the Laws speak the truth, or not?[4]

The death of Socrates as Plato relates it, however, created the indelible memory of the city at fault, the beginning of its decline – a memory reinforced by the fact that Socrates' death was more or less coincident with Athens' defeat by Sparta after thirty years of war. Although Athens continued to thrive for five long centuries, "Athens" is fixed in the collective western memory by its "classical" period of democratic self rule. Greek writers of a much later period (such as Plutarch, Lucian, Dio Chrysostom, and Philostratus) exalted the image of this classical Athens by adapting its distinctive dialect (Attic), imitating its important writers (Thucydides, Plato, and Demosthenes), and retelling its myths of exceptionalism. It is to Plutarch that we owe the "lives" of great Athenians including Cimon, Themistocles, Pericles, and Demosthenes, and even the mythic Theseus.

Alexandria

Unlike Athens or Rome, whose poets could celebrate a mythic past, Alexandria was founded in historical time – by Alexander in 332 or 331 BCE as he passed through on his way to Babylon. The story is related by the historians of Alexander, Arrian, and Quintus Curtius, as well as the fantasy-filled *Alexander Romance*, whose reception in the later antique and medieval world rivaled only that of the Bible. Located on an earlier Egyptian coastal fortification, Alexandria was among the first great megacities of antiquity, with a population of around 300,000 by 200 BCE.[5] From its foundation a city of mixed nationalities, it included Egyptians already resident on the site or immigrating for the advantages of the new place; citizens from other Greek or Macedonian cities such as Pella, Cyrene, or Athens; Greek speakers from North Africa, the Levant, and southwestern Turkey; and by the second century BCE, a large population of diasporic Jews (who were even given their own quarter of the city). Alexandria's ethnic mix and immigrant population is apparent in the city's earliest poets. Theocritus, for example, in his urban mime describes the crowded streets as two bourgeois ladies, immigrants from Syracuse, make their way to the royal palace for a festival of Adonis:

> Oh god, what a crowd. How and when are we going to get through this mess? Ants beyond number or measure. You have accomplished many marvelous things, Ptolemy, since your father became an immortal. No evildoer comes up to you like an Egyptian and does you harm – the tricks those men in their deception used to play – one as bad as another, nasty tricks, a cursed lot. Dear Gorgo, what will happen to us? The war horses of the king! Dear man, don't trample me![6]

Alexandria's harbors were dominated by its lighthouse, one of the seven wonders of the ancient world. The poet Posidippus celebrated it thus: "In Egypt there are not watchtowers on a mountain as on the islands, but the breakwater is low where ships are birthed. Therefore this tower, straight and upright from an immense distance is seen to cut through the air."[7]

If Athens had memorable civic spaces where democratic and philosophical debate took place, Alexandria had a palace quarter, whose resident monarchs were patrons of the arts, a Museum where scholars worked tirelessly at scientific inquiry and to preserve and understand the past, and the greatest library in the ancient world. The earliest testament to the city is found in a mime by Herodas:

> Everything that is and is produced is in Egypt: wealth, wrestling grounds, power, peace, renown, spectacles, philosophers, money, young men, the precinct of the Sibling Gods [Ptolemy II and his full-sister/wife, Arsinoe II], the best king, the Museum, wine, all the good things one might want, women ... more in number than the stars.[8]

The physical differences of the two cities function as reciprocals of their imagined characters – the one filled with resilient and versatile citizen soldiers, the other with monarchs and a lifestyle inclined toward luxury. The ruling order, the Ptolemies, engaged in the practice of brother-sister marriage, as did other of Alexander's successors, probably as a political measure to limit exogamous claims to the royal line. But it was the Ptolemies who became a byword for decadence. These kings also had themselves deified (e. g., the Sibling Gods), and images of their queens as goddesses graced the landscape. Arsinoe II was worshipped in conjunction with Aphrodite. Her mortuary temple can only be thought of as over-the-top: the roof was magnetized so that a statue of the deified queen could appear to float in the air as if ascending to heaven. The precinct was adorned with an obelisk brought from the great temple of Amun in Thebes (modern Luxor). Alexandrian poets wrote about their deified queen and her temples, and the poet Callimachus, whose influence on Roman poets was immense, immortalized another queen, Berenice II, the wife and cousin of Ptolemy III, for her victories in chariot racing at the Nemean games in Greece and for her dedication of a lock of hair for the safe return of her husband from war. At the opening of *Georgics,* book 3, Virgil recasts the central image of this victory hymn as praise of Augustus in his triumph over Egypt (a reference to the battle of Actium). The *Lock of Berenice* was imitated on many occasions by Roman poets, especially Ovid at the end of his *Metamorphoses*, and even translated into Latin by Catullus.

Yet the most characteristic monument of Alexandria is its library. Built under the first Ptolemies, it was designed to gather copies of previous Greek literature into one place and to serve as a focus of Greek pride and identity for the new immigrants. But it was also an act of cultural imperialism – Galen records that Ptolemy pledged fifteen talents of gold to Athens to borrow Athens' official state copies of its tragic productions (the plays of, among others, Aeschylus, Sophocles, and Euripides), but in the event he kept the originals and forfeited the talents.[9] The story, probably untrue, was told because of its symbolic value: the physical passing of the most distinguished literary production of the Athenian state to Egypt marked the waning of the former's power and the rising influence of the new city.

This library and its fate have led a rich fantasy life in the popular imagination. The *Letter of Aristeas*, written about 200 BCE, is the first to mention the foundation of the library under the first Ptolemies; it also claims that Jewish elders were sent to Alexandria to translate the *Septuagint* into Greek. This seems to have been an attempt by Jews immigrant in Alexandria to bolster the value of their sacred texts by having them attached to the prestige of the library.[10] In 1980, Carl Sagan devoted an episode of his popular TV series, *Cosmos*, to the library. It ends with another apocryphal story, taken from the thirteenth-century Arab historian, Ibn al-Qifti, who claimed that, at the instruction of the caliph, the library's books were given over to the public baths of Alexandria, where they were used for fuel. It took six months to burn the mass of material, and only the books of Aristotle were spared. The library had most certainly fallen into disrepair and neglect long before the Arab conquest of the city, but the story persists because it reflects the commonplace and unexamined antithesis of the west (read Greeks) as the inventors of certain kinds of intellectual activities – history, philosophy, open intellectual inquiry, and the Arab world as repressors of anything that is novel or unimagined by the Koran. Yet even the Arab Egyptian government cashed in on the popularity of the library as an icon of intellectual achievement when, in October 2002, it built the New Alexandrian Library on what archaeologists think may have been the site of the original. In front of that building, the state has displayed one of the colossal statues of a

Ptolemy dressed as a pharaoh, a statue recently found in the underwater excavations of the city.

Rome

In contrast to the cultured, exotic, and occasionally decadent image of Alexandria, Rome lives in our imaginations for its realization of power – its civil wars, its imperial reach – but equally its crowded urban spaces where prostitutes and gladiators and Christians compete for our attention. Popular film and television series such as the American productions *Rome* (2005) and *Spartacus* (2010) operate within these cultural clichés by nicely blending historical events with sex, violence, and war. (Athens has never been so figured in the popular imagination.) The very origin of Rome was conceived in discord and blood. Romans traced their history back to the story of the half-divine twins Romulus and Remus, who, when exposed by their mother, were suckled by a she wolf – and a bronze casting of the wolf and the twins still sits upon the Capitoline hill in the center of the city. Romulus was credited with founding the city after a dispute in which he killed his brother, and the city's origins in fratricide is a theme often evoked by later writers as they chronicled the long history of internecine strife that was ended only by the dissolution of the Republic. In the Roman narration of their own history, they initially endured a long reign of kings descended from Romulus, but threw off the monarchy and became a republic around 510 BCE.[11]

Rome was convulsed by a series of civil wars from the early 80s until 30 BCE. The writings of Sallust and especially Cicero provide eyewitness narratives of the struggles of the late Republic and they, like their successors – the historians Livy and Tacitus – project the Roman past as formed by homely courage, moral rectitude, and selfless service to the state in contrast to the violence and venality of the present order. The climactic event for Roman history was the murder of Julius Caesar by his fellow senators in 44 BCE in the Senate chamber, on the grounds that he intended to become king. Caesar's murder has come to stand symbolically for the end of the Republic as the very men who strove to maintain it could only do so by a treacherous act. The moment is preserved by many ancient historians, but it is Plutarch, in his *Life of Caesar*, who gave the story the shape that we have inherited, most obviously through William Shakespeare in *Julius Caesar* (1599).

Also implicated in the end of the republic was Cleopatra, the last queen of Egypt, who had become Julius Caesar's lover when he entered Alexandria in 48 BCE. She was in Rome at the time of Caesar's death, beat a hasty retreat, and later engaged in a liaison with Marc Antony, who had taken over most of Caesar's armies. To him she bore three children. The struggles of Marc Antony with Octavian were finally resolved in the latter's favor, and subsequently both Antony and Cleopatra committed suicide in Alexandria, another famous event immortalized in Plutarch's *Life of Antony*, the basis for Shakespeare's *Antony and Cleopatra* (ca. 1607). Octavian, with the resources of Egypt now at his disposal, went on to become the first Roman emperor. His reign lasted nearly forty years and effectively concluded the long period of civil war.

The Augustan age was the high point of Latin literature, through which the image of Rome and the contours of its past were refracted, and Virgil was by far the most influential of the Augustan writers. This is how he depicts the battle of Actium in a famous description of Aeneas' shield from the *Aeneid*:

> In the center [of the shield] it was possible to see bronze galleys, the battle of Actium … here was Caesar Augustus leading the Italians in battle along with the country and the people, and with the gods of hearth and home, and standing upon the lofty deck… Opposing him in barbaric splendor is Antony with various troops, as victor from nations in the land of the Dawn and the Red Sea, Egypt, bringing men of the Orient and furthest Bactria with him, following (shame!) his Egyptian wife [Cleopatra]… In the midst the queen summons her battle lines with her native sistrum. Not yet does she see the twin snakes at her back.[12]

Horace, too, takes up the theme in his justly famous "Cleopatra ode":

> Now is the time for drinking, now for stamping the ground with liberated foot, now to adorn the couches of the gods with a Salernian feast, friends. Before it was shameful to pour out vintage wines when the queen with her brood of men foul with disease plotted mad ruin against the Capitoline.[13]

In contrast to Virgil, Horace, and Ovid, who wrote under Augustus and celebrated the *pax Romana*, an end of civil war, and a new age of prosperity, writers of the next generation, especially Juvenal in his satires, give us a Rome of corrosive poverty, contaminated by outsiders, particularly cults of foreign gods, a cesspool of violence and disease. In this excerpt, Roman matrons, who have turned away from Roman deities, indulge in adultery and seek forgiveness via worship of the jackal-headed Egyptian god, Anubis, "who runs along with his linen-wearing and bald crew, a mocker of the weeping public. He obtains a pardon for wives who do not abstain from sex on days that should be kept holy and demands a large payment for the violated marriage bed."[14]

The novelist Petronius provides an unforgettable picture of the wealth and excess of the early empire in his description of Trimalchio's dinner party. Trimalchio was among the growing number of freed slaves whose entrepreneurial acumen allowed them to amass great wealth, which they displayed in banquets that served as theaters of excess:

> Servants entered and spread embroidered coverlets in front of our couches; these depicted men with nets and spears, the whole rigamarole of the hunt... Spartan hunting dogs entered and began to circle the table. A tray was carried holding a boar of the largest size ... and on its tusks were hung two little baskets woven from palm leaves, one filled with dried dates, the other with fresh. Around it were suckling pigs made of cakes as if hanging from its teats – these were the party favors.[15]

Next a servant dressed as a hunter plunged his knife into the beast's side, when out flew a bevy of quail. Fowlers stationed around the room then caught them in nets so that each guest might be served his own.

But the true theater of excess was the Roman Colosseum. With its displays of exotic beasts to be slaughtered and its gladiatorial games, it has become an enduring trope for brutal violence and conspicuous consumption. Tacitus and Suetonius write at length about the depravity of the emperors: Nero poisoning off members of his family, Tiberius feeding those who displease him to his carnivorous eels, Caligula whom Suetonius labels a "monster" – all are fare for later retelling as in the book and later television series, *I, Claudius* (1976). Later Roman writers reinforce these images of moral decline – it was Dio Cassius who in his *Roman History* provided the information that the emperor Commodus liked to compete as a gladiator, an image now familiar from Ridley Scott's film, *Gladiator* (2000). Christian apologists excoriating the games and stories of Christians martyred, condemned, and exhibited – often naked – to defend themselves unarmed against wild animals, complete the picture. Rome, once the epicenter of the civilized order had so fallen into decline that Augustine, in his *City of God* (426), meditated on its "fall" as a reminder of the hollowness of earthly life as he proposed a turn to the spiritual, for Christians to consider their true home not Rome, not an earthly city, but the heavenly city of God.

Jerusalem

Jerusalem first enters western letters in the first century CE. The Jewish historian Josephus, writing in Greek for a Roman audience, describes at length the horrors of the sack of Jerusalem by Titus in 70 CE and the destruction of the temple.[16] The arch of Titus in Rome depicts the booty taken from the temple (including the Menorah and the Table of the Showbread). The subsequent growth of Christianity gave Jerusalem another dimension – a sacred place where Jesus walked, taught, died, and rose from the dead. This Jerusalem became a place of pilgrimage for the well-to-do believer.

Cultural appropriation of the city as a Christian sacred space almost entirely overshadows the city of David and Solomon described in the Hebrew Bible. Since that collection of writings becomes widely disseminated only via its attachment to the Christian narratives of the New Testament, what was the historical city of the Jews became a place whose meanings could only be fulfilled by the later events of Jesus' life and death. Even more than the Christian recasting of Rome, the Jerusalem of Josephus and that of the gospels have almost nothing in common. For Josephus, the destruction of the temple is a defining crisis for an entire people, and in its wake Jews in great numbers once again left the city. This later event inevitably called to mind the much earlier destruction of the temple by Nebuchadnezzar in 587 BCE, with its attendant deportation of prominent Jews in three successive waves to Babylon, lamented in Psalm 137: "By the rivers of Babylon we sat, sat and wept, as we thought of Zion." If for Jews it is the temple, for Christians Jerusalem consists of the route sacralized by Jesus, his crucifixion and death; the location of the tomb from which he was said to have risen from the dead is the site of a Christian church in the old city. But both of these ancient accounts of the city converge in a sense of loss with the destruction of a holy place or a holy man, and competing desires to reclaim it.

Gibbon's narrative of the decline and fall of the Roman empire takes a negative view of the rise and eventual dominance of Christianity, but the seed of his argument is anticipated by Augustine. The opening of the *City of God* is a meditation on the sack of Rome by Alaric the Visigoth in 410, a destabilizing reminder that even a city as powerful and secure as Rome had been for five centuries was not impervious to destructive forces. By Augustine's time, Rome had long accommodated Christians as well as pagans: the founders of the Church – Saints Peter and Paul – were supposedly martyred and buried there, and churches were built over their tombs.[17] If neither Jerusalem nor Rome could escape the fate of invasion and desecration of sacred spaces, it was time to reimagine the idea of the city itself. For Augustine it becomes the eternal city that all the faithful will inhabit after death. Yet his was not a Christian polemic but the deliberate blending of the deep learning of late antiquity with the experience of a committed Christian (and bishop) – twenty-three books that reordered the events of human history to project a new and otherworldly trajectory realized in the trope of a heavenly city as the city of destiny.

Not surprisingly, Augustine could imagine the culmination of human events as fulfilled only in a city. Ancient cities were not simply large aggregations of people or seats of political power, they also enabled the growth and flourishing of culture. Cities did not come to an end – Rome, like Athens and Alexandria and Jerusalem, continued to exist and even thrive for thousands of years – but what did come to an end about the time that Augustine wrote the *City of God* was a concentrated and high level of literary activity in any one place. Not until the rise of Byzantium in the east and, later, the western Renaissance does a literature (and with it a sense of the importance of a city as place) reemerge.

NOTES

1 Virgil, *Aeneid*, book 6, lines 847–53. All translations in this chapter are the author's.
2 Thucydides, *The Peloponnesian War*, 2.41.1–2.
3 Aristophanes, *Lysistrata*, lines 574–86.
4 Plato, *Crito*, 51a7–b5, c3.
5 In contrast, Athens probably had a total population of 60,000–100,000. Rome was a city of several million.
6 Theocritus, *Idyll* 15, lines 44–52.
7 Posidippus of Pella, *Posidippi Pellaei quae supersunt omnia*, ed. Colin Austin and Guido Bastianini (Milan: Lettere Economia Diritto, 2002), 115.2–6 AB.
8 Herodas, *Mime* 1, lines 26–33.
9 See Galen's commentary on Hippocrates' *Epidemics* in Karl Gottlob Kühn, ed., *Claudii Galeni Opera Omnia*, 20 vols. (1821–33; Hildesheim, Germany: Olms, 1964–5), 17A.606–7.
10 See Erich S. Gruen, "Jewish Literature," in James J. Clauss and Martyne Cuypers, eds., *A Companion to Hellenistic Literature* (Chichester, UK: Wiley–Blackwell, 2010), pp. 419–21.
11 See, e.g., Livy, *ab urbe condita*, book 1, and Diodorus Siculus, *The Library of History* 8.2.4–6.
12 Virgil, *Aeneid*, book 8, lines 675–80, 685–9, 696–7.
13 Horace, "Cleopatra Ode," 1.37.1–10.
14 Juvenal, *Satire* 6, lines 533–7.
15 Petronius, *Satyrica* §40.
16 Josephus, *The Jewish Wars*, 6.220–70; Tacitus, fragment 2.
17 These stories are preserved in the *Apocryphal Acts of Peter* and of *Peter and Paul*.

3

KAREN NEWMAN

The Medieval and Early Modern City in Literature

The medieval and early modern city poses a paradox that urban historians have long tried to understand. The Middle Ages experienced urbanization on a greater scale than would be seen again until the nineteenth-century Industrial Revolution, which means that the cultural and commercial achievements we associate with the Renaissance occurred in a context of de-urbanization. Paradoxically, however, early modern *capital* cities grew prodigiously and threatened both the countryside and the thriving medieval towns, or as James I famously complained, "with time, *England* will onely be *London*, and the whole countrey be left waste." [1] London and Paris became in the early modern period not only capital cities but cultural capitals.

Symbolic cities were very important to the medieval and early modern urban imaginary. St. Augustine begins *De Civitate Dei* (426) by evoking the glorious *City of God* that is his title, an eschatological city associated with the biblical New or Heavenly Jerusalem and the community of Christian faithful destined to inherit the world beyond. Yet despite its title, Augustine's text is largely concerned with Rome, the earliest ancient city, except perhaps for Baghdad, to have more than one million inhabitants, to face the challenges any large urban settlement presents, and to be represented in several literary genres, from the poetry of Juvenal and Horace, to the comedies of Plautus. Augustine defends Christians blamed by pagans for the sack of Rome and the city's – and empire's – decline.

Although by the Middle Ages Rome was no longer the metropolitan center it had been in the ancient world, throughout the medieval and the early modern period it remained an iconic city to which writers turned for myths of origin. Myths of the second Rome and of the New Jerusalem enabled medieval and early modern writers to explore the classical and imperial past, to negotiate narratives of decline and loss, and to produce new foundational stories of national identity. Thus, while Petrarch (Francisco Petrarcha) was offered the laurel crown for poetic achievement by admirers in Paris, Naples, and Rome, he chose Rome in which to be crowned, both to reclaim a public place for poetry and to reestablish ancient Roman greatness. For Petrarch, and later for poets such as Pierre de Ronsard, Joachim Du Bellay, Edmund Spenser, and even John Milton, Rome remains the symbol of a lost cultural legacy they seek to access and to transmit in what is sometimes termed *translatio studii*: literally, the bearing across of knowledge over time and geographic space – from Jerusalem, to Athens, to Rome, and westward.

Medieval and early modern writers not only represent these symbolic cities; they also begin to represent the burgeoning medieval and Renaissance cities and towns to which people flocked that were centers of long-distance and local trade, of specialization and technological development, of social differentiation, and often of political independence from imperial or religious powers, or in the medieval period, from surrounding territorial lords. The twelfth century, as Eugene Vance has pointed out, is marked not only by "a decisive demographic revolution where human collectivities assumed new proportions and articulated a self-consciousness that wrought dramatic changes within the framework of feudalism, but also a spread of literacy among sectors of the population other than the clergy."[2] Such changes altered social patterns, weakened the military priorities of the nobility, and gave rise to new literary forms such as romance, in which the aggression of a warfaring elite is transformed into an ethic of desire.[3]

Medieval vernacular writing represents such "human collectivities" in conventional ways that persist into the early modern period and beyond: few architectural details, a focus on the geographical site of the city, its walls and defenses, its bustle and busy market, and finally, its most important buildings, often churches. The twelfth-century cleric William Fitz-Stephen thus begins his well-known description of London, "Amongst the noble and famous cities of the world, this of London, the capital of the kingdom of England, is one of the most renowned, on account of its wealth, its extensive trade and commerce, its grandeur and magnificence."[4] Fitz-Stephen then goes on to detail the city's features in turn. In the early modern period, the older epideictic descriptions of urban praise give way to the new form of the survey and, finally, the guidebooks with which we are familiar. Antiquarians such as Gilles Corrozet, Jacques Du Breul, John Stow, and the compilers that came after them continue the genre of city description well into the eighteenth century.

The city-states of Italy, particularly Florence and Venice, were among Europe's most important urban centers. In several letters, and famously in his *Divine Comedy,* Dante excoriates Florence and the mercantile Florentines for their violence, factionalism, and conspicuous consumption. In *Paradiso* XVI, he alludes to both the bloody murder on Easter Sunday 1215 at the entrance of Florence's Ponte Vecchio that precipitated the long battle between Guelfs and Ghibellines, and the sacrifice of Christ that gained the faithful admission to the heavenly city. Medieval Florence was devastated not only by the bitter strife of its feuding families but also by plague: one reason for the decline of medieval towns throughout Europe was the Black Death that wiped out 30–60 percent of the population, a loss that took more than 150 years to restore. The Black Death provided Giovanni Boccaccio with the pretext for his *Decameron,* the collection of one-hundred stories supposedly told over ten days by ten well-born young Florentines who have fled the city to avoid the plague. The frame begins in 1348 "when in the illustrious city of Florence, the fairest of all the cities of Italy, there made its appearance that deadly pestilence."⁵ Was it the scourge of God? The influence of celestial bodies? Whatever the reason, the Florentines took every precaution to prevent its spread; Boccaccio regales his reader with contemporary epidemiological theories, with descriptions of the effects of plague on the bodies of the sick, with the breakdown of social distinctions brought about by fear of disease, and with its impact on urban life. But ironically, in driving the Florentine youth from the city and its pleasures to refuge on a country estate, the plague provokes them to storytelling, and thus produces the *Decameron* itself.

What made Florence fair and illustrious were its flourishing cloth trade and its banking industry, both of which – through trade routes and fairs – connected cities throughout Europe: Lyon, Antwerp, even London. Chaucer's *Canterbury Tales* is also a collection of stories told by a group of city dwellers, but Chaucer's storytellers are pilgrims making their way to Canterbury. Chaucer was himself a Londoner, the son of a prosperous merchant, and a member of the emergent middling estate that was able to take advantage of the social mobility that followed the Black Death. Chaucer's works show him to have been at once situated in the city of London – he served for many years in the important position of controller of the wool custom, wool being then England's major trade commodity – but also connected to the court (he married a lady of the Queen's household and served in various diplomatic capacities). The Prologue to the *Canterbury Tales* begins famously with an evocation of spring and the natural world, but moves quickly to the local and particular, to Southwark and the Tabard Inn on the south bank of the Thames, where the pilgrims gather to start their pilgrimage to Canterbury. The *Canterbury Tales* are sometimes termed "estates satire" for portraying the three medieval estates: knights, the clergy, and plowmen or "churls." Boccaccio's storytellers are all members of the elite, but Chaucer's religious motive allows him to mix the different *condiciouns* or estates in a dialectical structure that interweaves each individual pilgrim's tale with the fiction of the pilgrims' interactions, their appearance, upbringing, and rivalries along the route. The *Tales* open with the hierarchically appropriate Knight's Tale, but when at its conclusion the Host of the Tabard Inn turns to the Monk, next in degree to the Knight, the Miller interrupts with a low tale of cuckoldry in the fabliau tradition. The Host attempts to avert argument and to keep the company together, but his failure – the Miller prevails – suggests the difficulty of imposing order and the challenge to hierarchy posed by the social mobility and rapidly changing world of the city in which Chaucer lived and worked.

In the aftermath of the Black Death, dearth in England led to the Uprising of 1381 in which a group of peasants, small landowners, and craftsmen entered London and executed the Archbishop of Canterbury. The Middle English allegorical narrative poem we refer to as *Piers Plowman,* roughly contemporaneous with Chaucer, also satirizes the different estates and London life in this period. The poem alludes frequently to London locales – Will, the dreamer protagonist, awakens from his first dream vision in Cornhill; mention is made of many principal places in London: East Cheap, Cock Lane in Smithfield, Shoreditch, Tyburn, and Southwark, and Will reveals a detailed knowledge of the legal processes of late medieval London and the abuses to which they often gave rise.

As medieval cities grew and drew immigrants from the countryside, and as social hierarchies were challenged, cities and towns began to confront urban ills: filth, noise, crowding, dearth, and crime. What little is known of the Paris-born French poet François Villon provides some insight into the life of a student at the University of Paris in the mid-fifteenth century. Born to an impoverished family, he was adopted by one Guillaume de Villon, later a professor of ecclesiastical law at the University where Villon became a student at age eleven. In and out of prison for brawling, theft, and murder, often hungry and cold, Villon was repeatedly exiled from Paris and was finally sentenced to hanging. His best-known poems, *Le petit testament* (1456) and *Le grand testament* (1461), are examples of the well-known medieval genre of the mock testament in which a dying man leaves parts of his body to others, often to obscene or anticlerical effect. Villon draws on the medieval *ubi sunt* ("where are they?") motif to meditate on life's transience, the fragility of fame and beauty that he situates in Paris, but the language of his poems often draws on the slang of medieval Paris, the argot of thieves and gamblers.

The Medieval and Early Modern City as Theater

Throughout Europe from at least the thirteenth century, rituals and entertainments of various kinds were mounted by cities to celebrate accession, coronation, dynastic weddings and births, royal visits, and military victories. In the mercantile cities of the Low Countries, civic pageants and festivities celebrated guilds and their trades as well as religious holidays and are said to have been the prototypes for civic pageantry. The most important of such civic celebrations in London were the Lord Mayor's shows, often dubbed "Triumphs," thus trading on the humanist prestige of the Roman triumph. Held annually to celebrate the new Lord Mayor's election, the shows were commissioned by the City's guilds to honor a duly elected member. Although some form of inaugural ceremony had celebrated the installation of London's mayor as early as the twelfth century, the inaugural shows accompanied by pageants with scripts written by leading dramatists date from the 1540s. They marked not only the expansion of civic power that accompanied London's dynamic growth and the decline of religious ceremony following the Reformation but also what Lawrence Manley has termed the "theatricalization of London's traditional civic ceremonies" that developed in tandem with the rise of public theatre.[6]

In his essay "Walking in the City," the theorist of urban space Michel de Certeau contrasts the view from the top – the prospect, the panorama – with the everyday practices of city dwellers "down below" who traverse the city on foot, taking part in civic ceremony, but who escape "imaginary totalizations produced by the eye" that views from above.[7] Among such images are the recycled city views found in the Nuremberg Chronicle (Figure 1), representations of ideal cities (Figure 2), city scenes representing tragedy and comedy (Figures 3, 4), and the prospects of artists and engravers such as Václav Hollar, Claes Janszoon Visscher (Figure 5), Abraham Bosse, and Stefano della Bella (Figure 6) that "master" the city with the eye/I. Early modern writers produced instead what de Certeau calls "spatial stories" in various literary forms including pamphlets, almanacs, broadsides, and chapbooks, as well as more traditional poetic forms such as drama, epic, and satire that show the streets of early modern cities filled with criers, tradesmen, servants and apprentices, thieves and vagabonds, and teeming multitudes of immigrants seeking their fortune. Among them was the fabled Dick Whittington, whose success story – from servant to Lord Mayor of London – was recounted in popular ballads and plays. It was this migration that fueled the extraordinary growth of Europe's capital cities and the rich and varied popular literature bemoaning that growth. In Donald Lupton's city guide, *London and the countrey carbonadoed* (1632), for example, urban description is replaced by comic allegory – London is a woman turned gluttonous, an expectant mother whose beauty is marred by her size; cony-catching pamphlets regaled the reading public with tales of con artists, vagabonds, and country rubes. In the early modern city, writers began to pursue literary careers, for cities also generated new forms of dissemination:

Figure 1. Views of Damascus, Ferrara, and Verona, from *Nuremberg Chronicle* [*Registrum huius operis libri cronicarum cu[m] figuris et ÿmagi[ni]bus ab inicio mu[n]di*] (1493). Courtesy of the Kislak Center for Special Collections, Rare Books and Manuscripts, University of Pennsylvania.

Figure 2. Piero della Francesca, *Ideal City* (ca. 1470). Courtesy of National Gallery of The Marche, Urbino / Getty Images.

Figure 3. Sebastiano Serlio, "Tragic Scene," from *Libro... D'Architettvra* (Venetia 1566). Courtesy of the Heidelberg University Library.

a burgeoning print culture, an increasingly literate reading public, expanded manuscript circulation, and new ideas of authorship itself.

The early English poet Isabella Whitney uses the medieval mock testament deployed earlier by Villon, in which a dying Christian settles his or her affairs. Her "Wyll and Testament," part of her collection *A Sweet Nosgay* (1573), begins, "The time is come I must departe, / from thee ah famous Citie," and it proceeds to blazon the city and to explore the relation of women to property. The speaker walks through London's streets and lanes describing its markets and shops – the Fleet, Bridewell, Bedlam, the Thames, Cheapside, and the

Figure 4. Sebastiano Serlio, "Comic Scene," from *Libro... D'Architettvra* (Venetia 1566). Courtesy of the Heidelberg University Library.

Mint – passing the buildings and landmarks that a woman in service would have known and frequented. By presenting her walk as her last will and testament, Whitney dramatizes her plight as an impoverished woman who has lost her place in multiple senses. As she moves from place to place, she bequeaths goods and services, activities, professions, even crimes, to their appropriate London locations: wool to "Watlyng Streete and Canwyck streete," linen to "Friday streete," jewels and plate to Cheape, hose in Birchin Lane, tailors to Bow Street, and artillery at Temple Bar. She lovingly describes the fashionable luxury goods for sale at the Royal Exchange, London's earliest shopping mall: "French Ruffes, high Purles, Gorgets and Sleeves." To the booksellers – "because I lyke their Arte" – she leaves money, to wealthy widows she leaves young gentlemen, and to young gentlemen at the Inns of Court she leaves books

> to furnish them withall.
> And when they are with study cloyd:
> to recreate theyr minde:
> Of Tennis Courts, of dauncing Scooles,
> and fence they store shal finde.

Figure 5. Claes Janszoon Visscher, "Long View of London" (ca. 1625). Courtesy of the Folger Library.

Whitney's final legacy offers a perspective on the poem's rhetorical stance in which London is represented as a rejecting lover. Whitney produces poetic authority through disfranchisement. Her movement through the city is far removed from that of the leisured flâneur of the nineteenth-century capital city, which is closer to the walk represented in John Donne's first satire. Whitney, like most of the city's inhabitants, is excluded economically, socially, and by her sex from the urban temptations and attractions that Donne describes.[8]

The Inns of Court were a gathering place for young men pursuing civility, letters, and preferment. Unlike Whitney's young gentlemen "with study cloyd" who take pleasure in the city's recreations, Donne's speaker must be seduced by a friend to walk out into the London streets. Donne's poem begins with a spatial opposition between the speaker's study and the city's peopled streets filled with a cross-section of London's inhabitants and ranks: the court, the military, the judiciary, apprentices, school boys, the homeless. The speaker and his companion meet a young man famous in the capital for dancing divinely and another said to excel the Indians in smoking tobacco. Tobacco, so ambivalently popular in the 1590s, was one of many foreign luxury imports newly available in London. Consumer goods and services are retailed and popular London sights mentioned, yet despite the variety of persons encountered, the London population depicted in Donne's satire, unlike many contemporary urban texts, is peculiarly homogeneous: few are the shopkeepers and small craftsmen, criers and watermen, beggars and urban poor that made up the largest proportion of the city's population. The speaker's companion evaluates the persons they meet and hails each

according to his level of conspicuous consumption. Even walking in the city had its protocols: the companion claims the privileged place inside, "to the wall," presumably protected by overhanging eaves from the ever-present danger of mud and filth jettisoned from windows or clogging conduits and streets.

Donne's poem can be fruitfully compared to the French poet and critic Nicolas Boileau's sixth satire. Formal satire is usually said to present an encounter between an "I" and its adversary who drives the satirist to speech. In Boileau's poem, that encounter is with the city itself. The poem opens with a question: "Qui frappe l'air, bon Dieu! De ces lugubres cris?" ["Who beats the air, dear God, with these mournful cries?"].[9] The speaker is awakened by the noise of the city and driven into the Parisian streets, where he is buffeted by the teeming crowds, gutter cats and thieves, coaches and carts, lackeys and blacksmiths, groans and gunshots, bombarded by sense impressions as he stumbles through the city, thwarted by a nightmarish traffic jam.

Cities on the Early Modern Stage

Cities figure prominently in popular and learned drama. In Niccolò Machiavelli's comedy, *Mandrogola* (1526), modeled on classical precedents, the hero returns from years living in Paris to his native Florence, where he and his wily servant concoct a scheme to win the love of a young married woman. Florence is portrayed conventionally – it is made up of streets, thresholds, and a church. *The Merchant of Venice* (ca. 1596) and *Othello* (1604), Shakespeare's two plays set in Venice – which the playwright never visited but knew through reading and by report – represent the city in its

Figure 6. Stefano della Bella (1610–1664), "Perspective of the Pont Neuf in Paris." Chisel engraving, 1646. Paris, Musée Carnavalet. Copyright ©. Musée Carnavalet / Roger-Violett.

more modern aspects. Venice was the richest city in Renaissance Europe, a fabled commercial center where Jews, Christians, and aliens or strangers – Turks, Arabs, Africans – lived and traded throughout the Mediterranean in an atmosphere of relative tolerance. A crossroads between east and west where goods from Asia could be exchanged with western Europe, its wealth depended on such tolerance. When Shylock the Jew determines to exact his pound of flesh from Christian Antonio, who has borrowed on credit to help his friend Bassanio woo the wealthy Portia, Antonio himself recognizes that "The Duke cannot deny the course of law, / For the commodity [trade] that strangers have / With us in Venice, if it be denied, / Will much impeach the justice of the state, / Since that the trade and profit of the city / Consisteth of all nations."[10] He also represents Antonio as disdainful of lending money at interest – usury – as practiced by Shylock (since Jews were often banned from other trades and professions), although Christian merchants in London in fact lent money at interest. In short, although in the language of the play Christians distinguish spiritual motives and values from economic ones, in fact they are inextricably intertwined. Both Bassanio and Portia describe their love in metaphors of credit and exchange, and Antonio's friendship with Bassanio depends on Antonio's loans. Shakespeare presents a near fantastic city of venturing, rich argosies, silks and spices, exotic merchandise – an urban commercial center contrasted with Portia's country seat. But that opposition collapses as Portia and Bassanio pledge their love using the very language of counting, credit, and exchange that characterizes commercial Venice. In both country and city, human relationships and feeling are constantly described in economic terms.

Othello also portrays Venice as a commercial crossroads, a suture between east and west. Othello is a Moor, an African mercenary hired by the Venetian government to protect its commercial interests from the predatory Ottomans. Venice is portrayed as a sophisticated city where, Iago persuades Othello, women "let God see the pranks, / They dare not show their husbands" and where Desdemona questions Emilia, "Dost thou in conscience think – tell me, Emilia – / That there be women do abuse their husbands / In such gross kind?"[11] Shakespeare's Venice betrays the English Protestant prejudice against Catholic Italian cities imagined to be hotbeds of adultery, deceit, and murder.

Shakespeare portrays London in his plays mostly "disguised" as another city, but we see glimpses in the histories. In *Henry VI, part* 2 (ca. 1596–9), the playwright presents the popular revolt of Jack Cade, who led a "ragged multitude" from Kent in opposition to changes brought about by urbanization and mercantile expansion. Having taken London by force, Cade vows to reverse inflation, criminalize the watering down of beer he associates with town trade, and pull down London's chief commercial district, Cheapside, where he will graze his horse. Cade's brief victory and rampage are chronicled through London place names – some contemporaneous with Cade's Rebellion, others anachronistic – from Shakespeare's London.

But London became the setting of choice for the genre known as city comedy – practiced by Ben Jonson, Thomas Middleton, Thomas Dekker, and others – that has been of particular interest to recent commentators who have argued that the commercial theatre depended on the city's unprecedented demographic growth and commercial vigor for its development. Dekker's early *Shoemaker's Holiday* (1599) has received renewed attention for its double plot showcasing urban social mobility: in the romantic plot, the aristocratic Lacy falls in love with a prosperous grocer's daughter whom he woos while disguised as a shoemaker, a theatrical version of unions between wealthy citizen daughters and impoverished gentlemen, while in a "city" plot on the Dick Whittington model, the citizen hero, shoemaker Simon Eyre, tipped off and financed by Lacy, disguises himself as an alderman to purchase commodities from a distressed Dutch merchantman, thereby achieves his fortune, and is duly elected Lord Mayor. The play dramatizes the distance between fiction and history since London's Lord Mayor was always chosen from the most prosperous guilds, not from among the humble shoemakers. And as Jean Howard has noted, Eyre's success, like that of Dick Whittington, comes not from hard work but from "the labor of unseen workmen in foreign lands."[12] Dekker also collaborated with Middleton on another London comedy, *The Roaring Girl* (ca. 1608), based on the notorious London transvestite whore, bawd, and cutpurse Mary Frith, who was a skilled swordsman, roarer, and gang boss. Middleton and Dekker make their literary Moll a kind of Robin Hood who robs the rich to help the poor. The play also presents a host of urban characters, from grasping city fathers to citizen shopkeepers and their wives plying their trades selling luxury goods: feathers, tobacco, and cutwork. In such plays as *The Alchemist* (1610), *Epicoene* (1609), and *Bartholmew Fair* (1614), Jonson similarly represents the London trades and fairs, city con men and women, and the rivalry among city gallants who squander their lands to buy velvets so as to see and be seen parading down a favorite London walk, the main aisle of St. Paul's Cathedral.

English city comedy is concerned with urban subcultures: vagabonds, apprentices and tradesmen, prostitutes, country bumpkins, and young heirs, types whose existence was bound up with the capital's development. By contrast, French city comedy was concerned with a young urban elite in search of romance, urban pleasures, fashion, and entertainment. City comedies such as Pierre Corneille's *Menteur* (1644), *Place Royale* (1634), and *Galerie du Palais* (1632) employ a language of exchange and value for affective relations that suggests the impact of what has been termed the "consumer revolution" taking place in Europe in the seventeenth century, an impact seen as well in the so-called English town comedies that limn the development of London's posh West End.

Unlike Jonson, Middleton, Dekker, and their fellow playwrights, Edmund Spenser neither set his epic romance in London nor anchored it in quotidian city life. The city in Spenser's *Faerie Queene* (1590–6) is a symbol of human community on earth and in heaven, drawn from both literary and scriptural sources. The poem depicts both the new Jerusalem and Cleopolis, the earthly city that allegorizes Spencer's native London; both figure human aspiration. Like Spenser's Redcrosse Knight, the everyman, "Christian," in the seventeenth-century religious allegory *Pilgrim's Progress* (1678) journeys from his native city modeled on London and dubbed the City of Destruction to the Celestial City that is to come.

This reinvigorated metaphoric journey between earthly and heavenly cities figures in what might be termed a transatlantic "translatio studii." In a well-known lay sermon preached on shipboard, John Winthrop admonished the soon-to-be founders of the Massachusetts Bay Colony that their community would be "a city on a hill" watched by all the world,[13] a phrase that President John Kennedy repeated more than two hundred years later in describing his vision for the United States. The Renaissance humanists' vision of a civilized life was urban: the trope of the city remains a model of human community, aspiration, and achievement, but also of failure.

NOTES

1 *The Political Works of James I*, ed. C. H. McIlwain (Cambridge, MA: Harvard University Press, 1918), p. 343.
2 Eugene Vance, "Signs of the City: Medieval Poetry as Detour," *New Literary History* 4 (1973), 557.
3 Ibid., p. 573.
4 William Fitz-Stephen, *Fitz-Stephen's Description of the City of London* (London: B. White, 1772), p. 21.
5 Giovanni Boccaccio, *The Decameron*, trans. J. M. Rigg (London: A. H. Bullen, 1903), p. 5.
6 Lawrence Manley, *Literature and Culture in Early Modern London* (Cambridge: Cambridge University Press, 1995), p. 212.
7 Michel de Certeau, *The Practice of Everyday Life*, trans. Steven F. Rendall (Berkeley: University of California Press, 1984), p. 93.
8 Isabella Whitney, "The Author (though loth to leave the Citie) upon her Friendes procurement, is constrained to departe ... and maketh her last Wyll and Testament ...," in Danielle Clarke, ed., *Isabella Whitney, Mary Sidney and Amelia Lanyer: Renaissance Women Poets* (New York: Penguin, 2000), pp. 20, 18, 21, 24, 26.

9   Nicolas Boileau, *Oeuvres I: Satires, Le Lutrin*, ed. Jerôme Vercruysse (Paris: Garnier Flammarion, 1969), p. 75; translation by the author.

10 William Shakespeare, *The Merchant of Venice*, in *The Norton Shakespeare*, ed. Stephen Greenblatt, 2nd ed. (New York: Norton, 2008), p. 1155.

11 Shakespeare, *Othello*, in ibid., pp. 2155, 2178.

12 Jean Howard, "Material Shakespeare/Materialist Shakespeare," in Lloyd Davis, ed., *Shakespeare Matters: History, Teaching, Performance* (Newark: University of Delaware Press, 2003), p. 38.

13 John Winthrop, "A Model of Christian Charity" (1630), in Andrew Delbanco, ed., *Writing New England: An Anthology from the Puritans to the Present* (Cambridge, MA: Harvard University Press, 2001), p. 11; Winthrop's figure invokes the Sermon on the Mount (Matthew 5:14).

4

ALISON O'BYRNE

The Spectator and the Rise of the Modern Metropole

"I live in the World, rather as a Spectator of Mankind, than as one of the Species." So declares Joseph Addison and Richard Steele's authorial persona in the opening essay of their enormously popular and highly influential periodical *The Spectator* (1711–14). Mr. Spectator's position as a detached observer, afforded to him by the gentlemanly status that leaves him free from having to pursue any specific occupation, allows him to slip in and out of various conversations and social spaces in the city. "I have made my self a Speculative Statesman, Soldier, Merchant and Artizan, without ever medling with any Practical Part in Life," he tells readers of the first issue, explaining that he is "very well versed in the Theory of an Husband, or a Father, and can discern the Errors in the Oeconomy, Business, and Diversion of others, better than those who are engaged in them."[1] This disinterested position grants him the ability to see and to comprehend all, and his essays seek to organize and to order the social and cultural world of his readers, allowing this audience to situate themselves in the urban milieu. In *The Spectator* – and indeed, as we shall see, in a wide range of eighteenth-century accounts of the metropolis – the city is a place to see and in which to be seen. In eighteenth-century London, the focus of this chapter, writers and artists frequently turned their lens on a city distinguished by its size, its continuing growth, and the diversity of its population, and it was possible for them to see the metropolis both as the site of a polite, refining sociability, and as a den of vice, chaos, and social disorder.

Although certainly the most famous, Mr. Spectator was not the only surveyor of London in this period. In the decade before *The Spectator*'s publication, Ned Ward's monthly periodical *The London Spy* (1698–1700) entertained readers with an account of a new arrival's experiences in the metropolis. A philosopher who throws aside book learning in order to see life, the spy takes a tour through London led by an old school friend who serves as his guide. As an observer of the manners and morals of urban society, Ward's naive country philosopher renders the familiar strange to the periodical's metropolitan audience. Disoriented by the city's lights, overwhelmed by its stench, and unable to understand what he hears, his ability to present the city accurately is compromised. The sensory overload confounds him, often leading to moments of unintentionally comic misrecognition. At one point, the waterman's cry of "'Oars' and 'Scullers'" to tout for business is misconstrued by the spy as "'Scholars, scholars, will you have any whores?'" offering him evidence that London is indeed a "wicked place." Elsewhere, he feels threatened by what he sees. Walking through the Royal Exchange, the hub of international commerce, Ward's spy is "jostled in amongst a parcel of swarthy buggerantoes" before being "squeezed … through a crowd of bum-firking Italians" in a hyperbolically xenophobic account of national differences.[2] Throughout, the spy's friend demystifies the scenes encountered and sets him to rights. The pair's observations on everyday life in the capital allow readers already in the know to laugh at the spy's initial mistakes as he tours the metropolis; unlike *The Spectator*, the *London Spy* is not interested in promoting the reform or regulation of its readers.

It was not only in the pages of Ward's *London Spy* that readers could find negative portrayals of the city. Whereas Mr. Spectator offers an account of polite sociability in London that is purged of dirt and disorder, Jonathan Swift's poem "A Description of a City Shower" – first published in 1710 in *The Tatler*, Addison and Steele's predecessor to *The Spectator* – scratches the veneer of the periodical's often sanitized view of city living. In Swift's poem, the only thing that unites the people of London is their desire to protect themselves from their environment, which implacably opposes any attempt to be polite. That the city is always already dirty is suggested by the poet-speaker's encounter with the "careless quean" who soils the clothing of the pedestrian with the mop she has used to wash the stairs, and by the reference to the cloud "that swilled more liquor than it could contain, / And like a drunkard gives it up again," vomiting rain over the city.[3]

The initial confusion of a naive observer like Ward's spy and the frustrations of Swift's poet-speaker throw Addison and Steele's project of ordering and making sense of the city into sharp relief. Whereas *The London Spy* and "A Description of a City Shower" might be seen to display the "Tory anarchy" of Ward and Swift in the face of Whig ideals of progress and reform, *The Spectator* clearly commits itself to the improvement of its readers.[4] By learning to read the city and to respond to its people, spectacles, and entertainments as Mr. Spectator does, the periodical's audience were themselves able to participate in the cultural world of eighteenth-century London. In *The Spectator*, according to the influential formulation of Jürgen Habermas, "the public held up a mirror to itself" and "read and debated about itself," taking part in discussions about good conduct and appropriate manners, whether by talking about the essays published or contributing letters for publication.⁵ For Habermas, the periodical's readers thus determine – via reading and conversation – what it means to be a polite consumer of the material and cultural offerings of the world's preeminent commercial city.

In eighteenth-century London, the coffeehouse played an especially important role in generating the improving sociability that *The Spectator* describes. First developed in Britain in the mid-seventeenth century, these "penny universities" offered visitors access to a range of newspapers and conversations for the price of a cup of coffee. The coffeehouse was thus a quasi-public realm in contrast to the more private, intimate, and exclusive world of the Parisian salon, which was more closely associated with the domestic realm.⁶ By the start of the eighteenth century, there were more than four hundred coffeehouses in the metropolis.⁷ Each had its own character: White's had a reputation for high stakes gambling, St. James's for the debating of politics, and those around Covent Garden – including Will's and Button's – as locations of literary discussion. Many were places of business as well as sociability: the insurers Lloyd's of London, for example, began as Lloyd's Coffeehouse in 1687. In Habermas's theorization of the "bourgeois public sphere" – the scene of private individuals coming together as a public outside the authority of the state – the coffeehouse features as the exemplary site of critical rational debate, where men from all backgrounds could come together and debate, shaping consensus and defining bourgeois norms.

More recently, historians have begun to challenge this story as an idealization. As Brian Cowan has suggested, for example, *The Spectator*'s project to "refashion the coffeehouse as a center of respectable male manners for eighteenth-century Britain" was a response to how codes of politeness "were so often breached in daily practice" rather than a reflection of coffeehouse life.⁸ Irrespective of the actual reality, these sites of news and conversation are central to the social world mapped by Addison and Steele's periodicals; indeed, as a work like Justus van Effen's *Hollandsche Spectator* (1731–5) suggests, in other cities, too, works based on Addison and Steele's *Spectator* were closely connected to a local coffeehouse culture. The first issue of *The Tatler* datelines its news items from coffeehouses in which such topics were discussed, while Mr. Spectator's authority on a wide range of topics is presented as a result of his ability to mix with different groups of people in London's coffeehouses, where he listens to the varied conversations as a spectator of men and manners. Mr. Spectator is also at home "in the Theaters both of *Drury-Lane*, and the *Hay-Market*," and he refers to having been "taken for a Merchant upon the *Exchange* for above these ten Years."⁹ At the Royal Exchange, Mr. Spectator delights in the idea of passing for "a *Dane, Swede*, or *French-Man*" and he imagines himself "a Citizen of the World" in an account of global commerce as an extended, mutually improving dialogue that rewrites Ward's account of the same place.[10] "[W]here-ever I see a Cluster of People I always mix with them," Mr. Spectator declares, "tho' I never open my Lips but in my own Club."[11] The club's diverse membership – including a Whig, a Tory, a retired military captain, a lawyer with literary aspirations, a fashionable man about town, and a clergyman – reflects the mixed society that might be found in London's coffeehouses, offering readers a model of male sociability applicable to people from across a range of backgrounds.

At the heart of *The Spectator*, then, is an imagined ideal of polite conversation that brings men – and frequently women – together in scenarios that provide opportunities for mutual improvement. For some writers of the Scottish Enlightenment, too, for whom Edinburgh rather than London was their primary reference point, the city was the key locus of civility. In his essay "Of Refinement in the Arts" (1752), the philosopher David Hume argues that

> The more ... refined arts advance, the more sociable men become: nor is it possible, that, when enriched with science, and possessed of a fund of conversation, they should be contented to remain in solitude, or live with their fellow-citizens in that distant manner, which is peculiar to ignorant and barbarous nations. They flock into cities; love to receive and communicate knowledge; to show their wit or their breeding; their taste in conversation or living, in clothes or furniture. Curiosity allures the wise; vanity the foolish; and pleasure both. Particular clubs and societies are everywhere formed: both sexes meet in an easy and sociable manner; and the tempers of men, as well as their behaviour, refine apace.[12]

Referring to "refinement" rather than the more pejorative "luxury," Hume here presents the city as a scene of natural sociability. As if to pre-empt Jean-Jacques Rousseau's famous critique of modernity, Hume attributes a positive role to spectatorship: as men become spectators of one another in the city, each begins to live in the eyes of the world, displaying taste, wit, and talents while conscious that his performance is observed by others.

James Boswell certainly regarded himself as living in the eyes of others during his visit to London between 1762 and 1763. Eager, anxious even, to be seen as a gentleman, he records in his diary his attempts to reinvent himself in the metropolis. Since coming to London, he notes, "I have begun to acquire a composed genteel character very different from a rattling uncultivated one which for some time past I have been fond of. I have discovered that we may be in some degree whatever character we choose. Besides, practice forms a man to anything." For Boswell, the key was to fake it until he could make it, and he often put his attempts to pass for a gentleman to the test. On one occasion, desiring to buy a silver-hilted sword but finding he had left his money at home, he determines "to make a trial of the civility of my fellow-creatures, and what my external appearance and address would have"; after initial misgivings, the tradesman allows him to buy on credit, "much to my honour." Boswell's concern to perform gentility as frugally as he can is evident in the way in which he debates where to live: "Sometimes I considered that a fine lodging denoted a man of great fashion, but then I thought that few people would see it and therefore the expense would be hid, whereas my business was to make as much show as I could with my small allowance." When his current landlord offers him the option to determine what he wants to pay rather than to lose him as a lodger, Boswell is pleased to take this as "very strong proof of my being agreeable."[13]

For Boswell, Mr. Spectator offers a model of masculine spectatorship and deportment in the city. He frequently references the periodical in his diary, styling himself "a person of imagination and feeling, such as The Spectator finely describes, [who] can have the most lively enjoyment from the sight of external objects without regard to property at all."[14] Boswell cites *The Spectator*'s essays on the pleasures of the imagination, in the first of which Addison describes the "Man of a Polite Imagination," who, among other attributes, "often feels a greater Satisfaction in the Prospect of Fields and Meadows, than another does in the Possession."[15] Addison's model of imaginative "satisfaction" appears to inform Boswell's account of how in London, "where men and manners can be seen to the greatest advantage ... a young man of curiosity and observation might have a sufficient fund of present entertainment, and may lay up ideas to employ his mind in age." Boswell delights in the connections between the London of the 1760s and the city described in Addison and Steele's periodical fifty years earlier. Riding through the city in a carriage, he describes himself as "full of rich imagination of London, ideas suggested by The Spectator." He especially enjoys the historical and cultural associations of particular locations that he visits, noting in his diary Mr. Spectator's links with coffeehouses such as Will's and Child's. At the latter, he remarks that "[t]he Spectator mentions his being seen at Child's, which makes me have an affection for it. I think myself like him, and am serenely happy there."[16]

Boswell's hopes to be like Mr. Spectator are not always realized, however. At Drury Lane Theatre for a performance of *Macbeth*, Boswell states that he and his companion "endeavoured to work our minds into the frame of the Spectator's, but we could not. We were both too dissipated." Such a frank acknowledgment of "dissipation" is also evident in Boswell's account of entertaining a couple of prostitutes in a tavern. Boswell states here that he "thought myself Captain Macheath," the highwayman in John Gay's

The Beggar's Opera (1728), and this identification suggests something of Boswell's ease of moving between the urban identities of polite gentleman and debauched rake. He certainly had no qualms about publicly "engag[ing]" with a prostitute on Westminster Bridge, recording of the experience that "the whim of doing it there with the Thames rolling below us amused me much."[17]

Boswell adopted "genteel" manners, aware of their currency, as part of his efforts to gain favor with social superiors who might help him to secure a commission in the foot guards. For other commentators on urban life throughout the century, however, the idea that the city provided opportunities for self-reinvention was a cause for concern. In an environment where people were strangers to one another, it was recognized that claims to social status were dependent upon appearances, especially in relation to dress and the company one kept.[18] According to Erasmus Jones, in his *Luxury, Pride and Vanity, the Bane of the British Nation* (1736):

> People where they are not known, are generally honour'd according to their Clothes, and other Accoutrements they have about them; from the *Richness* of them we judge of their *Wealth*, and by their ordering them we guess at their Understanding. It is this which encourages every body, who is conscious of his little Merit, if he is any ways able to wear Clothes above his Rank; especially, in large and populous Cities, where obscure Men may hourly meet with fifty Strangers to one Acquaintance, and consequently have the Pleasure of being esteem'd by a vast Majority, not as what they are, but what they appear to be.[19]

True worth and merit might, some suggested, always shine through, but the management of one's appearance could go an awfully long way. Daniel Defoe's eponymous heroine in *Moll Flanders* (1722), for example, makes use of a wide variety of disguises to undertake her criminal acts, most frequently masquerading as a gentlewoman. As she proudly explains, when she went out thieving she "always went very well Dress'd." On one occasion when her attempt to steal a lady's watch fails, she escapes detection by pretending that her own watch was also attempted, "for you are to observe," she tells the reader, "I had very good Cloaths on, and a Gold Watch by my Side, as like a Lady as other Folks."[20] Moll's success as a thief depends on her ability to read the city and its people; as a result, she develops a sharp sense of the best escape routes and an ability to anticipate how individuals and groups might behave.

Moll's range of disguises and her knowledge of the city and its people offer her a freedom of movement not normally granted to genteel women in the city. Half a century later, Frances Burney's *Evelina, or, the History of a Young Lady's Entrance into the World* (1778) presents mobility in the city as exposing a young woman to sexual danger. Evelina quickly learns that, in London's public places, women are a spectacle for men to enjoy. At her first assembly, for example, she notes with displeasure the way that "[t]he gentlemen, as they passed and repassed, looked as if they thought [the ladies] were quite at their disposal." During her two trips to London, one with the Mirvans, the other with Madam Duval and the Branghtons (the latter presented as typical "cits" – a derogatory term for City tradespeople whose knowledge begins and ends with trade, despite their pretensions to gentility), Evelina sees two very different sides to the city. Yet her difficulties arise in part because these two worlds are not wholly distinct. Even while staying "at *an Hosier's* in *High Holborn*" and attending the Branghtons at their favored spaces of entertainment, Evelina still crosses paths with her former acquaintances in the city's less exclusive, and thus more socially mixed, pleasure gardens at Vauxhall and Marylebone. As an orphan, Evelina's seemingly indeterminate status – made more pronounced by her movement between the social world of the Mirvans and that of the Branghtons – makes her an object of curiosity to some of the men she encounters. When Willoughby finds her lost in the dark walks of Vauxhall, he takes this as a sign that Evelina might indeed be sexually available to him. Rather than offer protection, he leads her further along the walks where, he explains, "'we shall be least observed.'" If his conduct to her differs radically depending on the company she keeps, Orville's conduct is unwavering. He treats her "with the same politeness and attention with which he had always honoured me when countenanced by Mrs. Mirvan," even when finding her in the company of prostitutes at Marylebone Gardens.[21]

Despite her lack of knowledge of urban manners, Evelina is presented from her arrival into London as a woman of taste and a discerning judge of the people she encounters, laughing at Lovel's foppishness and displaying her wariness of Willoughby's gaiety. Yet the free-ranging forms of spectatorship described by Mr. Spectator and adopted by Boswell are clearly unavailable to young women like her. Instead, concerned to behave correctly and always uncertain about the rules of polite conduct, Evelina finds that her sense of being looked at and judged on her behavior, and on faux pas in particular, leads to a heightened self-consciousness in the company of others. Her awareness of being watched by Orville allows Evelina to think about how she appears in the eyes of someone whose taste, politeness, and critical judgment she trusts, and she aligns her sense of good conduct to his. Despite Evelina's sense of the pleasures of London experienced on her first trip with the Mirvans, the novel retreats to the countryside at the end. This rejection of the city suggests that only in the country can Evelina and Orville's polite sociability be untroubled by the likes of upstarts such as Madam Duval and the Branghtons, and rakish libertines like Lord Merton and Sir Clement Willoughby.

The epistolary format of Burney's novel allows the reader to see and to experience London through the eyes of Evelina, whose letters to her guardian in the country are only briefly interrupted by Mr. Villars's concern for the safety of his adopted child. Other epistolary novels of the period, however, explore a wider range of voices and accommodate a greater variety of perspectives on life in the city. Tobias Smollett's *The Expedition of Humphry Clinker* (1771) consists of letters written by a Welsh party touring Britain. Led by Matt Bramble, whose travel plans are prompted by his ill health, the party also includes his sister, her maid, and Bramble's niece and nephew. In Bramble's account of the metropolis, the social interaction that, for Hume, led to "refinement" instead corrupts everyone concerned. In London, he finds that the social order is under threat in a city where men and women of different ranks "*all tread upon the kibes of one another.*"[22] Appearances are frequently liable to deceive: looking fashionable, he laments, is sufficient to gain someone a reputation for taste and politeness. "The gayest places of public entertainment are filled with fashionable figures; which, upon inquiry, will be found to be journeymen taylors, serving-men, and abigails, disguised like their betters," he complains, before summing up that "[i]n short, there is no distinction or subordination left – The different departments of life are jumbled together." In place of Hume's model of sociability as mutually improving, the coming together of different types in the metropolis is here presented in terms of "justling, mixing, bouncing, cracking, and crashing in one vile ferment of stupidity and corruption."[23] Bramble's voice, though, offers only one response to the city. Win Jenkins, Tabitha Bramble's maid, finds that London generates excitement as well as confusion, leaving "my poor Welsh brain … spinning like a top" as she tries to take in all of its sights.[24] Similarly, for Bramble's niece Lydia Melford, the metropolis is an enchanted realm – a city full of "superb objects," the most striking of which are "the crowds of people that swarm in the streets." "I at first imagined," she explains to her correspondent, "that some great assembly was just dismissed, and wanted to stand aside till the multitude should pass; but this human tide continues to flow, without interruption or abatement, from morn till night." For Lydia, the magnificence of London, its "wealth and grandeur," is almost indescribable and can be expressed only via comparisons with "the Arabian Night's Entertainment, and the Persian Tales."[25]

Lydia's comparison between London and eastern cities that she knows from descriptions in works of fiction – "Bagdad, Diarbekir, Damascus, Ispahan, and Samarkand" – serves to highlight her sense of both the opulence and the strangeness of the capital.[26] The perceived foreignness of the metropolis, the hub of an increasingly global empire, could also, however, be expressed in less romantic terms. In his account of the city in Book VII of *The Prelude* (1805), William Wordsworth finds the streets of London teeming with people from across the globe:

> … all specimens of man
> Through all the colours which the sun bestows,
> And every character of form and face:
> The Swede, the Russian; from the genial south,
> The Frenchman and the Spaniard; from remote
> America, the Hunter-Indian; Moors,
> Malays, Lascars, the Tartar and Chinese,
> And Negro Ladies in white muslin gowns.[27]

In Wordsworth's account, as Saree Makdisi explains, "[t]he space of London itself turns into the space of empire."[28] In the Preface to the 1800 edition of *Lyrical Ballads*, Wordsworth famously cites "the encreasing accumulation of men in cities, where the uniformity of their occupations produces a craving for extraordinary incident" as one of the "multitude of causes unknown to former times [that] are now acting with a combined force to blunt the discriminating powers of the mind, and unfitting it for all voluntary exertion to reduce it to a state of almost savage torpor."[29] In Book VII of *The Prelude*, Wordsworth finds the city to be a series of bewildering spectacles and soon discovers that even law courts, churches, and the Houses of Parliament are also sites of performance. The most striking thing about the city for Wordsworth, here, is the experience of alienation. Walking along the crowded streets, he describes how

> One feeling was there which belonged
> To this great city by exclusive right:
> How often in the overflowing streets
> Have I gone forwards with the crowd, and said
> Unto myself, 'The face of every one
> That passes by me is a mystery.'

Anonymity does not offer Wordsworth the opportunities for reinvention that it provides Boswell. The young Wordsworth felt only "lost / Amid the moving pageant."[30] Yet, for the poet, London could still be a place of order and harmony. As a spectator of the city looking out toward St. Paul's Cathedral in "Composed upon Westminster Bridge, 3 September 1802," Wordsworth finds that the scene vies with "valley, rock, or hill" in its quiet majesty – albeit that it is only because its "mighty heart is lying still" and its streets are empty of people that the city can inspire in the poet "a calm so deep."[31]

In the work of Wordsworth, as in the writing of the other authors considered here, the practice and representation of spectatorship in the city provides ways of thinking about the relationship between the individual and the social world. For Addison, Hume, and Boswell, for example, spectatorship offers individuals a means to improve themselves by observing others and performing for them in turn. The sociable encounters that the city affords play a crucial role in their understanding of refinement; for Addison and Hume especially, scenes of polite conversation improve the manners of all who participate. The idea that living in the eyes of others leads to refining improvement, however, was always attended by the critique that an emphasis on manners and external appearance invites individuals simply to mimic polite behavior. In Henry Mackenzie's *The Man of Feeling* (1771), for example, the world of moral virtue appears to be fundamentally at odds with urban manners. Harley – a quintessential man of sensibility who cannot hide his feelings behind a polished exterior – has mixed fortunes in his attempts to interpret the people he encounters in London, and his lack of worldliness leaves him potentially vulnerable to the city's con men and tricksters.

This tension between self and society is also at the heart of Wordsworth's presentation of London in *The Prelude*. Yet for other Romantic period writers like Charles Lamb and William Hazlitt, the urban crowd in which Wordsworth felt lost is an important prompt to the individual to look beyond personal needs and to consider the broader public. In a lighthearted response to an invitation from Wordsworth to join him in the countryside, Lamb declared, "Separate from the pleasure of your company, I don't much care if I never see a mountain in my life. I have passed all my days in London, until I have formed as many and intense local attachments, as any of you mountaineers can have done with dead nature."[32] Lamb goes on to describe his local attachments through an account of the pleasures of the urban crowd – pleasures that are also at the heart of his essay on "The Londoner" (1802), which attempts to carve out a distinct identity for inhabitants of the city. For Lamb, the crowd is a "multitudinous moving picture" that is a cure for ills like melancholy and hypochondria.[33] For Hazlitt, too, the urban crowd forces the inhabitants of the city – including the much derided figure of the cockney, characterized in the period as a kind of pert city type "who has never lived out of London, and who has got all his ideas from it" – to think beyond their individual needs.[34] In his essay "Of Londoners and Country People" (1823), Hazlitt argues that Wordsworth's concerns about men not knowing their next-door neighbors in London are irrelevant because in cities men "meet together generally and more at large." "In London," he stresses, "there is a *public*" and by having the idea of "the *People*" continually called forth to one's mind, "and by having our imaginations emancipated from petty interests and personal dependence, we learn to venerate ourselves as men, and to respect the rights of human nature."[35]

For both Hazlitt and Lamb, urban spectatorship connected the individual to a larger sense of community. By the dawn of the Victorian era, however, such a position would be increasingly difficult to maintain. The population growth that had taken place in the first few decades of the nineteenth century would transform the metropolis from a potential site of individual improvement that could be conducive to the public good into, in Gregory Dart's words, "a problem to be solved."[36] In nineteenth-century writing, the figure of the flâneur offered a new model of urban spectatorship that emphasized the experience of the individual spectator, rather than the possibilities for sociable encounters afforded by the city. As the terms of the debate about urban life shifted, the refining forms of sociability imagined by eighteenth-century writers, and the positive aspects of the urban crowd described by Lamb and Hazlitt, would no longer seem viable.

NOTES

1 *Spectator* 1 (March 1, 1711), Joseph Addison and Richard Steele, *The Spectator*, ed. Donald F. Bond, 5 vols. (Oxford: Clarendon Press, 1965), vol. 1, pp. 4, 5.

2 Ned Ward, *The London Spy* Part III, *The London Spy*, ed. Paul Hyland (East Lansing, MI: Colleagues Press, 1993), pp. 46, 58–9.

3 Jonathan Swift, "A Description of a City Shower," *Jonathan Swift: The Complete Poems*, ed. Pat Rogers (New Haven, CT: Yale University Press, 1983), p. 113.

4 Carol Houlihan Flynn, "Where the Wild Things Are: Guides to London's Transgressive Spaces," in Regina Hewitt and Pat Rogers, eds. *Orthodoxy and Heresy in Eighteenth-Century Society: Essays from the DeBartolo Conference* (Cranbury, NJ: Associated University Presses, 2002), p. 30.

5 Jürgen Habermas, *The Structural Transformation of the Public Sphere: An Inquiry into a Category of Bourgeois Society*, trans. Thomas Burger (Cambridge: Polity Press, 1992), p. 43.

6 Dena Goodman, *The Republic of Letters: A Cultural History of the French Enlightenment* (Ithaca, NY: Cornell University Press), pp. 120–3.

7 Markman Ellis, *The Coffee House: A Cultural History* (London: Weidenfeld & Nicolson, 2004), p. 172.

8 Brian Cowan, *The Social Life of Coffee: The Emergence of the British Coffeehouse* (New Haven, CT: Yale University Press, 2005), pp. 255, 260.

9 *Spectator* 1, vol. 1, p. 4.

10 *Spectator* 69 (May 19, 1711), vol. 1, p. 294.

11 *Spectator* 1, vol. 1, p. 4.

12 David Hume, "On Refinement in the Arts," *Selected Essays*, ed. Stephen Copley (Oxford: Oxford University Press, 1998), p. 169. The essay was first published under the title "Of Luxury."

13 James Boswell, *Boswell's London Journal, 1762–1763*, ed. Frederick A. Pottle (New Haven, CT: Yale University Press, 1992), pp. 47, 60, 58, 59, 68.

14 Ibid., p. 68.
15 *Spectator* 411 (June 21, 1712), vol. 3, p. 538.
16 Boswell, *London Journal*, pp. 68–9, 130, 76.
17 Ibid., pp. 240, 264, 255. See also Erin Mackie, *Rakes, Highwaymen, and Pirates: The Making of the Modern Gentleman in the Eighteenth Century* (Baltimore, MD: Johns Hopkins University Press, 2009), pp. 84–5.
18 Dror Wahrman, *The Making of the Modern Self: Identity and Culture in Eighteenth-Century England* (New Haven, CT: Yale University Press, 2004), pp. 202–11.
19 Erasmus Jones, *Luxury, Pride and Vanity, the Bane of the British Nation* (London: printed for J. Roberts, [1736]), p. 12.
20 Daniel Defoe, *The Fortunes and Misfortunes of the Famous Moll Flanders*, ed. David Blewett (Harmondsworth, UK: Penguin, 1989), p. 277.
21 Frances Burney, *Evelina, or, The History of a Young Lady's Entrance into the World*, ed. Edward A. Bloom (Oxford: Oxford University Press, 2002), pp. 30, 207, 198, 239.
22 Tobias Smollett, *The Expedition of Humphry Clinker*, ed. Lewis M. Knapp (Oxford: Oxford University Press, 1984), p. 88.
23 Ibid.
24 Ibid., p. 108.
25 Ibid., p. 92.
26 Ibid.
27 William Wordsworth, *The Prelude: 1799, 1805, 1850*, ed. Jonathan Wordsworth, M. H. Abrams, and Stephen Gill (New York: Norton, 1979), p. 238.
28 Saree Makdisi, *Romantic Imperialism: Universal Empire and the Culture of Modernity* (Cambridge: Cambridge University Press, 1998), p. 31.
29 Wordsworth, Preface, in Wordsworth and Samuel Taylor Coleridge, *Lyrical Ballads*, ed. R. L. Brett and A. R. Jones (London: Routledge, 2005), p. 294.
30 Wordsworth, *The Prelude*, pp. 258, 260.
31 Wordsworth, "Composed upon Westminster Bridge, 3 September 1802," in *William Wordsworth*, ed. Stephen Gill (Oxford: Oxford University Press, 2010), p. 236.
32 Charles Lamb, "Letter to Wordsworth, 30 January 1801," *Selected Writings*, ed. J. E. Morpurgo (New York: Routledge, 2003), p. 160.
33 Lamb, "The Londoner," ibid, pp. 162–3.
34 William Hazlitt, "Of Londoners and Country People," *Metropolitan Writings*, ed. Gregory Dart (Manchester, UK: Carcanet, 2005), p. 82.
35 Ibid., pp. 93–4.
36 Gregory Dart, *Metropolitan Art and Literature, 1810–1840: Cockney Adventures* (Cambridge: Cambridge University Press, 2012), p. 28.

5

CATHERINE NESCI

Memory, Desire, Lyric: The Flâneur

Around me the street deafeningly screeched.
Tall, slender, in heavy mourning, majestic grief,
A woman passed, with an imposing hand
Raising, swinging a scalloped hem;
Agile and noble, her leg was like a statue's.
As for me, contorted like an extravagant, I drank
From her eye, pale sky where a storm germinates,
The sweetness that enthralls and the pleasure that kills.
A lightning flash … then night! – Fugitive beauty
By whose glance I was suddenly reborn,
Will I see you no more before eternity?
Elsewhere, far, far from here! too late! *never* perhaps!
For I know not where you fled, you know not where I go,
O you whom I would have loved, O you who knew it too![1]

With "To a Woman Passing By" (1859), Charles Baudelaire created a modern myth of lasting depth and melancholy, a powerful miniature drama that intertwines old myths with present urban conditions. In this sonnet, love at first sight is also love at "last sight," in Walter Benjamin's apt expression, an impossible love born out of a fugitive encounter.[2] The urban setting deeply alters the traditional figure of the woman as muse. While the crowd – represented here by the street that imprisons the poet in its deafening roar – magically offers the woman passerby to the poet's vision, it immediately reclaims her. The lyrical poet who experiences the city's ephemeral gift of love links his writing of the poem to a process of loss (prefigured by the woman's mourning attire), particularly the poignant loss of love. Portraying himself as an "extravagant" wanderer searching for love and his own identity, the peripatetic poet feels in seconds the intense shock and quasi-death inflicted

I wish to thank Kevin McNamara, whose generous suggestions and masterful editorial changes have helped the shaping of this chapter throughout. I am much indebted to his inspiring feedback and immense knowledge.

by love at first/last sight and his own rebirth after the majestic, grieving woman has moved on. Recreating this trajectory of love and frustrated desire, the sonnet transforms the "fugitive beauty" into the addressee of the poem and the soul mate with whom the poet communicates beyond distance and death. As spectators of the poem's miniature drama of melancholy intimacy, we, too, become passersby; as readers, we also reenact the poet's quest to arrest the image and object of his mobile, ever-unfulfilled desire.

The mid-nineteenth-century Paris in which Baudelaire wrote was undergoing drastic transformation to adapt the city to the needs of a population that had doubled between the end of the eighteenth century and the 1850s. The process is known as "Haussmannization," after its master architect, Baron Georges-Eugène Haussmann, the prefect of the Seine, who commenced it soon after Napoleon III declared himself emperor in 1852. Creating the new cityscape involved leveling decaying districts of the old city and its serpentine streets, and erecting tall apartment buildings with uniform, ornate facades on new tree-lined boulevards in order to showcase Paris as an emblem of the industrial age, to enhance the circulation of goods and bodies, and, in the wake of the Revolution of 1848 and the coup d'état of 1851, to facilitate surveillance and control of all inhabitants, especially the working classes.[3] During this lengthy work of modernization, Parisians witnessed the destructive transformation of the historical city, while artists and writers lamented the erasure of collective memory and the uprooting of a bohemian quarter and a large underclass. The enigmatic *passante* of the love sonnet may allegorize Paris itself as a passing city.

Baudelaire's Parisian writings testify to the "drama and trauma" of urban modernization; Marshall Berman argues that Baudelaire's work "shows us something that no other writer sees so well: how the modernization of the city at once inspires and enforces the modernization of its citizens' souls."[4] To understand how Baudelaire's urban poetry expresses this ambivalent process of psychological and spiritual conversion to the modernist project, the parts that memory and desire play in the lyricism of the modern urban realm Baudelaire invented in the mid-nineteenth century, and the mediating roles the poet and flâneur embody in the culture of modernization, we will examine his poetic vision of the modern city. We will then turn to Walt Whitman's poetry of urban interactions and desires, and will briefly consider the twentieth-century reinvention and gendered revisions of street-rambling, memory, and desire.

Toward the Urban Lyric: The Flâneur as Avant-Garde

As an art critic, Baudelaire first attempted to define urban modernity and the heroism of his own age in his writings of the late 1840s. In his 1845

Salon, a review of that year's official exhibition of academic paintings, he complained of artists' lack of engagement with the present and the forward movement of his time: "To the wind that will blow tomorrow, no one pays attention; and yet the heroism of modern life surrounds and presses in on us."[5] A year later, he ended his Salon with a section "On the Heroism of Modern Life," in which he summoned artists to the fluid beauty of the cityscape: "Parisian life is rich in poetic and marvelous subjects. The marvelous envelops and soaks us like an atmosphere, but we do not see it."[6] A decade later, with the drastic remaking of the capital city at full speed, Baudelaire developed in his poetry the program he laid out in the Salons and other writings: the creative appropriation of urban experience. Scholars usually consider the second edition of *The Flowers of Evil* (1861), with its new section entitled "Parisian Tableaux," as when Baudelaire realizes his urban lyric, in such poems as "To a Woman Passing By," "The Swan," "The Little Old Women," and "The Seven Old Men." However, contemporary readers discovered these poems a few years earlier in the periodical press, a medium that deeply influenced Baudelaire's invention of new lyrical forms.

Baudelaire's urban poetics owes much, indeed, to the prepublication of his work as feuilletons in mass-circulation dailies, the satirical press, and arts magazines. Starting in the 1830s, columns in the dailies and satirical newspapers focused on the social world and reported everyday issues, all of which influenced the literary works that were published in the press. As Alain Vaillant points out, poetry published in newspapers had to face "the test of the news": whereas Romantic poetry fostered inner feelings and idealism, poetry in the daily press sat alongside political polemics and prosaic news as well as cultural and social notes. Poetry was thus immersed in "the trivial and insignificant rhythm of the dailies and the everyday."[7] Yet, rather than follow the speedy flow of the news, Baudelaire's flâneur injects reflective, contemplative, and allegorizing practices in the heart of the press.

Like the press itself, the invention of the flâneur was rooted in the emerging consumer culture and the urban milieu of the time. With the increasing use of gaslit streetlamps in the 1820–40s and electrical light in the 1880s, material changes in illumination prompted city dwellers to adapt their senses, daily rhythms, and mental lives to proliferating visual stimuli and increasingly intense lighting. New technologies of visual and commercial display multiplied the sights of commodities and advertisements. Popular attractions such as panoramas offered spectacles of optical illusions made of hyperrealist paintings, depicting famous historical battles and panoramic views of cities on a gigantic, 180-degree circular canvas; in the 1820s, Louis Daguerre opened his dioramas, which simulated lifelike movements and changing impressions of daylight by the rotation of the spectators' platform and the manipulation of light on curved panes of figurative paintings. With its busy streets and elegant boulevards, cafés and shopping arcades, wealth of entertainments, and, starting in the 1850s, department stores in new luxurious districts, Paris created an ever-changing cityscape, which testified to the lure of the artificial world of capitalist markets, visual pleasures, and artificially lit cities. The development of public transportation in large cities and the advent of railroad travel mediated the access to a flow of fleeting visual perceptions while installing movement and speed at the heart of modern life.[8] Although the flâneur predates most of the technological changes that shaped modern experience, he early on grew into a heroic character who browsed the streets, scanned and read the crowds; he became a recording device of progressively more complex and wider fields of vision.

Indeed, the flâneur became identified with the Parisian popular culture of the 1830s–40s, symbolizing a heroic potential of urban civilization. As a passionate, invisible, male observer of diurnal and nocturnal life in the arcades, parks, boulevards, and cafés he identified with the public spaces of the city. In his 1930s contextual reading of Baudelaire's works, Benjamin suggested that, to the flâneur, public spaces represent an interior space.[9] Yet he interpreted the genre of the urban sketch, which he termed "panoramic literature," as innocuous and "socially dubious": "The leisurely quality of these descriptions fits the style of the flâneur that goes botanizing on the asphalt."[10] Recent research, however, has granted cognitive value to the vignettes, physiologies, and caricatures that depicted the everyday, ordinary characters and social types, thus representing modern life and a new public space in the early nineteenth century. Mary Gluck argues that the flâneur was committed to the representation of modernity in all its ambiguities and diverse manifestations: "What he accomplished was to render legible and transparent the bewildering heterogeneity of urban life and, in the process, to create a viable model for an epic imagination in modernity."[11]

Edgar Allan Poe's tale "The Man of the Crowd" (1840), which Baudelaire translated and published as feuilletons in the daily Le Pays (1855), exemplifies the obsessive-compulsive process of reading the city, and points to the failure of the flâneur's urban sketch to achieve a legible public landscape by reading metropolitan surfaces and social types. In the first part of the tale, the narrator, recovering from a sickness, sits in a coffeehouse on a main London thoroughfare and tastes the intoxicating pleasure of observing the tides of swelling crowds lit by gaslight. Working as a physiologist, his mind classifies the pedestrians he observes into social and psychological categories, from the predictable higher classes to the more interesting lower classes and the criminal underworld. The rapid pace at which pedestrians go by presents no obstacle to the narrator's feverish clairvoyance:

The wild effects of the light enchained me to an examination of individual faces; and although the rapidity with which the world of light flitted before the window, prevented me from casting more than a glance upon each visage, still it seemed that, in my then peculiar mental state, I could frequently read, even in that brief interval of a glance, the history of long years.[12]

The narrator is able to read passersby through the minute details of their public appearances until a challenge to his mastery of social signs and production of urban taxonomies suddenly arises in an old man who defies all categories and mixes frightening or incompatible features: "vast mental power," "coolness," "malice," and "supreme despair."[13] Frantically pursuing the intractable, erratic character through the nocturnal city and into the next day, the narrator-turned-prowler and detective is unable to decipher the unrelenting wanderer and revenges himself upon the man by labeling him "the type and the genius of deep crime. He refuses to be alone. *He is the man of the crowd.*"[14] However, the narrator himself embodies the "man of the crowd," despite that his traits and intentions run counter to those of the old, decrepit man who cannot leave the teeming crowds.

In his celebrated essay *The Painter of Modern Life* (written in the late 1850s, published in *Le Figaro* as feuilletons in 1863), Baudelaire signals his own relation to the city when he invokes Poe's convalescent narrator as, even despite himself, a sensory subject who wishes to breathe in "all the odours and essences of life" and to remember all his past sensations, as he has just come back from the dead.[15] For the trivial life of the city and its moving crowds to be perceived in their concrete singularities, and not as commonplaces, Baudelaire contends, the artist must set aside mastery for the perception of a convalescent or the unmediated curiosity of a child, to whom everything appears in its newness. Then again, he argues that the experience must be modulated. When Baudelaire considers how the graphic artist "Mr. [Constantin] G[uys]" transposes into art the perceived, raw material of a real and trivial life, he presents the work as mediated by memory and the hand that draws the work of art. Away from the crowd, the painter of modern life gives visual form to the eternal beauty he has distilled from the ephemera of modern life. We thus understand that Baudelaire was not interested in the minutiae of the empirical city and its social categories but in its aesthetic presentation. When he added a new section entitled "Parisian Tableaux" to the 1861 edition of *The Flowers of Evil*, he certainly paid homage to the panoramic literature of the early nineteenth century, which multiplied representations of social types and the myriad appearances of a new public life anchored in a culture of commodities. However, Baudelaire did so at a time when the physiologies and other visual and written forms of social texts had lost their attraction and relevance: "Modernity had ceased to be a social text, that waited to be deciphered by the urban writer; it had become an aesthetic text, that needed to be freshly created through the artist's imaginative act," Gluck comments.[16] Baudelaire's poems make readers think about and feel the destruction and shattering of the present moment; but they also represent the lyrical process of aesthetic creation that resists the modern project of progress and city planning.

Heroes of Modern Life: Strolling Down Memory Lanes

Honoré de Balzac, whom Baudelaire much admired, established the archetype of modern desire in the 1830s Parisian novellas *Ferragus* and *The Girl with the Golden Eyes*, texts in which passing, mysterious female protagonists embody the object of longing and knowledge for young men in search of their identities in the modern city. Faced with the unsettling forces of urban life, male heroes experience self-loss or disillusionment in unexpected, hazardous confrontations with the sexualized city and its elusive women, who – like Paris itself – end up sacrificed to the restoration of social order. According to William Chapman Sharpe, the biblical heritage of Babel, Babylon, and the New Jerusalem still underlies the sexualization of modern cities and their passing women, identified as Whore or Virgin, or an ambivalent mix of both.[17]

More generally, large cities furnish artists and writers with what John Jervis has called "the imaginative framework of the modern experience"; it operates "through the dualisms that both capture that experience and constitute it *as* experience; it is a condition of the modern experience that can hardly be grasped *in* experience, yet forces one to make the attempt."[18] Existential exile in the midst of the new city, which Baudelaire expresses in "The Swan" (1860), provides a remarkable example of such an unstable framework. A "fertile memory" helps the poet to fight a sense of loss, which he experiences as the gap between memory and experience in a fast-forwarding city shedding its old spiritual and material forms. In a famous parenthesis, the poet laments this accelerated process of change and its corollary amnesia: "The old Paris is no more (the form of a city / Changes more quickly, alas! than a mortal's heart)."[19] Memory, then, shields the poet against the forgetfulness and devastation brought about by the modern project of technological progress and rational urban planning – a project some have claimed was heroic in its own right.

Starting with the Trojan Andromache, a majestic and sullied figure of antique grief, and a figure of modern dislocation, the swan itself – once mythical, now a circus animal stranded in a Parisian gutter – "The Swan" unrolls a thread of apostrophes and longings that turn the poet and his readers into pensive subjects of unfulfilled desires and nostalgia. Filled with references to alienation and loss, this lyrical tableau stands in opposition to the present city experienced by the poet-flâneur as he crosses the new Carrousel, a site that was the ground zero of Haussmannization. Haunted by memories, he thinks "Of whoever has lost that which is never found / Again! Never!"[20]

The poet displaced by the new Paris addresses himself to the exiled, grieving Andromache, caught in a sublime gesture of melancholy and resistance as she waters with her tears a "false Simoïs" (Simoïs is a Trojan river), and he recalls a marooned swan, escaped from its cage, which he makes an allegory of himself as it wanders in search for sustenance but finds only a dusty, dry pavement that soils its "white plumage." Nevertheless, the bird does not passively accept its fate; it rebels in the allegorical language of poetry, which can say what heavily censored news cannot in the repressive political climate of the 1850s:

> I see that hapless one, strange and fatal myth,
>
> Toward the sky at times, like the man in Ovid,
> Toward the ironic and cruelly blue sky,
> Stretch his avid head upon his convulsive neck,
> As if he were reproaching God![21]

Yet there seem to be two divergent results of the lyrical transfiguration of the changing city, as if the poet's memories testify to an irreversible loss while his language expresses desire for meaning and fulfillment. On the one hand, Ross Chambers argues that by comparing modern Paris with ruined Troy, Baudelaire presents the city as "both unfinished and residual: the rubble of its construction sites coexists with its bric-a-brac, the leftovers of the past that figures the materials of memory, rejected by-products of a history of progress that has no time or place for them."[22] On the other hand, the poet makes his poetic work into a simulacrum of Paris similar to Andromache's tear-filled Simoïs, and he transforms his weighty but "dear memories" into the sounds of music and lyrical poetry. Such transfiguration is lost in translation, but in French, sonorities are reversed between the arresting and heavy "rocs" (rocks) and the final breath/sound of the endless echo of the "cor" (French horn), the sonorities of which are emphasized by the final rhyme and non-closure of the poem on the adverb "encor" (still more):

> Ainsi dans la forêt où mon esprit s'exile
> Un vieux Souvenir sonne à plein souffle du cor!
> Je pense aux matelots oubliés dans une île,
> Aux captifs, aux vaincus! ... à bien d'autres encor!
>
> [Thus in the forest to which my exiled mind withdraws,
> An old Memory sings out a full note on the horn!

I think of the sailors forgotten on some isle,
– Of the captives, of the vanquished! … of many others more!]

Baudelaire ends his poem with a collective form of lyricism, as the poet's fellows in exile and addressees become plural and anonymous. Perhaps the most poignant figure of dislocation and deprivation is an anonymous woman of color who generates the poet's caring empathy and reinforces the sense of a meaningless exploitation at the heart of the western modern project. After recalling twice the well-known, dignified, but fallen heroine of antiquity and the "ridiculous and sublime" swan, Baudelaire places a "negress" as the midpoint figure in his chain of apostrophes – "… wasted and consumptive, / Treading in the mud, searching with haggard eye / For the absent coco-palms of superb Africa" – before the concluding apostrophes to a set of unidentified exiles. In this position, she embodies the enduring desire for an irrecoverable past and place of ideal plenitude and beauty.[23]

The two other long poems of the "Parisian Tableaux" section reinforce the poet's estrangement from the modern city and his failed quest to grasp the meaning of his identity in the present. "The Seven Old Men" and "The Little Old Women," published under the title "Parisian Ghosts" in *La Revue contemporaine* (1859), couple a crippling and a creative encounter with the crowd, pointing to the ambiguity of the aesthetic project in the age of modern urbanization. In "The Seven Old Men," the urban milieu becomes a "Teeming city, city full of dreams / Where the specter in broad day grabs hold of the passer-by!"; in that hellish, hallucinatory space, the wandering poet loses the protection of invisibility and mastery of the urban spectacle as he suddenly faces the wounding gaze of seven old men and finds himself on the verge of mental alienation.[24] Turning his back on the spectacle to protect himself, he withdraws to his home where his tired, old soul cannot recover from the disturbing encounter.

Yet in "The Little Old Women," the poet is a happier flâneur who forges an imaginary kinship with old, decrepit women and, through them, a limited sense of belonging in the city as he crosses "the limits assigned to Poetry" (according to the anonymous presentation of the poems in the *Revue contemporaine*), to roam "In the sinuous folds of the old capitals, / Where all, even horror, turns into enchantments." Depicting himself in search of "singular creatures, decrepit and charming," the strolling poet unfolds myriad vignettes of old women, whom he turns into mobile heroines of modern life, split subjects of past glories and present decay. Whereas their age, social status, and lost beauty drive them to the margins of the Parisian "teeming tableau," they become the spiritual center of the poem and the anchor of the poet's soul and desires. Deprived of their femininity and even humanity, they seem "monsters" or mechanical puppets to indifferent onlookers.

To the empathetic poet, however, their eyes encompass an extraordinary range of human feelings, which he captures in brief sketches expressing their resolute fight for survival, divine grace, mysteries, sorrow, and love. As in "The Swan," memories of a glorious past and extreme torments confirm the heroic stature of the little old women, who are portrayed as avatars of Andromache in a movement of collective lyricism: "They all could have made a river with their tears!"[25] As figures of existential homelessness, the eponymous women become the poet's kindred spirits, but at the cost of his engagement with the actual city and its modern, soulless landmarks. The little old women allegorize the passing of the decaying city.

In his prose poems, Baudelaire abandons the flâneur's heroic stance and renders the abject material and moral misery of the modern city, now severed from its past. The poet focuses on destitute, distanced mirror images of himself, which he catches in drifting through Parisian streets and public gardens, or sitting in a glittering café as in "The Eyes of the Poor." The bygone city can no longer be memorialized; the flâneur's gaze on the present and site of amnesia turns into "a spiritual contemplation," Laure Katsaros suggests.[26]

The Flâneur's "Holy Prostitution"

In the 1990s, feminist scholars began debating whether the urban walker, observer, and modern artist is an exclusively male figure. In "The Invisible Flâneuse," cultural sociologist Janet Wolff stated that the "literature of modernity describes the experience of men."[27] In "The Invisible Flâneur," Elizabeth Wilson replied that Wolff overlooked the inherent contradictions of the flâneur, who "represented not the triumph of masculine power, but its attenuation… The flâneur represents masculinity as unstable, caught up in the violent dislocations that characterized urbanization."[28] The poems we have read so far support the interpretation of melancholic and impotent masculinity in Baudelaire; the late prose poems of Paris Spleen present even more conflicting visions of masculinity and selfhood on trial.[29] Whereas in "The Little Old Women" the poet assumes a loving and fatherly position toward the old women, in "Widows" the poet's gaze on the women is detached and voyeuristic; the prose poem enhances feelings of estrangement in the midst of the crowds. Such dissonances and reversals pervade the prose poems, in which Baudelaire pushes yet further the frontiers of the lyric to create, according to the dedication to Arsène Houssaye, "the miracle of a poetic prose, musical without rhythm and without rhyme, supple enough and rugged enough to adapt itself to the lyrical impulses of the soul, the undulations of reverie, the jibes of conscience." Alternating images of harmony, discord, and shock, which translate the jagged movements of the soul, the new hybrid language records the poet's immanent presence and passage in the metropolis, which Baudelaire describes as the experience of contingency, offering endless possibilities of crossings and collisions: "It was, above all, out of my explorations of huge cities, out of the medley of their innumerable interrelations, that this haunting ideal was born."[30]

The prose poem "Crowds," which enacts a dualist poetics of mastery and incompletion between the poet and the eroticized, feminized city, condenses the contradictions of Baudelairian masculinity and poetic self. However, it does so with a sense of jubilant exuberance in the illicit, reversible, unexpected, and yet religious couplings the poet as invisible flâneur performs:

> The poet enjoys the incomparable privilege of being able, at will, to be himself and an other. Like those wandering souls seeking a body, he enters, when he wants, into everyone's character...

> What people call love is awfully small, awfully restricted, and awfully weak, compared with that ineffable orgy, that holy prostitution of the soul which gives itself totally, poetry and charity, to the unexpected which appears, to the unknown which passes by.[31]

Such scripts of omnipotence, penetration, role playing, and unobstructed freedom express the same male, bourgeois or aristocratic, fantasies that Baudelaire grants to Mr. G. in *The Painter of Modern Life*:

> For the perfect *flâneur*, for the passionate spectator, it is an immense joy to set up house in the heart of the multitude, amid the ebb and flow of movement, in the midst of the fugitive and the infinite. To be away from home and yet to feel oneself everywhere at home; to see the world, to be at the center of the world, and yet to remain hidden from the world... The spectator is a *prince* who everywhere rejoices in his incognito.[32]

A male projection of the feminized, sexualized city is clearly at work here. If at the end of "Crowds" the peripatetic flâneur and lover of the crowd is able to withdraw from the city to identify with celibate, chaste men, one can hardly conceive of a nineteenth-century woman who could likewise exit at will and unblemished. Nonetheless, the exchanges between outer and inner worlds, urban landscape and mental landscape, are neither stable, predictable, nor risk-free, and they always go beyond the balanced dialectic of self and other that "Crowds" celebrates in its redemption of prostitution.

In *Paris Spleen*, the self-effacing flâneur drifts from one chance or shock encounter to another in the desolate cityscape and its degraded world. From the anonymous character of the first prose poem, "The Stranger" to the last one, "The Good Dogs," in which the poet provides a parodic and lyrical physiology of the dogs haunting the streets of Paris and Brussels, most characters as well as the narrator-poet are nameless, impersonal, indistinct; they form the fragmented, unfinished collection of ephemera and *curiosa* of a precarious modern life. In "The Stranger," the brief dialogue between two unnamed interlocutors produces a mysterious answer to questions regarding the favorite attachments of the "enigmatic man," who admits he has no family, friends, or fatherland: "I love clouds ... drifting clouds ... there ... over there ... marvelous clouds!"[33] In the guise of a ragpicker, poor man, or sadist, the poet catches sight of short-lived heroes, most of whom keep their secrets, as does the old woman whose story the poet imagines in "Windows." Seeing her from above, over waves of rooftops, her window closed, he conceives her "legend" and mimics the self-assurance of the urban sketch: "With her face, her clothing, her gestures, with almost nothing, I have refashioned that woman's history, or rather her legend, and sometimes I tell it to myself weeping."[34] The poet does not tell his readers the woman's legend; yet he confides that such made-up "legend" ensures his own sense of self.

The last passing woman of *Paris Spleen*, the deranged prostitute of "Miss Scalpel," who is obsessed with doctors and blood-stained surgeons, grabs hold of the poet as he is "reaching the edge of the city outskirts, under flashing gaslights." Like Poe's narrator in "The Man of the Crowd," he goes along, hoping for some revelation: "I passionately love mystery, because I always hope to untangle it. So I allowed myself to be dragged off by that companion, or rather by that unhoped-for enigma." Irritated as the poet is by his failure to solve the mystery of Miss Scalpel's mad obsession, he simply adds, in a self-reflective note: "What weirdness you find in big cities, when you know how to walk about and look! Life swarms with innocent monsters!"[35] In this uncanny interaction, at the suburban edge of the gaslit city, the hapless flâneur reaches the frontier of the lyrical age and passes the threshold that leads him into the psychopathology of everyday life and sexual perversions, but by urging the absolution of *innocent* monsters, he signals his difference from Poe's narrator, who needs to define and condemn the inscrutable man of the crowd.

Flâneurs among the Multitude, from Walt Whitman to the Postmodern City

Similarly "To a Woman Passing By," Walt Whitman's short poem "To a Stranger" (1860, from the "Calamus" poems) reenacts love at last sight and envisions a future encounter. Whereas the passing woman of Baudelaire's sonnet is forbidden to the poet, he still celebrates the melancholic image of his unfulfilled desire, encapsulated in a stunning snapshot. Whitman's dual address leaves undecided the gender of the stranger, pointing both to heterosexual and same-sex loves: "Passing stranger! You do not know how longingly I look upon you, / You must be he I was seeking, or she I was seeking." In the space and fleeting moment of the urban encounter, passing glances and close proximity bring the poet back to a shared past, uncannily turning the unfamiliar person into a familiar one. The self and non-self merge in dreams and intense corporeal exchanges: "You grew up with me, were a boy with me, or a girl with me, / I ate with you, and slept with you – your body has become not yours only, nor left my body mine only / You give me the pleasure of your eyes, face, flesh, as we pass." At the close of the poem, the belief that the future will bring back the stranger compensates for the lack of verbal communication with him or her in the transient present: "I am not to speak to you, I am to think of you when I sit alone or wake at night alone, / I am to wait, I do not doubt I am to meet you again, / I am to see to it that I do not lose you."[36] As readers, we incarnate the stranger Whitman's poem conjures up as he pulls us into his textual crowds.

Whitman's poems of delightful belonging to the urban throng often carry the same exhilaration as the poet bathing in the multitude in Baudelaire's "Crowds." "Song of the Broad-Axe" (1856), and "City of Orgies," "Among the Multitude," and "Poem of Joys" (all published in 1860), blend sexual and textual gratifications through ephemeral encounters, with onlookers often glancing back at the strolling observer. In "Among the Multitude," Whitman's crowds include both men and women; however, the "lover and perfect equal" who picks the poet "out by secret and divine signs" may also perform, to modern readers, the recognition of gay lovers' sexual cruising.[37] In poems of *Leaves of Grass* devoted to ideal cities of free and open love, Sharpe argues, "Whitman's dream permits the repressed sexuality of the present to become the future city's central life force."[38] Whitman's best-known poem of the metropolis, "Crossing Brooklyn Ferry" (1856), develops the poet's physical, mental, and spiritual immersion in the city, which his fertile glance, amorous strolling, and lyrical language create anew. Young lovers and readers memorialize the intimate name of the urban bard: "Gaze, loving and thirsting eyes, in the house or street or public assembly! / Sound out, voices of young men! Loudly and musically call me by my nighest name!"[39] Whitman also faced up to the dissonances and degradation of urban life in New York, of which, as a journalist, he was accustomed to read and write; contrary to Baudelaire, he included the trivial and the criminal in his poetry in a quite direct fashion.[40]

In another time and space, when the film camera started capturing the motions and fluctuations of ever-fluid metropolitan life, tireless flâneurs and flâneuses nevertheless continued roaming the ever-changing cities of modernity. Transfigurations of city strolls in Virginia Woolf's works, such as the short *Street Haunting: A London Adventure* (1930), open the way to a female flânerie as a form of mobile creativity that blends street-rambling and street-writing; the recording of stories displays lyrical, life-affirming images of London life, quite dissimilar from the male pessimist, modernist visions of Woolf's time. While some lament the diminution of human experience in the urban setting, others confront the trying task of preserving memory in urban environments that lose their pasts through the "creative destruction" of urban development or the massive destruction wrought by highly tech-nologized warfare. In the 1930s, Benjamin built his inquiry into the modern city on collective and personal memories and images, the anxious selves of inhabitants lost in urban labyrinths, and the salvation of discarded objects and architectural forms, such as the obsolete European arcades.

Surrealism, in particular Louis Aragon's *Nightwalker* (*Le Paysan de Paris*, 1926), provided the initial inspiration to Benjamin's project. Different from Baudelaire, the Surrealists rejoiced in their break with a past civilization and its religious beliefs and moral constraints. With its ephemeral adver-tisements, luminous commercial displays, endless circulation of bodies in strolls, tramways and buses, cafés from which to observe passersby and meet women, and still mysterious buildings and decrepit shopping arcades, Paris provides the Surrealist flâneurs with aimless, infinite promenades and chance encounters. From their walks and random interactions in the city, they generated a new literary language of erotic and illogical dreamscapes and collages that celebrate urban civilization, explore the unconscious, and spawn a modern mythology of daily life – the "everyday marvelous" – thus achieving Baudelaire's 1840s project. Examples include, in addition to Aragon's *Nightwalker*, Philippe Soupault's *Last Nights of Paris* (1928) and André Breton's *Nadja* (1928).

Flânerie in contemporary North American poetry took the form of col-lage and free-verse lines, as in William Carlos Williams's city poem *Paterson* (1946–58), whose fifth book features his own passing woman. Traversing the male urban sphere, she incarnates the quintessential city, the union of expe-rience and innocence, of art and life, of ever-frustrated desire and longings. In Frank O'Hara's lunch poem of midtown Manhattan, "A Step Away from Them" (1957), the flâneur strolls through the vibrancy of the lunch hour, evoking in the present what comes in his field of vision and bodily sensations: the sights and sounds of yellow cabs, workers eating sandwiches and drink-ing Coca-Cola. Moving along, he memorializes the contradictory images of postwar, multiethnic New York: a "Negro" in a doorway observes a "blonde chorus girl"; "beautiful and warm" Puerto Ricans take the poet's mind away from his dead friends. Yet death comes back with the final snapshot of the Manhattan Storage Warehouse, "which they'll soon tear down."[41]

The flâneur need not be a native or limited to a single city, especially in an age of diaspora and air travel. So we close with the destruction brought about by ethnic conflict and Aleksandar Hemon's reappropriation of urban spaces in his 2011 autobiographical tale of two cities, "Mapping Home." Feeling at first disoriented in suburban Chicago after leaving his native Sarajevo, Hemon uses his memory of Baudelaire's flâneur as a survival strategy in order to make sense of street life and find himself at home in the American metropolis. The practice of the "low-wage, immigrant flâneur" in Chicago replicates Hemon's prior artistic and existential flânerie in Sarajevo before the war: "I collected sensations and faces, smells and sights, fully internalizing Sarajevo's architecture and its physiognomies. I gradually became aware that my interiority was inseparable from my exteriority, that the geography of my city was the geography of my soul."[42] In this blending of self, city, and text via flânerie and memories, Hemon testifies to the resilience of artists and historical subjects who mourn a lost past and a lost city, and, in the process, recover from the most crippling experiences of violent, painful separation and infinite grief.

NOTES

1 Charles Baudelaire, "To a Passer-By," *The Flowers of Evil*, trans. William Aggeler (Fresno, CA, Academy Library Guild, 1954), p. 311; translation modified by the author.

2 Walter Benjamin, "The Paris of the Second Empire in Baudelaire," *The Writer of Modern Life: Essays on Charles Baudelaire*, ed. Michael W. Jennings, trans. Howard Eiland, Edmund Jephcott, Rodney Livingstone, and Harry Zohn (Cambridge, MA: Belknap-Harvard University Press, 2006), p. 77.

3 The interpretation of Haussmannization and its outcomes are as numerous as they are conflicting. See, for example, David Pinkney, *Napoleon III and the Rebuilding of Paris* (Princeton, NJ: Princeton University Press, 1972), and David Harvey, *Paris, Capital of Modernity* (New York: Routledge, 2003).

4 Marshall Berman, *All that is Solid Melts into Air: The Experience of Modernity* (New York: Penguin, 1982), p. 147.

5 Baudelaire, "Salon of 1845," *Art in Paris, 1845–1862: Salons and Other Exhibitions Reviewed by Charles Baudelaire*, ed. and trans. Jonathan Mayne (London: Phaidon Press, 1965), pp. 31–2; translation modified by the author.

6 Baudelaire, "Salon of 1846," in ibid., p. 119; translation modified by the author.

7 Alain Vaillant, "Baudelaire, artiste moderne de la 'poésie-journal,'" in Guillaume Pinson and Maxime Prévost, eds., *Penser la littérature par la presse*, special issue of *Études littéraires* 40.3 (Autumn 2009), 46; author's translation.

8 For all these technological advances, see Wolfgang Schivelbusch's books, *The Railway Journey: The Industrialization of Time and Space in the Nineteenth Century* (Berkeley: University of California Press, 1986) and *Disenchanted Night: The Industrialisation of Light in the Nineteenth Century* (Oxford: Berg, 1988).

9   Benjamin, "The Flâneur," *The Writer of Modern Life*, p. 68.
10 Ibid.
11 Mary Gluck, "The *Flâneur* and the Aesthetic Appropriation of Urban Culture in Mid-19th-century Paris," *Theory, Culture & Society* 20.5 (2003), 65.
12 Edgar Allan Poe, "The Man of the Crowd," *The Selected Writings of Edgar Allan Poe*, ed. G. R. Thompson (New York: Norton, 2004), p. 235.
13 Ibid., p. 236.
14 Ibid., p. 239.
15 Baudelaire, *The Painter of Modern Life and Other Essays*, trans. Jonathan Mayne, 2nd ed. (London: Phaidon Press, 1995), p. 13.
16 Gluck, "The *Flâneur*," 77.
17 See William Chapman Sharpe, *Unreal Cities: Urban Figurations in Wordsworth, Baudelaire, Whitman, Eliot, and Williams* (Baltimore, MD: Johns Hopkins University Press, 1990), pp. xii–xiii, 1–15.
18 John Jervis, *Exploring the Modern: Patterns of Western Culture and Civilization* (Oxford: Blackwell, 1998), p. 65.
19 Baudelaire, "The Swan," *Flowers of Evil*, p. 289.
20 Ibid., p. 293.
21 Ibid., p. 291. For a political reading, see Richard Terdiman, *Present Past: Modernity and the Memory Crisis* (Ithaca, NY: Cornell University Press, 1993), pp. 106–48.
22 Ross Chambers, *Loiterature* (Lincoln: University of Nebraska Press, 1999), pp. 241–2.
23 Baudelaire, "The Swan," p. 293; translation modified by the author.
24 Baudelaire, "The Seven Old Men," *Flowers of Evil*, p. 295; translation modified by the author.
25 Baudelaire, "Little Old Women," ibid., p. 305; translation modified by the author.
26 Laure Katsaros, *New York-Paris: Whitman, Baudelaire, and the Hybrid City* (Ann Arbor: University of Michigan Press, 2012), p. 109.
27 Janet Wolff, "The Invisible *Flâneuse*: Women and the Literature of Modernity," *Feminine Sentences: Essays on Women and Culture* (Berkeley: University of California Press, 1990), p. 34.
28 Elizabeth Wilson, "The Invisible Flâneur," *New Left Review* 191 (1992), 109.
29 Baudelaire hesitated between several titles: *The Solitary Wanderer, The Parisian Prowler, Nocturnal Poems*. The posthumous volume is now known as either *Paris Spleen* or *Little Prose Poems*.
30 Baudelaire, "To Arsène Houssaye," *Paris Spleen*, trans. Louise Varèse (New York: New Directions, 1970), pp. ix–x, x.
31 Baudelaire, "Crowds," *The Parisian Prowler: Le Spleen de Paris, Petits Poèmes en prose*, trans. Edward K. Kaplan (Athens: University of Georgia Press, 1989), p. 21.
32 Baudelaire, *The Painter of Modern Life*, p. 9.
33 Baudelaire, "The Stranger," *Parisian Prowler*, p. 1 (ellipses in the original).
34 Baudelaire, "Windows," ibid., p. 93.
35 Baudelaire, "Miss Scalpel," ibid., pp. 115, 118.
36 Walt Whitman, "To a Stranger," *Leaves of Grass*, ed. Sculley Bradley and Harold W. Blodgett (New York: Norton, 1973), p. 127.

37 Whitman, "Among the Multitude," *Leaves of Grass*, p. 135.
38 Sharpe, *Unreal Cities*, p. 79.
39 Whitman, "Crossing Brooklyn Ferry," *Leaves of Grass*, p. 164.
40 See Katsaros, *New York-Paris*, pp. 52–4.
41 Frank O'Hara, "A Step Away from Them," *The Collected Poems of Frank O'Hara*, ed. Donald Allen (Berkeley: University of California Press, 1995), pp. 257, 257, 258, 258.
42 Aleksandar Hemon, "Mapping Home: Learning a New City, Remembering the Old," *The New Yorker* (December 5, 2010), 47, 42.

6

STUART CULVER

Social Science and Urban Realist Narrative

In 1845 Friedrich Engels published *The Condition of the Working Class in England*. Confronting his readers with the stark realities of life among the working poor in Manchester, an exemplary city of nineteenth-century industrialism, Engels offered closely observed details of the conditions of life among factory workers, noting the one-room huts with dirt floors in which families crowded, the miasmic gases rising from the river Irk, the piles of debris and refuse lining the river's shores. Engels was not only interested in making his reader see the city's industrial wasteland; he wanted also to show how Manchester's comfortable classes experienced their city: "The town itself is peculiarly built so that a person may live in it for years, and go in and out daily, without coming into contact with a working people's quarter, or even with workers ... without ever seeing that they are in the midst of the grimy misery that lurks to the right and the left," hidden by a facade of brilliant shops along the city's central boulevard. An unplanned but nonetheless significant cityscape prevents the prosperous citizens from perceiving the misery of the working classes, much less recognizing those conditions as the necessary complement of their own wealth. As they move up and down the boulevard and experience the public spectacle of the modern city, they are unable to grasp their city as a functioning whole or to see clearly their own place in the social system. Engels noted the "brutal indifference" with which Manchester's citizens confronted one another in public, in part because old customs had been "obliterated" and new ones not yet found.[1]

Engels was not alone in suggesting that the massive centralization ushered in by industrialization – the new urban environments and class relations that accompanied economic and technological progress – demanded a new approach to conceptualizing human society. Others in the industrialized west began to wonder whether there could be a legitimate science of the social and if such a science could discover ways to maintain order or to guide attempts to reform material conditions and interpersonal relations in the emerging urban system. Might social science need to begin by identifying the fundamental laws that necessarily underlie any social formation? Clearly there was an acceleration of associated life, and social relations were becoming increasingly complex. Was this an inevitable and healthy consequence of progress or a danger to any authentic sense of solidarity? The understanding of human agency and responsibility was being transformed by new tools and situations. Identities were themselves becoming more fluid as populations were mobilized by industrialization and new relations among social classes emerged. At the dawn of the twentieth century, Georg Simmel identified a tension in urban society between centripetal and centrifugal forces, between the pull on the individual to be deeply implicated in a complex system, on the one hand, and the sense of one's self as isolated and anonymous on the other hand. Was it the place of a professionalized science to overcome this tension?

When the Industrial Revolution was just underway, and in the aftermath of the French Revolution's radical challenge to traditional notions of order, Charles Fourier presented what he believed was a scientific approach to the social questions. Fourier's theory of associated man understood the human soul as essentially a collective phenomenon realized only when all "passional" types are assembled "in graduated proportions, arranged in classes, orders, genera, species and varieties."[2] Fourier assumed that all passions and character types that could be discovered should be included in their proper proportion in the Phalansterie, the residential and productive structure that served as the basic unit of Fourier's utopian colony. His analysis identified 810 types, which represented for him the scientifically determined building blocks of associated life. Fourier inspired utopian settlements, particularly in the United States, but his theory did not call for a flight from the city so much as a reconstruction of industrial society from the ground up, replacing the still-emerging modern cities with networks of Phalansteries. A generation later, Auguste Comte differed from Fourier by seeing social order as "something to be perfected, not created," by a "wisely and actively applied" social science.[3] Although social phenomena are always open to modification, the extent and character of successful political intervention must be limited in each epoch by a clear understanding of the form of social consensus, the underlying belief system that determines social relations and authority. Comte assumed that civilization inevitably passed through three distinct stages – the theological (fictional), metaphysical (abstract), and scientific (positive) – each of which supported a different kind of social consensus. Political institutions could be truly rational, but only when they were grounded on the consensus actively at work in a given social organization.

In his key contributions to the discipline of sociology, Herbert Spencer argued against Comte's notion of scientifically informed intervention. For

Spencer, the job of the social scientist was first to identify the laws at work behind social phenomena and second to challenge any misguided efforts to interfere with or modify those laws. As his American disciple, William Graham Sumner argued in "The Absurd Effort to Make the World Over" (1894), "Nine-tenths of the socialistic and semi-socialistic, and sentimental or ethical, suggestions by which we are overwhelmed come from failure to understand the phenomena of the industrial organization and its expansion. It controls us because we are all in it."[4] Other sociologists differed on the role social scientists ought to play or presented different theories of the fundamental social bond. If, for some, society was held together by resemblance and assumptions of identity, for others, including Emile Durkheim in *The Division of Labor in Society* (1893), it was precisely the opposite: advanced societies were held together by perceptions of lack, difference, and dependence. There was an increasing division of labor in social science itself as new fields of expertise arose to diagnose and regulate emerging social problems: Sigmund Freud's analysis of hysteria, Cesare Lombroso's account of the criminal type, and Durkheim's study of suicide all viewed the modern urban environment as in some sense the cause of distinctly modern disorders. The discussion to follow traces some of the key documents in the development of this discourse while examining the role that literary realism played in advancing and challenging some of the key premises involved in these attempts to establish a scientific study of social relations.

The urban realist narrative emerged alongside this discourse, and some writers, most notably Émile Zola, came to consider themselves social scientists. Zola conceived each of his Rougon-Marquart novels as an experimental study of human action in a specific social context, a study of the interaction between character, understood as a bundle of inherited traits and acquired propensities, and a clearly delineated environment. What unfolds in a plot should be what must have happened and would always have happened. Not all the novels discussed in this chapter are examples of Zola's naturalism, although each is an instance of urban realism if only because it aims to represent the modern city as a complex fabric of life. The five central novels – Honoré de Balzac's *Père Goriot*, Charles Dickens's *Our Mutual Friend*, Zola's *The Ladies' Paradise*, William Dean Howells's *A Hazard of New Fortunes*, and Frank Norris's *McTeague* – share a number of compositional strategies: they use a large canvas, juxtapose and crosscut among narrative threads, portray characters as complexly interdependent, and present setting as environment or a source of contagious influence. More significantly, in taking the urban milieu as its subject, each novel engages some of the key claims of the emerging discipline of sociology; each variously reflects, extends, and challenges the assumptions about how the industrialized modern city embodies a social whole.

Gemeinschaft and Gesellschaft

A generation after Comte insisted on the importance of social consensus, Ferdinand Tönnies introduced the distinction between *Gemeinschaft* and *Gesellschaft* as an analytic tool to identify a significant transformation of consensus under urban industrialism. *Gemeinschaft* (usually translated as "community") identifies the stable customs and folkways, familial obligations, and religious duties that hold traditional societies together. *Gesellschaft*, which Tönnies described as "the indispensable ground of modern urban life," refers to a network of negotiated, transitory bonds or contracts between individuals who confront one another as strangers and potential rivals: "One goes into *Gesellschaft* as one goes into a strange country."[5] Tönnies acknowledged that there had always been some elements of *Gesellschaft* in every social formation, if only in the chance encounters and negotiations between nomadic tribes. In the modern city, however, *Gesellschaft* had become the dominant mode of interaction, and if there is a new sense of equality and freedom among citizens who are no longer defined by traditional status relations, it comes at the expense of any clear or comfortable understanding of social identity. In the sphere of *Gesellschaft*, one enters into multiple relations with others, but in every case the goal is not to achieve equity or balance but to get the better of one's temporary partner. Tönnies looked nostalgically on a world of uncontaminated *Gemeinschaft* in which social roles and obligations were more clearly defined and more apparently reciprocal. He described the family dinner for those still living under *Gemeinschaft* as a communal ritual that affirms this system of values: "The table is the house itself in so far as everyone has his place there and is given his proper share." Conversely, in the city, "the household become[s] sterile ... a mere living place" and the family members become a loose association of wage earners with no clear-cut duties or responsibilities to one another.[6]

Balzac's seminal novel of urban realism, *Père Goriot* (1835), can be seen as analysis of the growing effects of *Gesellschaft* on post-Revolutionary Paris. The novel's central "character" is really a milieu, the Maison Vauquer, a seedy Left Bank boarding house filled with downwardly mobile elder Parisians and a few young men on the make, all of whom meet each other with indifference mingled with suspicion as they struggle to assert their own respectability. Balzac characterizes the boarders thrown together about the Maison's dinner table as restless and discontent, struggling to "demonstrate their superiority by making fun of the fare to which their penury condemns them."[7] Unlike the family table that Tönnies describes, the boarding-house table fails to affirm or to stabilize identities and relationships: a daughter disowned by her father sits at the table with a father exploited by his daughters. Balzac's narrative works by exploiting these juxtapositions and accidental doublings as it documents the dissolution of this provisional community and the revelation that the boarders had harbored in their midst a criminal mastermind.

Balzac's narrative finds its center in the story of a young man from the provinces, Eugene Rastignac, who is asked to choose between two substitute fathers, the doting and exploited Goriot, who will bankroll Eugene's affair with his daughter, and the criminal Vautrin, who would involve him in a murderous scheme to marry an heiress. Rastignac would like to believe that in choosing Goriot, he continues to respect the filial obligations and traditional values he brought with him from the provinces, even as his Parisian exploits are bankrupting his own family; however, at novel's end, he stands over Goriot's grave in Père Lachaise, looking down on the city of lights:

> His eyes fastened almost hungrily on the area between the column in the Place Vendôme and the dome of the Invalides, home to that fashionable society to which he had sought to gain admission. He gave this murmuring hive a look which seemed already to savour the sweetness to be sucked from it, and pronounced the epic challenge, "It's between the two of us now!"
>
> And as the first shot of the war he had thus declared on Society, Rastignac went to dine with Madame de Nucingen.[8]

Having internalized Vautrin's predatory vision, Rastignac has become for Balzac a monstrous symptom of what it means for a society to be given entirely over to *Gesellschaft*.

Contract

Whereas Tönnies and Balzac struggled in their different ways to preserve and to defend *Gemeinschaft* – or at least to criticize the predominance of *Gesellschaft* in urban life – Herbert Spencer, keeping faith with British Enlightenment political theory, argued in *Social Statics* (1854) that freedom of contract must be understood as the fundamental building block of any civilized society. Spencer celebrated the substitution of honesty for loyalty as the central virtue in liberal society; in place of *Gemeinschaft*'s respect for status relations and traditional obligations, the ground of modern society lay in keeping promises and acknowledging the equal rights of others. Society flourishes only when "man may claim the fullest liberty to exercise his faculties compatible with the possession of like liberty by every other man."[9] The question for social order was not whether an individual's actions harmed another, but whether they unfairly limited another's free actions. When conditions of life change, as they had in the industrialized city, it is the job of each individual to adjust his or her desires and actions to that environment.

The task of the Spencerian social theorist is essentially a negative one: to identify the fundamental social law – freedom of contract – and to defend it against reformist legislation. Spencer does, however, acknowledge that there needs to be a brake on mankind's predatory activity, and he believes that sympathy plays this indispensable social role. Paradoxically, he contends that sympathy is actually a by-product of selfish activity that flourishes best where there is most freedom: "Those who have the strongest sense of their own rights will have the strongest sense of the rights of their neighbours."[10] Sympathy, as Spencer defines it, is the recognition of resemblance and therefore develops most when all social relations are negotiations among equals. If sympathy is the crucial regulator of social behavior, the question facing the Spencerian social scientist is how best to promote and develop this virtue, which is not innate to pre-social man. Believing that sympathy is grounded in direct personal relations with others, Spencer identifies two dangers in any system of state-administered charity: first, it subverts the process of social evolution, and second, it undermines the individual's capacity for fellow feeling, which is the real ground of social harmony.

Spencerian sociology can appreciate literary narrative as one way that fellow feeling and the capacity to acknowledge resemblance in general are fostered and promoted. However, to become an active social virtue and a means of regulating social behavior, Spencerian sympathy must involve an immediate personal experience and not a represented one. One need only recall Ebenezer Scrooge's odyssey in *A Christmas Carol* (1843) to recognize the ways in which Dickens explores and promotes the workings of sympathy and fellow feeling in his fiction. A key episode in *Bleak House* (1853) seems to endorse Spencer's critique of delegated charity. The reader encounters Mrs. Jellyby, who is so caught up in her plans for building a model colony on the shores of the Niger River that she is blind to the needs of her own children and the deplorable state of her household. Clearly her "telescopic philanthropy," the effort to understand social reform and charitable duty in an abstract or theoretical way, has blocked her ability to see the real world in front of her and to respond immediately and personally.

Nevertheless, it would be a mistake to read Dickens as an uncritical proponent of Spencerian social theory, particularly in the complex late novels that deploy strategies of urban realist narrative. In *Our Mutual Friend* (1865), arguably Dickens's most significant effort to map the industrial city, the trope of mutuality traces a very different social bond from Spencerian sympathy. The novel opens by juxtaposing two nighttime scenes in London, two distinct urban milieus: mudlarks scour the river for valuable items among the refuse left by daytime commerce while a formal dinner is hosted by the Veneerings for a company of nouveau-riche pretenders to social status. It becomes the novel's job to bridge this impossible gap, and the narration unfolds complexly by withholding crucial information, leaping forward and cutting back so that the reader assumes the burden – and pleasure – of tracing out the lines of implication that show how apparently accidental encounters are, in fact, moments of mutuality.

Bella Wilfer, fearing she is becoming a fortune hunter who will sell herself to the richest suitor, has taken to looking in her mirror and speculating on her worth to others or her true value, but her chance encounter with Lizzie Hexam offers her another image of herself and of mirroring or resemblance in general. Lizzie understands love as giving another something to trust in and to care for, thus enabling her beloved to become "better and happier." In other words, the mutual exchange does not seek either the equality of Spencerian contract or its fundamental independence, so when Bella asks her mirror if she is, "for ever to be made the property of strangers" and an object of their speculation, Dickens's answer is yes.[11] Just so, the titular "friend," John Rokesmith, learns that we cannot leave others alone when we act in a social world.

The unearned increment of value that comes with mutuality is echoed by Dickens's account of urban economics in the novel. Borrowing from Henry Mayhew's *London Labour and the London Poor* (1851), Dickens describes a counter-economy on the city's streets where things are not produced but recycled or resituated, where bill brokers try to squeeze money out of bad paper, and rags become the clothes for dolls sold back to the children of fashion. At the novel's center are the "dust" heaps that represent wealth that is not created but discovered and appreciated amidst the debris of urban life. In this complex narrative economy, Dickens extends the novel-reader's burden, challenging that reader not only to recognize the identity or resemblance key to Spencerian sympathy but also to acknowledge how one's identity is entangled with and dependent on the other.

Imitation

While Spencer's sociology found important proponents in Britain and the United States, a school of French thought insisted on the pre-rational bonds that made social relations possible. Gabriel Tarde's *Laws of Imitation* (1890) opens with an explicit rejection of Spencer. Tarde argues that prior to any contractual or economic relationship, a social group is brought together by members' propensities to imitate one another or simply because they recognize in each other traits they share in common. This sense of resemblance and imitative drive underlies and enables social institutions and practices in the way "that tissues precede organs." Tarde rejected the assumption shared (but differently understood) by Comte, Tönnies, and Spencer that interpersonal relations inevitably become more rational as society develops: "we err in flattering ourselves that we have become less credulous and docile, less imitative, in short, than our ancestors."[12] Indeed, imitation becomes both more pervasive and more diverse in "the exaggerated and concentrated social life" of the modern city: "The noise and movement of the street, display of shop windows, and the wild unbridled rush of civilization arrest [city dwellers] like magnetic passes."[13] In this volatile imitative environment, individuals are less aware of when and what they are imitating.

The process of socialization accelerates, but for Tarde it represents both an enabling condition for social order and a threat to it. For some observers, such as Gustave Le Bon, whose *The Psychology of Crowds* appeared in 1895, the modern city unleashes irrational modes of association: "The sovereign force of modern times" is the urban crowd, formed spontaneously on the street by unconscious impulses, shifting and vaguely understood opinions, and the general atmosphere of imitation and contagion. The modern crowd is not the expression of a racial genius or deeply held, customary values and beliefs, but is moved by words and images that are projected in the city's image environment "like the slides of a magic lantern show." Le Bon argues that French schools – "factories of degeneration" – have exacerbated the social crisis by producing "frivolous" bourgeois and discontented proletarians who have acquired "a violent dislike for the state of life in which they were born, and an intense desire to escape" their everyday identities.[14] Tarde himself criticized Le Bon's argument, claiming that modernity was the age not of crowds but of publics that were formed not through immediate and emotional contact on the streets but more impersonally by reading the same newspapers and magazines. Still, Tarde was concerned about "capricious publics" and the increasingly subtle currents of influence, and he suggested that sociologists need to study the laws governing imitation in general and the difference made by the city's new media in the scale and intensity of imitation.[15]

In the Rougon-Marquart novels documenting the rise and fall of the French Second Empire, Zola frequently begins his narrative with a sustained and painstakingly documented description of a specific milieu – a train station, a coal mine, the food markets of les Halles, the stock exchange, and, in *The Ladies' Paradise* (1881), the recently developed department store. Each of these environments operates for Zola as both an arena for new types of public association and an organ in the city's circulatory or digestive system. They are sites where crowds are formed and the imitative forces Tarde both celebrated and feared are peculiarly activated. *The Ladies' Paradise* opens at the moment of a frenzied sale; the chaotic activity is brought into focus by the gaze of Denise Baudu, a young woman recently arrived in Paris from the provinces, who finds the spectacle at once horrifying and attractive. The reader will encounter and interpret the workings of the store through Denise's experience of it. Theodore Dreiser will deploy the same narrative device in *Sister Carrie* (1900) as he presents metropolitan Chicago through Carrie Meeber's enthusiastic reactions. But while Dreiser's Carrie goes on to embody uncritically the imitative spirit of the new city, Denise instinctually resists the department store – or at least the logic of fashion at its heart. By kinship she is linked to the owners of the small specialty shops that are being swallowed by the monstrous store; at the same time, Denise's hereditary sense of order or tidiness is attracted to the innovations in the retail system, such as selling at fixed prices instead of haggling, and relying on higher turn-over to lower profit margins. The problem for Denise is the hysteria incited by the store's display and advertising, the enticements to buy that unleash "a terrible spending agency, ravaging the households, working up the fashion-able folly of the hour." The novel goes on to document various pathologies of consumer desire – impulse buying, shoplifting, compulsive bargain hunt-ing – that threaten to undermine the fabric of middle-class life in the city. To Denise, the store appears alternately as a pagan "temple raised to the extrav-agant folly of fashion" – a machine for deranging and devouring women – and, at least potentially, "the phalansterium of modern commerce."[16]

Denise herself becomes a member of a unique social class, the "counter-jumpers" and shop girls, most of whom, like Denise, have recently moved to the city, live in a barracks-like dormitory above the store, take their meals in the basement cafeteria, and find their amusement in public: in the parks or along the boulevards of Haussmann's Paris. They occupy a specific imi-tative relationship to fashionable society: "by their daily contact with the rich customers [they] assumed certain graces, and finished by forming a vague nameless class, something between a work-girl and a middle-class lady."[17] The department store forms a type of metropolitan who is superfi-cially fashionable and uncertainly placed in the social system. *The Ladies' Paradise* is anomalous among the Rougon-Marquart novels for its conven-tional happy ending. At novel's end, Denise is to marry and domesticate the store's ambitious, innovative owner, and thus will be allowed to reform the conditions under which the counterjumpers labor. She introduces profit sharing, health care, classes, and libraries – in effect, aiming to render the superficial imitations of manners more authentic. But even as she improves the lives of this distinct urban class and makes the workings of the store in many ways more rational, Denise does nothing to reform the unreason that drives the fashion system, nor can she save her relatives who are symbolically buried in their small, dark shop.

A decade later, in the United States, Bradford Peck published a novel entitled *The World a Department Store* (1900), which finds in the well-run, thoroughly rationalized big store a model for a broader utopian order, in effect completing Denise's project. Peck's fantasy is one of a number of quickly written responses to Edward Bellamy's *Looking Backward* (1888). This set of utopian romances can be read as an alternative discourse to urban realism. Typically they discover the essence of the new order in a feature of contemporary society. Bellamy himself glimpsed the germ of the future utopia in the army, in particular in the parades of Civil War veterans. The novel's industrial army emulates the military: labor is presented as a patriotic act of self-sacrifice for the nation; one competes not for more money than others but for a higher rank and more visible prestige. Bellamy believed he had solved the central tension between individualism and subordination by embracing it: labor would always be irksome and servile, but the utopian quickly retires to a life of private, idiosyncratic consumption. For William Morris, this solution amounted to a "cockney paradise" in which labor ultimately would disappear and productive activity would always be disparaged.[18] Morris's alternative was to locate utopia in the artisanal world of the medieval village. In the end, Bellamy's romance had less influence on American political and economic arrangements than on the collective vision of what a city could be, as reflected in such late nineteenth-century forays into urban planning as the White City at Chicago's 1893 Columbian Exposition, which served a generation of Americans as the model of what urban public space might become.

Traffic

Toward the end of the century, a school of American sociologists led by Lester Ward began to challenge the influence of Social Darwinism. Ward argued that social scientists could "accelerate social evolution" by developing a "collective telesis," a conscious commitment to a future social system instead of the backward-looking notion of consensus or folkways championed by Sumner.[19] Edward Ross's *Social Control* (1901), dedicated to Ward, opens by evoking "the juncture of crowded city thoroughfares" and the ways in which pedestrians and drivers adjust to avoid collisions, expecting from the other not aid or sympathy but "reliable, predictable conduct."

Traffic doesn't involve on the spot negotiation or Spencerian contracts, but a common commitment to orderliness that is not instinctual according to Ross, but a "fabric" (a term he uses often) woven by the group's "craving for an impersonal solution." Ross contends that more searching and pervasive means of control will be required given the ever-increasing scale of industrial organization, and he advocates establishing in the society "radiant points of social control" capable of "fit[ting] people to deal kindly and honestly by one another."[20]

William Dean Howells's 1890 novel *A Hazard of New Fortunes* responds to both an 1889 streetcar strike in New York City and the author's own move from Boston to New York the year before. In the novel's climactic scene, several characters converge by chance on what Ross would call "the juncture of crowded city thoroughfares." The streetcars are running, manned by scabs; the streets are lined with strikers and police, and amidst the chaotic exchanges, two characters are killed by the police although neither posed any direct threat. In short, the system of social control fails. The State Board of Arbitration – described by the novel's central character, Basil March, as "the greatest piece of social machinery in modern times" – is unable to get the companies to compromise with their workers; the police present "a mere image of irresponsible and involuntary authority," and March is left to bemoan the ways in which "this economic chance world in which we live" fails to satisfy our rational assumptions about what a society should look like.[21]

March, like Howells himself, has come to New York to edit a new magazine, one that promises to create a new public space, to become one of Ross's "radiant points" of cultural authority. However, he finds it difficult to manage the traffic in opinions, the competing and clashing visions of society. The problem is borne out when the editorial staff find that they cannot agree about what it means for the magazine to do "good." Is it a question of finances, morality, political theory, or aesthetics? If the "noisy typography" of the dailies fails to make the strike itself clear, the magazine (or Howells's novel itself) is left with the challenge accurately to represent the chance world without contributing to its chaos and unreason. Perhaps it was just this anxiety about the novel as a representational form that led Howells in the mid-1890s to experiment briefly with Bellamy-inspired utopian romances. The Altrurian Romances, however, were less devoted to projecting possible future societies than they were with developing perspectives on the contemporary scene; that is, the visitor from utopia provides Howells with a lens for identifying the latent promises and the dangers in America's emerging metropolitan culture and, in Howells's hands, the utopian romance became a way of perfecting the representational project of urban realism.

Blasé Encounters

As the twentieth century dawned, Georg Simmel suggested that social scientists needed to attend to the psychological conditions unique to the modern city that were ushering in "an entirely new rank order in the world history of the spirit." According to Simmel, the metropolitan feels like "a mere cog in an enormous organization of things and powers" surrounding him and therefore harbors a psychic urge to assert his individual identity in the face of this overwhelming objective culture and threat of anonymity. At the same time, he endures on the city street "the *intensification of nervous stimulation* which results from the swift and uninterrupted change of outer and inner stimuli." The metropolitan overcomes this sensory overload by adopting a blasé attitude while also building up a flamboyant, fashionable public persona. There is in Simmel's account a crucial gap between the mask and the calculating private person behind it; the performance is, in fact, a strategy of self-distancing. Lacking any radiant points of authority to help him fit in or even to understand what fitting in might mean, the metropolitan pursues individual projects of display and concealment in order to find some comfort in an incomprehensible world; flamboyance becomes a strange species of social self-control, the mask that allows the individual to hold something in reserve. Simmel remarks that "the inner aspect of this outer reserve is not only indifference but, more often than we are aware, it is a slight aversion, a mutual strangeness and repulsion, which will break into hatred and fight at the moment of a closer contact."[22] Beneath the blasé surface is a fundamentally antisocial temperament.

In *McTeague* (1899), Frank Norris tells the story of a man's absolute failure to keep up his blasé front or to manage "the swift and continuous shift" of stimuli of his metropolitan milieu. The novel is set primarily on San Francisco's Polk Street, and Norris carefully describes the sights, sounds, and smells of this corner of the city as he documents McTeague's everyday life, the habits and creature comforts that keep him tied to a routine. Adopting Zola's naturalist strategies, Norris presents this social life as a flimsy veneer spread over a set of bestial impulses. Indeed, throughout McTeague's seedy neighborhood the walls prove too thin, the social performances never as polished as they need to be to contain the aversions or passions of Polk Street. McTeague, an unlicensed dentist unable to cope with the emerging regulatory system, is never able to negotiate public spaces without fearing that he is being "ma[d]e small" by officious others or becoming a spectacle for them.[23] Seeing himself not just as a cog in a vast social machinery but also as an object of derision, McTeague is unable to manage the blasé social performance Simmel describes and so provides for Norris's reader a vicarious experience of the emotional intensity of his writhing battle with his antisocial self.

McTeague famously ends up a wanted man handcuffed to his dead rival in the middle of Death Valley. Subtitled "A Story of San Francisco," the novel achieves a zero degree of social life and a sort of nightmare inversion of the mutuality that Dickens endorsed; the reader sees McTeague not alone but inescapably bound to another, albeit as purely a dead weight. At the core of the key works of urban realism – and the social theories these narratives complement and criticize – is the question of what constitutes the fundamental social bond and how the emerging environments and practices of metropolitan life disrupt, endanger, promote, or merely modify that bond. At a moment when the novel achieved its greatest prominence in western literary culture, the urban realists took as the object of their representation the city itself as a new structuring of social relations and encounters, and whether, like Balzac, they described the city as the negation of genuine social ties or, like Dickens, they found in the streets the promise of new kinds of mutuality, they shared a sense that their fiction participated in a larger project of interpreting and analyzing associated life and the effects that modern urban environments have on that life.

NOTES

1 Friedrich Engels, *The Condition of the Working Class in England*, trans. Florence Kelley-Wischnewetsky (Oxford: Oxford University Press, 1999), pp. 57–8, 37.

2 Charles Fourier, "The Individual, An Incomplete Being," *Harmonian Man: Selected Writings of Charles Fourier*, trans. Mark Poster (Garden City, NY: Anchor, 1971) p. 116.

3 Auguste Comte, *Course in Positive Philosophy*, trans. Margaret Clarke, in *The Essential Comte: Selected from Cours de philosophie positive*, ed. Stanislav Andreski (New York: Barnes and Noble, 1974), pp. 157, 156.

4 William Graham Sumner, "The Absurd Effort to Make the World Over," *On Liberty, Society, and Politics: The Essential Essays of William Graham Sumner*, ed. Robert C. Bannister (Indianapolis: Liberty Fund, 1992), p. 252.

5 Ferdinand Tönnies, *Community and Society*, trans. Charles P. Loomis (Mineola, NY: Dover, 2002), p. 34.

6 Ibid., p. 54, 162.

7 Honoré de Balzac, *Père Goriot*, trans. A. J. Krailsheimer (Oxford: Oxford University Press, 2009), pp. 4–5.

8 Ibid., p. 223.

9 Herbert Spencer, *Social Statics* (New York: D. Appleton, 1873), p. 94.

10 Ibid., pp. 116–17.

11 Charles Dickens, *Our Mutual Friend* (London: Penguin, 1997), p. 518.

12 Gabriel Tarde, *The Laws of Imitation*, trans. Elsie Clews Parsons (New York: Henry Holt, 1903), pp. 73, 77.

13 Tarde, "The Public and the Crowd," *Gabriel Tarde on Communication and Social Influence*, ed. Terry N. Clark, trans. Terry N. Clark and Priscilla P. Clark (Chicago: University of Chicago Press, 1969), p. 284.

14 Gustave Le Bon, *The Crowd: A Study of the Popular Mind* (Mineola, NY: Dover, 2002), pp. 30, 53.

15 Tarde, *Laws of Imitation*, p. 84.

16 Émile Zola, *The Ladies' Paradise*, trans. Kristin Ross (Berkeley: University of California Press, 1992), pp. 69, 347, 315.

17 Ibid., p. 138.

18 William Morris, Review of *Looking Backward*, by Edward Bellamy [1889], reprinted in *Science Fiction Studies* 3 (1976), 287–9.

19 Lester F. Ward, "Collective Telesis" (1897), *Outlines of Sociology* (New York: MacMillan, 1899), p. 262.

20 Edward Alsworth Ross, *Social Control: A Survey of the Foundations of Order* (New York: MacMillan, 1901), pp. 1, 12, 24, 77, 434.

21 William Dean Howells, *A Hazard of New Fortunes* (New York: New American Library, 1980), pp. 355, 368, 380.

22 Georg Simmel, "The Metropolis and Mental Life," *The Sociology of George Simmel*, ed. and trans. Kurt Wolff (New York: Free Press, 1950), pp. 423, 422, 410 (italics in original), 415–16.

23 Frank Norris, *McTeague: A Story of San Francisco* (London: Penguin, 1982), p. 95.

7

BART KEUNEN AND LUC DE DROOGH

The Socioeconomic Outsider: Labor and the Poor

The socioeconomic outsider is an inherent part of modernity, as we have known since the second half of the nineteenth century. This figure is as inherent to the city as are the phantasmagoria of the commodity and the grandeur of urban architecture. Yet as we examine the literary representation of the urban working class, things become more opaque. The identity of the working class has been primarily defined as a non-identity overrun by elements pertaining to heterogeneous identities: the working class is variously constructed as oppressed, subversive, unhygienic, morally weak, and so forth. Nevertheless, for cultural and literary theory, this referential ambiguity should not pose an obstacle to insight. Rather, precisely this construction of a generic identity sheds a fascinating light on how the western intellectual community has handled the complex cultural situation we call *modernity*. This chapter intends to uncover the logic in the volatile literary image of the working class, and to elucidate both the contribution made by a predominantly middle-class discourse on the urban working class to enlarging our understanding of social justice and the central role played by literary representations in this process.

The development of the representation of the socioeconomic outsider (that is, of the poor and the working class) throughout this period is from a vigorous political construction toward an identity less politically potent. Referring to the way in which the early Marx portrays the proletariat, Alain Badiou argues that

> [t]he question of the political process is always a question ... of finding something that is, paradoxically, a generic identity, the identity of no-identity, the identity which is beyond all identities. For Marx, "proletariat" was the name of something like that. It's not an identity. It's ... humanity as such, because the working class is something generic and not a pure identity.

But today, Badiou suggests, "[p]robably that function of the working class is saturated."[1] Badiou's characterization will serve as a guideline in this chapter, because his thesis lends coherence to a large variety of phenomena as authors seek to construct that *generic identity* and make the problem of the socioeconomic outsider the key to reform of the modern world.

Urban poverty and the emancipation of marginal groups pose the general problem of social modernization with singular acuity as the integration of the outsider into the history of mankind. The representations of the outsider offered here arise at different moments in the history of city literature yet as they crystallize, these representations coexist side by side or overlap – even within one text. A first strategy, indebted to the work of German Romantic intellectuals, employs an idealistic-individualistic discourse to impose a generic identity on the socioeconomic outsider that grants him or her a place in a global narrative of emancipation. Through a *parti pris* for the underdog (characters such as Charles Dickens's Oliver Twist and Victor Hugo's Jean Valjean), the middle-class intellectual propagates a historical struggle for the liberation of individuals irrespective of descent or education. A second strategy represents the outsider's emancipation as a matter of community values. Within this discourse the concept of the working class is discussed for the first time. The central idea is that capitalist society isolates individuals and deprives them of qualitative values. Outsiders from the working class constitute a challenge for community development to be met by moral edification of the whole community. Both of these strategies are strongly marked by moral sentiments and show that in the nineteenth century, before the advent of sociology and social psychology, fiction served as a form of opinion journalism in which value judgments interrupt the "neutral gaze."

Only within a third discursive formation does objectivity become a fundamental component of the literary strategies of representation. Throughout the late nineteenth and early twentieth centuries, quasi-sociological and quasi-anthropological judgments characterize the positivistic discourse that followed the journalistic revolution of the era. The most outspoken works – naturalistic texts, for example – are marked by a radically different interpretation of progress and human development. Spiritual development and the reconciliation of classes are supplanted by a belief in progress through knowledge. This shift in emphasis is clearly visible in the representation of the outsider. Gradually, however, the nineteenth-century emancipatory project gives way to skepticism and disillusionment. To a Schopenhauerian naturalist or an existential modernist, the main issue becomes not the representation of the outsider as a political generic identity but the problematic nature of the reformist or revolutionary project itself.

The Outsider as the Underdog

Fairly soon after the first signs of proletarianization of the western metropoles, some writers became aware that access to public space was restricted and the conditions under which a steadily growing group of people lived contrasted sharply with the dominant image of the city. For the elites and, increasingly, the middle classes, public space had become a space of visual consumption, of "promenaders" observing commodities and other passersby, of nightlife on boulevards or in and around theaters. Picturesque sketches of street life continued to appear, but now and then a new figure stepped into the limelight: the socioeconomic outsider. As the middle classes were confronted with the growing pauperization of certain urban enclaves and proletarianization of the historical city's outskirts (or in the United States, some of its older neighborhoods), some writers began to perceive the urban world as fundamentally split between increasingly prosperous citizens and harrowingly destitute stragglers who lived in what Benjamin Disraeli dubbed *The Two Nations* in the subtitle of his 1845 novel *Sybil*. The phenomenon is strikingly recapitulated in Charles Baudelaire's "The Eyes of the Poor" (1869), where a ragged threesome (an adult man, a *gamin* or rascal, and a child) gorge themselves on the festively lit facade of a restaurant on one of the new boulevards while the speaker and his darling enjoy the climax of a romantic day. He becomes angry because she wants the threesome removed by the waiter, while he is inclined to sympathize with them and to share their indignation. This existential spleen found a continuation in the melancholic empathy toward victims of socioeconomic exclusion that became the paragon of numerous literary responses to the urban working class and poor whose narrators identify with the underdog and project their antibourgeois sentiments onto their characters.

This representation of the outcast was fostered by an affective abhorrence or indignation aimed at the modern political system, which, after the wave of democratization, gave free rein to a rampant market economy. The dialectical counterpart of this system may be found in a philosophical project that considered idealistic individualism to be of paramount importance. Indeed, interest in the poor is not explained only by the fact that the poor increasingly made their existence known; the discourse of the outsider must also be viewed against the background of the creation of a new, typical modern discourse about poverty. Authors of urban novels who were influenced by this discourse observed how a generic identity was kindled in the poor, one that connoted "lack of freedom" and as such emanated a historical power. The putative source of this philosophical discourse is found among intellectuals who completed the revolution of Romanticism. To Hugo and

Dickens, two authors with a distinctive predilection for the moral power of the underdog, the urban outsider was what Egmont was to Beethoven, Napoleon to Stendhal, and the Greek freedom fighter to Lord Byron.

In this view, characters like Oliver Twist are not merely marginal social figures who work their way up but also representatives of a population claiming its place. In *Les Misérables* (1862), Hugo was inspired by the rising group of industrial workers who lived in poor conditions inside the faubourgs. In a remarkable passage that identifies the powers that will be with a little rascal or *gamin* from the suburbs who is depicted as the opposite of the old-world society, Hugo refers almost explicitly to the Romantic cult of freedom. The aristocratic good-for-nothing, who is characterized by "the passive acceptance, which contents itself with gazing," has had his time, Hugo claims. His successor was waiting in the form of

> This pale child of the Parisian faubourgs [who] lives and develops, makes connections, "grows supple" in suffering, in the presence of social realities and of human things, [and is] a thoughtful witness. He thinks himself heedless; and he is not. He looks and is on the verge of laughter; he is on the verge of something else also. Whoever you may be, if your name is Prejudice, Abuse, Ignorance, Oppression, Iniquity, Despotism, Injustice, Fanaticism, Tyranny, beware of the gaping gamin.
> The little fellow will grow up.[2]

The working-class *gamin* symbolizes the historical force that, once summoned by its dialectical antipode, would bring forth a new social synthesis. For Hugo and other authors inspired by Romanticism, the underdog was a figure with a "generic identity," not only an individual but also a "species" that symbolizes the course of history and the quality of mankind as a whole. It is no coincidence that Hugo took his stand at the left of the political spectrum and that he published his *Discourse on Misery* (1849) in the same decade that he was working on his great social novel.

In Hugo and Dickens, many characters fulfill the specific function of the underdog. They demonstrate that the truth of the modern world, which is the ultimate goal of the idealistically inspired author, does not coincide with the viewpoint of the bourgeoisie – who seem to have substituted political despotism with economic despotism, thereby pushing the working class into the slums. Valjean, for example, is an underdog who, surrounded by figures from the urban lumpenproletariat, wages war against the old and new forces. The cruel treatment of Oliver Twist illustrates the relation of tension between a genuine underdog personality and social constraints (child labor, the use of children in criminal activities). For that matter, Dickens's work abounds with characters of this sort. In *Our Mutual Friend* (1865), Charley and Lizzie Hexam are underdogs characterized as strong personalities who put up a successful defense against a hostile society despite their lack of education and thereby symbolize the group's potential. In the same novel, however, Betty Higden falls victim to the social system. Through this contrast, Dickens adds luster to the underdog as a symbol of freedom.

When surrounding the underdog with minor characters who become the social system's victims and offering a precise description of their social environment, the writer never fights shy of a miserabilistic tone: "Nobody in an industrial novel laughs, makes jokes or dances, and nowhere is this negative characteristic more apparent than in Dickens," who often went all out in depicting pitiful surroundings.[3] In the tradition of William Hogarth, he frequently represents London as a dark wilderness where his marginal characters – scum of the earth – live in the midst of waste and rubbish. Thus, in *Oliver Twist* (1838), he exposes the ugliest and morally most offensive end of London. Dragged along by Dawkins, Oliver observes:

> The street was very narrow and muddy; and the air was impregnated with filthy odours. There were a good many small shops; but the only stock in trade appeared to be heaps of children, who, even at that time of night, were crawling in and out at the doors, or screaming from the inside. The sole places that seemed to prosper, amid the general blight of the place, were the public-houses; and in them, the lowest orders of Irish were wrangling with might and main.[4]

Other examples include the poor living conditions of Betty and the Hexams in *Our Mutual Friend* and life in Bleeding Heart Yard, and the fate of the Plornishes in *Little Dorrit* (1857). Miserabilism is even more evident in the urban landscape of Coketown, the "ugly citadel" of *Hard Times* (1854), "where Nature was as strongly bricked out as killing airs and gases were bricked in."[5] Such descriptions create a specific setting ideal for illustrating the underdog's exceptional nature: The more robust the urban wilderness, the more just the struggle; the more inhumane the urban environment, the more humane the characters who fight against it.

The Outsider as Moral Problem

An attempt to characterize the second, idealistically inspired discourse about the urban outsider might start from the contrast between Dickens and the other representatives of the social novel in England. The latter group was certainly also guided by a Romanticism-infused discourse of the underdog. Yet, there was an additional concern. Authors of industrial novels, a rising genre in the 1840s, engage with "the social question" by trying to determine the social place and function of outsider groups. Although Dickens or Hugo may discuss these questions, it is fair to say that their paramount concern is "elements of human nature – personal kindness, sympathy, and forbearance,"[6] rather than the unchecked capitalism that concerns Elizabeth Gaskell, Disraeli, and later authors who focus on workers in the industrial slums, as in the American naturalistic novel. Through such social movements as Chartism in England, and waves of migration to the United States, the outsider acquires a new and recognizable face: the face of the worker.

In a somewhat anachronistic move, we will name the discourse emerging from these texts *communitarian*. The term is of twentieth-century origin and used by political philosophers (e.g., Alisdair McIntyre, Michael Sandel, Michael Walzer, and Charles Taylor), but it derives from the 1840s term *communitarian* coined by Goodwyn Barmby at the time of the Chartist uprisings. Both sets of writers criticize capitalist modernity and the latent anomie spreading in capitalist cities. Authors writing within this perspective consider the capitalist economy and its physical substratum – the metropolis – the primary subject of research. Stephen Morley, one of the characters in Disraeli's *Sybil* and an adherent of the Chartist movement, offers a fine summary of the nineteenth-century communitarians' image of the city:

> In great cities men are brought together by the desire of gain. They are not in a state of cooperation, but of isolation, as to the making of fortunes; and for all the rest they are careless of neighbours. Christianity teaches us to love our neighbour as ourself; modern society acknowledges no neighbour.[7]

Whether it concerns religious communal values (as in many industrial novels) or an equilibrium between ethnic traditions and urban existence (as in the American slum literature of the 1890s), at the heart lies the wish to cultivate a communal ethos. Both the working class and the middle class are presented with pedagogical ideals. The laborer should become the object of an educational project in which hygiene and schooling are of paramount importance, while the middle class, the dominant audience of readers, is instructed on the notions of generosity and tolerance and led to revise its all-too-stereotypical conception of the outsider group. Working-class heroes are portrayed in such a way that the middle-class audience understands that the seeds of moral regeneration are already present and their maturation lies soundly within the scope of possibility. As a result, these heroes emerge as individuals who are "basically no different from other people," but require care: "they need help, ... they shouldn't drink, ... more schools, hospitals or workhouses ... should be built for them."[8]

In order to stimulate such a change in mentality, fictions paint a vivid picture of the conditions of life for the working class. Gaskell's *Mary Barton* (1848) arguably offers "the most moving response in literature to the industrial suffering of the 1840s ... the effort to record, in its own terms, the feel of everyday life in the working-class homes," and Charles Kingsley's *Alton Locke, Tailor and Poet* (1850) deals with "sweated labour in the 'Cheap and Nasty' clothing trade" and the experience of "apprenticeship in the sweating-rooms."[9] Nevertheless, the ultimate goal of these novels is not to present knowledge about the other but to integrate the outsider group through the tale of moral progress. This dynamic holds for an entire series of Victorian texts in which "[t]he author's concern with social antidotes has weakened the power of his documentary realism[, which] ... leads to a manipulation of the characters' actions, motives and speech, in order that they may be used finally to justify a class theory held by the author."[10]

Such representations of the urban working class lack socio-philosophical depth. The working class is not looked upon as a collection of different social groups, but is reduced to a monolithic identity governed by the ideal of moral progress. This mentality, a clear product of the communitarian construction of a generic identity, is widespread in the second half of the nineteenth century. We encounter it with Henry Mayhew, a journalist who in the 1840s arguably enjoyed greater fame than many novelists from the same period, thanks to his series of reports published as *London Labour and the London Poor* (1851). Mayhew was deemed an impartial, neutral "social explorer" by almost everyone; yet he, too

> wished to impress upon his audience that the circumstances of slum life produced certain kinds of individuals and, by implication, to suggest that conditions would have to be transformed before individuals could be redeemed or "civilized." He had to convince his public that the people of whom he wrote were *of* English society though separate from it, *related* to the middle class but a "race" apart from it, fellow inhabitants of the same city but members of a different "tribe."[11]

The "uncivilized" nature of the urban working-class quarter is highlighted in an even stronger fashion by nonfiction literature of the 1880s and 1890s, when London's East End suffered the consequences of the European economic crisis: massive unemployment, workers' uprisings, and occasional outbursts of violence. The socioeconomic outsider is at this time portrayed in terms that describe his quarter of the city as an almost mythical "dark, labyrinthine, threatening and benighted" realm contrasted with the "other London" of clarity, openness, and enlightenment.[12]

A similar inconsistency – moral commitment toward the fate of the poor and distanced wonder before the strangeness of the workers' world – marks novel production. To be sure, sympathy for the underdog and fondness for staging blighted urban conditions persist. This time, however, characters' spiritual maturation becomes embedded in a discourse of moral education that "originate[s] in a popular religious tradition." Alton Locke, Kingsley's fictional tailor, joins the Chartist movement and thus experiences a conversion that runs deeper than a mere political U-turn. The working-class hero becomes the carrier of an idea of humanity that has its most concrete shape in the image of a society of morally mature individuals. This tendency becomes very strong in the Manchester novels of the second half of the nineteenth century, in which "[a] child, often an orphan, almost always without a conventional social or domestic background, moves from humble origins in the slums to a position of material and moral maturity."[13]

Communitarian writers thus mediate the opposition between individual and system, shifting focus from the lower classes' lack of freedom to the moral immaturity of the outsider, who has much to learn before he or she can be accepted into the community as a full member. Nineteenth-century melodramas tend to exploit this idea without moderation; the trademark of popular novels is cheap moral judgment. In more sophisticated novels, melodramatic staging of moral maturation lays the foundation for reconciliation between the classes and pleads for mutual understanding. In Walter Besant's *All Sorts and Conditions of Men* (1882) and *Children of Gideon* (1886), the individual's fight with his world is embedded in a plot that features a high-born person who lives in disguise among the slum populace, foreshadowing a new community in which rich and poor live harmoniously together. The same desire for reconciliation and tolerance lies at the heart of American immigrant novels around the turn of the century. The Irish, Italians, and Jews gradually made their way into the novel in the later nineteenth century. In immigrant ghettos, authors found material that they could also often use in their journalistic work (most, indeed, combined both writing activities). Irish longshoremen, Italian pushcart peddlers, and Russian-Jewish sweatshop workers are described within their environment; their heroic perseverance and courage is often highlighted. As in the Manchester novels, the protagonists are characterized by "the struggle toward the light of autonomous and educated consciousness."[14] Some of these works are melodramatic pleas for compassion and for reconciliation between the classes, in particular, for the melting-pot reconciliation of Old and New Worlds. They may also target the decline of moral values as both cause and effect of the ghetto's harsh economic situation. The work of social-work pioneer, social reformer, and America's first female public philosopher Jane Addams may have influenced some of these novels and certainly exemplified their ethos of respect for cultures and traditions. Influenced by Carlyle and Dickens, and by her visit to England (especially Reverend Samuel A. Barnett and Walter Besant's Toynbee Hall) she founded at Hull House in 1889 her own experimental settlement house. In *Twenty Years at Hull House* (1910), she articulates her communitarian ideals, offers insightful analyses of the mutual benefits of interaction between the ethnic poor and middle-class reformers, and observes the superiority of political machines and ward bosses to political reformers in their understanding of, and care for, vulnerable urban denizens.

The decline of moral values was played up in a second aspect of the communitarian discourse of the socioeconomic outsider's inherent "strangeness" that attributes his violence to deficiencies in his personality structure. In Eugène Sue's *The Mysteries of Paris* (1842–3), which popularized the plot of the aristocrat in disguise among the workers, Prince Rodolphe descends into the Parisian underworld and does battle with small- and big-time criminals. Fredric Jameson concludes that "[s]uch a gesture surely expresses the deepest middle-class anxieties about the 'mob' and the urban lumpenproletariat, at the same time that it functions as a grim warning of the lengths to which a terrorized propertied class was willing to go."[15] In *Mary Barton*, John Barton is not only a union man. He is also a killer. And in a famous scene from Gaskell's *North and South*, John Thornton is "baited by a mob of strikers possessed with 'the demoniac desire of some terrible wild beast.'"[16] In his *Monday Tales* (1873), Alphonse Daudet, a pioneer of French realism, depicts Arthur as a worker who has the habit of drinking his way through his wages on Saturdays and subsequently beating his wife; on Sundays, however, he "play[s] the agreeable, was the leading spirit" and seems to be "one of those model mechanics who are constant attendants at evening-school." His wife, "somewhat subdued by the effects of the beating the night before, regard[s] him admiringly." The middle-class audience would have been able to see the joke, yet at the same time, they would have been concerned about the fact that Arthur "declaim[s] fragments of ideas ... concerning the rights of the working man, the tyranny of capital," and that he chants seditious songs "full of artificial tears and the working-man's inane sentimentality" (rather than refined middle-class sentimentality).[17] This fear was very real as the middle classes were faced with workers' uprisings at the time of the Paris Commune (1871), the strikes and Chartist revolts in Manchester in the 1830s and 1840s, and the later rebellions in London's East End during the 1890s. It should therefore be no surprise that fictions in which heroes grow into morally mature individuals were the order of the day. Not infrequently, ladies of position, moved by reading this sort of literature, suited actions to words and ventured into neglected neighborhoods to hand out flowers. Much to their astonishment, they were not received with open arms, which, in turn, called up those eternally latent reactions of fear.

The Sociology of the Outsider

In the final decades of the nineteenth century and in the first decade of the twentieth, the growth of urban economic outsiders was of such magnitude that, coupled with a series of economic depressions and ensuing poverty, the optimistic tone of the Romantic-individualistic and communitarian discourses no longer seemed justified. Meanwhile, social scientists proposed that individuals were subject to merciless social and psychological forces. The upshot was that a new discourse was added to those that already existed: a positivistic discourse that analyzes individual fate in terms of social and psychological determinants. This discourse lends a different meaning to the generic identity of the outsider, who is an epistemic object, a member of a group whose values can be objectively studied and contrasted with those of other groups. No longer one of "the people" or an individualist underdog, the outsider represents the working class.

In his Rougon-Macquart novels, Émile Zola shows that the outward lifestyle, the language, customs, and cultural habits of the working class deviate from those of the petty bourgeois, the aristocracy, and the nouveau riche. Likewise, George Gissing, a middle-class author who sought residence in London's East End because of marriage troubles, can be considered a fine sociologist. It is far from a coincidence that both men worked as journalists. Just as in older journalistic interventions (e.g., Mayhew's), these novels offer thickly described, semi-anthropological depictions of the outsider, a trend helped along by a cadre of writer-journalists. In *Tales of Mean Streets* (1894), Arthur Morrison, from a working-class family in London's East End, writes candidly and with nuance about the mores he observed. With *Miss Grace of All Souls* (1895), W. E. Tirebuck, another child of workers who became a reporter, furnishes evidence of changes in urban literature forty years after *Hard Times*. Describing a small industrial city in the north of England, Tirebuck attends to the sociological and economic laws that govern characters' actions. In doing so, he reacted "against the attempts by earlier novelists to play down the existence of the workers as a separate power group" because he had "no interest in uniting the two nations."[18]

The novelty adduced by the new positivistic discourse can be illustrated by comparing Zola's naturalistic program with Hugo's Romantic underdog discourse. Of *Les Misérables*, Mario Vargas Llosa writes, "in its analysis of social problems, this subversive, horrifying book does not go any further than recognizing that society is imperfect because '[t]he saintly law of Jesus Christ governs our civilization but has not yet permeated this civilization.'"[19] In *L'Assommoir* (1877), Zola reveals the lives of Parisian workers through descriptions that purport to be, in his own words, at once "frightening" and "very precise." In his notebooks, Zola writes that he wants to describe the outsider as he truly is – "with his garbage, his hasty little life, his rude language."[20] But, he continues, he does not merely want to show; he also wants to explain the outsider's mores through an anthropological portrayal of life and customs that pays attention to typical and representative customs. In the fictional Montsou of *Germinal* (1885), the working class may very well rise in revolt as a natural force, and the violence is as monstrous as the industrial machinery that exploits the workers, yet it is impossible to hold that Zola is marked by the middle-class anxiety that set the tone of the Manchester novels. Zola offers a precise account of the economic factors that determine the behavior of industrialists and workers. He conducts a detailed investigation of the social consequences at all stages of development. In these novels, the reader gets a fairly accurate image of "the abstract forces of capitalism" and "the concrete experience of laboring under the Second Empire."[21] Zola shows the reader the sociological laws of the segregation and the transformation of the industrial city's landscape.

As the old definitions of outsider identity make room for sociological, social-psychological, and economic definitions, the outsiders themselves become a social factor, an active element in the play of social and economic forces that determines the history of society. In Margaret Harkness's novels, "the ordinary working man, not merely the exceptional artisan, fully understands what is at stake: he knows who his enemies are, and that time is on his side."[22] Her *In Darkest London* (1889) speaks slightingly of Besant's "pretty stories about the East End," and one of her characters explicitly formulates this self-confident view about the social and historical function of the outsider: "The West End is bad, or mad, not to see that if things go on like this we must have a revolution. One fine day the people about here will grow desperate; and they will walk westwards cutting throats and hurling brickbats, until they are shot down by the military."[23] The work of engaged intellectuals such as Jane Addams and a number of innovating works in American immigrant literature likewise put worker characters within a broader framework of social forces. When Isaac Kahn Friedman describes the Homestead Strike of 1892 in *By Bread Alone* (1901), the working class acquires an identity through its position in the socioeconomic network of factors and determinants. Strikes are a factor in the real balance of power, not an opportunity to draw attention to a moral problem, as in the industrial novel. When Upton Sinclair stages the exploitation of workers in the meat factories of Chicago in *The Jungle* (1906), he works from a broader view that posits the contrast between the rural traditions of the Lithuanian immigrants and the conditions of the industrial city. Like the representatives of communitarian discourse, Sinclair levels his criticism against modernity gone astray and the inherent injustice of industrial capitalism. Yet his novel wants to make its diagnosis by pursuing the causes and effects of the wage slavery that victimizes these immigrants. Moreover, he uncovers the role played by class solidarity in social history when, at the novel's end, he allows Jurgis Rudkus to join the socialist family. Jewish immigrant literature also contains traces of a positivistic discourse of the outsider. In Abraham Cahan's *The Rise of David Levinsky* (1917), for example, the economically successful main character is portrayed as an uprooted, lonely soul, who cannot thrive in a world governed by competition for profit.

Structural analysis of social problems is typical of this positivistic discourse. Early in his career, Gissing spoke positively about the Marxist project, but a reformist political disposition was never a necessity. Many authors link their positivistic approach to Social Darwinism; Gissing's later work can be read from this perspective, as can Theodore Dreiser's urban novels, set in a world where survival of the fittest is the only moral law left for mankind. Dreiser, an admirer of Herbert Spencer, uses his journalistic experience to illustrate the socioeconomic pressure on characters, but he also uses it to express his belief in evolutionary, materialistic determinism.

The Tragic Outsider in the Modernist Discourse of Alienation

In twentieth-century literature, the generic identity of the outsider becomes problematic, as do the historical implications that go with it. In a sense, they anticipate Badiou's observation that the concept of the proletariat is saturated. If the proletarian novel continued the discourse of reform or revolution, with the advent of modernism, authors shifted toward phenomenological description of the human condition. Addressing the issue of the outsider, they cultivated a discourse about individualized personalities divergent from the individualism of Romantics such as Hugo. They offered a meticulous study of the concept of individuality vilified by communitarians: the atomized, alienated individual barely able to enter into intersubjective relations or to govern his behavior, who takes social values as his cue. In this way, the working class ceases to play its role as trailblazer or explosive *force*.

High modernism offers relatively few representations of the urban working class or other socioeconomic outsiders. On these occasions, they appear as existentially suffering individuals – outsiders who meet a tragic downfall after succumbing to the temptations of the capitalist city and the anomic forces of modernity. On its face, this relative absence is surprising because only from the 1960s onward does a service economy gradually outstrip industrial production. Preoccupation with stylistic innovation alone cannot sufficiently explain this absence. Indeed, it is not because of their poetics that the modernists do not expect much good to come from revolutionary pathos, moralism, or the positivism previously discussed. It is rather a generally implicit, but sometimes articulated, awareness that the generic identity of the working class can easily evaporate. Equally important in this respect seems to be the rise of social democracy, and – as Richard Hoggart's *The Uses of Literacy* (1957) illustrates – the apparent sweeping domestication of the urban workers that goes with it. The advent of social programs coupled with postwar economic growth meant that poverty and misery stopped seeming sufficiently harrowing. Some novels feature individuals who seem to struggle with existential questions that are explicitly related to the viability of socialism. In others, the process of alienation that unfolds is more latent; they merely illustrate how the mechanisms of solidarity fundamental to the older workers' culture are slowly breaking down. Indeed, throughout the twentieth century, the saturation of the generic possibilities of the working class became the main issue. For the modernists, in a manner of speaking, Victor Hugo's *gamin* has grown up – unfortunately, not as Hugo predicted he would. Along the way, he seems to have lost many of his tricks.

The decline of socialism and workers' culture form the key issue in Karl Bednarik's utopian novel about postwar Vienna, *Omega Fleischwolf* (1954) and in the double novel *Chapel Road/Summer in Termuren* (1953/1956) by Flemish modernist Louis-Paul Boon. The son of industrial workers from Alost, Boon took stock of 150 years of workers' struggle in Flanders' textile industry and the generalized condition of alienation. Ondine, the protagonist, is a nineteenth-century working-class girl incapable of joining its grand social project. She stands aside, dreaming of marriage to the factory owner's son. She grows embittered and craves bourgeois success. In the novel's semi-autobiographical frame tale, the author stages himself as a writer and journalist in the first years after World War II and addresses the decline of the generic identity of the working class, alerting us to the risk of its vanishing and blaming its disappearance on increased social complexity and the gentrification of workers. Other authors who address the economic outsider also emphasize their protagonists' existential isolation. John Dos Passos's Jimmy Herf in *Manhattan Transfer* (1925), Alfred Döblin's Franz Bieberkopf in *Berlin Alexanderplatz* (1929), and John Fante's Arturo Bandini (in a cycle of novels), emerge as icons of the outsider's alienated existence. More recent examples include the 1960s novels of Gruppe 61 authors Max von der Grün, Bruno Gluchowski, Christian Geissler, and Günter Wallraff, and the 1950s novels of Britain's "Angry Young Men," such as Alan Sillitoe's *Saturday Night and Sunday Morning* (1958). Even more recent examples include novelist Pat Barker, whose work offers a strongly feminist description of urban workers' lives in *Union Street* (1982), *Blow Your House Down* (1984), and *The Century's Daughter* (1986), Parisian François Bon's *Factory Exit* (1982), Irishman Roddy Doyle's *The Snapper* (1990), and the recent story collection *Growing Up Poor* (2002).

The disconnection of the concepts of outsider and worker is also apparent in the single most important current in contemporary urban literature: ethnic minority literature. This time around, the subject is not reconciliation; rather, it engages such issues as increased social complexity, political powerlessness, and the "underclass" that rightist social scientists claim exists within "a culture of poverty" – which is itself a pseudo-concept that Liam Kennedy describes as a "myth of behavioral deficiencies and combined common assumptions about poverty and race" that "generates images of criminals, delinquents, crack addicts, and unwed mothers, and ... an urban scene in which crime, drugs, unemployment, welfare dependency, indiscriminate violence, and educational failure are norms of existence."[24] Novels broaching this subject submit the perverse representation of the racial outsider to a critical examination. Communitarian lines of reasoning hold a prominent place, yet there are also connections with the problem of individual alienation and positivistic discourse. Claude Brown's *Manchild in the Promised Land* (1965) and the novels of Hanif Kureishi exhibit an "existential" interpretation of outsider identity. Non-fiction such as Alex Kotlowitz's *There Are No Children Here: The Story of Two Boys Growing Up in the Other America* (1991) exhibits an anthropological line of approach that turns the underclass into an epistemic object.

While the four formations outlined in this chapter have been presented historically, it would be a mistake to imagine that we are no longer inclined to feel a romantic indignation à la Hugo or Dickens, foster communitarian longings for greater solidarity and social peace, have stopped wanting to understand the social determinants of marginalization, or ceased to project the tragic fate of the outsider onto our own alienated existences. This, of course, results in a split attitude toward the generic identity of late modern outsiders, a desire to view them as participating in a historical project that points toward a better world balanced by skepticism about every line of thinking or acting that would deliver us. The ultimate but open question is: How will outsiders be represented in a globalized and urbanized world that, in the title of his 2006 book, Mike Davis has called a *Planet of Slums*?

NOTES

1 Alain Badiou, "The Saturated Generic Identity of the Working Class" (2006), InterActivist Info Exchange, http://interactivist.autonomedia.org/node/5400.

2 Victor Hugo, *Les Misérables*, 5 vols., trans. Isabel F. Hapgood (New York: Thomas Y. Cowell, 1915), vol. 3, p. 4.

3 P. J. Keating, *The Working Classes in Victorian Fiction* (London: Routledge, 1971), p. 8.

4 Charles Dickens, *Oliver Twist* (Oxford: Oxford University Press, 1999), p. 60.

5 Charles Dickens, *Hard Times*, ed. Paul Schlicke (Oxford: Oxford University Press, 1998), p. 82.

6 Raymond Williams, *Culture and Society, 1780–1950* (Harmondsworth, UK: Penguin, 1961), p. 106.

7 Benjamin Disraeli, *Sybil, or the Two Nations* (New York: Oxford University Press, 2008), p. 65.

8 Keating, *The Working Classes*, p. 2.

9 Williams, *Culture and Society*, pp. 99, 111.

10 Keating, *The Working Classes*, p. 4.

11 Deborah Epstein Nord, "The Social Explorer as Anthropologist: Victorian Travellers among the Urban Poor," in William Sharpe and Leonard Wallock, eds., *Visions of the Modern City* (Baltimore, MD: John Hopkins University Press, 1989), pp. 132–3.

12 Epstein Nord, "The Social Explorer," p. 123.

13 Trefor Thomas, "Representations of the Manchester Working Class in Fiction 1850–1900," in Alan J. Kidd and K. W. Roberts, eds., *City, Class and Culture: Studies of Social Policy and Cultural Production in Victorian Manchester* (Manchester, UK: Manchester University Press, 1985), p. 194.

14 Ibid., p. 194.

15 Fredric Jameson, "Authentic *Ressentiment*: The 'Experimental' Novels of Gissing." *Nineteenth-Century Fiction* 31 (1976), 131.

16 Keating, *The Working Classes*, p. 227.

17 Alphonse Daudet, "Arthur," *Monday Tales*, trans. Marian McIntyre (Boston: Little, Brown, 1901), p.218.

18 Keating, *The Working Classes*, p. 238.

19 Mario Vargas Llosa, *The Temptation of the Impossible: Victor Hugo and Les Miserables* (Princeton, NJ: Princeton University Press, 2007), p. 109, quoting Hugo, *Les Misérables*.

20 Emile Zola, "L'ébauche de *L'Assommoir*," in H. Massis, *Comment Emile Zola composait ses romans* (Paris: Fasquelle, 1906), p. 100; translation by the authors.

21 David Harvey, *Paris, Capital of Modernity* (London: Routledge, 2006), p. 171.

22 Keating, *The Working Classes*, p. 243.

23 John Law [Margaret Harkness], *In Darkest London* (London: W. Reeves, 1890), pp. 189–90.

24 Liam Kennedy, "Representations of the Underclass: Race, Poverty, and the Postindustrial Ghetto," in Ghent Urban Studies Team, eds., *The Urban Condition: Space, Community and Self in the Contemporary Metropolis* (Rotterdam: 010 Publishers, 1999), p. 266.

8

JAMES R. GILES

The Urban Nightspace

Modern western cities evolved in a variety of ways. Richard Lehan points out that "medieval Paris lasted well into the nineteenth century."[1] But several interrelated factors produced the western city as we now envision it. Chief among them, the eighteenth-century Industrial Revolution in Europe shifted national economies from agrarian to industrial models as manufacturing surpassed farming in Great Britain and on the continent. In Britain especially, this economic shift devastated the countryside with a resulting exodus from rural areas into London, Birmingham, Manchester, Edinburgh (then "auld reekie"), and other manufacturing centers. Throughout Europe, cities expanded rapidly in an unplanned manner as impoverished individuals migrated to them seeking economic survival, with the result that an extreme contrast between urban wealth and dire poverty became apparent. Urban growth followed a similar pattern in the United States and, later, in other parts of the globe.

London's East End and New York City's Five Points neighborhood rapidly became centers of extreme poverty and criminality. Discussing Robert Louis Stevenson's sensational 1886 novella *The Strange Case of Dr. Jekyll and Mr. Hyde*, Irving S. Saposnik describes late Victorian London as the perfect setting for Stevenson's exploration of mystery and violence: "in the 1880's, London society could not have been much different from Michael Sadleir's description of it some twenty years before …: 'London in the early 'sixties was still three parts jungle… There was no knowing what kind of a queer patch you might strike, in what blind alley you might find yourself, to what embarrassment, insult, or even molestation you might be exposed.'"[2] Of course, the urban jungle was the most dangerous at night; Oliver Twist is only one character who discovers how easy it is to become lost and disappear as night falls in the city.

Despite the extremes of wealth and poverty associated with it, the Industrial Revolution also produced a large urban middle class possessing sufficient time and money to seek entertainment, both legitimate and illegitimate. At night, the middle class sought relief from the daytime pressures of earning a living. Thus, the urban nightscape emerged as a space to seek widely diverse forms of pleasure, ranging from elite horseback dining to the legitimate theater to assignations with prostitutes, many of whom were newly arrived refugees from impoverished rural areas.

In the literature of France, England, and the United States, urban nightspace has often been depicted as simultaneously tempting and frightening, intriguing and dangerous. It is where vice unapologetically emerges often accompanied by criminality. In *City of Dreadful Delight,* Judith R. Walkowitz discusses Victorian London as a city where social, geographical, and psychological boundaries were being challenged and even overturned, resulting in an increasingly insecure society. She sees the Jack the Ripper murders, all of which occurred at night in the lower-class areas of London, as encapsulating the perverted sexuality and frightening criminality that resulted from the dissolving of traditional Victorian values and mores.[3]

In *The City in Literature,* Lehan backgrounds his study of the modern city with a discussion of the rise of Athens and an accompanying retreat from nature that produced a reaction against Dionysus: "The worship of Dionysus was eventually taken over by those on the margins of the city... The god is driven underground, repressed by the forces of institutional authority, to console the marginalized and foreshadow urban revolt." Lehan argues that in literature the repressed Dionysus subsequently appears in the urban landscape in a variety of guises ranging from "the masked participant at the carnival" to Dracula.[4] Certainly, the repressed and often perverted Dionysus is never more at home than in the urban nightspace. As first realism and then naturalism assumed dominance over Romanticism, the literary depiction of urban nightspace increasingly emphasized the violent, the sordid, and the grotesque.

In poetry and fiction, the suppression and perversion of Dionysus is often associated with either literal or metaphoric death, and frequently death is linked to the night. In addition, the night often functions as a metonym for desire and the unconscious. Thus, the internal repressed nightspace is often the source and sometimes the site of Dionysian energy. Few passages in literature convey the deadly effects of the urban perversion of Dionysus more powerfully than the first and final scenes of Émile Zola's naturalist masterpiece, *Nana* (1880). The first chapter is an account of the initial theatrical triumph of Nana, Zola's personification of female sexuality. That the scene takes place in a theater is appropriate since the literary treatment of urban nightspace often has a theatrical aspect, not uncommonly containing elements of the grotesque.

In this opening chapter, the largely unknown Nana plays in *The Blonde Venus,* an absurd farce depicting ridiculous interactions among the classical gods. Zola overtly makes the audience representative of Paris:

> All Paris was there, the Paris of literature, of finance, and of pleasure. There were many journalists, several authors, a number of stock exchange people, and more courtesans than honest women. It was a singularly mixed world, composed, as it was, of all the talents, and tarnished by all the vices, a world where the same fatigue and the same fever played over every face.[5]

Here a feverish and wearied Dionysus is indeed perverted. In fact, the symbolic associations of the audience transcend Paris to include all of Second Empire France, a society that is fatally corrupted by selfish excess in the twenty volumes of the Rougon-Macquart series.

No one, including the theater manager, pretends that Nana has any talent, but, as she reappears in varying stages of undress, her control over the audience, especially its male members, increases, until she takes the stage nude, covered only by a thin veil. In this climactic moment, "[s]uddenly in the bouncing child the woman stood discovered, a woman full of restless suggestion, who brought with her the delirium of sex, and opened the gates of the unknown world of desire. Nana was smiling still, but her smile was now bitter, as of a devourer of men."[6] This scene foreshadows much of the rest of the novel, since the rich and powerful men whom Nana will seduce and then discard are seated in the audience.

The mood of *Nana*'s final scene differs greatly. In it, Nana, disfigured by smallpox, lies dying at night in a bare hotel room, viewed by her former male victims and female rivals, as if at another theatrical performance. The crowds on the darkened streets outside are falling prey to another illness, the lust for war, and can be heard shouting, "To Ber-lin! To Ber-lin! To Ber-lin!"[7] Nana's death foreshadows that of the Second Empire in the Franco-Prussian War. Zola envisions a repressed and perverted Dionysus taking control of the night, infecting an entire nation.

In *Maggie: A Girl of the Streets* (1893; 1896), the American naturalist Stephen Crane created another prostitute who encounters death in the urban nightspace. Until her early death, Maggie's life differs significantly from Nana's. Maggie is a product of New York City's impoverished ghetto, her life determined not only by her environment but also by abusive parents and an exploitive brother. We see Maggie plying her trade as a prostitute in only one brilliantly condensed chapter: An out-of-fashion Maggie, now Mary, unsuccessfully attempts to attract a client as richly dressed crowds leave the theaters. Crane succinctly contrasts the appearance and mood of the theatergoers with Maggie's barely contained desperation: "an atmosphere of pleasure and prosperity seemed to hang over the throng, born, perhaps, of good clothes and of two hours in a place of forgetfulness." Maggie, "neither new, Parisian, nor theatrical," fails to attract any of the men crowding the streets. She leaves the theater district for the increasingly dark and ominous streets near the East River. In Crane's original, privately printed 1893 version of the novel, she meets at the edge of the river a grotesque "fat man"; he perhaps murders her. In the 1896, commercially published edition, the fat man disappears. Here Maggie is described as entering "into the blackness of the final block" and approaching "the deathly black hue of the river"; she seems most likely a suicide. Whether murder or suicide, she dies in a darkened area pervaded by actual or latent violence.[8]

While the naturalism of Zola and Crane made them especially qualified to write such grotesque scenes, the essentially Romantic English novelist Charles Dickens often envisioned his own kind of perverted, even criminal, urban nightspace. An implied theatricality is inherent in some of his most memorable depictions of the London night. In Dickens, the night is often the province of the city's marginalized victims. "The Streets-Night," in *Sketches by Boz* (1836), although primarily focused on the behavior of the common, ordinary denizens of a London night, offers a glimpse of this urban Dionysus as a "wretched woman," infant in her arms, attempts to sing "some popular ballad, in the hope of wringing a few pence" from passersby; "[a] brutal laugh at her weak voice is all she has gained." The unfeeling response overwhelms her: "the tears fall thick and fast down her worn pale face; the child is cold and hungry, and its low half-stifled wailing adds to the misery of its wretched mother, as she moans aloud, and sinks despairingly down, on a cold damp door-step."[9] The victim of this drunken, mocking laughter, the desperate, probably starving mother is even more ignored by those few who pass her by than is Crane's Maggie. She is truly one of the urban marginalized, and her desperate attempt to arouse generosity gives the brief scene an aspect of the theatrical grotesque. The contemptuous attitude may well indicate that she is a prostitute whose illicit sexuality is made manifest by the baby she carries.

Despite its sentimental plot, criminality is central to Dickens's *Oliver Twist* (1838) with its gang of boys recruited as pickpockets by the villainous Fagin. For while Dickens was a Romantic, he was also devoted to protesting social injustice, largely because of his childhood. Although the boys necessarily work primarily in daylight, they report to Fagin's sordid dwelling at night. Fagin, himself, possesses the power to darken any scene. Fittingly, Oliver's meeting with an imprisoned Fagin awaiting execution occurs at night. The most memorable night scene in the novel, however – the murder of Nancy by Bill Sikes – does not directly involve Fagin. But, in one graphic and grotesque night scene, he is shown brooding over his betrayal by Nancy: "he looked less like a man, than like some hideous phantom, moist from the grave and worried by an evil spirit." The description of Nancy's murder is equally graphic: "[Sikes] beat [his pistol] twice with all the force he could summon, upon the upturned face that almost touched his own... [Nancy] was a ghastly figure to look upon. The murderer staggering backward to the wall, and shutting out the light with his hand, seized a heavy club and struck her down."[10] Much as Crane does with Maggie's death, Dickens makes the reader something of a privileged spectator of Nancy's murder. In Victorian times, his freedom to make overt a sexual relationship between Sikes and Nancy was limited, but it seems at least implicit. The murder, then, is a perverted Dionysian act.

Urban nightspace and its mythic associations are also central to the modernist imagination. In *Death in Venice* (1912), German novelist Thomas Mann sets his account of the disintegration and eventual death of a distinguished writer in a city long associated with romance. Mann's protagonist, Gustave Aschenbach, has lived a life devoted to an Apollonian creed of rationalist restraint. He has instinctively fled from pleasure, fearing a surrender of control. But as the novel opens, Aschenbach is beset by "a longing to travel" that is associated with "desire" mixed with "the marvels and terrors of the manifold earth": "he beheld a landscape, a tropical marshland, beneath a reeking sky, steaming, monstrous, rank."[11] He journeys to Venice, where he is obsessed with a fourteen-year-old Polish boy, Tadzio, whom he associates with Apollonian perfection in life and art. Yet he is pleased to note the boy's imperfect teeth, a sign of mortality. Ironically, it will be Tadzio who summons Aschenbach to death.

Tadzio's teeth are a key element in the novel's complex pattern of symbolism. Their link to mortality is associated with both a plague of cholera that city officials try to hide and Aschenbach's urge to surrender to the intensifying pull of Eros. The scent of the pestilence is part of Venice's frightening nightspace:

> Evenings one saw many drunken people, which was unusual. Gangs of men in surly mood made the streets unsafe, theft and assault were said to be frequent, even murder; for in two cases persons supposedly victims of the plague were proved to have been poisoned by their own families. And professional vice was rampant, displaying excesses heretofore unknown and only at home much farther south and in the east.

Deeply unsettled by the bizarre performance – sometimes lascivious and sometimes mocking – of some street musicians one evening, Aschenbach dreams of an orgiastic ceremony that echoes Dionysus' revenge on Pentheus in *The Bacchae*, in which "a whirling rout of men and animals" forms a ring "about the obscene symbol of the godhead" and they begin to devour each other. It concludes in particular horror:

> Yes, it was he who was flinging himself upon the animals, who bit and tore and swallowed smoking gobbets of flesh – while on the trampled moss there now began the rites in honour of the god, an orgy of promiscuous embraces – and in his very soul he tasted the bestial degradation of his fall.[12]

Aschenbach's degradation is completed when, one afternoon after a cosmetic attempt to remake himself as a young man succeeds only in making him look grotesque like the fop he found revolting on the boat ride to Venice, he follows Tadzio and his family through the streets of Venice, trying to be invisible, hiding in doorways and behind buildings and people's backs.

Rooted in classical mythology, *Death in Venice* recounts the destruction of an artist who has attempted, in his writing and in his life, to live on a strictly Apollonian plane. Mann's theme is that a merger of the Apollonian and the Dionysian is essential to art and life; but, when confronted with a contaminated vision of the Apollonian in Tadzio and the diseased nightspace of Venice's cholera-plagued streets, Aschenbach, as shown in his Dionysian nightmare, is unable to effect such a merger. He succumbs to the "disease" that has infected him and the city. Rather than romantic, Venice's nightspace is deadly in Mann's novel.

In T. S. Eliot's London, the alienated citizens search unsuccessfully in the night for meaning or mere human contact where the Dionysian has become enervated and sterile. J. Alfred Prufrock walks through "certain half-deserted streets"

> When the evening is spread out against the sky
> Like a patient etherized upon a table.[13]

In *The Waste Land* (1922), the woman in the pub is forced to abandon her harangue about Lil and her "demobbed" husband by the call of "HURRY UP PLEASE ITS TIME." In fact, it's time for the woman to retreat to the isolated streets of the "Unreal City." The typist and the "carbuncular" clerk have meaningless sex after which the woman thinks, "Well now that's done: and I'm glad it's over."[14] In *Dickens and the Unreal City*, Karl Ashley Smith links the Romantic novelist with Eliot. Dickens, he writes, "was acutely aware of the disjunction between the renewing power of Christianity as described in the New Testament and the sterility of its modern manifestations." Like Eliot, he argues, Dickens was concerned with discovering whether New Testament "discourse, including its language and symbols," had relevance in a secular world.[15] Unlike Dickens, however, Eliot approached this question from a perspective of ironic detachment and borrowings from classical mythology that he shared with Mann and other modernists.

In sharp contrast, an exuberant prose celebration of raw sensuality appears in the opening pages of Claude McKay's *Home to Harlem* (1928), an African-American novel published six years after *The Waste Land*. Jake, one of McKay's two central protagonists, has just returned to Harlem after serving in the US Army in France for two years. On his first night back, he luxuriates in a rediscovered Harlem nightspace:

> The deep-dyed color, the thickness, the closeness of it. The noises of Harlem. The sugared laughter. The honey-talk on its streets. And all night long, ragtime and "blues" playing somewhere, … singing somewhere, dancing somewhere! Oh, the contagious fever of Harlem. Burning everywhere in dark-eyed Harlem…[16]

During this night of celebration, Jake has sex with a prostitute and discovers the next morning that she has returned his money. A benevolent Dionysus is indeed above ground in nighttime Harlem. The novel's other central protagonist – Ray, an immigrant from Haiti – is the character closest to McKay, himself a Jamaican. Although Ray tries to resist Harlem's sensual pull, McKay describes him as "a reservoir of that intense emotional energy so peculiar to his race" and has him remember "the melancholy-comic notes of a 'Blues' rising out of a Harlem basement before dawn … he was sweetly, deliciously happy humming the refrain and imagining what the interior of the little dark den he heard it in was like."[17]

In his poem "Harlem Shadows" (1922), McKay again treats the subject of prostitution in Harlem, but quite differently than in *Home to Harlem*'s opening scene:

> I hear the halting footsteps of a lass
>> In Negro Harlem when the night lets fall
> Its veil…
>
> …
>
> The dusky, half-clad girls of tired feet
> Are trudging, thinly shod, from street to street.
>
> Ah, stern harsh world, that in the wretched way
>> Of poverty, dishonor and disgrace,
> Has pushed the timid little feet of clay,
>> The sacred brown feet of my fallen race![18]

McKay expresses compassion for the prostitute's suffering and exploitation, envisioning the Dionysian as being not so much repressed as perverted by a racist, capitalist system. One remembers Malcolm X, describing in his *Autobiography* the large numbers of white males who came to Harlem in search of nighttime vice.

Male prostitution is the focus of John Rechy's 1963 novel, *City of Night*, a path-breaking work of gay American literature. Admittedly autobiographical, *City of Night* depicts the experiences of an unnamed "youngman" who leaves his El Paso, Texas, birthplace to become a gay hustler in New York City, Chicago, Los Angeles, San Francisco, and New Orleans. In these cities, he becomes involved with desperately lonely clients and experiences the subculture they inhabit. The novel opens with a retrospective summary of the world he has explored:

> Later I would think of America as one vast City of Night stretching gaudily from Times Square to Hollywood Boulevard – jukebox-winking, rock-n-roll-moaning: America at night fusing its darkcities into the unmistakable shade of loneliness...
>
> One-night sex and cigarette smoke and rooms squashed in by loneliness...
> And I would remember lives lived out darkly in that vast City of Night, from all-night movies to Beverly Hills mansions.[19]

James Thomson's 1874 poem *The City of Dreadful Night* provides Rechy with the epigraph to his novel, "The City is of Night; perchance of Death, / But certainly of Night..." For both Thomson and Rechy, death constitutes an ever-present concern. Rechy's unnamed "youngman" has been haunted by death since he witnessed the body of a beloved pet dog that was buried but subsequently uncovered by the relentless West Texas wind. Rechy depicts gay urban American life as a night-shrouded landscape haunted by desperation, loneliness, and guilt. Especially in the descriptions of Mardi Gras and the "youngman's" encounter with the sadist Neil, the Dionysian is distorted into the grotesque and frightening. Finally, however, Rechy refuses to condemn the City of Night, or the world itself for that matter. He understands that Neil's self-hate is forced on him by the dominant heterosexual society. The destructive guilt and loneliness experienced by the inhabitants of Rechy's gay urban nightspace come from outside. While determined not to become emotionally involved with them, the "youngman" is never remotely as contemptuous of the men with whom he has sex as Zola's Nana is with the men whom she seduces and destroys.

In "The White Negro" (1957), Norman Mailer celebrates the "hipster" as, among other things, "a frontiersman in the Wild West of American night life," and Mailer's phrase serves as an apt description of the protagonists of *City of Night* and many of Rechy's subsequent novels.[20] They are all committed to an existentialist vision that refuses to deny death or to accept any promise of an afterlife but, rather, seeks to find in anonymous sexuality a "substitute for salvation." Mailer's prophecy was perceptive. The 1960s saw the emergence of a group of American writers devoted to a frank exploration of aspects of American experience that had previously been repressed in American literature and largely denied in mainstream American culture. Hubert Selby's savagely naturalistic description of life in Brooklyn's Red Hook ghetto, *Last Exit to Brooklyn,* was published the year after *City of Night.* Selby's novel, like Rechy's, is an exploration of the suppressed frontiers of American life, and it, too, is a distinctly nighttime text.

Exploration of the city at night continues in postmodernist fiction. In fact, perhaps the most memorable night scene in American literature is Oedipa Maas's journey through the streets of San Francisco pursuing the muted post-horn sign of a medieval postal system called Tristero used by the disinherited Americans of Thomas Pynchon's *The Crying of Lot 49* (1965). Conspiracies are best unraveled at night, so Oedipa wanders the streets watching for the post horn, soon believing that she sees it, although never quite certain: "in Chinatown, in the dark window of a herbalist she thought she saw it on a sign among ideographs. But the streetlight was dim."[21] Throughout this scene, Pynchon makes use of the exoticism of nighttime San Francisco for his suburban protagonist as Oedipa's sightings become increasingly disturbing and uncertain: "Riding among an exhausted busful of Negroes going on to graveyard shifts all over the city, she saw scratched on the back of a seat ... the post horn with the legend DEATH ... somebody had troubled to write in, in pencil: DON'T EVER ANTAGONIZE THE HORN." She discovers other frightening signs perhaps related to Tristero: "In one of the latrines was an advertisement by ACDC, standing for Alameda County Death Cult, along with a box number and post horn. Once a month they were to choose some victim from among the innocent, the virtuous, the socially integrated and well-adjusted, using him sexually, then sacrificing him." Oedipa's encounters become progressively more grotesque and alienated, and "[d]ecorating each alienation, each species of withdrawal, as cufflink, decal, aimless doodling, there was somehow always the post horn."[22] Maybe. Or perhaps Oedipa projects a world that does not exist outside her imagination. An additional possibility is that a former lover manipulates her in an elaborate game. No more than she herself, the reader can never be certain of the existence of Tristero signs, much less Tristero itself. In Pynchon's nightscape, the Dionysian, along with much else, remains shadowy.

The margins of the night are central to another postmodern novel, Roberto Bolaño's *Amulet* (1999), whose narrator begins with an ominous warning: "This is going to be a horror story. A story of murder, detection, and horror... Told by me, it won't seem like that. Although, in fact, it's the story of a terrible crime." Bolaño's protagonist is Auxilio Lacouture, an Uruguayan émigré to Mexico City and survivor of the 1968 student massacre and the government occupation of the National Autonomous University of Mexico, which furnish the backdrop of *Amulet*. The government-ordered massacre and the occupation, in fact, constitute interrelated crimes that haunt Auxilio throughout her narrative. It was the occupation of the university that most directly affected her: "I am the only one who held out in the university in 1968, when the riot police and the army came in. I stayed there on my own in the Faculty [building], shut up in a bathroom, with no food, from the eighteenth to the thirtieth of September, I think, I'm not sure any more."[23]

After her isolation, Auxilio joins the bohemian nightlife of Mexico City's young poets. She becomes a close associate of Arturito Belano, Roberto Bolaño's frequent fictional stand-in for himself. A close bond grows between the young Mexico City bohemians, although they all feel haunted by the events of September 1968. One especially memorable chapter captures the sense of vulnerability. She recounts nights of drinking with the young poets during which she envisions "the future from my obliterated cave in the fourth-floor women's bathroom" of the occupied Faculty. One night, having left the bar alone, she feels that someone "who desired my death" is following her. She tries desperately to attract help, but she is initially unable to do so and, now terrified, once again imagines herself back in the Faculty bathroom. Then, "other shadows appeared in that street, which could have become the epitome of all the terrifying streets I had ever walked down." When the "shadow" following her passes her, however, and looks back and walks on, he is "an ordinary-looking Mexican guy fresh out of the under-world and with him passed a breath of warm and slightly humid air that conjured up unstable geometries, solitudes, schizophrenia, and butchery." Soon Arturito Belano and another young poet appear, and she feels safe again. Later, Belano tells her that he had also seen "the shadow that was fol-lowing my shadow," but he laughs when Auxilio tells him that "it was the shadow of death."[24]

Especially in this scene, *Amulet* makes some of the most original use of urban nightspace in postmodern literature. Auxilio's slipping in and out of her memory of the Faculty bathroom, Arturito's laughter when she says that the figure following her represented "the shadow of death," and her description of the figure conjuring up schizophrenia make the whole scene highly subjective. Maybe no one has been following her or, if so, it truly was only an ordinary night-person. But Belano, who is, after all, the author's stand-in, *does* see the figure; and, in her closing vision of a multitude of sing-ing "ghost-children" marching together before falling into an abyss, Auxilio extends the theme of the novel to include not just the brutal 1968 Mexico City government repression but also the long history of Latin American repression and brutality. In both the earlier street scene and in the narrator's concluding vision, Bolaño elides the boundary between reality and fantasy, the actual and the imagined, just as Pynchon does in his account of Oedipa Maas's nighttime journey through the streets of San Francisco.

Of course, not all visions of urban nightscape in literature end ominously. The city of night has been depicted as a site of romance, adventure, and fascinating mystery. One example would be Frank O'Hara's 1964 poem "Present," which, in its first three stanzas, seems to promise a vision of a doomed Eros. The speaker sees "you" in New York's Union Square during a snow-filled night: "head bent to the wind / wet and frowning, melancholy" and knows "we'll meet in even greater darkness / later." But in a subsequent stanza, the speaker remembers "you" as he

> shake[s] the snows
> off onto my shoulder, light as a breath
> where the quarrels and vices of
> estranged companions weighed so bitterly
> and accidentally ...[25]

In the poem's concluding lines, the speaker feels that, along with "you," he will "explore some peculiar insight / of the heavens for its favorite bodies / in the mixed-up air" (353). After the poem's ominous beginning, Dionysus is not only affirmed but gives the city a magical redemptive power.

Except for McKay's *Home to Harlem,* such affirmation is absent in the other texts discussed in this chapter. In Zola, Crane, and Dickens, the figure of Dionysus – a force classically associated with unspoiled and uncomplicated sexuality – has been repressed in the city but struggles to reemerge at night. The Dionysian succeeds, however, only in perverse and distorted ways, if it succeeds at all. The naturalists Zola and Crane discovered a diseased and deadly sexuality in the urban nightspace. For Dickens, London at night was characterized by suffering and criminality. Eliot equates the urban night with sterility and life-in-death. Mann depicts it as contaminated by a perverse attempt to deny Eros. Rechy's "youngman" and Mailer's "frontiersman of the night" encounter a corrupted beauty while the postmodernists, Pynchon and Bolaño, merge reality and fantasy, leaving it impossible for their readers to be certain what, if anything, truly exists in the city at night.

NOTES

1 Richard Lehan, *The City in Literature: An Intellectual and Cultural History* (Berkeley: University of California Press, 1998), p. 53.

2 Irving S. Saposnik, *Robert Louis Stevenson* (New York: Twayne, 1975), p. 89.

3 Judith R. Walkowitz, *City of Dreadful Delight: Narratives of Sexual Danger in Late-Victorian London* (Chicago: University of Chicago Press, 1992), pp. 192–201.

4 Lehan, *The City in Literature*, pp. 19–20, 20.

5 Émile Zola, *Nana* (New York: Grosset & Dunlap, n. d.), p. 12.
6 Ibid., p. 31.
7 Ibid., p. 507.
8 Stephen Crane, *Maggie: A Girl of the Streets*, in *Maggie and Other Stories* (New York: Washington Square Press, 1960), pp. 57–8, 58, 59.
9 Charles Dickens, *Sketches by Boz* (London: Penguin, 1995), p. 77.
10 Dickens, *Oliver Twist* (Oxford: Oxford University Press, 1999), pp. 377, 383.
11 Thomas Mann, *Death in Venice*, in *Death in Venice and Seven Other Stories*, trans. H. T. Lowe-Porter (New York: Vintage, 1959), p. 5.
12 Ibid., pp, 65, 67, 68, 68.
13 T. S. Eliot, "The Love Song of J. Alfred Prufrock," *The Complete Poems and Plays, 1909–1950* (New York: Harcourt, 1952), p. 3.
14 Eliot, *The Waste Land*, in *Complete Poems and Plays*, p. 41, 39, 44.
15 Karl Ashley Smith, *Dickens and the Unreal City: Searching for Spiritual Significance in Nineteenth-Century London* (Houndmills, UK: Palgrave, 2008), p. 4.
16 Claude McKay, *Home to Harlem* (Boston: Northeastern University Press, 1987), p. 15.
17 Ibid., pp. 265, 266.
18 McKay, "Harlem Shadows," *Selected Poems of Claude McKay* (New York: Bookman, 1953), p. 60.
19 John Rechy, *City of Night* (New York: Grove Press, 1963), p. 11.
20 Norman Mailer, "The White Negro," *Advertisements for Myself* (New York: Putnam, 1959), p. 339.
21 Thomas Pynchon, *The Crying of Lot 49* (New York: Harper, 1986), p. 117.
22 Ibid., pp. 121, 122–3, 123.
23 Roberto Bolaño, *Amulet*, trans. Chris Andrews (New York: New Directions, 2006), pp. 1, 172.
24 Ibid., pp. 65, 66, 67, 67, 69.
25 Frank O'Hara, "Present," *The Collected Poems of Frank O'Hara*, ed. Donald Allen (Berkeley: University of California Press, 1995), p. 353.

9

CHRISTOPHE DEN TANDT

Masses, Forces, and the Urban Sublime

The Realization of Multitudinous Humanity

Observers of the urban scene in nineteenth- and early twentieth-century fiction are recurrently confronted with what the American novelist Robert Herrick called "the realization of multitudinous humanity": the city defeats their powers of perception.[1] In William Dean Howells's *A Hazard of New Fortunes* (1890), this experience is triggered by masses of immigrants. Gazing from an elevated train in Manhattan, upper-middle-class editorialist Basil March discovers slum dwellers with disquieting features – "small eyes, ... high cheeks, ... broad noses, ... cue-filleted skulls." As Basil's ethnic clichés cannot keep up with this diversity, he seeks comfort in Social Darwinist generalities; the streets, he ventures, are ruled by the "play of energies" in "the fierce struggle for survival."[2] If Howells's urban observer dared to immerse himself into the crowd, he would likely share the plight of Avis Everhard, the heroine of Jack London's dystopia *The Iron Heel* (1908), whose perceptual distress is compounded with disgust and terror. Trapped in a riot of the Chicago underclass, Avis must thread her way through the "awful river" of a subhuman mob made up of "carnivorous ... apes and tigers, anaemic consumptives and great hairy beasts of burden."[3] In other texts, the object of urban dread is industry. French science-fiction pioneer Jules Verne's *The Begum's Fortune* (1879) features gothic depictions of a city designed by German gun manufacturers: Stahlstadt is "a dark mass, huge and strange," whose "forest of cylindrical chimneys ... vomit forth clouds of dense smoke."[4] Likewise, north England towns in Benjamin Disraeli's *Sybil, Or the Two Nations* (1845) are "wilderness[es] of cottages ... interspersed with blazing furnaces."[5] For Émile Zola, steam engines in coal mines are "vile beast[s] ... gorged on human flesh."[6] American investigative journalist Rebecca Harding Davis called manufacturing towns the "Devil's place."[7] This nightmarish apparatus of production sustains economic processes beyond human measure. American novelist Frank Norris's

The Octopus (1901) and *The Pit* (1903) map the gigantic economic traffic whereby wheat is produced and exchanged. Harvested from the "Titan" earth, wheat unleashes speculation frenzies displaying the "appalling fury of the Maëlstrom."[8] At the far end of these economic chains, Zola's *The Ladies' Paradise* (1881) and Theodore Dreiser's *Sister Carrie* (1900) examine how customers fare in the urban market. In newly built department stores, Zola's and Dreiser's shoppers experience the "drag of desire" exerted by commodities with untraceable origins.[9]

These passages are instances of the urban sublime: they picture cities as objects of fascination and terror. The urban sublime, they suggest, interweaves two strands of discourse: oceanic metaphors that evoke magnitude and urban-industrial gothic that stirs accents of abject dehumanization. Edmund Burke and Immanuel Kant have provided the classic analyses of the psychological and philosophical stakes of the sublime. Burke's definition revolves around power and terror: we should regard as sublime "whatever is fitted in any sort to excite the ideas of pain and danger, that is to say, whatever ... operates in a manner analogous to terror."[10] For Burke, sublime terror paradoxically induces delight: subjects of the sublime enjoy fear by proxy. Kant's view of sublimity, relying partly on Burke, is concerned with the dynamics of cognitive processes. For Kant, the sublime arises whenever reason produces an idea of infinity that cannot be objectified by understanding and imagination, whenever the mind struggles with a concept of "absolute totality" with which it cannot catch up. This experience gratifyingly intimates that human subjects may perceive absolutes, albeit in "supersensible" form.[11] In light of Burke and Kant, the city's human aggregates are sublime because they inspire ambivalent feelings, mingling exhilaration with a threat to selfhood. Also, just as sublime landscapes hint at a divine presence in nature, cityscapes spark off epiphanies about multitudinous humanity. Urban novels suggest that the spectacle of the mass allows observers to perceive what late nineteenth-century American essayist Henry Adams calls the "economies ... of force," the latent play of energies in the social field.[12]

The urban sublime occupies a median position between the sublimes of Romanticism and postmodernism. For William Wordsworth and Samuel Taylor Coleridge, the chief object of wonder was nature. Under postmodernism, sublime distress is caused by what Fredric Jameson has called the "impossible totality" of technologically mediated social bonds.[13] In broader epistemological terms, the postmodern sublime arises from the mismatch between strategies of representation and their "[u]npresentable" objects.[14] Among the sources of sublime dread and wonder, Romantic nature and the postmodernist breakdown of representation have enjoyed more attention than the city. The critical corpus investigating urban sublimity is limited and mostly recent. It can be broadened by taking into consideration discourses cognate to urban experience – the industrial, the technological, even the nuclear sublime.[15] This apparent neglect may originate from the suspicion that the discourse registering the city's sublimity developed as an after-thought to Romanticism; it merely involves a "transfer" of sublime affects "from a natural to an urban ... scene."[16] Still, looking backward from post-modernism, the value of the urban sublime resides in its capacity to sig-nal that the epistemological crisis of (post)modernity is perceptible in the materiality of built-up space: the metropolis is the visible token of the resis-tances to representation caused by complex social interconnections. Unlike romantic nature, yet in agreement with postmodernist skepticism, the city manifests this epistemological breakdown in a cultural context that renders the mystical resolution of the sublime unavailable.

The primary corpus of the urban sublime ranges from architecture, the social sciences, literature, and film to such popular attractions as panoramas. Some of the earliest discussions of urban sublimity focused on architecture and urban planning. In his history of English architecture, Nikolaus Pevsner discerned a potential for fascination and dread in Victorian buildings – a phe-nomenon Nicholas Taylor described as the "Awful Sublimity of the Victorian City."[17] Similar reflections have been elaborated about skyscrapers and twentieth-century urban development, yet only a limited grasp of the urban sublime can be derived from architecture alone. Buildings and metropolitan sprawls are awe-inspiring not solely by virtue of their highly visible pres-ence in space. The fascination they exert is due to the fact that they serve as material tokens for principles that defy objectification. Spatial structures are indeed fragments in a profusion of urban stimuli whose full extent is never present to the observer's gaze. Thus, much as gothic cathedrals are expressions of the medieval community of believers, or as Versailles showcases absolute monarchy, the sublime metropolis gestures toward a social fabric perceived as a tangle of indeterminate masses and forces. The full deployment of the urban sublime therefore requires that architecture and the graphic arts be complemented by media able to name this imperfectly glimpsed background. From the nineteenth century to World War I, for instance, the urban sublime appears as the combined offshoot of the city's architectural configuration and its literary, journalistic, and sociological representation.

Thus defined, the corpus of urban sublimity yields its own principle of periodization. For the urban sublime to emerge, observers of the metropolis must possess some awareness of demographic and industrial development; the urban sublime is thus unlikely to appear before Adam Smith's treatises on economics or Thomas Malthus's reflections on populations. This places its onset no earlier than the first half of the nineteenth century, when the impact of the Industrial Revolution on city life was exposed in the "Blue Books" of Victorian social investigators, in treatises of political economy such as Friedrich Engels's study of the Manchester working classes, and in reform novels by Charles Dickens, Disraeli, and Elizabeth Gaskell.[18] Conversely, we must consider, if not the disappearance of the discourse of urban sublimity, at least its qualitative change under modernism and postmodernism. The social structure of the metropolis is no less opaque today than at earlier stages of urbanization. Yet it less often inspires the discourse of masses and forces that dominated previous stages of urban culture.

From the Picturesque to the Sublime

In Burke and Kant, the sublime exists by virtue of its contrast with the beautiful: excess and dissonance instead of balance and harmony. Similarly, the "City Sublime," Elizabeth Wilson has argued, coexists dialogically with "an essentially moderate and 'civilised' approach to urban living."[19] Urban planners often seek to restore what Lewis Mumford calls the city's "illumination of consciousness ... [and] stamp of purpose."[20] Alan Trachtenberg pointed out, for instance, that Frederick Law Olmsted, the designer of Central Park, aimed to "teach the metropolis about itself, to clarify its parts."[21] Verne's *The Begum's Fortune* contrasts grimy Stahlstadt with tree-lined France-Ville, an urban Eden evocative of turn-of-the-twentieth-century garden cities. Likewise, in documentaries and social-science reports, the portrayal of cities beyond control serves as a preparatory shock tactic for sociological analysis and reform. Jacob Riis's late nineteenth-century photographs of New York slums expose poverty of gothic proportions in order to advertise a program of housing regulations. Jack London's *The People of the Abyss* (1903), a muckraking investigation of London's East End, legitimizes a socialistic agenda.

The development of nineteenth-century urban fiction may be narrated on the basis of the pattern of dialogization just outlined: city novels developed according to writers' efforts to manage the spectacle of sublimity. Urban dread and wonder were either contained by the strategies of classic realism and the picturesque, or set to work for mapping urban space in the idiom of the romance. Honoré de Balzac's realist classic *Père Goriot* (1835) features surprising traces of the urban sublime, both oceanic and gothic. "Paris," Balzac writes, "is a veritable ocean" whose depths contain "flowers, pearls, monsters ... unheard of, forgotten by the literary divers."[22] Likewise, *Père Goriot* swerves into blood melodrama in its portrayal of a spine-chilling convict hiding at the boarding house that serves as the novel's main locale. These are, however, scattered flashes in a text mainly concerned with scanning what Amy Kaplan, citing Raymond Williams, called the "knowable community" of realist fiction, its determinate lifeworld.[23] Balzac fulfills the realist agenda by resorting to the mechanics of the novel of manners, which cannot accommodate unfathomable motives and social forces. Any oddity affecting the boarding house, a building initially labeled a "curious monstrosit[y]," is no sooner evoked than neutralized by the reassuring accents of the picturesque.[24]

As city novels shift from realism to naturalism, they increasingly rely on sublime rhetoric. I have argued elsewhere that the appropriation of this Romantic idiom is a definitional feature for naturalism as it splits off from realism.[25] In naturalism, the sublime is no longer the accursed portion of the image of the city; naturalist authors assume, as American novelist Abraham Cahan puts it, that the metropolis must be both "great" *and* "strange."[26] The sublime thus becomes a paradoxical asset in the mapping of what James Naremore, in a study of film noir, felicitously called "the social fantastic" – areas at the periphery of the knowable lifeworld.[27] Thomas Weiskel's reflections on the Romantic sublime, if transposed to urban fiction, indicate how a literary idiom concerned with obstacles to representation may paradoxically contribute to the exploration of social space. Weiskel described the sublime as a moment of perceptual excess that triggers either a metonymical or a metaphorical resolution. The metonymical variant fits the (post)modernist variant of urban sublimity, as we shall see. Its metaphorical counterpart, already predominant in Romanticism, informs most city fiction until World War I. The metaphorical sublime turns perceptual distress into what Weiskel called an "intuition of *depth*."[28] The representational breakdown, in this case, originates from an excess of stimuli – of signifiers – for which no determinate signifieds are available. Yet the excess comes to stand as a token for a signified of a deeper order: sublime distress gestures toward an indeterminate metaphorical tenor. For city fiction, this distress implies that aspects of the metropolis that resist the analytical strategies of documentary realism are evoked connotatively, as ungraspable energies and forces emanating from the totality of urban experience.

Dreiser's and Zola's representations of the subject's relation to the metropolis illustrate the dynamic of the intuition of depth. Realist certainties have a limited scope in *Sister Carrie*. The heroine's initial grasp of economics is shallow; she understands "the meaning of a little stone cutter's yard" in her native small town, yet knows "nothing" about the "strange energies and huge interests" informing businesses in the Windy City. The men she meets embody forces beyond representation, be it the energizing appeal of "the city's hypnotic influence" or, conversely, the destructive drag of urban life. Commercial salesman Charles Drouet radiates with "the mesmeric operations of super-intelligible forces"; tavern manager George Hurstwood is led to suicide after an eerie voice – the city's diffuse call – urges him to steal from his employer.[29] Zola, in *Money* (1891), seems more intent than Dreiser on portraying the urban economy analytically. Yet he swerves into gothic as he characterizes the ruthless speculator Saccard and his illegitimate son, raised among the Paris underclass. Young Victor is a sadistic, incestuous pervert – the living metaphor of his father's implicitly criminal will to power. In Dreiser's *The Financier* (1912), similar gothic allegories depict speculator Frank Cowperwood as the evolutionary kinsman of a lobster meticulously devouring a squid, or the "Mycteroperca Bonaci," a predatory fish with chameleon-like powers of simulation.[30] To some extent, as the two writers sound these sublime accents, they foreground their difficulties in turning perceptual breakdown into determinate revelation; they hesitate before settling on a metaphor fitting the city's sublime power. Still, they eventually give a solid outline to what might have remained a blurry intuition. Carrie's Chicago, we learn, is the playground of "the forces of life."[31] Likewise, Cowperwood, as he discovers the Windy City in the opening of *The Titan* (1914), describes it as a place where "life [i]s doing something new."[32] Zola's Saccard, after dragging his shareholders into bankruptcy, exclaims: "Does life concern itself about that?"[33] The object of sublime intuition is therefore life embodied in the urban field.

As urban novels equate the mysteries of the metropolis with life itself, they avail themselves of a mapping tool endowed with flexible fuzziness and the capability to picture their object either as fascinating or repellent. Thus, any enigmatic aspect of the city may stand for various manifestations of life energies. Economics and demographics, because they defy understanding, are equivalent to the equally puzzling processes of biological reproduction. Capitalism and crowds are thereby caught up in a gendered economics. In Norris's *The Octopus* and *The Pit*, the wheat acts as a reproductive principle informing labor activity, trade, and the protagonists' mental processes; one single material acquires the status of a vital principle acting as token for the totality of the urban economy. Gold plays a similar part in Norris's *McTeague* (1899), as does meat in Upton Sinclair's *The Jungle* (1906), where the Chicago stockyards are the emblem of capitalist exploitation. Yet these energizing life cycles may veer into degenerative forces. Norris's wheat is both creative and destructive. More spectacularly, the biological traffic of sublime cities becomes a cesspool of abjection as it reaches the slums. Disraeli describes a city of metal workers whose streets are "reservoirs of leprosy and plague";[34] Sinclair's Chicago reeks with the metamorphoses of meat; in Jack London's East End documentary, the English capital accommodates a monstrous biological and economic traffic whereby rural England's "flood of vigorous strong life … perishes by the third generation."[35]

The Politics of the Urban Sublime

In Romanticism, Weiskel contended, ideology seeps into the sublime at the moment when a specific label is assigned to the awe-inspiring intuition of depth.[36] By a mechanism akin to Derridean logocentrism, subjects of the sublime transcode the indeterminate stimuli of distress into determinate concepts drawn from preexisting ideologies. In late nineteenth-century urban novels, the ideological resolution of the sublime is secured not only by naming life as the city's latent force but also by conceptualizing that force in light of Social Darwinism. When Darwinism still carried the thrill of the new, the rhetoric of the struggle for survival made it possible to map populations in a fashion that seemingly met the requirements of both science and art. Phrased in this idiom, the urban scene appears as a segment of the social world where, to borrow Social Darwinian philosopher Herbert Spencer's mystical terminology, evolutionary processes unfold with the allure of the "Unknowable."[37]

Since Social Darwinism has served as ideological validation both of capitalism and scientific racism, one may suspect the nineteenth- and early twentieth-century urban sublime to be the handmaiden of political conservatism. Trachtenberg has endorsed this view, stating that late nineteenth-century social science and popular culture propagated "the image of the city as mystery, as unfathomable darkness and shadow"; this discourse was a "mystification" that encouraged urban dwellers to view monopoly capitalism as natural and unchallengeable. Trachtenberg's critique of the city's "new inexplicableness" is grounded in the Marxist concepts of commodity fetishism and reification.[38] Marx argued that capitalism, by the complexity of its mode of production, misleads subjects into believing that their social environment is "under the sway of an *inhuman* power." Instead of appearing as a human aggregate amendable by human effort, the social world seems invested with the alien impenetrability of things. Thus, discourses romanticizing the city's mysteriousness enhance "human self-estrangement" and abet strategies of domination.[39] In this logic, the rhetoric of urban wonder is guilty of the philosophical mistake Marxist critic Georg Lukács imputed to vitalism: it views history not as the deployment of reason but as the whimsical course of "the 'eternal essence of life.'"[40] Nor does sublime vitalism fare better at the hands of critics relying on Michel Foucault's reflections on biopolitics. Mark Seltzer and Walter Benn Michaels suggest that Dreiser's and Norris's gendered economics neutralize all strategies of resistance as they make instincts and desire indistinguishable from consumerist seduction.[41]

The contention that urban sublimity amounts to mystification and subjection faces several objections, however. First, the idiom of dread and wonder was appropriated by literary left-wingers such as Zola, Sinclair, London,

Ernest Poole, and H. G. Wells. Poole's *The Harbor* (1915) – a best seller among American Progressive-era novels of social reform – both testifies to the existence of this aesthetic/political choice and illustrates its contradictions. Poole's chronicle of New York narrates the shift from entrepreneurial liberalism to monopoly capitalism, and celebrates the promise of a socialist future. While the novel presents small entrepreneurs as obsolete, it makes monopoly capitalism and socialism equally fascinating. Advocates of scientific management, in their efforts to restructure the chaotic urban-industrial city, are "giant[s]" radiating "some queer magnetic force." To these icons of corporate glamour, labor opposes "the 'strike feeling'" – the capacity of industrial crowds to achieve self-organization.[42] Political commitment in this novel is therefore less a matter of demystification than of emotional surges; socialism will conquer if its energies surpass the romance of capitalism.

Second, as Poole's novel inchoately suggests, political thinkers with no inclination toward irrationalism may refuse to condemn sublimity as parasitical. In the early twentieth-century United States, Fredric Clemson Howe and Simon Nelson Patten developed visions of urban life praising the "crowding together of mankind" as a "social treasure":[43] the social interfacing made possible by urban masses creates a self-multiplying social surplus affording a "gain upon nature."[44] These thinkers anticipate the postmodern view according to which the city's indeterminacy, fluidity, and excess foster empowerment. Yet in the context of their time, their arguments were marginalized by the negative connotations clinging to urban masses. In *The Crowd, A Study of the Popular Mind* (1895), French sociologist Gustave Le Bon argued that the members of political crowds descend "several rungs in the ladder of civilisation."[45] They respond exclusively to leaders able to channel hypnotic intensities arising from the mass itself. Sigmund Freud reformulated Le Bon's argument by theorizing that crowd leaders achieve their dominion over groups by acting as the agglomerated subjects' "ego-ideal" (i.e., their superego).[46] Even pro-Socialist novelist H. G. Wells's *The War of the Worlds* (1898) suggests that streams of refugees are as much of a threat to Londoners as are the Martians. The novel's obsession with unruly masses is also noticeable in its visions of parasitical red weeds overrunning the ruins of London and colonies of bacteria lethal even to extraterrestrials.

Toward Postmodernism: Beyond Masses and Forces

The urban sublime survived the transition from realism/naturalism to modernism at the cost of several reconfigurations. On the one hand, the reshaping of cityscapes by architectural modernism and the International Style perpetuated the sublimity of masses and forces. This nineteenth-century discourse also found new outlets in emergent media such as film (Fritz Lang's *Metropolis* [1927], King Vidor's *The Crowd* [1928]), science fiction (Isaac Asimov's *The Caves of Steel* [1954], William Gibson's *Neuromancer* [1984], Ridley Scott's film *Blade Runner* [1982]), and comics (the Batman and Spiderman franchises). On the other hand, the romance of the mass was marginalized in literature and painting. As these artistic media turned toward formal abstraction and the inner world, urban sublimity in the realist/naturalist mode was deprived of its main channel of expression. The shift was no mere matter of aesthetic choice. It also testifies to the high-modernist belief that the urban world had become associated with culturally sterile or politically objectionable mass phenomena. Pam Morris indicates that modernism's critique of realism is rooted in writers' distaste for commercially oriented mass culture, for the visible face of the twentieth-century urban world.[47] More ominously, the spectacle of the mass acquired military or totalitarian overtones: the portrayal of sublime crowds experienced its demonic swan song in the visions of armies stranded in World War I trenches (the debacle in Ernest Hemingway's *A Farewell to Arms* [1929]), in the choreography of fascist hordes (Leni Riefenstahl's *Triumph of the Will* [1935]), and in the urban apocalypse of World War II bombings.

To the previous mode of the urban sublime, modernism opposed in the first place what we might call necropolitan terror and wonder. Romantic and postromantic sources such as Edgar Allan Poe's "The City in the Sea" (1845) and James Thomson's *The City of Dreadful Night* (1874) had long established an anxiety-ridden link between the city, loss of self, and death. Similarly, works of modernist poetry and fiction such as Joseph Conrad's *Heart of Darkness* (1899), T. S. Eliot's *The Waste Land* (1922), F. Scott Fitzgerald's *The Great Gatsby* (1925), and Franz Kafka's *The Trial* (1925) identified the metropolis with cemeteries or the circles of hell. This mode of the sublime reverses the vitalistic depiction of urban masses. The alienated necropolis – Conrad's "whited sepulcher," Fitzgerald's "valley of ashes," or Eliot's "Unreal City"[48] – is metaphorically equivalent to death, not life. Beyond literature, the necropolitan sublime flourished in the modernist and postmodernist iconography of the urban scene, from Edward Hopper's paintings to photorealist cityscapes by Richard Estes and Edward Burtynsky's photographs of industrial waste lands.

Simultaneously, postmodernism developed a variety of the urban sublime that is neither death-obsessed nor concerned with underlying forces. In this discourse, the city is the playground of what Jean-François Lyotard called the *"infinity of heterogeneous finalities."*[49] Its endless multiplicity is experienced as exhilarating, inducing only temporary anxiety soon overcome by new wonder. Nineteenth-century antecedents for this empowering mode of urban fascination appear in Charles Dickens's *Sketches by Boz* (1836), Poe's "The Man of the Crowd" (1840), and Charles Baudelaire's evocation of the Paris flâneur. Each of these texts suggests, with occasional spikes of guilt, that the city's endless stimuli are pleasurable. Within modernism, this structure of feeling informs John Dos Passos's urban novels, which weave potentially infinite narrative networks among dozens of fictional lives. In Weiskel's terminology, this variety of the sublime affords a metonymical, not a metaphorical, resolution. Weiskel identified its mechanism in the experience of writers faced with a crippling "excess of signified."[50] The blockage is overcome by producing new signifiers ready to accommodate new meanings. Thus, the metonymic movement of writing from one signifier to the next defeats paralyzing excess. Weiskel's reasoning can be transposed from the subject to the object of perception. In this perspective, the confusion caused by perceptual excess is resolved by the reassurance that the stream of stimuli will not cease; there will always be more of the world to mobilize observers' attention. Cities fitting the metonymical sublime therefore resemble the rhizomatic lattices freed from a unifying principle evoked by Gilles Deleuze and Felix Guattari.[51] Novels and films of the postmetropolis such as David Mitchell's *Ghostwritten* (1999) or Alejandro González Iñárritu's *Babel* (2006) celebrate this rhizomatic freedom. The fragmented, multifarious locales they evoke create ever more surprising connections among a planet-wide cast. In these cases, the engine of the urban sublime is no longer a transcendent force; instead, it is the very unfolding of time and space actualized in the form of human interconnections.

NOTES

1 Robert Herrick, *Together* (Greenwich, CT: Fawcett, 1962), p. 182.
2 William Dean Howells, *A Hazard of New Fortunes* (New York: New American Library, 1980), pp. 159, 160.
3 Jack London, *The Iron Heel*, in *Novels and Social Writings* (New York: Library of America, 1982), p. 535.
4 Jules Verne, *The Begum's Fortune*, trans. W. H. G. Kingston (Philadelphia: Lippincott, n. d.), p. 65.
5 Benjamin Disraeli, *Sybil, or the Two Nations* (New York: Oxford University Press, 2008), p. 139.
6 Émile Zola, *Germinal*, trans. Roger Pearson (London: Penguin, 2004), p. 482.
7 Rebecca Harding Davis, "Life in the Iron-Mills," in Nina Baym, ed., *The Norton Anthology of American Literature*, 7th ed., vol. B (New York: Norton, 2007), p. 2603.
8 Frank Norris, *The Octopus, A Story of California* (Harmondsworth, UK: Viking–Penguin, 1986), p. 131; Norris, *The Pit, A Story of Chicago* (New York: Doubleday, 1903), p. 80.

9 Theodore Dreiser, *Sister Carrie* (Harmondsworth, UK: Penguin–University of Pennsylvania Press, 1981), p. 23.

10 Edmund Burke, *A Philosophical Enquiry into Our Ideas of the Sublime and the Beautiful*, ed. James T. Boulton (Oxford: Blackwell, 1987), p. 39.

11 Immanuel Kant, *The Critique of Judgment*, trans. James Creed Meredith (Oxford: Clarendon Press, 1952), p. 119.

12 Henry Adams, *The Education of Henry Adams*, in *Novels, Mont Saint Michel, The Education* (New York: Library of America, 1983), p. 1066.

13 Fredric Jameson, *Postmodernism, or The Cultural Logic of Late Capitalism* (Durham, NC: Duke University Press, 1991), p. 38; see also Joseph Tabbi, *The Postmodern Sublime: Technology and American Writing from Mailer to Cyberpunk* (Ithaca, NY: Cornell University Press, 1995), pp. 11–13.

14 See Jean-François Lyotard, "Presenting the Unpresentable: The Sublime," trans. Lisa Liebmann, in Simon Morley, ed., *The Sublime* (London: Whitechapel Gallery–MIT Press, 2010), p. 130.

15 See Lauri Pauli, Kenneth Baker, Michael Torosian, Mark Haworth-Booth, and Edward Burtynsky, *Manufactured Landscapes: The Photographs of Edward Burtynsky* (Ottawa: National Gallery of Canada–Yale University Press, 2003); David E. Nye, *American Technological Sublime* (Cambridge, MA: MIT Press, 1994); Frances Ferguson, "The Nuclear Sublime," *Diacritics* 14.2 (1984), 4–10.

16 Carol Bernstein, *The Celebration of Scandal: Toward the Sublime in Victorian Urban Fiction* (University Park: Pennsylvania State University Press, 1991), p. 174.

17 Nicholas Taylor, "The Awful Sublimity of the Victorian City: Its Aesthetic and Architectural Origins," in H. J. Dyos and M. Wolff, eds., *The Victorian City: Images and Realities* (London: Routledge and Kegan Paul, 1973), p. 431; see also Lynne Walker, "The Greatest Century: Pevsner, Victorian Architecture and the Lay Public," in Peter Draper, ed., *Reassessing Nikolaus Pevsner* (London: Ashgate, 2004), p. 138.

18 Sheila Smith, "Introduction," in Disraeli, *Sybil*, p. x.

19 Elizabeth Wilson, *The Sphinx in the City: Urban Life, the Control of Disorder, and Women* (Berkeley: University of California Press, 1991), p. 20.

20 Lewis Mumford, *The City in History: Its Origins, Its Transformations, and Its Prospects* (New York: Harcourt, 1961), p. 576.

21 Alan Trachtenberg, *The Incorporation of America* (New York: Hill and Wang, 1982), p. 108.

22 Honoré de Balzac, *Père Goriot*, trans. A. J. Krailsheimer (Oxford: Oxford University Press, 2009), pp. 10–11.

23 Amy Kaplan, *The Social Construction of American Realism* (Chicago: University of Chicago Press, 1988), p. 47.

24 Balzac, *Père Goriot*, p. 11.

25 Christophe Den Tandt, *The Urban Sublime in American Literary Naturalism* (Urbana: University of Illinois Press, 1998), p. 33.

26 Abraham Cahan, *The Rise of David Levinsky* (New York: Harper & Row, 1960), p. 90.

27 James Naremore, *More Than Night: Film Noir in Its Contexts* (Berkeley: University of California Press, 1998), p. 16. Naremore borrowed the term from the French film critic Nino Frank.

28 Thomas Weiskel, *The Romantic Sublime: Studies in the Structure and Psychology of Transcendence* (Baltimore, MD: Johns Hopkins University Press, 1976), p. 24; emphasis in original.

29 Dreiser, *Sister Carrie*, pp. 17, 78, 78.

30 Dreiser, *The Financier* (New York: New American Library, 1981), p. 446.

31 Dreiser, *Sister Carrie*, p. 73.

32 Dreiser, *The Titan* (New York: New American Library, 1984), p. 12.

33 Zola, *Money*, trans. Ernest Alfred Vizetelly (New York: Mondial, 2007), p. 319.

34 Disraeli, *Sybil*, p. 165.

35 London, *People of the Abyss*, in *Novels and Social Writings*, p. 28.

36 Weiskel, *The Romantic Sublime*, pp. 44–8.

37 Herbert Spencer, *First Principles*, 2nd ed. (London: Williams and Norgate, 1867), p. [1].

38 Trachtenberg, *The Incorporation of America*, pp. 112, 103.

39 Karl Marx, *Economic and Philosophic Manuscripts of 1844*, trans. Martin Milligan (New York: International Publishers, 1964), pp. 156 (emphasis in original), 135.

40 Georg Lukács, *The Historical Novel*, trans. Hannah and Stanley Mitchell (London: Merlin, 1989), p. 181.

41 Walter Benn Michaels, *The Gold Standard and the Logic of Naturalism: American Literature at the Turn of the Century* (Berkeley: University of California Press, 1987), pp. 63–5; Mark Seltzer, *Bodies and Machines* (New York: Routledge, 1992), pp. 41–4.

42 Ernest Poole, *The Harbor* (New York: Macmillan, 1915), pp. 152, 315.

43 Fredric Clemson Howe, *The City, the Hope of Democracy* (New York: Scribner's, 1905), p. 294.

44 Simon Nelson Patten, *The New Basis of Civilization* (New York: Macmillan, 1907), p. 16.

45 Gustave Le Bon, *The Crowd: A Study of the Popular Mind* (Mineola, NY: Dover, 2002), p. 8.

46 Sigmund Freud, *Group Psychology and the Analysis of the Ego*, trans. James Strachey (New York: Liveright, 1967), p. 42.

47 Pam Morris, *Realism* (London: Routledge, 2003), p. 21.

48 Joseph Conrad, *Heart of Darkness* (London: Penguin, 2007), p. 11; F. Scott Fitzgerald, *The Great Gatsby* (Harmondsworth, UK: Penguin, 1979), p. 29; T. S. Eliot, *The Waste Land, The Complete Poems and Plays, 1909–1950* (New York: Harcourt, 1952), p. 39.

49 Jean-François Lyotard, "The Sign of History," trans. Geoff Bennington, *The Lyotard Reader*, ed. Andrew Benjamin (Oxford: Blackwell, 1989), p. 409, emphasis in original.

50 Weiskel, *The Romantic Sublime*, p. 29.

51 Gilles Deleuze and Félix Guattari, *A Thousand Plateaus: Capitalism and Schizophrenia II*, trans. Brian Massumi (London: Continuum, 2004), p. 7.

10

ARNOLD WEINSTEIN

Fragment and Form in the City of Modernism

"Make it new!" Modernism, even though it is a good century old now, is rightly understood as deeply cued to that stirring war cry. Yet the city has been the locus of literary fervor ever since there was literature. The relation of the individual to the polis is central and vexed as far back as the *Oedipus*, and darling conceits such as the appearance of a new urban type called the flâneur are likewise recycled, since this fellow can be spotted already in Nicolas Boileau's reflections on seventeenth-century Paris. It seems that the project of city-writing is virtually hardwired to notions of bristling change, even of looming crisis. What, then, is modern about modernism's city in literature, say, from the 1880s on through the 1920s?

No account of the modernist city in literature can avoid saluting the foundational nineteenth-century works that are its substratum: Edgar Allan Poe's "Man of the Crowd" and the Dupin tales, Nikolai Gogol's functionaries and grotesques, the supreme urban anatomies of Honoré de Balzac and Charles Dickens, Walt Whitman's "blab of the pave" and "barbaric yawp,"[1] Fyodor Dostoevsky's annunciatory Underground Man, and perhaps most productively of all, Charles Baudelaire's "Parisian Tableaux" and prose poems. These works convey the very rhythms and creatures of urban existence: spasmodic, lurching, awash in stimuli. In Georg Simmel's "The Metropolis and Mental Life" (1903), we see the lineaments of a new urban figure taking shape: an unmoored figure, protectively blasé in his manner, geared to the de-individualizing money calculus, enmeshed in a neural web, at once lost and free. Modernist writers will follow in his wake. Yet Baudelaire's significance for modernism is located on another plane as well: that of encoded time and history. The famous poem "The Swan" (1860) refers insistently to figures of classical mythology, but it quite overtly does so against the alienating backdrop of the new Carrousel, the Haussmann-produced Paris (of destroyed medieval alleyways and spacious new boulevards) now coming into view. But the heart remembers: "The form of a city changes faster, alas! than a mortal heart."[2] It is exactly this conjunction of personal and urban past that underlies and underwrites some of the major city narratives of modernism, and it stamps as well the most canonical of modernist city poems, T. S. Eliot's *The Waste Land* (1922), where the "broken narrative" of Baudelaire is given its boldest, most contrapuntal, and fragment-driven form.

How could it be otherwise? One thinks initially – but perhaps wrongly – that the privileged dimension of cities is *space*; after all, the cardinal fact of urban life is that the city outruns you, that you cannot (unless from space) "oversee" it. And the taxonomic injunctions of realist city narratives are in line with these spatial givens, as any novel of Balzac or Gustave Flaubert or Dickens or Dostoevsky will reveal. What is lacking in such a perspective is the element of *time*, a no less central axis of urban life. The city is a temporal container. Over and over we find that the modernist city text has a memorializing function, urging us to take larger and better measures of the reaches of both subject and setting. Thomas Mann's *Death in Venice* (1912) has a mythic underlay of this sort, but one especially recalls Sigmund Freud's description, in *Civilization and Its Discontents* (1930), of Rome's riddling dimensionality: How, Freud asked, can the *eye* do justice to the mind, when taking Rome's measure, since the visible "modern" city exists on the ruins of classical structures, themselves covering more primitive ones, going ever further back, irretrievable to human vision? (Such a model stands, of course, for Freud's view of mind itself, understood as possessing its own ruins and residues; what Freud failed to see is that it is also a formula for *writing*.)

Many scholars of modernism have placed a huge emphasis on subjectivity as its signature feature; *Nervenkunst* is a term sometimes applied to the German works of the period. *Fragmentation* – the hallmark of many modernist works – sends us into realms of time and space. Temporal sequence is annihilated in works that chart the back-and-forth neural commerce between past and present (and future and might-be). Realist and naturalist cities may be menacing and spectral, but they can seem outright docile and inert when contrasted to the kinetic renditions of the modernist city in literature, which wrecks our familiar assumptions about subject/setting, about inside/outside, about now/then and here/there. Boundaries no longer bind.

Eliot's famous 1922 essay on James Joyce's "mythical method" announces, as we know, much of his own program for *The Waste Land*, particularly the use of myth and counterpoint to make the "anarchy which is contemporary history" amenable to art.[3] The poem is justly famous for its disjointed bits of story, fable, citation, echo, and historical bric-a-brac, and, of course, Eliot's Notes make the case even more brazenly that the common reader has lost all direct access to the teeming yet esoteric cultural and literary debris on show here. All readers sense that the poem's form is its meaning: these shimmering bits of language are what is shored against ruin, thereby issuing a challenge to determine what, if anything, they actually contain, or, better, *conduct*. Here is a fair question to be put to the great modernist works: Are they *arterial*? Is the "poetics of fragment" in the service of a connective vision? This is no idle question. Must modernism's most famous works, of famously difficult access, be *decoded* – the labor of scholars – or do they still retain power and immediacy for readers? Might the *city theme* be the "Open Sesame" to such work, enabling us to posit the conditions of urban life as a cohering principle? In this light, *fragment* itself conveys not only the bedrock nature of city life as the flickering experience of heterogeneity and simultaneity (indeed, as the negotiating of Baudelaire's key binary, *solitude/multitude*), but it also propels outward – from shard to whole, individual to polis, present to past.

"Bearing fruit" is the vexed matter of *The Waste Land*, and Eliot finds many voices and strategies to convey his pervasive sense of sterility as the condition of both his moment and his city: the myth of the wounded Fisher King acquires modern pungency in the "demobbed" episode with its notes of false teeth and abortion. The loss of erotic vitality is figured in the Smyrna merchant's bid "in demotic French" for a homosexual tryst "at the Metropole," as well as in the automaton-like seduction of the typist by the "young man carbuncular," set against the sexual radiance that emanates from the references to *Antony and Cleopatra*. Eliot's depiction of the current run dry, the mechanization of feeling, comes at us in precise yet drab particulars: awaiting her rendezvous, the typist "clears her breakfast, lights / Her stove, and lays out food in tins" while "Out of the window perilously spread / Her drying combinations touched by the sun's last rays, / On the divan are piled (at night her bed) / Stockings, slippers, camisoles, and stays."[4] Here is a grittiness not found in Baudelaire, as well as an echoing ironic counterpoint unique to Eliot: the adverb "perilously" hints at the Notes' "Chapel Perilous," and the sweet rhyme of "rays/stays" accentuates the reduced scale of the contemporary urban love story: less "staying" even than a one-night stand, part of a dull day's work.

Such are the dalliances of the "unreal city," where the "human engine" throbs no differently from the taxi, where the belief-fed mating and purification rituals of the past have turned cheap and vulgar:

> But at my back from time to time I hear
> The sound of horns and motors, which shall bring
> Sweeney to Mrs. Porter in the spring.
> O the moon shone bright on Mrs. Porter
> And on her daughter
> They wash their feet in soda water
> Et, O ces voix d'enfants, chantant dans la coupole!

Eliot has turned Baudelaire's "layered" Paris into something more murmurous and complex: Andrew Marvell's sumptuous – even if ironic – carpe diem "To His Coy Mistress" now heralds, instead of "Time's winged chariot," the clanking metropolitan traffic, and the seasonal lovers' union issues into a mockery of cleansing, crowned by Paul Verlaine's line from his languorous poem, "Parsifal," where the questing hero had overcome sensual lures, and the song of children proclaims the healing of the Fisher King and the attainment of the Grail. Such renewal, given the poem's allusive network, can be signaled only as loss: The corpse planted in the garden will not bloom, the plaint of Philomel is reduced to "Jug Jug," the lovers' splendor found in Sidney and Shakespeare has devolved into bad nerves in rat's alley, London Bridge is falling down falling down, and Baudelaire's unreal city has become the generic site of destruction: "Falling towers / Jerusalem Athens Alexandria / Vienna London / Unreal."⁵ Time's winged chariot stops for no one, and Eliot's apocalyptic references scan a history from antiquity to World War I, but go on – for us today – to foreshadow the Blitz of 1940, and, more uncannily, the falling Twin Towers of 2001. Here is perhaps the nastiest of all features of cities: they can be targeted.

It has already been suggested that *The Waste Land* ranks as modernism's preeminent urban poem. Yet some might argue that Hart Crane's *The Bridge* (1930) constitutes a vibrant and equally ambitious American modernist performance, and it is well known that Crane found *The Waste Land*'s dystopian vision at once uncongenial and outright regressive. It is for certain that the sheer *force* of urban life is captured by Crane's hallucinatory evocation of New York and its prodigious Brooklyn Bridge. Whitman's signature is felt everywhere in Crane's ecstatic dithyramb, but most memorable perhaps is the haunting image of Poe – dark urban saint – imagined first as a peering subway icon, "eyes like agate lanterns – on and on / Below the toothpaste and the dandruff ads," and then as dying his real death in the streets "when they dragged your retching flesh, / Your trembling hands that night through Baltimore – / That last night on the ballot rounds," in the surreal "Tunnel" sequence of the poem.⁶ William Carlos Williams's *Paterson* (1946–58) belongs in these ranks as well, where London Bridge and New York's steel and girders yield to a denser and more *local* sense of place and perception, giving the poem a "grounding" and flavor quite distinct from either Eliot's or Crane's more mosaic-like and jagged work, even if delivered in the sharp, atomistic, syncopated fashion so dear to modernists.

Eliot's fragment-aesthetic looks outright cohesive, however, against what is arguably the most prodigious city-text that we have: Joyce's *Ulysses* (1922), for the Irish writer brought the dizzying inchoate whirligig of Dublin and its denizens to the forefront of his text, effectively cashiering those older paradigms of narrative closure and recognizable plot. Yes, *Ulysses* sports three central characters and a massive host of minor folks, but it refuses to grant them much representational authority. One might say that the individual story fights for its life in the textual cornucopia that Joyce fashioned, and one would then be justified in stating that this is the law of the city, as well as the modus operandi of modernism. Leopold Bloom might well be taken, at times, for the flâneur Baudelaire pointed to: he swims in the current of the metropolis, noting the signs and wonders of the streets he navigates, much like a traveling camera might, yet he is thinking and reflecting and remembering all the while. Reports from "inside" and "outside" cohabit in this book in the most formidable ways, and even though such a narrative practice wreaks havoc on our reading habits – we want plot, it seems – *Ulysses* delivers beautifully on the messy stereophonic reality of daily urban life.

Again the city theme rewards readers in a way that other features of Joyce's text – its encyclopedism, its Homeric references, its huge, learned echo chamber of historical, literary, and religious allusions – do not, for it offers "freebies" available to any flâneur-reader. One particularly choice instance of Joyce's street-poetry occurs when Bloom, eager to read Martha Clifford's little *billet doux* (which he fingers in his pocket) encounters M'Coy. Bloom is dressed in black because he will soon attend Paddy Dignam's funeral; M'Coy wonders if there's been a death in the family, realizes it is about Paddy instead, then proceeds to tell Bloom how shocked he was to learn of this death. This pitter-patter is counterpointed by (1) Bloom's impatience to get away (Martha's letter!), but also (2) Bloom's libido (as "interested" flâneur) espying the kind of little goodie he delights in (and which city streets offer prodigally): the sight of exposed flesh, in the form of a woman across the street mounting a carriage. Now, there is nothing remotely "significant" in this urban take, yet Joyce makes compositional "gold" out of it by sandwiching together M'Coy's palaver, Bloom's replies, *and* Bloom's increasingly aroused sense of a gratifying sight: "Watch! Watch! Silk flash rich stockings white. Watch!" Here is appetite's irrepressible voice, but poor Bloom is destined not to get his fill: a tramcar comes, blocking his view. The little sequence, lasting a good page and then some, filled with inconsequential things, closes with Bloom assenting to M'Coy's sad assessment of Paddy's death: "Another gone."[7] Joyce is our great environmentalist, inasmuch as *Ulysses* captures the *traffic* (human, neural, not just vehicular) on Dublin's streets and also captures its profoundly egalitarian nature, so that the disappearance from this earth of mortal Paddy Dignam and the bit of leg ascending into the carriage are accorded the same honors.

Other chapters come at city life in still more draconian fashion. "Aolus" regiments its utterances along newspaper lines, reminding us that the format of our dailies, with their disconnected bits of storyline sharing the same page, is not a bad representation of the crowded, pluralist, plotless city; in today's Internet culture, "Aolus" may acquire an unintended historicity. "Wandering Rocks" makes perhaps the strongest bid for capturing the city as space, and it, too, promotes an egalitarian discourse in which people and things come across as so many vectors plotted on a map, none authoritative. Dublin streets are written as pure topography. Other chapters of *Ulysses* are less overtly, but arguably more profoundly, readable as city inflected. "Lestrygonians'" savory restaurantese, "Cyclops'" bar room dramatics, and "Sirens'" musical loosening of the line all draw on the sheer energy of urban locales, bidding to shoulder Bloom's "story" out of the picture. One reads "Circe" as the carnival moment of the text, giving us the city as Nighttown, where all grids have come undone, and libido-fueled phantasms take over the stage. Above all, *Ulysses* differs tonally from *The Waste Land*: Eliot's dyspeptic, sometimes dystopian view contrasts with the vibrancy, ebullience, and zest of Joyce's novel; the book never shies away from darkness (the hauntedness of its two male leads, the baiting of Bloom, the vexed marriage, the refusal to promote any definitive moral view), but it remains the most textually affirmative book ever written.

That cities might contain, parse, and enrich the lives of their citizens, is nowhere more beautifully borne out than in Virginia Woolf's *Mrs. Dalloway* (1925), the most lyrical and generous of all modernist city texts. Woolf's full-throated style honors human feeling and imagination as the prime motors of life, and London has an upfront presence in *Mrs. Dalloway* that is outright celebratory: "In people's eyes, in the sing, tramp and trudge; in the bellow and uproar; the carriages, motor cars, omnibuses, vans, sandwich men shuffling and swinging; brass bands; barrel organs; in the triumph and the jingle and the strange high singing of some aeroplane overhead was what she loved; life; London; this moment of June." One hears Whitman's vigor here, and a quite comparable muscularity: *all* of London is to be sung, all of London is a song. Yet Woolf's emphasis on the *now* is complemented by references to the city "as the Romans saw it, lying cloudy, when they landed" yielding something of that temporality that is a signature of city culture. This novel is not afraid, either, to imagine a day when "death's enormous sickle" will have struck the city.[8] London bathes Woolf's novel, constitutes the "parade" into which her characters step and move and thrive, and everything (including the skywriting airplane) is part of its anthem.

Big Ben famously punctuates this novel – "the leaden circles dissolved into the air" is the recurring refrain – but the city frame reaches well beyond specific landmarks or salutes. *Mrs. Dalloway*, like *Ulysses*, is devoted to a single June day and plumbs the temporal reaches of its figures so that we end up knowing the separate histories of Clarissa, Peter, and Septimus; further, the city is imbued with a wonderful centripetal force so that the far-flung players in Clarissa's emotional life – Peter Walsh living in India, Sally Seton in Manchester – will be brought as if by magnetic force to Clarissa's party. Others, too, will be brought together in the city: Maisie Johnson will note the odd behavior of Septimus and Rezia Smith in Regent Park, and the Morrises from Liverpool will be struck by the worldliness of Peter Walsh, whom they meet at the hotel. In this, Woolf reminds us even of taut neoclassical writers such as Jean Racine, where all that can ever happen must happen in *that place*.

Hence, Woolf picks up the crucial "encounter-theme" of city texts and city life – you do not meet strangers when you inhabit a village – and works it into the magnificent closing spectacle of the novel: her party. Not only do so many of the various and sundry players make their way as guests to the party, but Clarissa's fatefully opposite number, Septimus Smith, also arrives – dead on arrival – through the story of his suicide, forcing Clarissa to come to terms with his dark tidings. Septimus is the book's dark angel, and whereas Clarissa feels the pulsating splendor of life on London streets, his toxic vision transforms it all into horror:

> vans roared past him; brutality blared out on placards; men were trapped in mines; women burnt alive; and once a maimed file of lunatics being exercised or displayed for the diversion of the populace (who laughed aloud), ambled and nodded and grinned past him … each half apologetically, yet triumphantly, inflicting his helpless woe.[9]

Woolf, remembering Lear on the heath, had the requisite breadth of vision to enlist the city experience as a source of mania, no less than of wonder. Perhaps, as Woolf had reason to know, mania is always the flip side of wonder. Each, in its way, is a tribute to the city.

The city as hallucinatory, overheated, *outré* verbal construct with a life of its own well describes Andrei Bely's *Petersburg* (1916), which Vladimir Nabokov judged one of the four greatest fictions of the twentieth century. In this book of shadows, fog, mania, and phantasms, the city of 1905, built on a swamp at a monstrous human cost by Peter the Great, becomes a site for all of Russia's conflicts: cultural, political, Oedipal. The plot centralizes a ticking bomb: Nikolai Ableukov, rich and bored bourgeois, is expected by the Party to execute (by means of said bomb) his own father, Apollon Ableukov, a highly placed, reactionary bureaucrat. Then there is Alexander Dudkin who has given him the bomb, Sofia Petrovna whom Nikolai courts, Sergei her feckless husband who fails at suicide, and the sinister operative Lippanchenko who works behind the scenes. Each of these figures is sufficiently nuanced and twisted to fill a different kind of novel. But one must be awfully clever to discern this fulsome plot because Bely has put everything possible between the reader and it: large doses of Russian history, copious literary echoes, storytelling so disjointed that you rarely know what is "happening" (even though each byte of narrative sports a Fielding-like heading), agents and double agents, elliptic conversations, depictions of consciousness so emancipated and zigzagging as to go wherever they please, and – to crown it off, everywhere one looks – Petersburg, with its mist-shrouded Neva, its grandeur and stone facades, smoldering islands, sovereign Nevsky Prospect, official protocols, social whirl, and dank garret-rooms. And a new species is at hand: "There were no people on the Nevsky, but there was a crawling, howling myriapod there. The damp space poured together a myria-distinction of voices into a myria-distinction of words… It hung above the Nevsky, a black haze of phantasmata."[10] Modernist city: brave new world.

Bely's city is a geometric yet adrenalin-filled fantasia of molting forms. And Bely's page is a wondrous thing: dashes, dots, italics, ellipses, citations, and virtually no "glue" to cohere them. Ultimately, Bely reminds us of Sterne even more than Fielding, for he likes to "shuffle" his story as if it were a deck of cards. Wordplay, authorial asides, "wildings" of every sort are on hand. Most of all, *anarchy* seems to stamp this text: in the rumors of strikes and the momentous, gathering political events of 1905, but also in the outbreaks of consciousness itself, which refuses to be "housed," flaunts its rebellious power, turns on its "owner," and revels in its own indigenous power. There are reaches here, giving the reader the sense that the city and its people are crammed with fissile energy. One of Bely's central metaphors is the tiny circle that is a dot – but a dot that radiates outward, pulsing in a concentric fashion into the world. Such a figure denotes the unfurling and "uncorralable" nature of thought, the centrifugal itinerary of rumor and print (including the government's various directives), the relation of Petersburg to Mother Russia, the trajectory of the statue of Peter the Great that leaves its pedestal and courses through the city (thereby saluting Pushkin), the bloated gaseousness of sordid, otherwise airless interiors (including the digestive precincts of Apollon Ableukov, always on the verge of "popping"), and the explosive energy of a ticking bomb waiting to go off. Baudelaire's and Eliot's "unreal city" is now exponentially more unreal, so it comes across as completely logical to read, "The biology of the shadow has not yet been studied,"[11] and to realize it is Alexander Dudkin's spectral "other" speaking to him, overcoming him.

Not unlike Joyce, Bely utilizes a "family plot" to impose at least some kind of human frame onto the energized and decentered world of his novel, but whereas Bloom and Stephen are dense, historied human figures, Apollon and Nikolai often enough verge on the caricatural, and neither escapes the withering satire – indeed, scorn – felt by the author. Somatically, his creatures are a sorry lot: women with incipient mustaches, froglike and flatulent men, chills and perspiration galore, fumbling and bumbling in their gestures and words. The comic angle is corrosive. In this regard, the Oedipal drama has a cardboard feeling to it, much like the political plot does, as if Bely were first and foremost committed to the spectacle of his own dazzling verbal wizardry (and the haunting power of his city). Is there a cost? The political and moral stakes of this book, co-opted by firing and misfiring synapses, tend to become ever more ghost-ridden, but Bely has won the wager that matters to him: the shadows – of both mind and metropolis – have acquired a neural and verbal life so intense, so solid, as to have their own heft, their own biology.

If Bely's book is unabashedly modernist in its packaging and manner, the sibylline tales and narratives of Franz Kafka would seem its very opposite: no shadows, no neural or verbal "wildings," no temporality as such, no play of consciousness – in fact, no cultural particulars of any stripe. We know this must be Prague, but would-be tourists will find no orientation in these stories. None. In Kafka's city texts, you are either lost or you cannot get there from here. In this respect, nothing surpasses the harrowing two-paragraph piece entitled "Give it up!" It starts benignly enough as the speaker is making his way through the city, en route to the station, but then glances at the tower clock, sees the "time" is different from that of his watch, espies a policeman, asks him for direction, and receives the news: "Give it up!" It is the archetypal lost-in-the-city tale, except that the lostness would appear to be more than cartographic: loss of meaning, loss of soul, loss of salvation. Kafka is as severe as Eliot when it comes to a desacralized world without grace, even if his manner hews utterly to the surface of things. The imperial message will never arrive; the man from the country will never make his way into the Law. You will never get your bearings.

The longer narratives, especially *The Trial* (1925), deliver more of the texture of things – the peculiarly seismic character of Kafka's scheme where the urban setting turns muscular, undoing any sense of individual authority: you are arrested without knowing why, the warders are there in the room, but you hadn't seen it coming, you are seeking the courtroom but cannot find it, you gain an audience with the lawyer but lose your focus, you seek out the painter but are stymied by the little girls, you are befriended by Leni but yield to Eros.

In a much earlier century, Kafka might have been Dante, but his recurring fable of *going under* is hauntingly mapped onto anonymous streets and grimy offices and dingy corridors, onto a cityscape where the soul has no perch. Further, as Robert Alter has argued, Kafka's city is the *coup de grâce* for that favorite city specimen, the flâneur, for he is not only undone by his setting (and this would be true of naturalist city texts as well), but he is also understood as contaminant, as source of projections, as participating in a discourse of paranoia.[12] Even Bely's flickering Petersburg is saturated with the density of history and culture; Kafka's city – teeming, but inhospitable and illegible – has lost all markers.

In thinking visually about modernism's city, films such as *Metropolis* (1927), *Man with a Movie Camera* (1929), and *Modern Times* (1936) come to mind, for they convey the fascination (and sometimes horror) elicited by modern forms of production and architecture, along with the dehumanizing effects related to them. Speed likewise dissolves the markers that would order city life, and the effect is amplified by the machine, which from Le Corbusier to movements such as Vorticism and Futurism is a key concept in understanding the city. In this regard, narratives such as John Dos Passos's *Manhattan Transfer* (1925), with their frenetic pace and disjointed medley of voices and discourses, make Joyce's Dublin, Eliot's London, and Bely's Petersburg look staid and almost homogeneous by contrast. New York's Lower East Side may retain its historical markers for David Shearl in Henry Roth's city-of-immigrants novel *Call It Sleep* (1934), but this Jewish lad confronts the scale and speed of the city via an "Englished" Yiddish that is quasi-biblical in its power; "alienation" acquires here a more virulent taste, and Joyce's Bloom – quasi-Jew looked at askance by Dubliners – seems utterly "native" in contrast to Roth's new arrivals: "I'm losted," young David moans when he strays out of the neighborhood and cannot pronounce the name of his "own" street, signifying a crisis that is verbal as well as spatial. One needs also to bear in mind what Maxim Gorky termed "the lower depths," as one imagines city life in the early twentieth century, and Alfred Döblin's *Berlin Alexanderplatz* (1929) tells us about the Calvary of one Franz Biberkopf against a teeming backdrop of bars, pimps, prostitutes, and low-life violence. But Döblin's rendition of these brutal forces has nothing in common with the work of a Zola or Crane, for it enlists the entire Joycean arsenal of narrative wizardry – blending the testimony of newspapers, myth, the Old Testament, and statistics – to convey the rumbling power of a new age.

Our final modernist narrative of city life, *Invisible Man* (1952) – explicitly remixing the earlier performances of Joyce and Eliot, while remembering Dostoevsky's *Notes from Underground* (1864) at every turn – takes the migrant story into new territory, indeed into virtually a new medium. Ralph Ellison's novel begins and ends in a light-blasted underground setting, linked to the "thinker-tinker" tradition of American thought, enabling us to see the protagonist as a modern version of Franklin and Edison, men who wrested secrets of power from the elements themselves, honoring perhaps the originary myth of Prometheus. But Ellison prophetically aligns his coming-of-age story with art forms other than literature. The double salute to Louis Armstrong – the man who "bends that military instrument into a beam of lyrical sound," as well as the man who's "made poetry out of being invisible"[13] – hints at the book's deepest allegiances: his urban Prometheus must grasp the nature of "black power," while the text works its blues and jazz improvisation on the canon.

Ellison has sprinkled his text with countless literary references – Ralph Waldo Emerson, Herman Melville, and Mark Twain, as well as Freud, Eliot, Joyce, and others – but his deeper structural tribute to modernism consists of a musical form that works via leitmotifs and associative logic of great daring. The early fireworks of the novel – the Battle Royal and Trueblood's tale of incest – broadcast an oneiric strain of displacement and libidinal subcurrents that are there to stay: sexual energy cargoed via black bodies made to dance, sexuality itself as figured in power plants and exploding machines (which is how Trueblood's dream casts the story of a black man having transgressive relations with his daughter/with the dreamed naked white woman). This roiling cluster of images recurs in the forced electroshock treatment meted out to the protagonist, a procedure that peels away his cultivated facade and leaves him with his core identity: black boy, Buckeye the Rabbit. Over and over we see the figures of black power – except that we don't actually *see* them; they are hidden in the dark, operating like Bledsoe at the college or Brockway at Liberty Paints – and we wonder just how and when our protagonist will take his place among them. That cannot happen until the Brotherhood (Ellison's Marxist group of New York political operatives) is rejected in favor of *brothers*, the black community that must be understood on its terms and must free itself.

Invisible Man flaunts in its very title the difficulty in seeing clearly, yet it seems to be telling us in the very form of jazz (improvisation, riffing) that the protagonist must come to see his kinship with his true "brothers": Ras the Exhorter (West Indian revolutionary *cum* organizer), Todd Clifton (Messiah-like figure who leaves the Brotherhood and is gunned down by the cops), and the mysterious Rinehart (figured as a ladies' man, numbers-runner, Reverend/Spiritual Technologist, and epitome of pure mask and freedom). This is what a modernist version of city life as jazz might look like: variations on a theme, portraits of possibility, serial sketches of black roles, and plural gestures toward black power. All of this comes to a head in the hallucinatory depiction of Harlem's 1943 race riots, where the city is momentarily reclaimed by its black victims, and the protagonist comes of age and moves underground.

Modernism's most famous texts are to be found in poetry and fiction. Perhaps the project of representing the city is alien to theatrical form, for how do you bring a city on stage? In this regard, not only narrative and poetry, both also painting and film, possess trumps that drama lacks. (The now dated plays of Elmer Rice sadly prove this point.) Yet, it can be argued that August Strindberg's plays announce – unlike the more traditional fare of Henrik Ibsen and Anton Chekhov – a new beginning for theater that is perhaps most brilliantly seen in *A Dream Play* (1901), where time and space are audaciously refigured, but no less potent in his phantasmal late "Chamber play" of 1906, *The Ghost Sonata*, which takes the familiar urban motif of "roof-lifting" (zooming in on a city building) and transforms it into a surrealist extravaganza. Strindberg's Thor-like old man inducts the young student into the horrors of the elegant Östermalm apartment, which turns out to be a viper's nest filled with the living dead who can neither die nor get clear of each other. We see a menagerie of geriatric grotesques, of whom the *vedette* is the mummy who lives in a cage, admiring the statue of herself as she looked thirty years earlier.

Dickens's Miss Havisham and Baudelaire's "little old women" have, as it were, come of age, and little in modern theater matches the antics of these creatures: the old man and the mummy converse in parrot-language; the "ghost supper" is conducted in silence because none of these ghouls can any longer fool the other; and the sexual and moral crimes of this group are so toxic that the young girl (illegitimate offspring of the old man and the mummy) is doomed. In Strindberg's hands, all buildings are haunted houses; if, in some sense, the city lives by remembering, the Swedish playwright suggests, then it can also die via the paralyzing force of memory and the damning past. Yet this saga of doom, deceit, and decay is electrifying in its musical, ballet-like form, its technical audacity: seeing and hearing are jumbled, scenes are in the "conditional" tense, figures metamorphose. Maybe theatrical performance can go no further than this; maybe, indeed, cinema is the right medium for the swirling Strindberg world, as Ingmar Bergman's entire oeuvre makes clear.

In flagrant contrast to *Ghost Sonata*, Bertolt Brecht's early, violent, quasi-mythic rendition of Chicago (Europe's favorite great city), *Jungle of Cities* (1924), has an outright pioneering/anarchic feeling to it: we see here the savage pre-Marxist Brecht (recognized already by the languid Hugo von Hofmansthal as ushering in the "new"), and he delivers an anatomy of the city that is stunningly prescient in its rendition of urban stigmata. Strindberg's bloodsuckers are all Swedes; Brecht's city drama sports class war, multicultural violence, ethnic and racial hatred, hard-to-package libido, all bundled with considerable literary pizzazz and echo. Brecht's superb metaphor for the city-agon is a sports stadium where raw force is pitted against raw force, and the ensuing combat becomes an echoing one, with links back to gladiatorial games and forward to today's wrestling matches and soccer hooligans.

But the force of Brecht's play stems also from its enduring murkiness: there is a homosexual subtext here that dodges expression and knowledge even as it fuels actions, and there is a persistent imagery of humans as *skin* – skin that comes in many colors, skin that is damageable, skin that is the only armor we have in the bruising and penetrating urban scheme that tends to cashier all ideals. *The Jungle of Cities* counts as modernist work also because it restores something of the mythic to our view of the city in a way that mimetic texts cannot easily manage. Consider this exchange between John and Manky (both minor figures):

> JOHN: These here cities, you can't tell what's going on in the house next door. And you can't even tell what it really means, when you read one of their damn papers.
> MANKY: Or when you have to buy a ticket to go somewhere.
> JOHN: Those people, riding around in them electric cars, they'll god knows end up with ...
> MANKY: Cancer of the stomach.
> JOHN: You just can't tell. But ain't it true, here in the States you can grow wheat all year round, summer and winter ...
> MANKY: But all of a sudden, and nobody's going to tell you, there is no dinner to eat. Or you go and take a walk with your kids in the street, and everything's fine and dandy, all according to the Fourth Commandment, and all of a sudden you find you're just holding the hand of your son or daughter, just the hand, and your son and your daughter have already sunk down into that sudden gravel, way above their heads.[14]

Much is humming in Brecht's exchange. We begin to sense what a city of immigrants might actually have felt like, how much the urban setting defies either control or understanding, as the sweet myths of America show their grisly, would-be-apocalyptic underside. Even the pathos of Roth's *Call It Sleep* seems more staid when contrasted with the virulence of Brecht's play, where all surfaces are subject to breakage or worse (they can open up; you could fall in), and one is entitled to see something at once violent and surgical here, as the dramatist probes into the urban body politic, peels away its epidermis, and displays its bubbling fluids and raw energies.

Finally, however, the city's hyper-modernity can do without tall buildings altogether, can be found in lower-to-the-ground sites such as early twentieth-century Paris, as is beautifully on show in Guillaume Apollinaire's upward-bound notation of Christ-aviator: "Behold the Christ who flies higher than aviators / he holds the world record for altitude." Hence – no surprise – the flâneur is now under vehicular threat: "You are walking in Paris alone inside a crowd / Herds of busses bellow and come too close." The Baudelairean crowd has become at once pastoral and motorized. The old forms have cracked. Something has come to an end, the poet realizes, and his famous closing lines take our romantic sunset to its final avatar: "Adieu Adieu / Soleil cou coupé" ["Goodbye Goodbye / Sun cut throated"].[15]

All the violence and vitality of modernism and the city are explosively freighted into Apollinaire's visionary line. As far back as François Villon, Paris was depicted with its gallows and death machinery. The modernist depiction of the city announces a radical shift in registers, emphasizing disjointedness, alienation, and the play of consciousness, but *adieu* is never possible in literature. The bleeding sun will also rise, as Ernest Hemingway and all the city-writers knew. The streets and the sky cargo life, whether it be crowds or planes, and the reader is required to take large measures. Modernist texts, more than those of other periods, ask us to ponder the plenitude of both time and space. Fragment, echo, shadow bespeak a poetics of linkage and connection and traffic, of what one might, in this context, even term *municipal bonds*. Here might be art's most profound response to the issues of the city and modern life.

NOTES

1 Walt Whitman, "Song of Myself," *Leaves of Grass*, ed. Sculley Bradley and Harold W. Blodgett (New York: Norton, 1973), pp. 36, 89.
2 Charles Baudelaire, "The Swan," *The Flowers of Evil*, trans. Keith Waldrop (Middletown, CT: Wesleyan University Press, 2006), p. 115.
3 T. S. Eliot, "*Ulysses,* Order and Myth," *Selected Prose of T. S. Eliot*, ed. Frank Kermode (New York: Harcourt, 1975), pp. 178, 177.
4 Eliot, *The Waste Land*, in *The Complete Poems and Plays, 1909–1950* (New York: Harcourt, 1952), pp. 43, 44.
5 Ibid. pp. 39, 43, 48.
6 Hart Crane, *The Bridge*, in *The Complete Poems of Hart Crane*, ed. Marc Simon (New York: Liveright, 2001), p. 99.
7 James Joyce, *Ulysses*, ed. Hans Walter Gabler (New York: Random House, 1986), p. 61.
8 Virginia Woolf, *Mrs. Dalloway* (San Diego: Harcourt, 1990), pp. 4, 24, 81.
9 Ibid., p. 90.
10 Andrei Bely, *Petersburg*, trans. Robert A. Maguire and John E. Malmstad (Bloomington: Indiana University Press, 1978), p. 179.
11 Ibid., p. 206.

12 Robert Alter, *Imagined Cities: Urban Experience and the Language of the Novel* (New Haven, CT: Yale University Press, 2005), pp. 141–59.
13 Ralph Ellison, *Invisible Man* (New York: Random House, 1989), p. 8.
14 Bertolt Brecht, *Jungle of Cities*, in *Jungle of Cities and Other Plays*, trans. Anselm Hollo (New York: Grove Press, 1966), pp. 33–4.
15 Guillaume Apollinaire, "Zone," *Alcools*, trans. Donald Revell (Middletown, CT: Wesleyan University Press, 1995), pp. 4, 6, 10.

11

MALCOLM MILES

Cities of the Avant-Garde

The last appearance of the avant-garde was probably during the events of May 1968 in Paris. Students occupied universities. Workers took over the running of factories; millions joined a national strike. But the insurrection was also "a revolution in social and cultural relations."[1] It was the *imagination* of a radically new, free society. As memories of the Paris Commune of 1871 were revived (when the painter Gustave Courbet oversaw the ceremonial dismantling of the Vendôme Column), student meetings mixed philosophical critique and political invective with poster graphics. In North America, meanwhile, campaigning against the war in Vietnam was characterized by protest songs, sit-ins, be-ins, and love-ins. In London, students occupied Hornsey School of Art in the summer of 1968. The model of the Maoist cultural revolution was appropriated (minus the violence of the original) to mean a continuous, ever-incomplete process of social, political, and cultural change. Running through all these events was a hope that the world could and would be changed as a new consciousness emerged through creative action. As radical philosopher Herbert Marcuse remarked, in May 1968, "the piano with the jazz player stood well between the barricades" while the new sensibility became "a political force."[2] But the creative insurrections of 1968 differed from earlier avant-gardism by almost erasing the division between leaders and participants.

The term *avant-garde* derives from Napoleonic military strategy, denoting a small force going ahead of the main army. Writers and artists who assumed this role in the nineteenth century saw themselves as having a privileged insight into future social forms. But in 1968, action was more spontaneous: the point was to be there, and to be there was itself transformative, as it was in the autumn of 2011 when Occupy became a worldwide resistance to neoliberalism. Occupy had neither leaders nor a program, neither did it have a cultural presence. In the years since 1968, radical art has itself become an art-market commodity within a broader cultural consumerism, and so the fortieth anniversary of May '68 was commemorated by T-shirts, scarves, and bags: a mix of designer goods and tourist souvenirs marking the avant-garde's encapsulation in history.

The Commune ended with tragedy as thousands of Communards were killed in the battles of May 21–22, 1871, and others later executed. Courbet was spared and charged with the cost of re-erecting the column – a piece of imperial art that Napoleon had commissioned to commemorate his victory at Austerlitz. Courbet died in poverty in Switzerland in 1874, the year of the first Impressionist group exhibition. For three decades, artists and writers withdrew into an aesthetic reality as an alternative to bourgeois society (drawing on the precedent set by the poet Charles Baudelaire in the 1850s). It was not until the early twentieth-century performances and manifestos of the Italian Futurists that avant-gardes resumed an active challenge to the bourgeoisie. But while Courbet saw himself as the fulcrum of ideological change, the modernist avant-gardes of the early twentieth century saw opposition to bourgeois culture's institutions as an attack by other means on wider bourgeois values and conventions; among their targets were the separateness of art forms, the passivity of art's relation to its audiences, and the status of high culture as morally above the noise of the street. Hence Futurist music used motor horns both for their intrinsically urban sound and as an impolite gesture to the audience.

Fusing visual, sonic, and literary performance in polemics and provocative gestures, Futurism drew a line under history to rub it out and start again for an era of speed and the excitement of danger. The audience was engaged, affronted, threatened. Art was no longer comfortable, a consoling retreat into a dreamworld; it was a shock. And it was shaped by metropolitan experience: the realm of rapid tramcars, electric lights, crowds, and the kaleidoscopic shifts of scene and mood that occur only in cities. Even in culturally conservative England, where the middle classes fled the city to suburban idylls, the Vorticists echoed Futurism's jagged forms and provocations. This phase was ended forcibly by the war of 1914–18, a war that the Futurists saluted as a purifying force but that materialized as an apocalypse far worse than anything they could envisage. In voluntary exile in Zurich, the Dadaist group of writers, artists, and performers used cabaret to produce an uncompromising refusal of the values of bourgeois society, which (unlike the Futurists) they saw as responsible for the war.

By 1968, tramcars and streetlights were nothing new; consumer capitalism offered spectacles more technologically advanced than those of art. Yet the city of the Commune became a fresh ground for dissent when the Situationists drifted through its marginal spaces and interstices in the new cultural form of the *dérive* (drift), moving on foot or in a taxi, sometimes drunk, to seek momentary liberations within the routines of capitalist society, purposely wasting time as a rejection of the society of productivity. Drifting might be thought of as a continuation, or renewal, of the strolling that characterized the arcades of Paris in the nineteenth century, viewed by Baudelaire as an explicitly modern activity as the stroller gazes on others gazing at shop windows. But the arcades housed shops selling mainly luxury goods, including imports from colonial countries, as well as fabrics, dresses, and such accessories as hats and gloves. Above them, the seamstresses worked and sometimes entertained illicit visitors. It was not until the 1920s that the theorist, translator, and critic Walter Benjamin saw the (by then semi-derelict) arcades as sites of wonder at the extraordinary in the ordinary. That, perhaps, is related to the drift, although for Benjamin the encounter awakened a utopian awareness of more distant futures, while the Situationists were rooted in the present and the political.

In the 1990s and 2000s, with enough retrospect to reassess Situationism, its literature expanded. Its actions were ephemeral, but its legacy may be more lasting as architects turn to city margins to seek alternatives to the realm of signature buildings, and writers (notably Iain Sinclair) celebrate the city's overlooked edges. Simon Sadler's *The Situationist City* comprehensively critiques the movement's origins and relation to Paris; David Pinder's *Visions of the City* examines the utopianism of Dutch artist Constant Nieuwenhuys, an associate of the Situationists, whose work included models for a future city. McKenzie Wark reconsiders Situationist theory in *The Beach Beneath the Street* (a title borrowed from the Situationists' own use of the idea of a latent, ludic realm accessible to anyone, while they borrowed it in turn from French Marxist Henri Lefebvre, for whom it was an idea and not the slogan the Situationists made of it). There were also republications of documents including the correspondence of the Situationist Guy Debord, his *Society of the Spectacle* (1967), and Raoul Vaneigem's *The Revolution of Everyday Life* (1967). Lefebvre's work has been translated into English; *Critique of Everyday Life* is the most relevant title for our purposes. In *'68 and Its Afterlives*, Kristin Ross argues that the narrative of '68 has since been depoliticized in a regrouping of the French Left. It is, as Ross says, too easy to see '68 as a student carnival; and it is too easy to read Situationism merely as an art movement. It was a new kind of politics, playful and irreverent, a serious interruption to routine equivalent to the shock tactics of the Dadaists – in which context, the republication of Michel Sanouillet's *Dada in Paris* offers extensive detail on Parisian Dada, and background material on Dada in Zurich, Berlin, and New York from 1916 to the 1920s. Theoretical contributions to discussion of the concept of the avant-garde include Peter Bürger's *Theory of the Avant-Garde* (1974), which takes collage and the manifesto as key avant-garde forms; and Matei Călinescu's *Five Faces of Modernity* (1977), which sets avant-gardism on a cusp between modernism and postmodernism.

The focus of this chapter is the modern avant-garde's efforts to create an alternative culture as metaphor for an alternative society, looking at art, literature, and urbanism. The borders between these fields were dismantled by the avant-gardes, and part of their legacy is that such borders are no longer policed. It uses three headings: interruptions of routine, ambivalence toward the city, and the building of a better world.

Interruptions

The Futurists used street noises in a new urban music, performing semi-scripted outbursts, and published their first manifesto in the Paris newspaper *Le Figaro* in 1909. The poet Filippo Tomasso Marinetti proclaimed that a racing motorcar was more beautiful than the *Winged Victory of Samothrace* (a classical Greek sculpture in the Louvre) after running his own car in a race with friends. As it happens, his car overturned. The Futurists were avid nationalists, too, although Italy was itself a relatively new entity, a nation-state formed in the 1860s. Those Futurists who survived the war mainly supported fascism, which has led avant-gardes to be linked to the specter of totalitarianism. But this is too simplistic. Umberto Boccioni's painting *The City Rises* (1910) conveys what may be a socialist message: a horse rears up, carrying workers on its rising force; the skyline consists of scaffolding and buildings under construction. Art historian Paul Wood writes of the image as "laced with a political rhetoric of anarchy, youth and aggression."[3] Boccioni's style used the multiple viewpoints of French Cubism, leading French poet and critic Guillaume Apollinaire to see Futurist art as a weaker reflection of Cubism. Yet, as Wood points out, the Futurists responded to a different modernity, employing the visual language of motion photography while ignoring the domestic space of Cubist collages – in the genre of still life – to celebrate outdoor, urban space as a site of change as new city districts were erected to house a workers' society. In Moscow after 1917, avant-gardism took the form of another sweeping away of the past, exemplified in a move from aesthetics to utility in Vladimir Tatlin's model for a *Monument for the Third International* (1919, not built): a set of revolving meeting halls for the Party, a politicized monument of modern engineering to rival the Eiffel Tower (which marked the centenary of the 1789 revolution). The *Monument* highlights a tension within avant-gardism between scrapping the past and building the future, and between gesture and practicality.

On the fifth anniversary of the revolution, Arseny Avramov's *Symphony of Factory Sirens* was performed in Baku, with the fog horns of the Caspian Sea fleet as well as bus horns and factory sirens.

The declaration of war in 1914 ended contacts between different avant-gardes. Several artists were killed, including Boccioni, the architect Antonio Sant'Elia, and the German Expressionist Franz Marc. Others took refuge in neutral Zurich where a group of artists, writers, and performers met in exile, their foreign status and opposition to the war being a common currency. Dada drew on Futurist performance, and on the use of typography as part of poetic language. Sanouillet recalls André Breton's meeting (as a medical orderly) in 1916 with Jacques Vaché, recently wounded, whose art took the form of full-time idleness in a proto-Situationism. Typical of a Dada event was the use of spoken sounds – like *da da* – of no explicit meaning, which stood for a parody of a world that had become absurd, and a creative refusal of the old languages by which that world had maintained its bourgeois illusions. After 1918, Dada spread to Berlin, Cologne, and New York, and merged into Surrealism in Paris in the 1920s.

While Dada exhibitions are necessarily documentary because Dada was ephemeral, the use of wit and confrontational tactics resurfaced with Situationism. When the Situationists appeared at London's Institute for Contemporary Arts in 1960, Maurice Wyckaert began by verbally attacking his hosts. Members of the audience stamped their feet. After one question – rudely denounced by Debord – Wyckaert and Debord walked out. Their message was, "We are waiting for you at the turning," which Sadler reads as "revolution."[4] The context then was the Cold War, the Soviet invasion of Hungary in 1956, and, a year later, the Berlin Wall. Left allegiances were questioned, but avant-gardism offered another way to denounce conventional society via a life of wandering idleness, a reoccupation of the city.

Situationist collages reflected a specifically urban environment. For instance, Debord's *Life Continues to be Free and Easy* (1959) reuses a screenprint by Debord and Asger Jorn, *The Naked City* – a scattering of bits of a Paris street atlas, a six-franc stamp torn in two, and hand-colored images of nineteenth-century soldiers plus arrows like those on military maps – and adds the title text as caption within the frame. Debord made it as part of his correspondence with Constant, mixing references to colonialism and the chance alignments of diversionary activity (*détournement*). Although such work took the city as its subject matter, even if it tore up the city map, one sees in retrospect that avant-gardes had ambivalent feelings about the cities to which they gravitated (usually as strangers).

Ambivalences

For artists and writers, the larger cities of Europe from the 1850s onward and of North America from the early 1900s, afforded a critical mass of support systems such as café society, the presence of critics and dealers, small magazines, and the anonymity and proximity of difference that was the defining quality of the metropolis. Railway networks and rapid communication between cities made the metropolitan the cosmopolitan as cities including Barcelona, Paris, Berlin, Munich, and New York became centers for transnational avant-gardes whose members could validate their work outside the restrictions of the academies of fine arts, using culture to reveal society's contradictions. But here ambivalence begins. Artists and writers who were all strangers found common cause as migrants in a solidarity of outsider status. The term bohemian denoted this in the mid-nineteenth century, although those who opted out of bourgeois conventions still relied on the market for an income. As opposition turned to disenchantment, the conjuring of an aesthetic reality in opposition to the regime of money widened the separation of avant-gardes from the targets of their invectives. Art for art's sake withdrew from the industrialized city, which also produced the only market for aesthetic objects, looking to rural culture in Brittany or to African masks imported by traders for new visual languages. One source for such inspiration was, ironically, the international exhibitions held in Paris and other European cities through the nineteenth century. But there was also a quality specific to city living: a frenetic ambience and volatility, a pervasive fluidity reflected in the dominance of money as an abstract, universal means of exchange. Sociologist Georg Simmel wrote in *The Philosophy of Money* (1907) of the new mentality in Berlin in the 1900s, in which money made city life the arena for fluidity and an unending renegotiation of values. What was culture's value then? Was beauty but a relative quality, counter to traditional (Kantian) aesthetics? In that situation, how could writers and artists pretend to have a privileged insight?

In Zurich, all the Dadaists were exiles. The poet Tristan Tzara and painter Marcel Jancu were Romanians; the artist and writer Raoul Hausmann, anarchist poet Hugo Ball, and the performer and poet (and Ball's wife) Emmy Hennings were German, as was the ex-medical student Richard Huelsenbeck, who organized various cabarets, while the painter Jean Arp was Franco-German. The boxer Arthur Cravan joined them from the United States. In another part of Zurich, Vladimir Illich Lenin wrote political tracts. The authorities watched both Lenin and the Dadaists, but they saw Dada as the greater threat to public order.

Dada could happen only in such a neutral city where nationals from across the war front could gather. After 1918, currents such as Expressionism and New Objectivity grew in Germany while in England, the poet, editor, essayist, and banker T. S. Eliot wrote in *The Waste Land* (1922) of an unreal city: a scene of desolation, fragmentation, and meaninglessness where older values and connectivities had collapsed. Eliot projected a personal crisis onto London, but the point is that London provided a credible screen for such a projection as the effects of industrialization, suburbanization, and social mixing (aided by metropolitan transport and the availability of home loans) produced a new kind of city, both diverse and de-centered. But if to be de-centered is also to fail to cohere, it was also London that had brought together Eliot, Ezra Pound, and William Butler Yeats in the 1910s. Yeats wrote his poem of a rural idyll, "The Lake Isle of Innisfree" (1890), after seeing a soft-drink fountain in a shop window. While Eliot mostly disdained the lower-class subjects he caricatured in *The Waste Land*, and Yeats looked to Sligo as his iconic home, the negative image of the city colored their work and led them to create alternative scenarios. Yeats found his in mysticism (his interest in the occult shared with Pound), Eliot in Christianity (adopting the reading voice of a high-Anglican cleric), and Pound, like the Futurists, in Italian Fascism. In contrast, modernist architects saw cities as sites of opportunity: to build a new society by design. If Eliot retreated from the city as a mirror of mental fragmentation, European architects and planners were driven by a need, after the 1914–18 war, to build a new, international society within which wars could not recur.

Rebuilding

Hence international modernism became a movement for a better society through rational design. In North America, the Chicago group of sociologists, untouched by the war, saw the city as a laboratory for social experiments. Repeated migration made transitional zones between the commercial center and executive suburbs. Industry and dwelling mixed there, and city life produced new personality types and ways in which to experience urban spaces. But growth also produced conflict between social or ethnic groups, requiring planners' mediation through rational tools of urban management.

Cities were seen by professionals as requiring expert ordering, but citizens were relegated to the role of users: passive recipients of the city, not its authors. Although the efforts of modern architects and planners were well intentioned, their legacy is ultimately as negative as that offered by bohemian writers and artists, epitomized by the concrete jungle and the tower block for social housing, not the mobility or the welfare state of which such images were once signs. It is not so much that all that is solid melts into air in modern cities, but that all that once seemed to be progressive and humane has melted into a new, bleak ennui.

After the slaughter of 1914–18 and the bombing of civilian targets in 1939–45, there was an imperative to replace what was destroyed – materially and mentally – by something better. Cities were to be hothouses of new social forms designed on a humane basis to counteract the memory and possibility of conflict, and conducive to social coexistence and conviviality. The International Congress of Modern Architecture (CIAM) met from the 1920s through the 1950s in order to develop this project; its members included Le Corbusier, Josep Sert, Siegrfried Giedion, Aldo van Eyck, Kenzo Tange, and the young English Brutalists Alison and Peter Smithson. Brutalism is a somewhat misleading term since the concrete walkways that the Smithsons designed into social housing blocks were meant as an equivalent for the village street where neighbors met, borrowed cups of sugar, and exchanged gossip. It never worked, but the vision was naive, not antisocial, and contrary to popular opinion the projects were, in most cases, well resourced. For families who moved into the new housing around London in the 1950s and 1960s, many having been bombed out of inner-city streets, the new kitchens and bathrooms, and the large windows of the blocks were wonderful improvements on previous conditions.

CIAM's concern in the postwar years was to reimagine the city, yet some of its meetings were held in semirural towns such as Bridgewater in southwest England in 1947, or Hoddesden, a small town north of London, in 1951. The theme at Hoddesden was "The Heart of the City: The Humanization of Urban Life," but the critique was conducted in this semirural periphery. An undercurrent of CIAM's postwar meetings was democracy – or a view of democracy as not-totalitarianism after the rise of Fascism in the 1930s and red totalitarianism in the Soviet Union – and modernism became entwined with a sense of accountability and responsibility, although CIAM remained a meeting place for a professional elite. In its time, nonetheless, CIAM was as progressive as the professional disciplines that formed it. The image of white tower blocks surrounded by green margins, and separation of roads from pedestrian spaces, is a caricature of the modernist city, criticized for lack of integration and over-functionalized space. This city of tower blocks derived from the ideas of Le Corbusier was also clean, orderly, and efficient – qualities regarded as absent in old cities. This perception of existing cities reproduces in new terms a nineteenth-century liberal myth of inner cities as sites of crime, sickness, and vice, and Le Corbusier had been either politically naive or opportunist enough to promote his plan for remodeling Paris and demolishing its old center by publishing it in a French fascist newspaper. But in another way, the ordering of the city in modernist architecture and planning counters the chaos that was one impression of the city of mobility, change, and volatility. While avant-gardes in art and literature celebrated flux and sought to undermine solidities they saw as bourgeois, modern architects and planners sought to reproduce solidity in a geometric rationalism for all. CIAM's members were not unanimous in their views, however; one tendency looked to a repositioning of the architectural eye in the street, echoing the street scenes of postwar cinema.[5] Another saw mass communication as tainted by propaganda and sought to strengthen the distancing of a professional viewpoint.

The former tendency softened the mathematical approach of grid-based plans, and relocated the architectural eye within, rather than above, the places where users lived and worked. For Lefebvre, who was critical of the new towns built in France in the postwar years, this was the realm of a lived space that overlaid – as counterpart to it – the space of plans. Still, CIAM was divided between concepts of wholeness and unity on one hand, and those of humanist individualism on the other hand. Barry Curtis notes that although Siegfried Giedion cited the leftist philosopher and Existentialist Jean-Paul Sartre in his closing remarks at Hoddesden, there was "little evidence of the dialectic demanded by Henri Lefebvre."[6] Concepts such as *Mankind* limited the scope of a reimagined urbanism, while functionalism undermined its utopianism by denying users the capacity of managing the spaces they used themselves. Now many progressive planners and some architects see user participation as a norm, and they rehabilitate the inner-city street as a mixed-use zone rather as, although for quite different purposes than, the Situationists revalidated it as a site of potential liberation.

The legacy of international modernism is not a better world, but the popular rejoicing that occurs when tower blocks are demolished. Oddly, or perhaps not, such demolitions could be images of Futurist or Dadaist chaos, or of Situationist deconstruction. But this is in the past now, and a failed dream. At the beginning of the modernist period, shortly before the 1914–18 war, the French poet Guillaume Apollinaire wrote, in his epic poem *Zone*, of a walk, part imagined and part remembered, to the city's margin – the zone of the title – where the poor wandered and sat around. On the way, he observed the crowds, motor transport, a sky filled with swallows in which an airplane represents the new era. Le Corbusier was also attracted to airplanes, similarly as a sign of the technological era he welcomed, his machine age. But Apollinaire seems to be ambivalent: he laments past beauties as well as celebrating new realities; he strolls, or drifts, or simply walks through Paris as Eliot had seen himself walking toward the crowds in London in *The Waste Land*. In this ambivalence is the fundamental question on which the modern avant-garde dwells repeatedly, and to which it offers different, irreconcilable responses.

NOTES

1 Hervé Bourges, Foreword, *The French Student Revolt: The Leaders Speak*, ed. Bourges, trans. B. R. Brewster (New York: Hill and Wang, 1968), p. 2.

2 Herbert Marcuse, *An Essay on Liberation* (Harmondsworth, UK: Pelican, 1972), p. 30.

3 Paul Wood, "The Avant-Garde in the Early Twentieth Century," in Wood, ed., *The Challenge of the Avant-Garde* (New Haven, CT: Yale University Press and The Open University, 1999), p. 196.

4 Simon Sadler, *The Situationist City* (Cambridge, Mass.: MIT Press, 1999), p. 41.

5 Barry Curtis, "The Heart of the City," in Jonathan Hughes and Simon Sadler, eds., *Non-Plan: Essays on Freedom, Participation and Change in Modern Architecture and Urbanism* (Oxford: Architectural Press, 2000), p. 57.

6 Ibid., p. 59.

12

ROB LATHAM AND JEFF HICKS

Urban Dystopias

The emergence of the urban dystopia during the second half of the nineteenth century coincided with – and responded to – an outburst of utopian writing, both fictional and nonfictional, centering on the city as a site of human perfectibility. The dystopian version instead depicted baleful imaginary societies in which cities themselves feature as the main symbols of negative possibility, as spaces of oppression, blight, and ruin. While such dystopias were initially in the minority, they gradually became the dominant tradition in the decades following the First World War, to the point that, today, grim and ominous visions of future cities vastly outnumber any rosier alternatives.

Many early urban dystopias were, in fact, anti-utopias, critiques of the blithe overconfidence in rational planning characteristic of utopian writers and thinkers, who saw the reorganization of urban space as a panacea for a variety of social ills. The Garden City Movement pioneered at the end of the century by Ebenezer Howard, for example, envisioned efficient transportation systems, strategically placed industrial and commercial areas, ready access to parks, and a communal stake in civic welfare as the levers that urban planners could manipulate in order to expunge the poverty, ugliness, and class strife endemic to the major cities of the time. Howard's ideal was profoundly shaped by Edward Bellamy's hugely influential 1888 novel, *Looking Backward: 2000–1887*, which contrasted the inequality and squalor of Boston at the end of the century with a utopian vision of what that city might become after a century of socialist reform. Bellamy's future Boston is a veritable earthly paradise: industrial wealth has been nationalized, citizens enjoy a harmonious prosperity whose fruits are equally shared, and the city itself is a culturally dynamic and physically beautiful place. The urban dystopia responded to such sanguine projections with a prophetic pessimism bordering on the apocalyptic.

Whereas William Morris's *News from Nowhere* (1890) reacted to Bellamy's idealization of a revitalized urbanism by retreating into a pastoral idyll, Ignatius Donnelly's *Caesar's Column* (1890) and H. G. Wells's *When the Sleeper Wakes* (1899; revised as *The Sleeper Awakes*, 1910) instead depicted future cities (Manhattan and London, respectively) governed by plutocratic elites and riven by rampant class warfare. Technological progress has brought undeniable marvels – airships and electronic newspapers in Donnelly, moving roadways and television in Wells – but also an exacerbation of social inequalities. Wondrous luxury coexists with brutalizing squalor. As a character in *Caesar's Column* puts it, "our civilization has grown to be a gorgeous shell; a mere mockery; a sham; outwardly fair and lovely, but inwardly full of dead men's bones and all uncleanness."[1] Both novels culminate in massive eruptions of revolutionary violence as the working classes rise up against their oppressors, although neither author has faith that the struggle will have a positive outcome. In Wells, the revolution is co-opted by a power-hungry thug, while in Donnelly, the pent-up fury animating the rebellious underclass unleashes an orgy of indiscriminate bloodletting. These two novels set the standard for grim depictions of dystopic plutocracies. Subsequent treatments such as Jack London's *The Iron Heel* (1908), which projects a centuries-long struggle between capitalists and proletarians set primarily in the San Francisco Bay Area, owe them a sizeable debt, although London is more confident that socialist revolution can redeem the blighted cityscape.

This pattern of sunny utopian blueprints spawning dire dystopian responses, which dominated Anglo-American futuristic literature, was repeated in other European traditions. In France, Jules Verne wrote perhaps the earliest full-fledged urban dystopia, *Paris in the Twentieth Century*, in 1863, in the midst of Baron Haussmann's epochal modernization of that city, yet the novel did not appear in print until 1994 because Verne's publisher found it too dark and depressing. Haussmann's remodeling helped to usher in a modern consumer society; his majestic boulevards facilitated the emergence of department stores and other mass-cultural institutions. Verne's novel depicts the results a century hence: classic literature and high art have died out, replaced by homogenous pap and relentless commercial advertising. Although Verne's novel at first seems utopian in its depiction of a high-tech metropolis of gas-powered cars and proto-fax machines, a dystopian animus manifests in its protagonist's persistently frustrated efforts to pursue a career as an artist in a society driven by utilitarian imperatives and the profit motive. This barren social wasteland achieves potent symbolization at the end of the story, as the advent of a new ice age brings the city to a freezing standstill.

In the same year that Verne penned *Paris in the Twentieth Century*, Russian author Nikolai Chernyshevsky published *What Is to Be Done?*, which outlines the struggles of young intellectuals working for a future revolution.

Chernyshevsky's heroine is visited in dreams by a mysterious spirit who leads her through a process of self-realization and eventual emancipation. When she asks what life will be like after the revolution, the spirit describes a massive building of glass, aluminum, and cast iron – the communal living space of thousands of people working together in harmony. This "crystal palace" – and the many others like it that have replaced traditional metropolitan conurbations – is a reference to the building of the same name designed by Sir Joseph Paxton and originally erected at Hyde Park as part of the Great London Exhibition of 1851.[2] The Crystal Palace was the world's largest freestanding glass structure, a monument to technological innovation and Britain's industrial might. In the dream of Chernyshevsky's heroine, it is the symbol of a rapidly approaching urban utopia, a shining promise of future prosperity and equality.

As with Bellamy's novel, *What Is to Be Done?* generated an immediate dystopian response: Fyodor Dostoyevsky's *Notes from Underground* (1864), in which the Crystal Palace emerges as the emblem of an arid, soulless determinism that has little room for human whims and foibles. This exchange of views would give birth – half a century later in the wake of a successful socialist revolution – to the greatest of early urban dystopias, Yevgeny Zamyatin's *We*, published in English translation in 1924. A scathing rebuke to Chernyshevsky, *We* takes place after the Two Hundred Year's War has wiped out 99.8 percent of the world's population and most survivors have moved into the glass city of OneState. To eliminate any trace of individuality, citizens are compelled to wear identical gray uniforms and are known only by their numbers; moreover, in a satire of Frederick Winslow Taylor's theory of scientific management, they must live out their lives – working, sleeping, even copulating – according to the rigid decrees of "The Table."[3] Obedience to OneState and its dictator, The Benefactor, is maintained by surveillance strategies facilitated by the perfect transparency of the city's glass walls: privacy is abolished, there is literally nowhere to hide, and nonconformists are swiftly eliminated. At the end, as resistance fighters from outside OneState begin to disrupt the social order, The Benefactor announces that every citizen will be forced to undergo a mandatory lobotomy.

The novel is a critique of the withering conformism and ruthless suppression of dissent the author saw as the likely outcome of the Bolshevik Revolution; unsurprisingly, it was banned by Soviet censors until 1988. Zamyatin worried that Russia after the revolution would become a brutal police state rather than the harmonious communal utopia posited by Chernyshevsky, and that it would punish creativity and use fear and intimidation to ensure compliance with the state's restrictive mandates. The novel served as a rebuke to those who believed that orderly city planning was the key to creating a utopian urban environment, showing instead that it was the potential harbinger of totalitarian rule. Zamyatin's bleak novel deeply influenced subsequent Anglophone dystopian writing, especially George Orwell's classic *Nineteen Eighty-Four* (1949), with its projection of the pseudo-benevolent autocracy of Big Brother and the cancerous growth of the surveillance state. Although Orwell's London is dismally drab and Zamyatin's OneState is gleaming, both convey a suffocating atmosphere of downcast gazes and averted eyes, of furtive intimacies and casual betrayals.

We and *Nineteen Eighty-Four* brought to fruition a strand of urban dystopia that forecasts the political devolution of the city into a tyranny of centralized administration and control. Yet even as the former was being published, modernist city planners were defending precisely these qualities as the harbingers of a utopian urban future of unparalleled order and prosperity. In 1925, Charles-Édouard Jeanneret, better known as Le Corbusier, released his earnest manifesto *Urbanisme* (translated into English as *The City of To-morrow* in 1929). In this ambitious work, the Swiss architect extrapolated the implications of new building technologies that allowed a massive vertical concentration of population, sketching the contours of a hyper-modern cityscape at once efficiently regulated and aesthetically sublime. Apparently unaware of Zamyatin's dystopian vision of stark crystalline towers, Le Corbusier evoked this new urban landscape of soaring glass-and-steel skyscrapers – which he would later dub the "Radiant City" – in the dreamy terms of utopian literature: "As twilight falls the glass sky-scrapers seem to flame... It is a spectacle organized by Architecture which uses plastic resources for the modulation of forms seen in light."[4] While his wildly extravagant schemes could never have been achieved outside a totalitarian system such as Zamyatin's, in which the urban planner could operate as a kind of unfettered "philosopher-king,"[5] his principles eventually came to inform more limited attempts at urban renovation, the worst of which – the cheaply built Brutalist designs of postwar public-housing projects such as Trellick Tower in London and Cabrini Green in Chicago – would summon a fresh wave of dystopian responses during the 1960s and 1970s, as we shall see.

During the 1920s–40s, however, Le Corbusier's utopian visions received a seemingly sympathetic audience in the burgeoning ranks of the science-fiction pulp magazines. Catering to a popular appetite for technological marvels, down-market publications that featured such awestruck titles as *Amazing Stories, Astounding Stories*, and *Wonder Stories* frequently evoked futuristic cities as majestically cyclopean as any modernist architect could wish. The prototype for the grandiose pulp city was Hugo Gernsback's 1911 novel *Ralph 124C 41+*, originally serialized in the author's own magazine,

Modern Electrics, before being released in book form in 1925. A triumph of technocratic planning, Gernsback's future Manhattan is an imposing complex of lofty high-rises traversed vertically by electromagnetic elevators and horizontally by aerocabs powered by massive solar generators, and graced by municipal parks for leisure and recreation – an image that would achieve visual expression in the dazzling urban vistas of Fritz Lang's film *Metropolis* (1927). Yet that movie's projection of a dystopic future city (echoed in Thea von Harbou's novelization of her screenplay) in which stark class divisions are encoded in the architecture itself – capitalists populate lofty high-rises while workers labor in subterranean depths – was more than counterbalanced by the idealized megalopoli showcased in the science-fiction pulps, several of which Gernsback himself edited.

These magazines were graced with bright, lurid covers by such artists as Frank R. Paul. They sometimes depict cities that literally soar because antigravity devices permit them to take flight. Floating cities appear in Edmond Hamilton's "Cities in the Air" (*Science Wonder Stories*, 1929), while Stanton A. Coblentz's "The Sunken World" (*Amazing Stories Quarterly*, 1928) features a domed underwater city and John W. Campbell's "Twilight" (*Astounding Stories*, 1934) a city run entirely by machines. Isaac Asimov's "Foundation Series" (*Astounding Science-Fiction*, 1942–50) portrays the planet Trantor, the administrative capital of a sprawling galactic empire, as a continuous global city, virtually every square foot of its surface area covered in a carapace of concrete and steel. Yet despite the technophilic optimism of such depictions, they are often haunted by an elegiac shadow: as the machine city is perfected in Campbell's tale, human culture declines into sterility and stagnation, while the most striking image of Asimov's Trantor follows a sack of the city-planet by an inferior civilization, with an agrarian society reasserting itself amidst the spectacular ruins. This vision of advanced cities fallen into decay – the monuments of their once-proud pasts subsisting as inscrutable relics in a world of industrial debris and reawakened nature – has been a fascination of dystopian writers since at least Lionel Jeffries's *After London* (1885). The most famous treatment of this theme in pulp science fiction is probably Clifford D. Simak's *City* (*Astounding Science-Fiction*, 1944–7), in which the Earth's bustling metropolitan areas gradually devolve into a decentralized, bucolic torpor dominated by intelligent dogs and ants.

The depiction of future cities in pulp science fiction thus manifests a decided ambivalence. On the one hand, the wonders of high technology are consistently evoked in near-magical terms; on the other hand, every form of progress seems at the same time a potential regression, a step down the road toward human obsolescence in a machine-driven false utopia. Laurence

Manning and Fletcher Pratt's aptly named "The City of the Living Dead" (*Wonder Stories*, 1930), for example, promises its citizens an epochal liberation from toil only to immure them in a regime of regimented leisure and synthetic experiences. "You must picture ... a world in which Machines had deprived men not only of labor, but of amusement, of adventure, of excitement – in short, of everything that makes life worth while. Oh they were terrible days of boredom! What was left? Only the frantic pursuit of artificial pleasures."[6] This abiding sense that some appalling decadence lurks at the heart of the utopian city would have a profound influence on postwar writers of urban dystopias. The knife's-edge closeness of the choice between utopia and its opposite is captured in Jack Williamson's *The Legion of Time* (*Astounding Science-Fiction*, 1938), where the protagonist's decision to pick up either a magnet or a pebble is the temporal fork in a road that leads, in one direction, toward the glorious kingdom of Jonbar and, in the other direction, toward the hive-like slave city of Gyronchi.

In the wake of the high-tech horrors of World War II, from the automated butchery of Auschwitz to the atomic flattening of Hiroshima, it seemed as if western culture had taken the darker path. In response, utopian depictions of city life all but vanished, and a host of new urban dystopias swarmed in to take their place. From the 1950s to the 1970s, widespread anxieties about looming dangers to civilized life were reflected in a spate of apocalyptic novels and stories depicting vaporized cities, polluted cities, overpopulated cities, hypertrophic or bureaucratically stratified cities, and cities suffering from social breakdown or moral malaise. The threat of nuclear annihilation revived the trope of the ruined city with a vengeance, yet most of the resultant stories do not qualify as urban dystopias per se because they tend to be set outside the blasted metropolitan cores, in small towns and rural areas that have escaped destruction, at least temporarily. Pat Frank's best-selling *Alas, Babylon* (1959), for example, focuses on a Florida hamlet quietly struggling to preserve civic order, its title suggesting a mournful verdict on the urban culture responsible for the conflagration.

The overpopulated city, on the other hand, is one of the classic postwar images of urban dystopia. Science-fiction writers began to respond to concerns about overpopulation as early as the 1950s, in such stories as Kurt Vonnegut's "Tomorrow and Tomorrow and Tomorrow" (1953), Frederik Pohl's "The Census Takers" (1955), and Cyril Kornbluth's "Shark Ship" (1958). The floodgates opened in the 1960s, however, as demographers and sociologists began warning about the possible effects of a "population explosion." *Time* magazine featured a cover story on the subject in 1960, and Paul Ehrlich's *The Population Bomb*, a runaway bestseller in 1968, exposed an even wider public to dire predictions of famine, overcrowding, and environmental degradation. At the same time, novels such as Anthony Burgess's *The Wanting Seed* (1962), Harry Harrison's *Make Room! Make Room!* (1966; filmed as *Soylent Green* in 1973), John Brunner's *Stand on Zanzibar* (1968), and John Hersey's *My Petition for More Space* (1974), with their vivid descriptions of cramped living spaces, unending lines, and government-enforced privation, collectively evoked an image of the over-crowded city as a swollen hive, a teeming site of scarcity, lack of privacy, and psychological terror.

The anguish of crowded bodies pressed together without hope of release is powerfully captured in Hersey's novel, which is set entirely in a miles-long line of petitioners seeking redress from the state: human relationships are formed solely on the basis of who is standing nearby, with everyone in danger of succumbing at any moment to an eruption of "line madness," a communicable form of temporary insanity resulting from limited personal space and decreased mobility. Given their jostling throngs of anonymous strangers, the threat of riot is never far away in these novels, and Brunner's *Stand on Zanzibar* features a pivotal street brawl that alters the destinies of two of its multitudinous characters. In *Make Room! Make Room!*, future New York is pushed to the limit of its resources by population pressures: food and water are strictly rationed, electricity is available only as a luxury item, and criminal operations sell meat from questionable sources. Although circumstances are constrained for all citizens in Brunner's and Harrison's novels, deprivation and need are unequally distributed, with the rich living measurably better than the vast urban underclass.

Tales of overpopulation often dovetail with depictions of oppressively overbuilt cities, as J. G. Ballard's 1957 story "The Concentration City" (aka "Build-up") demonstrates. On the surface, the tale offers an exaggerated conception of urbanization gone wild: the world consists of a single city, a grimmer version of Asimov's Trantor, with never-ending formations of apartment blocks stretching horizontally for thousands of miles, filled to capacity with human life. The protagonist takes a series of high-speed trains around the globe in a quest to find free space, only to discover at the end that he has returned to where he started. In a later Ballard story, "Billenium" (1962), 95 percent of the planet's population has migrated to urban centers due to the increasing amount of land needed for agriculture; as a result, unmarried residents of the city are forced to live within a space no larger than four square meters, with the threat of further restrictions constantly looming. Tenants fight tooth and nail to protect every inch of their living quarters; hallways and stairwells are crammed with people; and lines of pedestrians fill the sidewalks, making it nearly impossible to move. Amidst this crush, the protagonist discovers a hidden room "some fifteen feet square" that seems composed of "huge cliffs" and an "unconfined emptiness," an "absolute spatial freedom."[7]

Ballard continued his exploration of dystopic cityscapes into the 1970s, with his novel *High-Rise* (1975) centering on a luxury apartment building descending into chaos because of the deep-seated tensions and rivalries of urban existence. The setting is a forty-story glass-and-steel skyscraper on the margins of London, inhabited by a range of white-collar functionaries (on the lower floors), bourgeois professionals (in the middle), and elite techno-crats (on the top). This blatant recapitulation of prevailing class divisions, coupled with the hedonistic isolation of high-rise living, allows the "thinly veiled antagonisms" between these groups to be expressed without the usual filters of social deference and personal self-control.[8] Soon, the edifice has balkanized into clannish factions, enforced by vigilante violence that only escalates as the building's services – water, sewage electricity – begin to break down. Regressing to primal savagery, the groups are driven to survivalist extremes, fighting for control of the stairs and elevators, ambushing strag-glers who stray beyond their designated spaces, feasting on captured pets and, eventually, one another. A disturbingly surreal examination of the tenu-ousness of urban civilization, *High-Rise* – along with the author's other nov-els of the period, *Crash* (1973) and *Concrete Island* (1974) – set an unusually high standard for critically pointed interrogations of contemporary city life.

Ballard's work shows how closely intertwined were images of sweep-ing technocratic monumentalism on the one hand and irremediable deca-dence and breakdown on the other hand. Similar treatments include David R. Bunch's *Moderan* (1971), Robert Silverberg's *The World Inside* (1971), Thomas M. Disch's *334* (1972), Felix Gottschalk's *Growing Up in Tier 3000* (1975), and Charles Platt's *Twilight of the City* (1977). Silverberg, for example, depicts vast megalopoli (called "urbmons," short for urban monads) in a hypertrophic, over-regimented future marked, as in Ballard, by a tendency to regress to atavistic barbarism. Disch's *334*, the finest novel in this group, shows how development and decay, progress and poverty, are mutually constitutive realities in an overpopulated Manhattan marked by stark divisions of age, race, and class. Mocking the utopian Brutalism of Le Corbusier and pulp-era science fiction, Disch's eponymous building, located at 334 East 11th Street, houses 3,000 tenants in 812 apartments on 21 floors, not counting the homeless who shelter on landings and staircases. Its elevators have long since ceased to function, isolating the elderly and infirm in their cheerless aeries, visited only by social welfare agents and slumming sociology students. Disch's sympathies are clearly with the struggling inhab-itants of this dreary urban maze, whose hard-scrabble lives are sketched with an admirable meticulousness and intensity.

The urban dystopias of the 1960s and 1970s also focused on the growing pollution and environmental degradation plaguing large metropolitan areas after decades of virtually unlimited industrial growth. As awareness of the effects of smog, acid rain, and pesticides entered public consciousness, dystopian authors used projections of extreme environmental catastrophe to urge readers to push for environmental reforms. In John Brunner's 1972 novel *The Sheep Look Up*, for example, inhabitants of Los Angeles and New York are required to wear disposable masks if they plan to spend any time outside, while oxygen is conveniently offered at diners and drugstores. Drug-resistant strains of common diseases are reaching epidemic proportions, and cases of enteritis are often fatal. The overuse of ever-stronger pesticides, herbicides, and fertilizers has caused an agricultural collapse, pollution-induced birth defects are commonplace, and child mortality rates are skyrocketing. As a result of all this, urban areas have become epicenters of illness, starvation, and death. As the novel moves through the span of a single year, the plagues caused by environmental degradation become progressively worse until the government declares martial law in order to quell the urban riots. The novel ends with the smoke from burning American cities wafting across the ocean to Ireland.

Growing public anxiety about the ecological costs of technological progress led not only to a series of political reforms – culminating in the United States with the formation of a federal Environmental Protection Agency in 1970 – but also to a rare postwar outburst of urban utopianism during the following decades. The most famous of the resulting fictions was undoubtedly Ernest Callenbach's *Ecotopia* (1975), the title referring to a flourishing commonwealth in the Pacific Northwest organized around principles of ecological conservation and long-term sustainability. The scenes set in San Francisco, the capital of this secessionist republic, depict a free-spirited city powered by solar energy, collectively owned factories, organic food, and marijuana. Indebted to Callenbach but more ambitious in its aims is Kim Stanley Robinson's *Pacific Edge* (1990), the third volume of a trilogy that depicts different prospective futures for Southern California. The second volume, *The Gold Coast* (1988), offers a dystopian take on the dire consequences of unchecked urban sprawl, but *Pacific Edge*, by contrast, suggests that community-oriented, environmentally conscious living is still possible, even in Orange County. In Robinson's utopian version, water rights are systematically returned to their original owners, forcing the state to limit growth and to conserve existing groundwater supplies. Automobiles have been gradually eliminated for short-distance use, and volunteer laborers are busy tearing out roads and removing unused shopping centers, gas stations, and strip malls. More technocratically inflected but no less hopeful in its vision is Frederik Pohl's novel *The Years of the City* (1984), which provides a detailed plan for reclaiming New York from decades of urban blight.

Yet this wave of ecotopian urbanism was more than counterbalanced during the 1980s and 1990s by a cascade of dystopian writing about the city that emanated from the motley assortment of authors grouped under the banner of cyberpunk. Although none of these writers ever produced a full-fledged urban dystopia, most of them evinced an abiding fascination for the darker side of cities, which they evoked with an edgy, hallucinatory disquietude. The sum total of these depictions amounts to one of the most powerful portrayals of urban decadence in contemporary literature, on par with mid-century noir fiction and film – an aesthetic that heavily influenced many of the cyberpunk writers. Cyberpunk is, in essence, a form of high-tech noir: like noir, it gravitates toward clandestine scenes and criminal subcultures, marginal milieus inhabited by con men, grifters, loners, and freaks. But cyberpunk's shady underclass is more likely to trade in black-market software and bootlegged human organs than in the traditional noir vices of gambling, drugs, and sex. Cyberpunk also owes a debt to the classic dystopias of Zamyatin and Orwell in its extrapolation of sinister forms of urban surveillance – a monitoring, amplified by pervasive information technologies that can extend directly into the psyche itself via virtual-reality interfaces and "wetware" devices (cranial implants, nerve grafts, etc.).

The paradigmatic cyberpunk novel is undoubtedly William Gibson's *Neuromancer* (1984), whose opening scenes convey in condensed form the dystopian urban imagination characteristic of the movement. Set in a section of Japan's Chiba City known among locals as "Night City," the story follows a freelance hacker through a sleazy enclave of bars, arcades, and "black clinics" – underground wetware labs that cater to desperate types. To the protagonist, Night City seems like some "deranged experiment in social Darwinism, designed by a bored researcher who kept one thumb permanently on the fast-forward button. Stop hustling and you sank without a trace, but move a little too swiftly and you'd break the fragile surface tension of the black market."[9] Other scenes set in "cyberspace" (a term coined by Gibson) portray a navigable virtual-reality mindscape whose representations of looming data banks resemble a city skyline; like Night City, cyberspace is dominated by furtive forms of commerce among vast mega-corporations and their shadowy proxies. Other cyberpunk writers have drawn similar portraits of corrupt urban settings: Richard Kadrey's *Metrophage* (1988), for instance, provides a vivid tour of louche street life in a futuristic Los Angeles twitching with neon and danger, while in John Shirley's *City Come A-Walkin'* (1980), punk-era San Francisco achieves a kind of cybernetic sentience as a cynical, manipulative puppet master. The most well-known dystopian city in the cyberpunk canon, however, is filmic: the dank, febrile Los Angeles in Ridley Scott's *Blade Runner* (1982).

An even more extravagant take on urban dystopia is provided by an off-shoot of cyberpunk that has swiftly eclipsed its progenitor: steampunk. At least in its literary incarnations (it is also a mode of fashion and design), steampunk extrapolates retro-futuristic or alternative-historical technologies, as with William Gibson and Bruce Sterling's depiction of nineteenth-century steam-driven computers in *The Difference Engine* (1990). Many of the key texts of this subgenre – K. W. Jeter's *Infernal Devices* (1987), James P. Blaylock's *Lord Kelvin's Machine* (1992), China Miéville's *Perdido Street Station* (2000) – are set in an imaginary version of Victorian London, a brooding Gothic metropolis seething with weird new technologies. Miéville, a preeminent urban fantasist, is also the author of *The City & The City* (2009), a novel featuring twin Central European cities that somehow occupy the same physical space but are separated by socioeconomic and cultural traditions; to grow up in one involves the systematic "unsensing" of the other, a process that must be learned and ruthlessly self-policed.[10] Drawing equally on the *roman noir* and Kafka, the novel – like all of Miéville's work – evokes the city as a haunted place, a nexus of puzzling legends and half-told histories, wrong turns and spooky culs-de-sac, whose abiding mystery can never be fully dispelled.

Over the past three decades, cyberpunk and steampunk have generated some of the most compelling and influential images of dystopian urban spaces. They have also echoed – and in many cases inspired – work in other genres, especially in Japan, where the serialized comics known as *manga* are often set in bleak future versions of Tokyo. The most famous urban dystopia in Japanese manga is undoubtedly Katsuhiro Otomo's *Akira*, originally published in *Young Magazine* from 1982 until 1990; an *anime* film version appeared in 1988. *Akira* begins with the advent of World War III, which is instigated by the apparent nuclear devastation of Tokyo in 1992. The remainder of the story is set within the post-apocalyptic island city of Neo-Tokyo, against a backdrop of teen biker gangs and psychically gifted government pawns, with Otomo deploying hyperbolic images of disaffected youth, political intrigue, military aggression, and technology run amok to mount a powerful critique of contemporary Japanese society. Otomo's vivid and hallucinatory work set the tone for future dystopian manga, including Masamune Shirow's *Appleseed* (1985–9) and *Ghost in the Shell* (1989–90), both of which have strong flavors of cyberpunk. In the west, many of the better urban dystopias of the 1980s also took the form of graphic narratives: Alan Moore's ten-issue comic series *V for Vendetta* (1982–9) imagines a future London suffering under a repressive totalitarian government, while

Frank Miller's *Batman: The Dark Knight Returns* (1986) depicts a grim near-future Gotham City plagued by crime and wanton violence.

Yet despite these popular successes, the urban dystopia as a distinct form has palpably declined, at least by comparison with the outpouring of material during the immediate postwar decades. Ironically, this may be a consequence of the form's success: in essence, many of the basic elements of the urban dystopia have been disseminated throughout the body of contemporary literature, becoming a portable assemblage of aesthetic and ideological properties that can be incorporated into all manner of texts. Most literate people know what is meant by an "Orwellian atmosphere" or a "Ballardian landscape" or a "cyberpunk future" even if they have never read *Nineteen Eighty-Four* or *High-Rise* or *Neuromancer*. Moreover, the widespread experience of postwar urban life *as* dystopian has made the depiction of dark, foreboding, or oppressive cities in literature a matter of straightforward realism rather than an imaginative projection of a disturbing future. After more than a century of predicting the direst of possibilities, the urban dystopia is now hard pressed to find a darker vision than that evoked by the modern-day realities of shantytowns, dying downtown centers, and unchecked suburban sprawl.

NOTES

1 Edmund Boisgilbert [Ignatius Donnelly], *Caesar's Column: A Story of the Twentieth Century* (Chicago: Schulte, 1890), p. 40.

2 Nikolai Chernyshevsky, *What Is to Be Done?* Trans. Michael R. Katz (Ithaca, NY: Cornell University Press, 1989), p. 370.

3 Yevgeny Zamyatin, *We*, trans. Clarence Brown (New York: Penguin, 1993), pp. 12–13.

4 Le Corbusier, *The City of To-morrow and Its Planning*, trans. Frederick Etchells (Cambridge, MA: MIT Press, 1986), p. 178. *The Radiant City* appeared in 1935.

5 Robert Fishman develops this idea in *Urban Utopias in the Twentieth Century: Ebenezer Howard, Frank Lloyd Wright, Le Corbusier* (Cambridge, MA: MIT Press, 1989), p. 263. On Le Corbusier's relation to Fascism, see Simone Brott, "*Architecture et révolution*: Le Corbusier and the Fascist Revolution," *Thresholds* 41 (2013), 146–57.

6 Laurence Manning and Fletcher Pratt, "The City of the Living Dead," in Donald A. Wollheim and George Ernsberger, eds., *The 2nd Avon Fantasy Reader* (New York: Avon, 1969), p. 151. This story expands on E. M. Forster's pioneering critique of a seeming utopia of machine-guided leisure "The Machine Stops" (1909).

7 J. G. Ballard, "Billenium," *The Complete Stories of J. G. Ballard* (New York: Norton, 2009), pp. 274–5.

8 Ballard, *High-Rise* (New York: Popular Library, 1978), p. 13.

9 William Gibson, *Neuromancer* (New York: Ace, 1984), p. 7.

10 China Miéville, *The City & The City* (New York: Del Rey, 2009), p. 65.

13

NICK BENTLEY

Postmodern Cities

The opening shots of *Blade Runner*, Ridley Scott's 1982 film adaptation of
Philip K. Dick's novel *Do Androids Dream of Electric Sheep?* (1968) have
come to epitomize the postmodern city. Despite depicting a future world
where corporations have replaced governments and advertising has merged
with art, the towering and technological splendor of this late capitalist panorama offers its own kind of utopian beauty. The subsequent series of scenes
at street level, however, mark out the dystopian travails of the overcrowded,
Babelish populace in a permanent atmospheric gloom pierced only by flickering artificial light. Scott's film recalls an older filmic image of the city, Fritz
Lang's *Metropolis*, in which a similar dialectic of the utopian aerial view
and the dystopian lower levels is produced. In Lang's case, Metropolis, the
project of the city's architect and creator, dehumanizes and mechanizes its
inhabitants, whose labor is marshaled to maintain the privileged lifestyle of
an elite. If Lang's film can be identified in terms of a Marxist dystopia of
dehumanized labor, then Scott's vision is of a more ambivalent cacophony
of late capitalist images and simulacra.

The novelists discussed in this chapter deal with this vision of a vertigi-
nous, consumerist urban landscape in their representations of the postmodern city. For some of these writers, particularly Paul Auster, Orhan Pamuk,
Jorge Luis Borges, and Italo Calvino, the postmodern metropolis represents
a labyrinthine enigma that metaphorically stands in for the dizzying plurality of contemporary urban living. For others, it is the physical manifestation
of a culture of consumerist excess and bears the traces of earlier images of
the modernist metropolis in which an implicit critique of contemporary culture is manifest alongside the dehumanizing effects of hyper-urban living.
Postmodernism embraces ambiguity, however, and the image one gets from
the urban environment in writers such as Martin Amis, J. G. Ballard, Bret
Easton Ellis, and Chuck Palahniuk is a mixture of attraction and repulsion;
this ambivalence makes their cities darkly exotic and alluring, fascinated,
as those writers are, with the darker aspects of human psychology. A third

strand of writing on the postmodern metropolis emphasizes the city as a palimpsest of histories and narratives evoked in the psyche of the observer – the postmodern flâneur or flâneuse who attempts to disentangle its multiplicity of texts. This overlaying of multiple cities can be seen in the work of Haruki Murakami, Peter Ackroyd, Will Self, and Iain Sinclair. The latter three authors incorporate an interest in psychogeography into their fictional worlds, an approach also adopted by Doris Lessing and Angela Carter, who in addition to presenting mythical and emotional visions of the city, also introduce a concern with the way urban geographies are gendered.

While fictional representations often emphasize postmodern cities as disorienting, labyrinthine dystopias, this is certainly not true in other fields. In architecture – one of the disciplines that established postmodernism as a theoretical concept – postmodernism is often perceived (not unproblematically) as a utopian release from the debilitating, homogenizing effects of modernist architecture's rationalized cityscapes as exemplified in Le Corbusier's *Radiant City* (1935). In this account, postmodern architectural and planning practice is sensitive to the local needs of eventual users and combines a popular playfulness with responsiveness to the cultural locality of buildings. As Kevin Robins writes, "The postmodern city is then about an attempt to re-imagine urbanity: about recovering a lost sense of territorial identity, urban community and public space," although, as he notes, it cannot evade the pressures of consumerist economics and has even been accused of capitulating to it.[1] The cultural geographer David Harvey has stressed the unplanned and spontaneous nature of the postmodern city by evoking modernist tropes of the metropolis as unpredictable and potentially dangerous, where crime is rife and the darker human desires find release.[2] Other postmodern theorists have rendered this idea of the city's uncontrollable nature in a metaphor of the metropolis as a cybernetic organism. Charles Jencks, for example, talks of "fractal cities" that develop through a perpetual change of structure and shape and survive by jettisoning dead tissue in order for new growth to emerge. Jenks sutures a Darwinian rhetoric of natural selection with a focus on rapid technological change to produce a model in which the city ebbs and flows according to undiscoverable laws of fractal geometry.[3] This version of the postmodern metropolis exceeds the idea of a utopian vision and replaces it with a more ambivalent descriptive, rather than prescriptive, model of city development.

Many postmodern novelists have inherited aspects of the modernists' vision of the urban metropolis as an atomistic and fragmented space. The trope of an unsettling urban landscape experienced by an alienated observer is taken up in much postmodernist fiction, although the detached modernist flâneur is often replaced by a character intent on gorging on metropolitan excesses. This is especially true of Martin Amis's main protagonists in what has become known as his London trilogy of novels: *Money: A Suicide Note* (1984), *London Fields* (1989), and *The Information* (1995). Each of them presents an image of the urban metropolis as a sinister space in which a culture of excessive consumption and extreme behavior has become the norm. Amis's vision of the city is a component of his broader rhetoric of the decline of the west (and Britain in particular) in the late twentieth century. In *Money*, the representation of the postmodern city is split between London and New York, the former representing an environment that appears tired and exhausted, the latter pandering to the shiny barbarism of strip clubs and drinking dens: "On masculine Madison (tightly buttoned, like a snooker waistcoat) I took my left and headed north into the infinite trap of air. Cars and cabs swore loudly at each other, looking for trouble, ready to fight, to confront. And here are the streets and their outlandish personnel. Here are the street artists."[4] The aggressive urban streets initially appear to be the ideal location for the novel's narrator and antihero, John Self, a British filmmaker who made his reputation (such as it is) with commercials. Self is the epitome of a 1980s culture of conspicuous and onanistic excess; he wallows in an environment, epitomized in the novel by Manhattan, in which money is the driving force for all aspects of behavior: "Heat, money, sex, and fever – this is it, this is New York, this is first class, this is the sharp end."[5] In contrast to New York, London is represented in a state of terminal decline: "In summer, London is an old man with bad breath. If you listen, you can hear the sob of weariness catching in his lungs. Unlovely London. Even the name holds heavy stress."[6] Amis's London is filled with dark pubs and shady characters under an ominous sky that threatens millennial catastrophe. This distinction between the two cities in many ways represents a modernist/postmodernist dialectic: Britain's moribund capital is superseded by the emergent lure of New York for this lover of excess.

The new may well be a shock for Amis, but it is far from being celebrated. The critique of postmodernity can also been seen in J. G. Ballard's final novel, *Kingdom Come* (2006). Ballard's approach is to present the contemporary world as a near-future dystopia that offers a defamiliarized observation of everyday urban realities. His fictional worlds are not quite Michel Foucault's heterotopias – real spaces imbued with imaginary ideals – but more like "heterodystopias." At the beginning of the novel the main protagonist and narrator, Richard Pearson, travels by car to one of London's suburban towns, traversing a landscape that is at once devoid of real humanity and filled with threatening technological paraphernalia: "I was moving through a terrain of inter-urban sprawl, a geography of sensory deprivation ... Warning displays alerted each other, and the entire landscape was coded for danger. CCTV cameras crouched over warehouse gates, and filter-left signs pulsed tirelessly, pointing to the sanctuaries of high-security science parks."[7] In this description of the interstitial spaces of the postmodern metropolis, the culture of surveillance results in the absence of actual humans from the environment. This unsettling vision of metropolitan sprawl is contrasted with what at first seems to be the utopian vision of the shopping mall, represented in the novel by the Metro-Centre:

> Like all great shopping malls, the Metro-Centre smothered unease, defused its own threat and offered balm to the weary. I stood in the sunshine fifty yards from the south gate entrance, watching the shoppers cross the wide apron that surrounded the mall... In a few moments they would be bathed in a light more healing than anything on offer from the sun. As we entered these huge temples we became young again, like children visiting the home of a new schoolfriend.[8]

However, when Pearson probes beyond the surface of the Metro-Centre, he discovers a society bubbling with violence and what one of the characters describes as a "soft fascism" in which the overly stultified populace dream of (and are beginning to enact) outbursts of violence to alleviate the restraint placed on them by an all-encompassing consumerist desire: "All malls subtly infantilized us, but the Metro-Centre showed signs of urging us to grow up a little. Uniformed stewards stood by the entrance, checking bags and purses, a response to the tragedy in which my father had died. An elderly Asian couple approached the entrance, and were quickly surrounded by volunteers in St. George's shirts."[9] Commodity fetishism has reached a peak in Ballard's vision and becomes a quasi-religious narcotic. The novel dramatizes the resistance to pacification in its description of the populace's desire for acts of violence, what the novel's radical psychologist terms "elected psychopathy."[10] Ballard's style of inner-space fiction links these psychological effects on an urban population out of synch with the rapidly advancing techno-consumerism with the theories of the postmodern city put forward by Fredric Jameson, according to which

> we ourselves, the human subjects who happen into this new space, have not kept pace with that evolution; ... we do not possess perceptual equipment to match this new hyperspace, as I will call it, ... and we need to grow new organs to expand our sensorium and our body to some new, as yet unimaginable, perhaps ultimately impossible, dimensions.[11]

This image of the cloying psychological effects of consumer-led, metropolitan living is also a feature of two important American novels of the 1990s: Chuck Palahniuk's *Fight Club* (1996) and Bret Easton Ellis's *American Psycho* (1991). In *Fight Club*, the unnamed narrator lives in a world regulated by white-collar work practices that, although they provide the means to furnish his domesticity with the latest Ikea furniture, are ultimately psychologically debilitating. To escape the banality of his existence, he becomes involved in the fight club of the title, in which a group of men with similar lifestyles engage in underground fights in an attempt to reengage with the masculinity effaced by contemporary living. Tyler Durden, who organizes the club, epitomizes this desire for renewed physicality and danger, but only toward the end of the novel does the reader realize that Durden is a projected fantasy of the main character, revealing a psychotic split and wish fulfillment as an antidote to the banality of living in the postmodern city. *American Psycho* offers a similar narrative of violence as a way of coping with the pacifying effects of postmodern lifestyles. Ellis's novel traces the experiences of serial killer and psychopath Patrick Bateman in a world of young male executives where a sharp fashion sensibility and being seen in the most fashionable Manhattan restaurants with the right "hard-bodied" women is paramount. Postmodern identity is a "moveable feast," as Stuart Hall has defined it, and in Ellis's novel, the clone-like young corporate executives seem to meld into each other:

> "That's not Morrison," Price says.
> "Who is it then?" Preston asks, taking his glasses off again.
> "That's Paul Owen," Price says.
> "That's not Paul Owen," I say. "Paul Owen's on the other side of the bar. Over there."[12]

Because identity is located in income and appearances, not in individuality, it is interchangeable across individual human units, and names become transferrable ciphers. However, as with *Fight Club*, the ontological framework of Ellis's text is complicated by an uncertainty about what is real and what is a projection of Bateman's imagination. The possibility is thus raised in the text that the serial murders and sexual abuse Bateman undertakes are wish-fulfilling fantasies rather than actual violence.

In both of these texts, the ontological status of the characters and the worlds they populate are repeatedly questioned. In this sense they correspond to Brian McHale's definition of postmodern fiction as texts in which "epistemology is backgrounded, as the price for foregrounding ontology."[13] McHale cites science fiction as the paradigmatic form for postmodern fiction in contrast with the epistemological modernity of the detective novel, and several writers explore the limits of detective fiction as a way of signaling a postmodern concern with the limits of the Enlightenment project's rational epistemology. Paul Auster's novella "City of Glass," part of his *New York Trilogy* (1985–6), is perhaps the most representative example of this pushing of the detective novel beyond its limits. The text establishes the detective scenario when Quinn, the main character, receives a wrong-number telephone call in the middle of the night that initiates a desire to discover its meaning. However, the novel goes on to parody the drive of conventional detective fiction by repeatedly slipping between narratives in which the desire to discover withers away as another set of circumstances begins to preoccupy Quinn. It moves the reader from a convention in which epistemological knowledge is the imperative to an examination of the onto-logical nature of contemporary urban existence. This is hinted at in the first paragraph: "The question is the story itself, and whether or not it means something is not for the story to tell."[14] Meaning is thus demoted in favor of the action of storytelling itself. However, to reach this position Quinn first has to reject his previous conviction that the detective, like the writer, "is one who looks, who listens, who moves through the morass of objects and events in search of thought, the idea that will pull all these things together and make sense of them."[15] At one point, Quinn tries to find meaning in the apparently arbitrary by tracing the movements of Stillman, a character he follows around the New York streets. Stillman appears to be wandering in a random fashion; however, as Quinn traces his movements on a map of the city, he becomes convinced that Stillman's peripatetic journeys inscribe a pattern. When traced out over several days they appear to spell out "Tower of Babel." This is found to be Quinn's own imposition of an ordering frame-work, but the Babelian myth is obviously significant in that it gestures not toward clarity but to confusion and misunderstanding. New York itself is seen to be a spatial and temporal entity of such complexity that it resists rational explanation. As Stillman informs Quinn:

> The whole city is a junk heap. It suits my purpose admirably. I find the streets an endless source of material, an inexhaustible storehouse of shattered things. Each day I go out with my bag and collect objects that seem worthy of inves-tigation. My samples now number in the hundreds – from the chipped to the smashed, from the dented to the squashed, from the pulverized to the putrid.[16]

When asked what he does with these things, Stillman replies, "I give them names." This attempt to impose some kind of meaningful order on the amorphous complexity of New York existence is ultimately frustrated, as is every attempt to identify fixed meaning in the text. The novel in this sense dramatizes Jacques Derrida's poststructuralist theory about the way language operates as a system of endless deferral without the possibility of reaching a fixed point of meaning. In his 1968 essay "Difference," Derrida writes, "Within a language, within a *system* of language, there are only differences... The use of language or the employment of any code which implies a play of forms – with no determined or invariable substratum – also presupposes a retention and protention of differences, a spacing and temporalizing, a play of traces."[17]

The idea of a "play of traces" is also taken up in Orhan Pamuk's novel *The Black Book* (1990), which offers a representation of Istanbul as a city that defies fixed meaning in its constantly shifting narrative contexts. Like "City of Glass," Pamuk's novel is presented as a kind of detective story focused on the search by the central character, Galip, for his wife Rüya who has unexpectedly disappeared, leaving him a brief note and a confusing telephone call. Galip suspects that his wife is with his uncle Celâl, a famous Istanbul journalist who has also mysteriously disappeared. The text is divided between details of Galip's search for his wife and uncle, and extracts from Celâl's journalism, which ponders political, social, and philosophical questions. As with Auster, however, the novel deconstructs the epistemological logic upon which traditional detective narratives rely, and its use of shifting identities, copies, and doubles renders Istanbul as an imaginary space. This is presented most effectively in a scene in which Galip describes being given a tour of an underground mannequin museum in which the real city appears to be replicated and populated by copies of the people aboveground. This scene culminates in Galip confronting a mannequin version of Celâl, a simulacrum that evades the recovery of the real, just as the text itself resists the discovery of the meaning behind Rüya's disappearance and, by extrapolation, of Istanbul itself.

For Auster and Pamuk, then, the city becomes the ideal metaphoric landscape for the resistance to meaning and fixed grounding reflected in postmodern and poststructuralist thought. The urban landscape as a labyrinthine conundrum that exceeds the possibility of a determining order is a feature of the work of two other writers who have been highly influential for later postmodern novelists, Jorge Luis Borges and Italo Calvino. The stories collected in Borges's *Labyrinths* (1962) are not necessarily representations of cities per se, but in "The Library of Babel" (1941) the library becomes a metaphor for contemporary urban living. The library, in fact, represents the whole world, and knowledge becomes an endlessly deferred system in which people play out their lives seeking facts that are never fixed. Borges's library has become a seductive metaphor for a poststructuralist model of language and an implicit critique of the search for knowledge at the heart of modernity. The city as text is also an important aspect of Calvino's work. In *Invisible Cities* (1972), Calvino presents a series of fantastical cities whose appearance depends upon the point of view from which they are observed. In "Cities and Desire 3," for example, alternative perspectives produce completely different images of the city of Despina: when viewed by a camel driver approaching it by land, it resembles a ship, whereas a sailor arriving from the sea "discerns the form of a camel's withers." As Calvino explains, "each city receives its form from the desert it opposes."[18] Calvino's *If on a Winter's Night a Traveller* (1979) metafictionally refers to its own status as a work of fiction and traces the development of the narrative alongside the story itself, although it is probably more accurate to say that the conception and the telling of the story are what the narrative is about, as much as the characters and events it introduces. "The city outside there has no name yet, we don't know if it will remain outside the novel or whether the whole story will be contained in its inky blackness."[19] The constructed nature of the fictional city is itself foregrounded; however, the link is made to the sense of the ubiquity of contemporary urban existence: "there are no provincial cities anymore and perhaps there never were; all places communicate instantly with all other places, a sense of isolation is felt only during the trip between one place and the other, that is, when you are in no place."[20]

The descent of darkness plays an important function in José Saramago's novel *Blindness* (1995), which describes a city in which loss of sight suddenly becomes contagious and the authorities are forced to implement increasingly repressive measures in an attempt to contain it. Blindness thus becomes both an affliction for a marginalized group and a subversive threat to the prevailing ideologies of the urban environment. As blindness begins to spread throughout the city, the essence of the human condition is etched in acts of altruism and cruelty. Saramago's novel is a remarkable book that replicates the way in which space is rendered in fiction. The focus on the inability to see, and the consequent necessity of the characters to develop their imaginative understanding of their surroundings, replicates the act of reading about physical space itself. Cities and all spaces in novels, of course, remain invisible in the material sense, and the emotional response to location thus invited in the act of reading fiction is foregrounded in the conceit of Saramago's novel.

Japanese writer Haruki Murakami also renders contemporary cities as worlds whose corporeal solidity appears to falter as we encounter increasingly unlikely situations and characters. In *1Q84* (2009–10), two slightly altered cities coexist, one of which is accessed by the central character, Aoname, when she leaves a taxi stuck in a traffic jam on an elevated highway and climbs a service ladder to the street below. This action of descending into the pedestrian environment appears to land her in an alternative version of the city in which events of the past have been slightly altered, emphasizing the constructed nature of both the metropolis and the experience of living in it. It is never clear which of the city's appearances is the real one, despite the taxi-driver's invocation, "don't let appearances fool you. There is always only one reality."²¹ *1Q84*, and Murakami's fiction generally, is in the business of rejecting that belief.

The sense of dual cities overlaying each other recalls David Harvey's description of the postmodern city as "necessarily fragmented, a 'palimpsest' of past forms superimposed upon each other, and a 'collage' of current uses."²² This idea is pursued in the psychogeographies of writers such as Peter Ackroyd, Iain Sinclair, and Will Self, who have focused on representations of real and imaginary Londons. Self has described psychogeographers as "disciples of Guy Debord and those rollicking Situationists who tottered, soused, across the stage set of 1960s Paris" and share an understanding of the city that is "concerned with the personality of place itself." In a writer like Peter Ackroyd, Self argues, "while the physical and political structure of London may have mutated down the ages, as torrents of men and women have coursed through its streets, yet their individuality is as nothing, set beside the city's own enduring personification."²³ This kind of historical, palimpsestic city can be seen in Ackroyd's *The House of Doctor Dee* (1993), in which a fantastical exchange is carried out between the novel's two storylines; one set in the late twentieth century, the other in the sixteenth century. In Self's own novel, *How the Dead Live* (2000), ghosts continue to haunt the capital carrying on lives that parallel those they had lived before they died. In *The Book of Dave* (2006), Self pushes the idea of an alternative fantasy London into a future society in which the people worship Dave, who we discover in the alternating contemporary narrative is/was a twenty-first-century taxi-driver called Dave Rudman. This narrative setup allows Self to offer a critique of contemporary London by defamiliarizing the contemporary in the futuristic alternative. In The Year of Our Dave 523 the city has been flooded, leaving the region around West Ham in East London an island whose inhabitants find relics of the twenty-first-century world in the form of pieces of plastic that they call "Daveworks," which they imbue with spiritual value. Experts on hand distinguish between real and "toyist" or fake Daveworks. In the contemporary narrative, we learn that "toyist" is the word Dave uses with his young son Carl to describe the preponderance of fake architecture and city furniture they observe in a post-Thatcher London:

> on bad days almost everything could be toyist: the Bloomberg VDU on the corner of North End Road was an outsized Game Boy, the flaring torch outside the new Marriot Hotel at Gloucester Road a lit match. The buildings themselves were so many CD towers and hair-styling wands, while people walked the street with the jerky motion of puppets, visible strings lifting Styrofoam cups to their painted lips.²⁴

Contemporary London is presented as a Baudrillardian simulacrum in which the fakery of the environment begins to affect its inhabitants. Dave is revered because of his mastery of the Knowledge, the awareness London cab drivers need to find their way around the labyrinthine metropolis; as Dave explains in a section of internal monologue: "*I know it all – I hold it all. If all of this were swamped, taken out by a huge fucking flood, who'd be able to tell you what it was like? Not the fucking Mayor or the Prime Minister – that's for sure. But me, an 'umble cabbie.*" In a recurring postmodern trope, however, Dave's epistemological power is threatened by the ontological inevitability of his demise: "*Now I understand that I learned this city to hold in my mind for a while – then lose it to my boy. Without him it's starting to disappear.*"[25] Dave's knowledge is transformed into the religious frameworks followed by the "Hamsters" in 325 AD ("After Dave" – an ironic reference to the year of the Council of Nicea, which established the first Christian doctrine). However, Dave's ideas have been warped into a grand narrative of social control. The future narrative follows the exploits of Carl, a distant descendent of Dave, who attempts to rebel against the authorities.

The palimpsestic city is also a feature of Iain Sinclair's style of urban psychogeography, which combines postmodern narrative techniques with a critique of Thatcherite economics. In his 1991 novel *Downriver*, Sinclair describes a fragmented London of differing worlds some real, some fantastical: "Mother London herself was splitting into segments, the overlicked shell of a chocolate tortoise. Piggy hands grabbed the numbered counters from the table. The occult logic of 'market forces' dictated a new geography."[26] It falls to "Iain Sinclair," the narrator, to disentangle and decipher these interstitial spaces in his attempt to offer a route through the labyrinthine city. However, the narrator is often lost: "the townscape would not settle into any recognizable pattern. Disturbingly, everything was almost familiar – but from the wrong period. I was navigating with a map whose symbols had been perversely shifted to some arcane and impenetrable system."[27] As in Michel de Certeau's model of voyeurs – whose elevated position provides an Icarus-like view of the city that renders it readable – and walkers in the Daedalus labyrinth below – whose experience of its streets at close quarters allows the perspective to shift between multiple points of view and produce emotive representations of the city – walking the city does not equate to discovering meaning. It becomes an activity akin to writing, one that constructs an imagined landscape from the "arcane and impenetrable" semiotic fragments bombarding the urban wanderer.[28]

The psychogeography undertaken by Ackroyd, Self, and Sinclair recalls the theoretical model of urban postmodern geography propounded by Edward Soja, who calls for an extension of Marxist theory to include a socio-spatial dialectic because spatiality is not a fact but a cultural discourse that reveals present and historical power relationships.²⁹ Drawing in particular on the work of Henri Lefebvre and on Michel Foucault's theory of heterotopias, Soja's revision effectively produces a "trialectic" of history, space, and social discourse in which space is understood as a combination of the physical and the conceptual or discursive. For these theorists, the development of social space is bound up with the discourses of cultural politics. One effect of this focus, as Doreen Massey has pointed out, is that both urban space and postmodern theory and criticism show a masculine gender bias and disregard for the concerns of feminist criticism.³⁰ The writers discussed in this chapter thus far, for example, are all male. This gendering of city spaces is taken up by Deborah Parsons, who in her excellent book *Streetwalking the Metropolis* (2000) identifies the ways in which the city has often been a place of exclusion for women, and how certain women writers have addressed gender inequality by placing women in urban locations and offering alternative and potentially radical visions of the urban landscape from a position that takes gender politics into account. Parsons discusses in this context Doris Lessing's *The Four-Gated City* (1969), the last volume in her *Children of Violence* sequence, which moves formally from a broadly realist mode toward fantasy and inner-space fiction. The central character, Martha Quest, is initially presented as a modernist flâneuse in 1950s London, but later the text projects a future city in which a utopian ideal is curbed by increased fragmentation of social class; the four gates of the title represent the walled-off ideology of contemporary urban living.

Angela Carter is another postwar British writer conscious of the way in which the postmodern city is represented as a space of male construction and female objectification. In *The Passion of New Eve* (1977), the central character Evelyn, like John Self in Amis's *London Fields*, moves from London to New York and finds a city in which gendered identity is performed and ultimately becomes untethered from conventional associations: "Nothing in my experience had prepared me for the city... I imagined a clean, hard bright city where towers reared to the sky in a paradigm of technological aspiration... But in New York, I found instead of hard edges and clean colours, a lurid, Gothic darkness that closed over my head completely."³¹ The city, here, is clearly expressed in gendered terms distinguishing between the masculine image Evelyn expects and the feminized gothic space he finds. New York is represented as the first step in the gendered trajectory of the text as a whole, as Evelyn is eventually forced to have a sex change and then becomes the new Eve of the title. Within this narrative of fluid gender and sexual identity, Carter is able to interrogate the ways in which contemporary society constructs demarcated codes of behavior for men and women, and simultaneously to project the possibility of an alternative gender ideology.

In many of the works discussed in this chapter, the postmodern city is defined in terms of the narrative experience of both its material and imaginative spaces. The point of observation thus complicates any fixed definition of the urban. Fiction is a privileged form in this context as it allows for the manipulation of point of view through the deployment of partial and plural narrative perspectives. The complexity of contemporary urban space is thereby rendered in the postmodern novel through a pluralization of space, time, and social discourse, while the alienated modernist observer is replaced by multiple perspectives that produce heterogeneous representations of the city.

NOTES

1 Kevin Robins, "Prisoners of the City: Whatever Could a Postmodern City Be?" *Space and Place: Theories of Identity and Location* (London: Lawrence & Wishart), p. 304.

2 David Harvey, *The Condition of Postmodernity* (Oxford: Blackwell, 1990).

3 Charles Jencks, "The City that Never Sleeps," *New Statesman*, June 28, 1996, 26–8.

4 Martin Amis, *Money: A Suicide Note* (London: Jonathan Cape, 1984), p. 19.

5 Ibid., p. 49.

6 Ibid., p. 85.

7 J. G. Ballard, *Kingdom Come* (London: Fourth Estate, 2006), p. 6.

8 Ibid., p. 37.

9 Ibid.

10 Ibid., p. 103.

11 Fredric Jameson, "Postmodernism and Consumer Society," in E. Ann Kaplan, ed., *Postmodernism and Its Discontents* (London: Verso, 1988), p. 20.

12 Stuart Hall, "Introduction: Identity in Question," in Stuart Hall, David Held, and Tony McGrew, eds., *Modernity and Its Futures* (Cambridge: Polity Press, 1992), p. 277; Bret Easton Ellis, *American Psycho* (London: Picador, 1998), p. 35.

13 Brian McHale, *Postmodernist Fiction* (London: Routledge, 1987), p. 11.

14 Paul Auster, *The City of Glass Trilogy* (London: Faber, 1987), p. 3.

15 Ibid., p. 8.

16 Ibid., p. 78

17 Jacques Derrida, "Differance," *Speech and Phenomena: And Other Essays on Husserl's Theory of Signs*, trans. David B. Allison (Evanston, IL: Northwestern University Press, 1973), pp. 140–6.

18 Italo Calvino, *Invisible Cities*, trans. William Weaver (London: Vintage, 1997), pp. 14–15.

19 Calvino, *If on a Winter's Night a Traveller*, trans. William Weaver (London: Secker & Warburg 1981), p. 14.

20 Ibid., p. 17.

21 Haruki Murakami, *1Q84: Books One and Two*, trans. Jay Rubin (London: Vintage, 2012), p. 12.

22 Harvey, *Condition of Postmodernity*, p. 66.

23 Will Self, *Psychogeography* (London: Bloomsbury, 2007), p. 11.

24 Self, *The Book of Dave* (London: Viking, 2006), p. 47.

25 Ibid., p. 33 (italics in the original).

26 Iain Sinclair, *Downriver* (London: Vintage, 1995), p. 265.

27 Ibid., p. 51.

28 Michel de Certeau, *The Practice of Everyday Life*, trans. Steven F. Rendall (Berkeley: University of California Press, 1984), pp. 92–3.

29 Edward W. Soja, *Postmodern Geographies: The Reassertion of Space in Critical Social Theory* (London: Verso, 1989), pp. 76–93.

30 Doreen Massey, *Space, Place and Gender* (Cambridge: Polity Press), 1994.

31 Angela Carter, *The Passion of New Eve* (London: Virago, 1985), p. 10.

14

SETH GRAEBNER

Colonial Cities

Colonization is a centuries-old phenomenon, as the spread of Greek civilization throughout the Mediterranean demonstrates. The modern period of European colonization from the 1500s onward was global in scale, affecting European cities like Dublin and Prague, as well as cities on other continents. Overseas colonization has always produced very distinctive cities, as it has also transformed imperial metropoles through migration and trade. The distinctiveness of colonial cities persisted through the nineteenth and early twentieth centuries; the strangeness of earlier colonial cities (e.g., Goa, Mexico City, New York, or Salvador da Bahia) has merely worn off with the passage of time. French and British imperial colonialisms, which reached their apex at the turn of the twentieth century, tended to emphasize separation of ethnic and racial communities, often with consequences still visible today. While generalizations are thus possible across centuries, continents, and colonial administrations, the literature of colonial cities is deeply textured by differences of local culture and history that surpass the expertise of any single scholar and the scope of a single essay.

This chapter will focus on cities in the literature of authors living in North and West Africa, mostly writing in French, during the periods of colonization and struggle for independence. It concentrates on passages that actually describe urban settings or institutions, even though one might focus on such phenomena as modern trade, crowds, or anonymity. Attention to descriptions of the physical environment has the advantage of allowing readers to make connections with the other phenomena of urban life, all of which are influenced by the nature of the urban built environment. Much of the African literary canon might not strike casual readers as primarily concerned with, or situated in, cities – a notion reinforced by the litany of painful news from Africa in the world's media, which often focuses on rural tragedies. It therefore bears repeating that despite a relatively small population for its size (just more than a billion people living in 30 million square kilometers, an area bigger than China, India, Europe, and the continental United States combined), Africa has had cities for centuries, even if they have not always figured in literature in the way that the European example would lead one to expect.[1] Today, despite the well-known difficulties of intra-African travel, a broadening class of urbanized Africans views regional and transcontinental travel as a natural part of modern city life, while the Internet and recent political developments have also connected African cities in ways much more immediate than previously.

Moreover, these cities did not all originate under European rule, even if some of the largest (Lagos, Abidjan, Casablanca) owe the origins of their current organization to the period of colonial rule. In addition to its well-known portrayals of rural or village life, African fiction has developed an urban consciousness visible from the origins of modern literature on the continent. While much criticism of African novels has focused on what critics have called a struggle between "tradition" and "modernity," attention to the urban concerns of these texts moves readers beyond such limited notions. City life now has a long history in Africa, and the cultural and literary forms arising from it are neither traditional nor modern in the usual sense, but simply urban and contemporary, in ways that depend on their individual contexts.

The colonial establishment of "civil lines," *quartiers indigènes* or *européens* ("native" or European quarters), or "cantonments," at times separated by walls and unbuilt areas, has frequently left traces in the urban fabric of the cities involved. As a result of recent expansion in Rabat, Morocco (to choose one of the most extreme and frequently commented examples), a very large portion of the population lives and works in areas unaffected by the policies of colonial-era urbanism. The centers of many other cities in North and West Africa still show clear evidence of pre-colonial neighborhoods that were preserved and marked as "traditional" or "Arab" by colonial authorities. These older districts stand in stark contrast to the modern business and administrative districts alongside them, whose layouts are familiar to anyone who knows Paris or Washington, DC. Although this essay will focus on writers "native" to colonial cities, or at least to the countries in which those cities were built, writers from elsewhere also noted the bifurcated nature of colonial urban development: in Morocco, the French arch-exoticists Pierre Loti in *Au Maroc [Morocco]* (1890) and Jérome and Jean Tharaud in *Fez, ou les Bourgeois de l'Islam [Fez or the Bourgeois of Islam]* (1930) devoted a good deal of their urban descriptions to this very phenomenon.

Elsewhere in Africa, colonizers produced similar effects, if only by concentrating their money and administration on zones they built for themselves alongside African-inhabited population centers. With the exception of the British in Zanzibar, the French in Morocco and Tunisia were virtually the only colonizers who were at least partly motivated by a desire to preserve what they found "picturesque" about the already existing cities. Racial segregation was almost always high on the list of priorities for colonial urbanists. Yet segregation did not always occur in quite the way that either theorists of racial inequality or urban planners imagined that it would. First not every colonial city actually had a consistently functioning planning authority, or one that actually had the power to carry out its policies. Second, a number of areas in even the most segregated cities tended to escape the effects of segregationist policy, whether through neglect or resistance (active or passive) by inhabitants.[2] Third, some cities were simply too complex or contained too much preexisting construction for any colonial authority to divide. Cairo, for instance, had a religiously and ethnically diverse population (among both colonizers and colonized) that made an urban structure like that of Tunis, Dakar, or Nairobi impossible to engineer, so no one seriously tried. For all these reasons, one should not assume that colonial authorities invariably succeeded in creating two socially and architecturally divergent cities on the sites they occupied, even though visual and historical evidence demonstrates the general validity of a dual-core model for many colonial cities.

Nor should this chapter's focus on the colonial period suggest that no literature from or about African urban settings exists from earlier periods: some does, and it deserves notice. The earliest written literature arising in an urban context in Africa is probably the *Thousand and One Nights*. Although readers have associated these stories primarily with Baghdad, Cairo also played a major role in the compilation of extant manuscripts and the establishment of the collection, including both "canonical" and later-added stories. Several centuries later, Cairo again became the explicit subject of the earliest writing of the *nahda arabiya*, the nineteenth-century "renaissance" of Arabic literature. 'Alī Pāshā Mubārak, a French-trained technocrat, composed *Al-Khitāt al-tawfīqiyya al-jadīda li-Misr al-qahira* [*New Plans for Egypt under the Khedive Tawfiq: Cairo and Other Cities*] (1887), a multivolume description of the city's neighborhoods, as well as *'Alam al-Dīn* [*The Signs of Religion*] (1882), one of the first novelistic texts in Arabic, in which the story of the protagonist's study trip to Europe serves mostly as a vehicle for descriptions of European science and technology.[3] This text and its predecessor, Rifāʿa Rāfiʿ al-Ṭahṭāwī's travelogue about Paris, *Takhlīs al-ibrīz fī talkhīs Bārīz* [*translated as An Imam in Paris: Account of a Stay in France by an Egyptian Cleric*] (1834), also served to introduce the first notions of the appearance and daily experience of modern European cities to the Arabic-speaking world, explicitly comparing Cairo and Paris, and rhetorically "Egyptianizing" the French capital.[4]

Slightly later, Muḥammad al-Muwayliḥī's *Ḥadīth 'Īsā ibn Hishām* [*A Period of Time*] (1907) satirized developments in nineteenth-century Cairo by miraculously reviving a pasha of an earlier period to witness the habits of the social classes visible in the city. By the time of its publication, Cairo had a "new city," or at least a new residential and commercial neighborhood in the form of Heliopolis, begun in 1905 according to a design by the Belgian Baron Édouard Louis Joseph Empain, one of the principal industrialists behind the Paris Metro. In a very different literary mode from Muwayliḥī's, several North African cities (notably Algiers and Tunis) became the subjects of *qaṣā'id* (singular *qaṣīda*), lyric poems both celebratory and nostalgic for the beauties of a city before colonial intervention or the influx of peasants and montagnards, whom city dwellers apparently everywhere see as uncouth. Finally, no account of the city in modern Arabic literature can ignore the work of Naguib Mahfouz, who after early novels set in ancient Egypt, turned his attention to the modern period and to Cairo, most famously in *Khān al-Khalīlī* (1945) and the monumental *Cairo Trilogy* (1956–7), a three-volume panorama set between 1919 and 1944 but very aware of the city's heritage from earlier periods. African cities, despite their massive twentieth-century expansion, almost always have a previous history that has left its traces in literature.

Part of the casual reader's unfamiliarity with the topic of the city in African literature may stem from its relatively external role in, or absence from, many of the great foundational texts of Anglophone African literature – novels like Amos Tutuola's *The Palm-Wine Drinkard* (written 1946, published 1952) and Chinua Achebe's *Things Fall Apart* (1958), which take place in contexts quite distant from anything most readers today would call urban life. Critics have read both as, among other things, constructing a precolonial world antithetical to the conditions of modernity that we associate with the city in European literature. Yet with the exception of René Maran's *Batouala: Véritable roman nègre* [*Batouala, A True Black Novel*] (1921), the initial texts of African literature in French do not demonstrate such an exclusively rural focus. A certain number follow a pattern set by the Guinean Camara Laye's *Enfant noir* [*The African Child*] (1953), in which the city figures as a distant seat of power, visited and even briefly settled in, but only for limited periods, and never inhabited in the full sense of the word. Given the political arrangements of French colonial rule, this should not surprise us; regardless of the limited rights they enjoyed on paper after the Second World War, colonized peoples were generally barred from acting as full-fledged citizens. Principal characters in both Mouloud Feraoun's *Le Fils du pauvre* [*The Poor Man's Son*] (1950) and Mouloud Mammeri's *La Colline oubliée* [*The Forgotten Hill*] (1952) visit the city, and they end with, respectively, departure from, and failed return to, the protagonist's home village.[5] Even though none of these texts engages in any extended urban description, we can still draw conclusions from their use of the image of the town as a foil for their mostly village settings. The cities or towns in these novels are regional colonial administrative centers (even Camara's Conakry was not a capital but a subsidiary of Dakar).[6] For this reason, they were temporary stops on the path to education and success, never places of permanent habitation for these characters.[7] Readers get little impression of a town like Feraoun's Fort-National, Algeria (Larbaâ Nath Irathen today) as a place with a self-sufficient population and its own culture. Authentic culture in these novels comes from the natal village and is transmitted by and through the characters' parents, and especially via mothers, aunts, and grandmothers who never leave the village and its environs. The cities in these texts exclude such authenticity, and they discomfort the protagonists because only their schooling prepares them to live there; their parents could not conceivably survive in such alien places. These briefly evoked towns turn out to be almost entirely masculine spaces, which only adds to their temporary nature and precludes the development of familial roots.[8]

More distinctly "urban" texts existed from the beginnings of written literature in European languages in West and North Africa. Texts from as early as the 1920s in Algeria and the 1950s in Senegal have urban settings. Despite our expectations, these environments are not principally created or controlled by colonial powers. The plot of Khodja Chukri's *El Euldj, captif des Barbaresques* [*El Euldj, Captive of the Barbary Pirates*] (1929) unfolds in sixteenth-century Algiers, where local and Turkish authorities of mixed ethnicity hold a monopoly of power over the city's institutions and social life. In quite a different genre, Abdoulaye Sadji's *Nini, mulâtresse du Sénégal* [*Nini, Mulatto Woman from Senegal*] (1954) takes place in Saint-Louis, the sometime capital of colonial Senegal and Afrique Occidentale Française, and the center of power for the mixed-race bourgeoisie that dominated early Senegalese encounters with the Portuguese and then the French. Despite the presence in the novel of French authorities, the plot remains focused on the interests, culture, and institutions of this unique African urban class. While it might seem that a story about the protagonist's doomed attempt to "whiten" herself socially would merely confirm the power relations of colonialism, *Nini* actually demonstrates the diffusion of cultural power and prestige that occurs as one historical urban ruling class gives way to another. One could therefore draw a more convincing parallel with certain novels of Balzac or Thackeray than with North or West African novels of the rural persuasion. Yet one might also see Sadji's novel as a very Senegalese view of city life in the colony, constructing a local aesthetic of class representation.

These two lesser-known novels complement our understanding of several much more canonical texts of the colonial period in North Africa: the Moroccan Driss Chraïbi's *Le Passé simple* [*The Simple Past*] (1954) and the Algerian Kateb Yacine's *Nedjma* (1956). Both novelists composed these first and most famous novels of their careers in the immediate context of antico- lonial struggle. Moreover, both devoted much of their attention to observing the organization of urban life in their respective colonies, and to suggesting ways for city residents to inhabit the urban topography as citizens rather than subjects. Chraïbi's disaffected protagonist (also named Driss) moves freely about Casablanca and Fes, but he is fully conscious of when he is in spaces coded as "native" (*indigène*) or "European." He offers few descrip- tions of neighborhoods, but a great deal in the way of encounters on the street. His street-smart dealings with friends, his father's business associates, petty criminals, and beggars demonstrate mastery of two different sorts of city topography: the historic Arab city of Fes and the new French city of Casablanca. Far from feeling out of place in the modern urban landscape, Driss makes himself, if anything, more at home in Casablanca, a city that had from the beginning of the century furnished sites for staging colonial domination via displays of French administrative power. The city also pro- vided means for contesting that domination in a variety of "unauthorized" uses of space (begging, fraud, political demonstrations, nonstandard con- structions, etc.). Chraïbi shows this most vividly in the moments of nonsen- sical humor and hyperbole that punctuate the novel's mordant darkness: for example, the episode in which Driss assembles a mob of street characters and invades his own house, or when he "demonstrates" that because one inevitably loses money to commissions on a series of money-changing trans- actions, the savvy trader can make money simply by reversing the order of trades in a dizzying series of moves across the city.[9] Although Driss fails in his rebellion against his father (initially because of the pervasive reach of interlocking financial interests in the city), he succeeds in using his space creatively, as the novel moves toward the final scene of him departing the colony for France.[10]

Writing in a much less realist mode and with a far more disjointed chro- nology, Kateb Yacine similarly examines the possibilities for resistance to authority in the colonial city, the space ostensibly created by and for that authority, and serving primarily its interests. Unlike the ultimately compre- hensible order of Chraïbi's Casablanca, however, Kateb's Algerian cities of Bône and Constantine (today's 'Annāba and Qusantīna) prove sufficiently complex to resist comprehensible topographic description. Moreover, recent historical experience (the riots of May 8, 1945 and their brutal repression, particularly intense in these parts of eastern Algeria) make movement in any politically consequential way impossible in these cities. Simply put, the characters can neither accomplish nor resolve anything in the urban topographies they scarcely comprehend. As one of the four protagonists of *Nedjma* reaches Bône, Kateb provides a nearly surreal description of the railway terminus that will set the tone for his characters' apprehension of the city. He speaks of the

> somber future of the city decomposing in architectural islands, in oubliettes of crystal, minarets of steel screwed into the heart of ships, in trucks loaded with phosphates and fertilizer, in regal shop windows reflecting the unrealizable costumes of some century to come, in severe squares where human beings, makers of roads and trains, seem to be missing, glimpsed in the distance from the train's calm speed, glimpsed too behind the wheels of cars, masters of the road, adding to their speed the human weight ominously abdicated, at the mercy of a mechanical encounter with death, humming arrows following each other alongside the train, suggesting in series an ever-tighter schedule, bringing closer to the passenger the moment of the naked, demanding city which lets every movement break up within it as the sea fawns at its feet, tightens its knots of rails as far as the platform where all tracks ... converge and end.[11]

Readers are not surprised to find that this city remains figuratively and almost literally uninhabitable to most Algerians. The anachronistic mention of "oubliettes," dark holes or dungeons in medieval fortresses, suggests a power to impose amnesia coercively on visitors. While the city obviously cannot actually do this, the industrial landscape effectively dehumanizes the vision of modernity that new colonial cities like Bône supposedly presented. The power of Kateb's description easily matches any other twentieth-century Francophone description of an urban setting: it manages the sensitivity of Breton's *Nadja* or Aragon's *Paysan de Paris*, even as it demonstrates the inaccessibility to outsiders of meaning in the city.

The references to the future of the city, with shops selling the merchandise of "some century to come," seems to refer to no particular feature or planned development in Bône, but evokes nonetheless another trend in colonial urbanism. The French, especially, found their colonial cities, particularly in North Africa, to be ideal places to experiment with urbanists' ideas and scientific planning, which political, environmental, and economic conditions would have made it impossible to try in mainland France. *Urbanisme* developed in France as a technical discipline along with the modern social sciences around the turn of the twentieth century, just as new colonial sites were becoming available for experimentation, a coincidence noted by a number of historians.[12] The colonies thus became laboratories for testing the application of then-futuristic ideas of urban planners. (They would later serve as sites for the development of effective tactics of police intelligence gathering and repression that authorities would also import to France.[13]) Algiers provided the site for one of Le Corbusier's famous plans for restructuring an entire city, the Plan Obus of 1930. The dramatic curves of its massive buildings and access routes, imposed by the topography more than by any respect for local architectural tradition, at least presented more visual interest than the cruciform buildings he imagined for central Paris in the earlier Plan Voisin. The more human-scale development of colonial Rabat in the 1920s, together with the high-rise housing projects of 1950s Algiers, stand today as some of the most visible French planning interventions in the formerly colonized world. Readers of *Nedjma* may get the sense that for the novel's narrators Algeria is more or less entirely a construction site or a ruin, or both together; given the pace of development, this is a common impression in a great many of the literary presentations of colonial cities.

During the colonial period and around the time of independence, cities became gradually harder to "read" or to make sense of, as increasingly haphazard urban designs resulted from the galloping growth of new construction to house the population. Following independence, the most important developments in African literature coincided with the disillusionment that ensued from the well-known progression of African politics in the 1960s–70s: from parliamentary regimes to first presidential, and then military, dictatorships. African urban space and life changed during this period as well, as ever more rural people moved to regional and national capitals. Literary representation of urban life shifted as this process became pronounced. Increasingly corrupt national governments proved unable to meet the political expectations of any part of their populations not actually in power, and the cities became home to recently rural masses of the disaffected and dispossessed. While many novels arose from this state of affairs, the most famous probably remains Ahmadou Kourouma's *Les Soleils des indépendences* [*The Suns of Independence*] (1968), which depicts political corruption and the offended dignity of fallen elites against a background of the affairs of everyday urban survival, demonstrating new ways of understanding the role of the city in a failing national polity. This novel exemplifies the efforts of African fiction of its period to find aesthetic modes to convey the new realities of urban life, framed in a built environment and attendant social consequences largely left over from the colonial period.

Kourouma's unnamed capital city, while never explicitly the subject of the novel, clearly defines much of the first half of the story. The city shares much with Abidjan in Côte d'Ivoire: a central business district and moneyed neighborhoods on hills above a lagoon, separated by the water from low-lying popular neighborhoods facing them. Like Abidjan, it is home to large numbers of rural migrants, including a population of Malinké traders from the distant north substantial enough to have its own social networks and occasional friction with migrants from the city's immediate hinterland. Kourouma's city thus brings members of a number of ethnic groups into contact with each other, and here as almost everywhere else, it becomes the site of an initial experience of social diversity on a large scale. In an early scene, the protagonist Fama, an aristocratic Malinké, crosses the bridge over the lagoon, late for a seventh-day funeral rite:

> Faster and faster he walked, as if seized with diorrheoa. He was still at the far end of the bridge linking the white man's town with the African quarter, and it was time for second prayer...
>
> Everything conspired to exasperate him ... the people in the street! the bastards lounging about in the middle of the pavement as if it were their old man's backyard. You had to shove, threaten and curse your way past. All this in the midst of an ear-splitting din: horns hooting, motors racing, tyres flapping, passers-by and drivers shouting...
>
> He, Fama, born to gold, food in plenty, honour and women! ... What was he now? A scavenger... A hyena in a hurry.[14]

The city shows no respect for fallen aristocracy or Malinké traders ruined by the imposition of new international borders and trade barriers. While the focus on the heterogeneous and uncouth crowd, the traffic, and the noise is not especially African, the inclusion of bestial images (the casual simile with diarrhea, and the metaphor of the disreputable carrion eater) typifies Kourouma's aesthetic. The animal, for him, consistently invades urban living and its social and political pursuits, blurring the boundaries between the natural and built worlds: a particularly odd phenomenon in a large twentieth-century city. The passage also demonstrates another consistent feature of African literary city description: the split character of the city inherited from colonial rule and perpetuated by mass migration and great disparities in wealth. Strictly speaking, Kourouma's capital no longer has a separate neighborhood for Europeans, built at a distance from less-desirable zones reserved for Africans. Yet the text emphasizes the separation that prevails even after independence by calling one "the white men's town," although Africans would have begun to occupy it even before formal independence. The text also emphasizes the separation of "white" and "African" areas by focusing on one of the latter in particular – the one most visibly set apart from the European-built city by the lagoon and bridge. The terms actually seem to refer more to styles of construction (high-rise steel and glass vs. low corrugated iron and wood) and layout (rectilinear boulevards vs. courtyards and passages) than to the actual race of the inhabitants. Nonetheless, the African capital city continued to encode visually, at least in literature, an inherited racial distinction.

African literature as it developed during the twenty or thirty years following Kourouma's tone-setting novel has not always stressed this distinction in its treatments of urban life. Readers may not find it in the chaotic, absurdly complex cities of Sony Labou Tansi's *L'Anté-peuple* [*The Anti-People*] (1983) or *Les Sept solitudes de Lorsa Lopez* [*The Seven Solitudes of Lorsa Lopez*] (1985), or in Calixthe Beyala's *C'est le soleil qui m'a brûlée* (1987; translated as *The Sun Hath Looked Upon Me*). Yet two features of the aesthetics of urban description appear persistently enough to warrant notice here: the inter-penetration of the natural and built environments, and the continued, marked distinction between styles of urban construction and layout. Tansi's text provides ample evidence of the continuation of the first trend, as his characters generally move in an indeterminate semi-urbanized landscape of unpaved roads, high-rise towers, vacant lots, villas, and jungle. In a demonstration of the second trend, the Congolese satirist Henri Lopes's *Le Pleurer-rire* [*The Laughing Cry*] (1982) takes place in a pastiche capital that includes elements of Dakar, Abidjan, Algiers, and Brazzaville among others, and divides the city between quarters once again coded as "African" and "white":

> The city consists of two quarters: Moundié and the Plateau. Moundié is the African quarter of the colonial epoch, our Adjamé, our Treichville, our Poto-Poto, our Casbah or Medina. When the Uncles were in charge, we had no right to come out of it, except to go to work. If you look attentively at the map, you will see that the quarter is spread in the form of a Traveller's Palm. All the avenues converge on a central point, where a police post has stood ever since colonial times, which has long since become the Central Commissariat for the city.
>
> In Moundié, all the main streets bear the names of the most prestigious tribes of the continent, along with those of our rivers, our districts and our divisions. There are two exceptions to this rule, however: the Avenue Charles de Gaulle and the former Avenue of France, now renamed Avenue Ma Mireille. There circulates, along with a little water in the street fountains, a whole crowd of workers and idlers. Whatever their condition, they dance and sing, to relax, to seduce a girl, to forget, to weep for the dead at some wake.[15]

In the Plateau district, by contrast, the narrator notes that

> The panorama from the terrace of Daddy's [the President's] Palace never fails to move those privileged to view it, above all those of us who can compare it with colonial days. At that time, only "the building" displayed its six storeys above the low level of the other roofs. Nowadays, a clump ... of new skyscrapers announce to the visitor that the capital is no longer a bush village. The farthest off of these buildings is the headquarters of the University. Nearer at hand rise the towers of banks, insurance companies, mining cartels and airlines. On all of these, Daddy has imposed a minimum height of seven storeys.[16]

The description proclaims the similarities among African (and, indeed, other postcolonial) capitals, pointing out shared histories manifest in the contrast between the two broad types of quarter that comprise them. This assertion, ostensibly about styles of urbanization, has the effect of generalizing the novel's satire for the implied audience, one assumed to be familiar with major African cities. This familiarity would be combined with the knowledge of African history necessary to appreciate Lopes's political satire, as the narrator only rarely leaves explicit clues to identify the events to which his satire alludes, but if readers do not have it at the start of the novel, they will by its end. The novel constructs an audience "in the know" in a specifically African way – one that understands the texture and sophistication of the continent's urban life. The text also invites the informed reader to draw conclusions, reading against the grain the assertions of editorialists in the pay of their regimes, knowing the real reasons for the construction norms and new look of the cities in question, to say nothing of the renaming of streets for members of a dictator's family. In texts like this, African literature succeeds in creating not only its own aesthetic but also its own canon of urban references and experiences in the same way that other international cultural forms (e.g., jazz, modernist prose, hip-hop) have done.

These very few texts from North and West Africa demonstrate how writers during and immediately after the colonial period not only represented city spaces and urban concerns but also participated in the elaboration of urban culture across and beyond the continent. As Africa, like other formerly colonized territories, has since begun to develop its own "global cities" rather than merely sending emigrants to the global cities of Europe and North America, and as urban living becomes the norm in Africa, too, we may expect literary texts to grow ever more important as a means of understanding city life.

NOTES

1 An excellent graphic representation of the size of Africa is Kai Krause, "The True Size of Africa" (2010), http://statico2.mediaite.com/geekosystem/uploads/2010/10/true-size-of-africa.jpg. Africa's population density rises slightly above North America's (33.7 vs. 33.2 inhabitants/km²), but remains considerably below Europe's (72.5 inhabitants/km²). In mainland Africa, only Rwanda and Burundi come close to the population densities found in the Benelux countries or parts of East and South Asia, yet a number of African countries show densities in the European mainstream of 100–400 inhabitants/km². Moreover, a number of countries of low overall density (Algeria, Morocco, and Egypt) began in the colonial period, or long before, to concentrate populations along rivers and coasts.

2 The Océan neighborhood of Rabat demonstrates that even in a showpiece city of intentionally bifurcated development, some areas escaped the segregationist

tendency. For the concept of "passive resistance," see János Mátyás Kovács, "Rival Temptations and Passive Resistance: Cultural Gobalization in Hungary," in Peter Berger and Samuel Huntington, eds., *Many Globalizations: Cultural Diversity in the Contemporary World* (Oxford: Oxford University Press, 2002), pp. 146–82.

3   Mubārak's work coincided with the beginning of colonial rule in Egypt under the Anglo-French condominium. Timothy Mitchell's *Rule of Experts: Egypt, Techno-Politics, Modernity* (Berkeley: University of California Press, 2002) provides excellent historical coverage of this and later periods.

4   See Peter Gran, "Tahtawi in Paris," *Al-Ahram*, no. 558 (January 10–16, 2002), http://weekly.ahram.org.eg/2002/568/cu1.htm. The author thanks his colleague Anne-Marie McManus for this and other references concerning Egyptian literature.

5   Lucy R. McNair's recent translation (*The Poor Man's Son: Menrad, Kabyle Schoolteacher* [Charlottesville: University of Virginia Press, 2005]) restores text cut from the 1954 French edition.

6   From 1895 to 1902, when it was replaced by Dakar, Saint-Louis-du-Sénégal served as the capital of Afrique Occidentale Française, one of several forms of French government of the territories that included Guinea.

7   Mammeri's novel does not envision such success, as the protagonist dies on his way back to his village.

8   Patricia Lorcin demonstrates that colonial cities in Algeria and Kenya did in fact have visible female cultural actors. See her "Women, Gender and Nation in Colonial Novels of Inter-War Algeria," *Historical Reflections/Réfléxions historiques* 28, no. 2 (2002): pp. 163–84; and *Historicizing Colonial Nostalgia: European Women's Narratives of Algeria and Kenya, 1900–Present* (New York: Palgrave Macmillan, 2012).

9   Driss Chraïbi, *Le Passé simple* (Paris: Denoël, 1986), pp. 140–3.

10 Driss's friends refuse to house him after he has left home because their parents are also his father's business partners, and they will not risk irritating him.

11 Translation modified from Kateb Yacine, *Nedjma*, trans. Richard Howard (1961; Charlottesville: Caraf Books–University of Virginia Press, 1991), pp. 92–3.

12 See Paul Rabinow, *French Modern: Norms and Forms of the Social Environment* (Cambridge, MA: MIT Press, 1989); Gwendolyn Wright, *The Politics of Design in French Colonial Urbanism* (Chicago: University of Chicago Press, 1991); and Zeynep Çelik, *Urban Forms and Colonial Confrontations: Algiers under French Rule* (Berkeley: University of California Press, 1997).

13 Jim House and Neil McMaster demonstrate this in the early chapters of *Paris 1961: Algerians, State Terror, and Memory* (Oxford: Oxford University Press, 2006).

14 Ahmadou Kourouma, *The Suns of Independence*, trans. Adrien Adams (New York: Africana Publishing, 1981), p. 5.

15 Henri Lopes, *The Laughing Cry: An African Cock and Bull Story*, trans. Gerald Moore (London: Readers International, 1987), p. 37.

16 Ibid., pp. 38–9. Poto-Poto is a residential neighborhood in Brazzaville, Republic of Congo; Adjamé and Treichville are both in Abidjan. All three were begun under French rule. A number of North African cities have "Medinas" or "Casbahs" that predate colonial contact and have today become considerably poorer than the other neighborhoods the narrator mentions.

15

CAROLINE HERBERT

Postcolonial Cities

Questions of space, place, and territory have long been central to postcolonial studies. Nevertheless, postcolonial literary studies has been relatively slow to recognize the significance of urban space to configurations of colonial power and to negotiations of postcolonial subjectivity and citizenship. Even so, the public spaces of cities have often been important sites for material negotiations of national identity, citizenship, and belonging; they are, as James Holston and Arjun Appadurai note, "the place where the business of modern society gets done."[1] As recent protest movements across the Middle East, Europe, India, and North and South America show, cities often become the stage for debate and dialogue, where ideas of national identity, culture, and citizenship are challenged and reimagined. More recently, postcolonial literary studies has been marked by an identifiable urban turn, as scholars examine the city as a complex site of colonial and anticolonial struggle, postcolonial politics, and neo-imperial economies, and they consider the ways in which the city has frequently been understood as both a "real" and an "imagined" location – a "representational space," to borrow Henri Lefebvre's term – that is both lived and narrated.[2] Central to the discussion that follows is the complex relationship between the material and the imagined, the narrated, and the fictionalized: how the city is narrated by different constituencies, and how such imaginings are made real through spatial restructuring and urban displacements; what happens to those imagined as not belonging in the material spaces of the postcolonial city; and how writers have sought to intervene in these imaginings, or worked to reimagine the city in resistance to its various rebuildings.

The city's significance to negotiations of postcolonial citizenship, home, and belonging emerges from its importance to the colonial project itself. The city – in both the imperial center and in the colony – was a key site for policing relations between the colonizer and the colonized. It was in the city that the "imaginary and material spatialities" of the imperial project intersected. Thus, cities were key locations for the administration of empire, and for the production, consumption, import, and export of commodities. But they were also "important sites in the deployment of the technologies of power through which indigenous populations were categorised and controlled. Here, town planning became the mechanism by which colonial adjudications of cleanliness, civility and modernity were realised quite literally on the ground."[3]

Frantz Fanon's work brings into view the spatial formations of colonial modernity discussed in the previous chapter. In the opening section of *The Wretched of the Earth* (1961), Fanon positions the Manichean city as emblematic of the spatial, social, and economic ordering of the colonial world, which, he writes, is "cut in two." The "settler's town," Fanon asserts, is "a strongly-built town, all made of stone and steel." It is "brightly-lit," with streets that are "clean and even," and "is a well-fed town, an easy-going town; its belly is always full of good things." Adjacent to it is the "the native town," "a place of ill fame, peopled by men of evil repute." This town is "a hungry town, starved of bread, of meat, of shoes, of coal, of light," and in this "world without spaciousness," men's lives go unnoticed and unaccounted: "They are born there, it matters little where or how; they die there, it matters not where, nor how." The "native town," Fanon writes, is "a crouching village, a town on its knees, a town wallowing in the mire." Here, Fanon brings into view the spatial practices of the imperial imaginary. The "settler's town" is an embodiment of Enlightenment rationality, illuminated, ordered, hygienic, and healthy; its "easy" lifestyle is "protected" by organized material wealth. The "native town," by contrast, is overcrowded and dark, chaotic, and cramped. Against the plentitude and soaring architecture of the "settler's town," this almost subterranean space is marked by hunger and poverty.[4] Fanon thus makes clear the intersecting networks of injustice at work in the Manichean city, which becomes the space in which racial and economic inequalities and oppressions are mapped and materially experienced: "The cause is the consequence; you are rich because you are white, you are white because you are rich."[5]

By discussing the Manichean city so early in *The Wretched of the Earth*, Fanon establishes urban space as a key terrain of struggle for national liberation, decolonization, and postcolonial citizenship. It is here, across "the frontiers" of colonial urban space, that the oppressed "surge" to reclaim and to remake society.[6] Thus, urban space becomes a key site of colonial oppression but also of anticolonial resistance. The bifurcated spaces Fanon mapped are replayed and reworked in literary representations of the postcolonial city. These representations often foreground movements across the spaces of the Manichean city and articulate the instability of its spatial ordering. At the same time, they frequently register a note of caution, drawing attention to the ways that such spatial representations and experiences of power remain or reemerge in the present.

Fanon's accounts of the relationship between space and power, and the revolutionary "surge" of the colonized across the policed frontiers to reclaim space, resonates with Michel de Certeau's readings of panoptic power and subversive movements in *The Practice of Everyday Life* (1984). We need take care in bringing together work produced under the experience of French colonization and work produced in Paris because the apparent ease with which figures journey through the city in de Certeau's work is unavailable to Fanon's colonized subjects. Nevertheless, and with these contexts in mind, it is somewhere in the complex traffic between the material violence of the disciplined Manichean city mapped by Fanon and the melancholic and utopian writings of urban life offered by de Certeau that the city in postcolonial literature often emerges.

If Fanon works through a horizontal mapping of space, emphasizing adjacency, then de Certeau introduces verticality to his conceptualizations of the city. In his essay "Walking in the City," de Certeau contrasts the ordered and rational "Concept-city" with the "metaphorical city" produced by the everyday "spatial practices" of city dwellers. From above, authorities view the city with the panoptic gaze of a "voyeur-God," rendering the "complexity of the city readable" as a stable, functional, disciplined "place."[7] De Certeau contrasts this panoptic, panoramic view with the journeys and stories of the "ordinary practitioners" who "live 'down below,' below the thresholds at which visibility begins."[8] These city dwellers' movements through the streets resist and evade the authorities' disciplinary gaze and rewrite the city from below, transforming each space in the process – a process we repeatedly encounter in the texts discussed in this chapter. Movement is therefore crucial to de Certeau's understanding of the everyday experience of urban space. The act of walking brings into view the textuality of a "*migrational*, or metaphorical city" in which stories and experiences cross each others' paths and "weave places together" into an "urban 'text.'" Positioning walking as an enunciative act, de Certeau describes how the "rhetoric of walking" transgresses the authorized routes that structure the Concept-city and weaves together the diverse fragments of the city, exposing gaps and absences in the Concept-city even as it traces new trajectories that diverge from it.[9]

In the city that de Certeau describes, efforts to police space are continually negotiated, subverted, and resisted by the everyday activities of city dwellers, a process that offers some useful starting points for reading literary representations of postcolonial cities. The dynamic of visibility and invisibility that he traces – which resonates with Fanon's account of the "unseen, unknown" inhabitants of the colonized town – becomes a refrain of postcolonial texts that draw attention to those histories and bodies rendered "invisible" or illegitimate by officious discourses of city and nation, or, we shall see, made spectral by networks and flows of global capital. Postcolonial literatures also frequently place a "rhetoric of walking" at the center of their narratives to bring into view the sometimes hidden histories of postcolonial urban modernity, and to emphasize that the postcolonial city is continually remade, reread, and rewritten in ways that evade the surveilling gaze of the authorities. Although this argument tends to position the walker as a radical and revisionary figure, postcolonial urban literature also considers some of the limits of modernist flânerie as a universally available subject position. De Certeau suggests that walking establishes the experience of being in the city as "an immense social experience of lacking a place."[10] Postcolonial texts consider the implications of "lacking a place," bringing into view material experiences of homelessness and situating the experience in relation to fraught questions of citizenship, home, and belonging.

We begin our itinerary of city spaces in the former imperial metropolis, which, like the colonial city, was affected by the colonial process and by decolonization. In this light, perhaps the most well-established strand of postcolonial urban literary studies explores how writers invite us to "historicize the imperial (and neo-imperial) history of the production of space" in "postcolonial London," and to engage with the ways the former imperial centers are represented and rewritten by migrant and diasporic communities.[11] Salman Rushdie's *The Satanic Verses* (1988) is frequently positioned as the paradigmatic text of postcolonial London, amidst such other notable examples as Sam Selvon's *The Lonely Londoners* (1956), Grace Nichol's *The Fat Black Woman's Poems* (1984), Hanif Kureishi's *The Buddha of Suburbia* (1990), Bernadine Evaristo's *The Emperor's Babe* (2001), Zadie Smith's *White Teeth* (2000), and Gautum Malkani's *Londonstani* (2006). Through the intertwined narratives of two Indian migrants, Saladin Chamcha and Gibreel Farishta, Rushdie's novel looks beyond the "Proper London" of "Bigben Nelsonscolumn Lordstavern Bloodytower," to a "city visible but unseen" of migrant and diasporic communities, rewriting and remaking national identity in resistance to neo-imperial discourses of city and nation.[12] Frustrated by his inability to control London's cartography, Gibreel imposes Bombay's climate onto the English city, "rewrit[ing] the cultural cartography of the city" and "collaps[ing] the distinction" between imperial center and colonial periphery.[13] As John McLeod suggests, this tropicalization potentially repeats the dynamics of the colonial spatial imaginary, but in reverse.[14] However, Gibreel's actions are, in part, a response to his experience of material and cultural homelessness in London and his rereading of the architecture surrounding him as invested in the violence of colonial modernity. Gibreel walks through a "writing" and "unstable" city, seeing "essences instead of surfaces." From his migrant perspective, he rereads London's facades, transforming its gothic architectures into sites of, and monuments to, the violence of colonial capital.[15] This London, "stifled and twisted by the insupportable, unrejected past," has begun to decay as it refuses to recognize the continuities between its colonial past and its neo-imperial present. Navigating London's gothic spaces, Gibreel sees "a grand colonnade built of human flesh and covered in skin that bled when scratched." London is exposed as a "pandemonium of mirages," a labyrinth of buildings whose facades ooze with the bodily pain of those who, in the imperial centers and the colonized peripheries, labored to bring (the) imperial capital forth.[16] In Gibreel's movements, the "unseen, unknown and hardly thought about" foundations of the imperial metropolis that Fanon highlights are brought firmly into view.

Michael Ondaatje's *In the Skin of a Lion* (1987) offers an extensive rereading of the western metropolis to bring to light the violence of colonial modernity and lost histories inscribed into its architecture. *Skin* traces Toronto's emergence in the 1920s and 1930s, focusing on sites such as the Bloor Street Viaduct, Union Street Station, and the water filtration plant, as well as the relationship between the construction of the city by predominantly migrant laborers and Canada's colonial history. Built by workmen employed by the "DOMINION BRIDGE COMPANY," the viaduct is, on completion, "[c]hristened 'Prince Edward.'"[17] Ondaatje thus places Toronto's emergence within Canada's complex colonial past; at this time, Canadians remained subjects of the British empire but *Skin* demonstrates that the "Dominion of Canada benefit[ed] from the mistreatment of labourers, many of them foreign-born."[18] Recovering the stories of the immigrants, workers, and women absent from Toronto's official archives, *Skin* repositions the public works structures as public monuments to the lost histories and stories of the workers who built them. As in de Certeau's work, the authorized city is rewritten by illicit spatial practices, and space is remapped through the relationship between the visible and monumental and the invisible or subterranean experiences of the laborers. Toronto's Commissioner of Public Works, Rowland C. Harris, represents the authorized city in both senses of the word: he is a municipal official and is represented as imagining Toronto into existence. While Harris gives his name to Toronto's water treatment plant and is a visible presence in the city's history, the migrant workers are absent from its official archives, which "depicted every detail about the soil, the wood, the weight of concrete, everything but information on those who actually built the bridge." This archival absence is paired with a material absence;

by 1938, "over 10,000 foreign-born workers had been deported out of the country," their labor no longer required.[19]

Harris's buildings embody an idea of the city as rational, ordered, and clean. This is evident in the water filtration plant, whose role as a "palace of purification" connotes both sanitation and social cleansing; the "giant centrifugal pumps" housed within it are "more valuable than life."[20] With an entrance "modelled ... on a Byzantine city gate," the plant is the "immaculate fiction" of an "ideal city." As the plant emerges, Ondaatje brings into view "the other tentacle of [Harris's] dream," the tunnel that is dug underneath Lake Ontario to draw water.[21] In contrast to the smoothly "orchestrated" construction above ground, workers under the lake "grunt into hard clay"; the "purification" processes that the plant will house jar against the laborers' unsanitary working conditions: "All morning they slip in the wet clay unable to stand properly, pissing where they work, eating where someone else left shit."[22]

Ondaatje uses the dark, underground space of the tunnel to imagine the hidden histories of Toronto's laborers and to foreground the violence of urban modernity. At the same time, he depicts the migrant communities as occupying subterranean, nocturnal spaces in ways that reclaim the city from officious discourses. While Harris surveys the construction of the viaduct at night, Nicholas Temelcoff's acrobatic movements underneath it register an alternative spatial knowledge that works beneath the authorities' panoptic gaze. The Macedonian bar Temelcoff frequents, meanwhile, exists outside Toronto's officially Anglophone linguistic space. The bar re-imagines a small part of Toronto as a Macedonian street: not only the decoration, but the very "darkness represents a Macedonian night ... So when customers step in at any time, what they are entering is an old courtyard of the Balkans." Here, Toronto *becomes* Macedonia. Migrant communities also reclaim city spaces against their official functions with the nighttime meeting at the waterworks, "an illegal gathering of various nationalities" that, through its multinational and multilingual activities, transforms the plant into an alternative site of urban creativity and community. Silenced in Toronto's public spaces and in its archives, the workers claim belonging in this site they have created.[23] Through these illicit nighttime gatherings, Ondaatje transforms the waterworks from its official identification with Harris and, as Meredith Criglington argues, rededicates it as a site of "counter-memory" to the community of migrant laborers who risked and lost their lives to build it.[24] Through the tunnel, Ondaatje reminds us of the violence of colonial modernity, but through the gatherings, he transforms the waterworks from a symbol of purity into an emblem of an alternative "ideal city" formed by collaborations among different cultural communities.

The issues of memory and history raised by *Skin* in relation to the western metropolis gain a further set of complex meanings in the South African context, where the recent past of apartheid haunts the present of post-colonial Johannesburg. Ivan Vladislavić's *Portrait with Keys: The City of Johannesburg Unlocked* (2006) begins with two epigraphs whose concern with the dynamics of memory resonates with Ondaatje's text. The first, provided by Lionel Abrahams, states, "Memory takes root only half in the folds of the brain: half's in the concrete streets we have lived along." The second is de Certeau's claim, "Haunted places are the only ones people can live in."[25] Vladislavić thus establishes the city and its architecture as anxious sites of remembering and forgetting, but what are the implications of de Certeau's statement in the postcolonial context? What kinds of haunting take place in the postcolonial city?

Apartheid policies of social and racial segregation worked through forms of spatial control that echo Fanon's Manichean city. Disciplinary spatial practices such as forced removals, restriction of movement, pass laws, and the demarcation of townships and Bantustans all made material and reinforced the ideology of the apartheid state.[26] In *Portrait with Keys*, Vladislavić reflects on the traces of the spatial ordering of apartheid that remain in post-apartheid Johannesburg. In this formally experimental text, the postcolonial city emerges as a palimpsest of individual and collective memories and fragmented histories. Walking through Johannesburg, the narrator observes the legacies of its history as a series of gold-mining camps in the late nineteenth century. Road names such as Victoria and Empire bear witness to the imperial past, while their layout points to Johannesburg's origins in the colonial capitalist exploitation of land and labor: "Roberts and Kitchener, avenues in the uniforms of English soldiers, march away to the east, side by side" while "[a] spine of rock, an outcrop of the gold-bearing reef on which the city depends, blocks every thoroughfare between the avenues, except for Blenheim and Juno."[27]

While the city's colonial heritage is advertised by its cartography, Vladislavić reflects on what de Certeau might term the "presences of diverse absences" produced by efforts to create clearly demarcated racialized spaces.[28] Objects and artworks are important to this process. Fragment 60 describes Sue Williamson's installation, *Mementoes of District Six* (1993), made in response to the forced clearance of an area close to the center of Cape Town populated by predominantly black African communities. This piece is "a cabin made of resin blocks," each containing "an object or fragment that the artist ... collected among the ruins of District Six after the removals: a shard of pottery, a scrap of wallpaper, a hairclip, a doll's shoe." Here "worthless things [are] made to seem precious" and everyday objects are transformed into relics that carry within them lost histories and memories and that act as reminders of the absences of homes, families, and children produced by apartheid.[29] In Vladislavić's text, everyday, often discarded objects are invested with layers of individual and collective memory. If apartheid was an everyday experience of oppression, then, Vladislavić suggests, its memory haunts the everyday spaces and objects of the city itself.

In an interview, Vladislavić noted that "the actual physical structures of apartheid are going to be difficult, if not impossible, to erase, and that we're going to be living within those structures for a very long time."[30] This sense of the presentness of the past informs *Portrait with Keys*'s often ambivalent negotiation of processes of remembering and forgetting. Johannesburg continues, in Vladislavić's text, to be "a frontier city, a place of contested boundaries."[31] The spatial order of the past reemerges in tensions between communities concerning the occupation and control of space in the present-day city, as exemplified by the "boundary between Troyeville and Kensington ... two suburbs [that] turn their backs on one another." Fragment 8 explains how "[t]he recent history of the house at 22 Albemarle Street, strictly in Kensington, is ... typical of the frontier suburb which Troyeville has become, a contested zone between inter-city suburbs such as Fairview and New Doornfontein, which have evolved into black areas, and Kensington, which still holds on to its white identity."[32]

Alongside these continuing tensions, some of the optimism of the post-apartheid city emerges in fragments concerned with the painting of an Ndebele mural on a garden wall in Blenheim Street. As the spatial policing of apartheid gives way to an apparently more fluid sense of space, the narrator observes black Africans moving into the once predominantly white suburbs. The Ndebele mural is "bravely optimistic" and "suited the early nineties perfectly: Africa was coming to the suburbs in the nicest possible way."[33] The narrator's tone indicates the ambivalent and tentative nature of this movement and the continued tensions over space and belonging. A few years later, a subsequent owner paints over the mural, suggesting some of the limits of post-apartheid transformations while highlighting the postcolonial city as a palimpsest of histories, identities, and communities. Although the mural is painted over to render the house more marketable – the estate agent's advice was to "paint it white" – "it took a couple of coats" and "you could still see the African geometry developing, like a Polaroid image, as the paint dried."[34]

As this ghostly image suggests, while the postcolonial city is haunted by the spatial violence of the past, it is also marked by the exploitations and exclusions of the present: the Manichean city of colonialism reemerges in new forms in postcolonial urban space. In Fragment 43, "*Handwritten (Roll*

2)," the narrator reflects on the different landscapes of the suburb and the township. In terms that echo Fanon's, Vladislavić notes that the "white city is made of steel and glass, illuminated from within. It is printed on aluminium hoardings and Perspex sheeting. It is bolted down, recessed and double-glazed, framed and sealed, it is double-sided and laminated, it is revolving in the wind of a well-greased axle." This description of the "white city" as ordered, "illuminated," and clean, is couched within – or, in fact, written over by – two descriptions of the township that, in contrast, appears disordered and ad hoc. "The township," we learn, "is written in longhand across the printed page of the white city" with signs written "in felt tip, in chalk, in gaudy heeltaps of enamel" offering services that "[w]hite eyes appraise ... on flaking facades, accompanied by crude drawings." The township

> is made of cardboard and hardboard, buckling in the sunlight. It is hand-painted on unprimed plaster, scribbled on the undersides of things, on the blank reverses, unjustified, in alphabets with an African sense of personal space, smudged. Tied to a fence with string. leaning against a yield sign. propped up by a brick. secured with a twist of wire. nailed to a tree trunk.[35]

This fragment draws attention to continuing divisions within the city at the intersection between racial and socioeconomic difference. However, by emphasizing the sign as a palimpsest of writings in which one town overlays and interrupts the other, Vladislavić figures the towns as overlapping and interconnected – "the same space understood, imagined, and ... signifying *differently*." As he does throughout the text, Vladislavić invites the reader to reflect on the multiple and overlapping ways in which the city is experienced and imagined, and on the "socially-encoded structures of prejudice" that mark the relationship between the city walker and city reader.[36]

Fragment 43 draws attention to "the underside of things," the "blank reverses" of Johannesburg, articulating a concern that the economic discrepancies of apartheid Johannesburg continue to mark the spatial structures and experiences of the post-apartheid city. Like Ondaatje, Vladislavić turns to the notion of a subterranean city to explore the ways that Johannesburg's neoliberal restructuring produces invisible communities and spectral citizens in its present. In the Hillbrow area of Johannesburg, the narrator discovers that beneath the iron utility covers, the poor store clothes, food, and discarded items to be recycled in exchange for cash. Here, the resistant and subversive tactics of de Certeau's "ordinary practitioners" come into view, as subterranean niches created by public structures are transformed into secret, private dwellings, "known only to those who could see [them]." Yet, Vladislavić refuses a utopian celebration of this reuse of space, observing that "people are so poor they have to store their belongings in holes in the ground."[37]

Literary representations of other cities articulate similar anxieties about the uneven experiences of postcolonial citizenship and, as Vladislavić does, turn to tropes of invisibility and the ghostly to reflect on those rendered spectral by deregulated global capitalism. Fictional representations of Bombay/Mumbai often turn to tropes of spectrality and embodiment to explore the impacts of economic liberalization. In Rushdie's *The Moor's Last Sigh* (1995), for example, an "invisible work-force" builds the everywhere-visible skyscrapers of Bombay's post-liberalization economy.[38] Excluded from official census data, and thus positioned as noncitizens without rights or access to protection by the nation-state, these "wraiths ... kept the city going, building its houses, hauling its goods, cleaning up its droppings" before "simply and terribly dying ... unseen, as their spectral blood poured out of their ghostly mouths in the middle of the bitch-city's all-too-real, uncaring streets."[39] Chris Abani similarly deploys a language of spectrality in his depiction of Lagos in *Graceland* (2004), a novel that joins a growing body of literature concerned with the precarious lives of those living in the growing slum or informal housing areas of postcolonial cities. Its central protagonist, Elvis, appears as a spectral figure as he tries to scrape together a living in the city, "haunting markets and train stations, as invisible to the commuters or shoppers as a real ghost." Early on, Elvis even appears spectral to himself as "[h]is face, reflected back at him, seemed to belong to a stranger, floating there like a ghostly head in a comic book."[40]

According to Mike Davis, the slum is a key characteristic of the "megacity" and establishes the pattern of the urban future. "Cities of the future," he writes, "rather than being made out of glass and steel as envisioned by earlier generations of urbanists are instead largely constructed out of crude brick, straw, recycled plastic, cement blocks, and scrap wood. Instead of cities of light soaring toward heaven, much of the twenty-first-century urban world squats in squalor, surrounded by pollution, excrement, and decay."[41] A key concern of postcolonial literature is the precarious lives of the poor who inhabit informal housing, slums, and ghettoes, and the homeless pavement dwellers. In *Graceland*, Abani plays with the *bildungsroman* form to examine the "stark unevenness of development that persists within the postcolonial state."[42] The "suspended city" of Maroko, "half slum, half paradise,"[43] where Elvis lives a "suspended existence" emblematizes, for Sarah Harrison, the "stalled urban development" of Lagos in the 1980s as Nigeria faced rising debt, conditions imposed by International Monetary Fund loans, and political and financial corruption.[44] Following familiar representations of the city, Abani frames Lagos as a dual city marked by contrasts between extreme poverty and extreme wealth. Postcards advertise sites of economic and infrastructural development, and indeed Lagos "did have its share of rich people and fancy neighbourhoods" with "skyscrapers, sweeping flyovers, beaches and hotels" and "beautiful brownstones set in well-landscaped yards, sprawling Spanish-style haciendas in brilliant white and ocher." The cosmopolitan elegance and ordered landscape of Victoria Island, protected by "stone-faced guards armed with automatic rifles," contrasts with the adjacent "swamp city of Maroko." Here, "[h]alf of the town was built of a confused mix of clapboard, wood, cement and zinc sheets, raised above a swamp by means of stilts and wooden walkways."⁴⁵ It is clear that the proceeds of postcolonial development and global capitalism are not evenly distributed here, and *Graceland* emphasizes the parasitic nature of the different districts of Lagos. At one point, Elvis labors on one of Lagos's many construction sites, highlighting how circulations of local and global capital depend on those very city subjects who are excluded from its profits.

Perhaps the novel's most explicit critique of discourses of national development and postcolonial progress is its representation of the 1980s slum clearances, a key part of the government's "Operation Clean the Nation" that ostensibly sought to improve Lagos' sanitation and infrastructure. It is soon clear that the enterprise targets the poor as reminders of the failures of national development. Elvis's family is quick to puncture the narrative of national unity; the slum will be cleared, his father says, "[s]o dat dey can turn dis place to beachside millionaire's paradise." Moreover, the "Clean up" is reinterpreted as a cover-up for the failures of development projects funded by the IMF, the World Bank, and the United States: "Instead of dem to address de unemployment and real cause of poverty and crime, dey want to cover it all under one pile of rubbish."⁴⁶ Although he reverses the language of development by labeling the new constructions as "rubbish," the clearances show how the bodies of the poor become part of the rubble left by the operation, part of the debris in the ruins of urban narratives of postcolonial progress and global modernity.

After discovering his Maroko home has been destroyed, Elvis is left to walk across the city alone. With "no plans, no ideas about what to do or where he was going, he just walked. He wasn't going anywhere in particular, but at least he was not standing still."⁴⁷ De Certeau suggests that to walk is to lack a place and that urban walkers unsettle notions of dwelling and being at home. Postcolonial texts frequently explore the implications of "lacking a place" in the contemporary city, situating the experience of walking in relation to questions of citizenship, home, and belonging. In *Graceland*, Elvis's experience of walking the city is situated in relation to material experiences of homelessness, not Baudelaire's activity of making oneself at home in the crowd on the street. Elvis moves through spaces occupied by communities displaced by "Operation Clean the Nation," "seeing signs not normally visible": homeless and begging children, mutilated bodies, girls forced into prostitution.[48] Elvis's movements reveal that to "lack a place" in the post-colonial city might be to experience the material violence of homelessness, poverty, and dispossession.

In *Portrait with Keys*, Vladislavić explicitly takes up de Certeau's "rhetoric of walking" as a way of mapping the narrator's ambivalently shifting sense of Johannesburg as a space of familiarity and estrangement, home and belonging, during and after apartheid. "The 'long poem of walking,'" Vladislavić writes, "is a dialogue" in which "[t]he way and the walker ... are in conversation." This conversation produces Johannesburg as a provisional city that both changes and is changed by the experiences and interpretations of the pedestrian, who is often caught between familiarity with, and estrangement from, its built environment: "Everyday I trawl along my habitual routes ready to be startled by something else I have missed until now." The rereading of familiar space at work here is paired with the narrator's insistence elsewhere that "getting lost is not always a bad thing. One might even consider misdirecting a stranger for his own good."[49] As James Graham suggests, a key aspect of Vladislavić's interest in "finding the unfamiliar in the familiar" and in "defamiliarizing the city" is his concern to explore the ethics of walking in the city, "the difficulty of being a *citizen*, of living ethically in an increasingly unhomely city."[50] Walking, moreover, is central to the very structure of Vladislavić's innovative text, *Portrait with Keys*, which comprises 138 numbered fragments followed by 29 "Itineraries" that direct readers back through different sequences of fragments organized into "long," "moderate," or "short" "routes" that are ostensibly thematically connected. These itineraries offer alternative maps to Johannesburg and invite readers to reread and revisit urban spaces and subjects, emphasizing the provisionality and proliferation of interpretations of the urban text. Linearity, chronology, and fixity of space are disallowed by these itineraries, which direct (and misdirect) readers back through Johannesburg, creating "walkerly text[s]" that involve "reader-walkers" in the production of meaning and require them to reread scenes and spaces and their own responses to them.[51]

As Vladislavić's text demonstrates, formal experimentation and critical reflection on form are important aspects of postcolonial literature's search for alternative modes of mapping urban space and subjectivity. Sarnath Banerjee's graphic novel, *Corridor* (2004), uses the interplay between image and text to contrast the ordered spaces of Connaught Place in Lutyens's Delhi with activities that take place within and beyond its rational, concentric circles. Organized around a series of flâneur-like figures who move through the city in the hope of collecting the answers to their specific problems, *Corridor* maps Delhi through form and content as a palimpsestic space of layers, alleyways, circularities, and digressions, of chance encounters and connections, that resists the stability of the map. Here, the rational topography of New Delhi is placed in dialogue with the unplanned alleys of Old Delhi, where "the immeasurably old rub[s] shoulders with the very new," and the concentric circles of Connaught Place are crossed and complicated by images of spiral staircases and the double helix of DNA.[52] Thus, unlike the sort of flâneur who accrues sights and experiences like a collector "fanat[ical] for an illusory wholeness, for completing the set," the city itself comprises fragmented stories and spaces that cannot quite be connected to form a coherent, linear narrative of urban modernity.[53] In an Escher-like, metafictional moment toward the end of *Corridor*, Brighu – revealed as the graphic artist creating the narrative we read – is shown in a series of frames to move away from the rational cartography of the chess board to his complex drafting board on which he draws himself, drawing himself, drawing himself, while the text notes that "the city is about anonymity / Some people meet, talk, part / Some don't / and live with the frustrating knowledge that invisible bonds tie them together." If this sequence presents the city as a *mise-en-abyme* of stories and encounters, constituted by "invisible" connections, the novel frustrates the reader's desire to make sense of those connections or transform them into legible map. Instead, the novel ends with the reflection that "People are like Onions, Baba / They have layers and layers / But who will know? Who has time?"[54]

Although working in a conventional novel form, Kamila Shamsie experiments in *Kartography* (2002) with different modes of mapping the postcolonial city as she explores Karachi and Pakistani identity politics after the 1971 civil war that established Bangladesh. Shamsie represents Karachi as a site of memory and forgetting, whose present is repeatedly interrupted by the lingering pasts of the 1947 partition of India and Pakistan and the 1971 war. Exploring different modes of mapping these events' complex legacies, Shamsie produces what I have elsewhere called "lyric maps" that bear witness to the cartographic anxieties that affect contemporary Pakistanis' subjectivities and complicate those narratives of nation that would censor the loss of Bangladesh.[55] One of the central concerns of Shamsie's text is the ways that some narrative maps of the city exclude others. Thus, in a letter to Karim late in the novel, Raheen acknowledges his concern that "you can only know the stories of those to whom you've bothered to listen. What happens to all those streets that hold no stories for us? Do we simply stay away from them?"[56] Toward the end of *Kartography*, Shamsie gestures toward an alternative mode of mapping the city that is at once inclusive of and structured by difference and, at the same time, draws attention to its limits. Building up from a "basic street map," Karim proposes an "interactive map on the Internet" that would bring together a network of "links" to multimedia files "telling stories of what it's like to live in different parts of town."[57] By following these links, a viewer could access a diverse range of perspectives on the city that bear witness to its social, linguistic, and ethnic diversity without privileging any one community, area, or approach. Furthermore, such a map would emphasize the necessity of a shift in *form* to bear witness to the complexity of the city's past and present, comprising a network of narrative and nonnarrative, written and visual forms that together resist any linear organization of Karachi's spaces and archives. As a "lifelong project ... in a city that's always changing," the map would refuse closure and instead figure the representation of the city as a collaborative process that is constantly in motion, that is shared and interactive, and that is created through difference and debate.[58] In this sense, that map would embody an alternative approach to the city that, while certainly less radical and innovative, resonates with Vladislavić's formal experimentation in *Portrait with Keys*.

In these and other postcolonial city texts, then, debate, motion, movement, and interaction are not only characteristic of the experience of being in the city itself, they are also central to the very modes of imagining its present and future possibilities. "Ask a question of any intersection," Vladislavić writes, "and it will answer, not always straightforwardly, allowing a quirk of the topography, the lie of the land, a glimpse of a prospect to nudge you one way or the other. The conversation is one of the things that make city walking interesting."[59] In their formal play, then, and in their emphasis on dialogue and active engagement, literary representations of the postcolonial city reflect on the complex experience of postcolonial urban modernity – the experience of being in the city. But they also invite us to reflect on the experience of reading the city and on the ethical implications of imagining its past, present, and possible futures in collaboration and in conversation with other writers, readers, and reader-walkers.

NOTES

1 James Holston and Arjun Appadurai, Introduction, in James Holston, ed., *Cities and Citizenship* (Durham, NC: Duke University Press, 1999), p. 3.
2 See Henri Lefebvre, *The Production of Space*, trans. Donald Nicholson-Smith (Oxford: Blackwell, 1991), pp. 39–42.
3 Jane M. Jacobs, *Edge of Empire: Postcolonialism and the City* (London: Routledge, 2002), pp. 19–20, 20.
4 Frantz Fanon, *The Wretched of the Earth*, trans. Constance Farrington (London: Penguin, 1990), p. 30.

5   Ibid., p. 31.
6   Ibid., p. 31.
7   Michel de Certeau, *The Practice of Everyday Life*, trans. Steven F. Rendall (Berkeley: University of California Press, 1984), pp. 95, 93, 91, 93, 92, 117.
8   Ibid., p. 93.
9   Ibid., pp. 93, 97, 100.
10 Ibid., p. 103.
11 Rashmi Varma, *The Postcolonial City and It Subjects: London, Nairobi, Bombay* (London: Routledge, 2011), p. 32.
12 Salman Rushdie, *The Satanic Verses* (London: Vintage, 1988), pp. 38, 241.
13 Ian Baucom, *Out of Place: Englishness, Empire, and the Locations of Identity* (Princeton, NJ: Princeton University Press, 1999), p. 212.
14 John McLeod, *Postcolonial London* (London: Routledge, 2004), pp. 152–3.
15 Rushdie, *Satanic Verses*, p. 320.
16 Ibid., p. 327.
17 Michael Ondaatje, *In the Skin of a Lion* (London: Picador, 1987), pp. 25, 27.
18 Gillian Roberts, *Prizing Literature: The Celebration and Circulation of National Culture* (Toronto: University of Toronto Press, 2011), p. 56.
19 Ondaatje, *Skin of a Lion*, pp. 145, 209.
20 Ibid., pp. 103, 108.
21 Ibid., pp. 109, 110.
22 Ibid., pp. 105–6.
23 Ibid., pp. 37, 115.
24 Meredith Criglington, "The City as a Site of Counter-Memory in Anne Michael's *Fugitive Pieces* and Michael Ondaatje's *In the Skin of a Lion*," *Essays on Canadian Writing* 81 (2004), pp. 129–51.
25 Ivan Vladislavić, *Portrait with Keys: The City of Johannesburg Unlocked* (London: Portobello, 2006), pp. 6, 9.
26 See Sarah Nuttall and Achille Mbembe, "Introduction: Afropolis," in Sarah Nuttall and Achille Mbembe, eds., *Johannesburg: The Elusive Metropolis* (Durham, NC, and London: Duke University Press, 2008), pp. 1–33 (especially pp. 20–1); and Rita Bernard, *Apartheid and Beyond: South African Writers and the Politics of Place* (Oxford: Oxford University Press, 2007).
27 Vladislavić, *Portrait with Keys*, p. 17.
28 De Certeau, *Practice of Everyday Life*, p. 108.
29 Vladislavić, *Portrait with Keys*, p. 70.
30 Christopher Warnes, "Interview with Ivan Vladislavić," *Modern Fiction Studies* 46.1 (2000), 278–9.
31 Vladislavić, *Portrait with Keys*, p. 169.
32 Ibid., p. 19.
33 Ibid., p. 24.
34 Ibid., p. 57.
35 Ibid., pp. 60–1.
36 James Graham, "Ivan Vladislavić and the possible city," *Journal of Postcolonial Writing* 44.4 (2008), 341.
37 Vladislavić, *Portrait with Keys*, p. 46.
38 Rushdie, *The Moor's Last Sigh* (London: Vintage, 1995), p. 186.

39 Ibid., p. 212. For a detailed discussion, see Caroline Herbert, "Spectrality and Secularism in Bombay Fiction: Salman Rushdie's *The Moor's Last Sigh* and Vikram Chandra's *Sacred Games*," *Textual Practice* 26.5 (2012), pp. 952–4.

40 Chris Abani, *Graceland* (New York: Picador, 2004), pp. 14, 6.

41 Cited in Varma, *The Postcolonial City*, p. 20.

42 Sarah K. Harrison, "'Suspended City': Personal, Urban, and National Development in Chris Abani's *Graceland*," *Research in African Literatures* 43.2 (2012), 99.

43 Abani, *Graceland*, pp. 6, 7.

44 Harrison, "Suspended City," 99.

45 Abani, *Graceland*, pp. 7, 164, 6, 48.

46 Ibid., p. 248.

47 Ibid., p. 306.

48 Ibid., p. 306.

49 Vladislavić, *Portrait with Keys*, pp. 49, 49, 160, 13.

50 Graham, "Ivan Vladislavić and the possible city," 340.

51 Ibid., p. 337.

52 Sarnath Banerjee, *Corridor: A Graphic Novel* (New Delhi: Penguin India, 2004), p. 48.

53 Ibid., p. 7, quoting Jean Baudrillard.

54 Ibid., pp. 107, 111.

55 Caroline Herbert, "Lyric maps and the legacies of 1971 in Kamila Shamsie's *Kartography*," *Journal of Postcolonial Writing* 47.2 (2011), 159–72.

56 Kamila Shamsie, *Kartography* (London: Bloomsbury, 2002), p. 331.

57 Ibid., p. 337.

58 Ibid., pp. 337–8.

59 Vladislavić, *Portrait with Keys*, p. 49.

16

AZADE SEYHAN

The Translated City: Immigrants, Minorities, Diasporans, and Cosmopolitans

> There are certain forms of metamorphosis from which one never returns.
>
> Kate Braverman, *Palm Latitudes* (1988)

> Exile teaches you about individual fate with universal implications, because it is eternal and has always been with us.
>
> Breyten Breytenbach, "The Exile as African" (1991)

The urban spaces of the contemporary world stand as enduring emblems of our modernity. They signify the shifting landscapes, breakneck rhythms of daily life, and deepening conflicts between collectivities – national and ethnic – that all bear testimony to Karl Marx's memorable observation of 1848, "all that is solid melts into air."[1] Positioned in the fold of a paradox that represents both the security of home and the inevitability of migration, the city confronts the ethical imperative of settling its inhabitants as it allows for their differences. While this need for openness to diversity is a long-acknowledged characteristic of the city, its literary representation by writers living in contemporary diasporas has generated a new consciousness of the city as a site of continuous exchange, economic and monetary, as well as linguistic and cultural.

Challenges of Terminology

In contemporary critical usage of the term, *diaspora* has moved into a broadly defined semantic field. While the word originally signified the forced expulsion of major religious communities, such as the Jews and the Armenians, in our age the term has expanded to include in its purview many forms of exile. Can we consider diverse groups of refugees, immigrants, and exiles diasporans? If not, what distinguishes each group from the other?

Unless otherwise noted, all translations in this chapter are by the author.

And what is the function of each in the infinite calculus of movements in and out of cities? Definitions as well as self-definitions of groups have proven to be as diverse as the groups themselves. Hannah Arendt, the prominent philosopher who fled Germany when the Nazis came to power stated, "we don't like to be called 'refugees.' We ourselves call each other 'newcomers' or 'immigrants' ... A refugee used to be a person driven to seek refuge because of some act committed... Well, it is true we have had to seek refuge; but we committed no acts."[2]

Bharati Mukherjee, the award-winning Indian-Canadian-American author, identifies narratives of movement and transfer predicated on "expatriation, exile, immigration, and repatriation."[3] For Mukherjee, immigration is "the act of adopting new citizenship, of going the full nine yards of transformation," and it is one option a noncitizen can exercise. To expatriate, on the other hand, is to exercise "an act of sustained self-removal from one's native culture, balanced by a conscious resistance to total inclusion in the new host society." "In the case of *exile*," however, "the comparative luxury of self-removal is replaced by harsh compulsion. The spectrum of choice is greatly narrowed" because alternatives to exile may very well be torture, death, or imprisonment.[4] Like the mobile character of worldwide displacements of our age, definitions that aim to capture these movements shift and shape thus destabilizing any foundational concept. One approach to differentiating terms that collectively refer to all acts of im/migration would be to abstract the critical term from the real experience of movement, transport, and translation and its various modes of register by the experiencing subject.

Migrations occur within or without national borders when individuals as well as groups are forced to leave their homes when confronted with poverty, famine, or loss of jobs and employment opportunities and have to look for work elsewhere. One of the major causes of such necessary migration is loss of agricultural land and prospects. "Migration is the failure of roots," critic Juan Bruce-Novoa writes; "[d]isplaced men are ecological victims. Between them and the sustaining earth a wedge has been driven. Eviction by droughts and dispossession by landlords, the impoverishment of the soil or conquest by arms – nature or men, separately or together, lay down the choice: move or die." During the first quarter of the twentieth century, in the aftermath of the Mexican Revolution, Mexican farmers and peasants were ruthlessly exploited and driven away "by the impossibility of living humanely and humanly in Mexico" and headed northward to the United States.[5] Similarly, in another country far away from Mexico, the Turkish peasant, whose small farming land was either destroyed by natural forces or appropriated by landlords during the 1950–60 *Demokrat Partisi* rule, first migrated to major Turkish cities and then to German industrial centers in search of work. The

Chicanos, as the Mexican migrants in the United States came to be known, and the Turkish *Gastarbeiter* (guest workers) in Germany represent the traditional definition of the migrant: someone expelled from the hometown or homeland by natural or man-made calamities. While not always self-evident, the word migrant has connotations of unreliability and transience and implies a threat to established communities. Furthermore, it appears to define those hailing from a lesser culture or background. An American expatriate would certainly not be referred to as a migrant in Paris. In this field, terminology is tricky. Arjun Appadurai noted early on that "postnational formations" could not be defined within the lexicon of existing political vernaculars. "[N]o idiom has yet emerged," he states, "to capture the collective interests of many groups in translocal solidarities, cross-border mobilizations, and postnational identities."[6] We need to look for value-free terms to the extent this is possible, while remaining cognizant of their contingency. This chapter attempts to define the relational contact points of the terms as they are represented by specific groups and individuals.

Although the word *immigrant* differs from *migrant* by virtue of two initial letters, the two terms are separated by a wide semantic margin. The migrant usually seeks temporary or seasonal employment, which is usually found in the agricultural sector. If these temporary workers venture into the city, they work in construction or as caregivers in private homes. Whether out in the country or in the city, their participation in the life of the host land is invisible, partly because many of them also lack visas and work permits. While the image of the Mexican migrant worker in California's vast agricultural landscape is a familiar one, thousands of seasonal migrant workers in other distant locales are not as visible. Presently, in Istanbul, for example, there are close to a million women from the former Soviet republics working as caregivers to the elderly and as nannies. A great number of these women overstay their visas; however, no matter what the length of their stay is, they remain technically migrants. As migrant populations grow, some from the group may decide not to return home, and if the numbers of "guest workers" who eventually settle in the host land reaches a critical mass, then they constitute a minority. This is what has happened with the Turks of Germany. What began as a labor migration from Turkey to Germany at the end of the 1950s resulted, in the course of half a century, in the formation of a minority. Arguably, not every member of this minority started out as a migrant worker; there are also immigrants, political refugees, and academics, among others, in this minority population. Today, close to three million Turks are permanently settled in Germany. The creative talent of Germany's Turkish minority is concentrated in Berlin, which has become a desired site of affiliation not only for Turkish writers but also for numerous artists of non-German origin.

Immigrants, on the other hand, make a conscious choice to leave the home country and apply for permanent residency in the country of destination. They are looking for better working conditions and income, and often a better future for their children. They are in the host country to stay, and their opportunities are usually in the city. The work they seek requires them to have mastery of the language of the land, to transpose and to translate themselves into citizens of a new collectivity, and to translate the discourse of the "foreign" city into their own vernacular. In Salman Rushdie's words, immigrants like him are "translated men."[7] Writers and academics like Rushdie and Arendt see themselves as immigrants, for their – or in some cases, their parents' – choice to settle in the host land was neither accidental nor seen as a short-term solution to a crisis they wanted to escape. In the final analysis, it is neither possible nor desirable to offer clear-cut definitions of *migrant*, *immigrant*, and *minority*, as these states alternately diverge and overlap in time. However, narratives of exile demonstrate by example what it means to write as diasporans or cosmopolitans and how such writing is conditioned by, and connected to, the metropolis.

Writing/Translating Berlin

"*Wahlberliner*" is the preferred designation assumed by many writers and artists of non-German origin who currently live and write in Berlin, among them Turkish-born novelist and actress Emine Sevgi Özdamar, journalist and poet Zafer Şenocak, writer Yadé Kara, and film director Ayşe Polat; the Russian-born satirist Wladimir Kaminer; and from Romania, Carmen-Francesca Banciu, Nobel laureate Herta Müller, and her ex-husband, the novelist Richard Wagner. Literally, the word means "Berliner by choice," as the artists who have chosen to become citizens of Berlin see this metropolis as an imagined community where they are free of ethnic and national biases. The metropolis offers the writer in diaspora an alternative home and a space in community. For authors exiled or displaced from their respective nations, another national affiliation poses the threat of obedience to exclusionary practices. Whether New York, Los Angeles, London, Berlin, or Istanbul, the city where capital and transnational movements are spatially concentrated and citizenship is not one of state but of the city itself, has become the preferred destination of moving populations in search of refuge or opportunity.

In one of her stories about Berlin, Özdamar famously remarks, "In a foreign tongue, words have no childhood."[8] However, it is in German, her foreign language, that she remembers the stories of her childhood, as these intersect with the history of the nation. Özdamar's status as a German resident of non-German origin exemplifies the impossibility of classifying people who have left their homelands in any clear-cut category. She came to Germany in the mid-1960s as a temporary worker, then became a permanent resident and thus, naturally, part of the existent Turkish minority. However, as a multilingual Berliner author, playwright, and actress who has performed at Bertolt Brecht's Berliner Ensemble and the Comédie Française in Paris, has been the subject of international academic conferences, and has given workshops as writer-in-residence at American universities, she is also undoubtedly a citizen of the world and a cosmopolitan.

In current usage, cosmopolitanism has emerged as the term of choice for progressive political positions and figures prominently in a diverse range of social theories. It is seen as an alternative to both narratives of nationalism and an identity-driven multiculturalism. Despite the desirable connotations of cosmopolitanism, however, many discussions of this concept include some disclaimer about being able fully to define it. A more nuanced understanding of the concept with regard to transnational writing would need to consider cosmopolitan writers' reliance on cultural translatability. These writers study cultural differences and convergences not only between geographical entities, but also between different temporalities, and they translate them into terms intelligible to the reader. Translation and self-translation also allow exiled writers to bring to language what they could not say in their own languages or what was censored in their own countries. Özdamar's work both re-members fragments of Turkish history and, in the free world of Berlin, dares to reveal its silenced and censored voices.

A first-generation Kurdish/Turkish-German, Özdamar writes in German which, as her second or possibly third language, is already a translation. Some of her politically charged work would likely have been subjected to censorship if written in Turkish. Translation reveals something that censorship or fear of persecution holds back or hides. Özdamar's stories disclose banned chapters of modern Turkish history, put Turkish and German pasts into an open dialogue, and retell suppressed or forgotten tales that help decipher the apparently inscrutable signs of other cultures. In her self-declaredly favorite novel, *Das Leben ist eine Karawanserei hat zwei Türen aus einer kam ich rein aus der anderen ging ich raus* (1992) and its sequel, *Die Brücke vom goldenen Horn* (1998) – translated as *Life is a Caravanserai, Has Two Doors, I Came in One, I Went Out the Other* (2000), and *The Bridge of the Golden Horn* (2007) – Özdamar renarrates the history of the long stretches of political oppression in Turkey, which she witnessed as a child and later as a young woman, in fragmented experiences of her immediate world. The form of her renarration in *Karawanserei*, cloaked in folkloristic wisdom and accented with echoes of *A Thousand and One Nights*, resists any external censorial intervention. At the same time, in the German context, her stories gain resonance by her ability to read them against the memories of Germans; in the juxtaposition of these parallel national pasts (Turkish and German), she sees a repeating trauma that can be brought to a level of consciousness only in writing in translation.

Özdamar's life story and her work represent an ongoing dialogue between different cultures and define her as a translator across national, ethnic, and linguistic divides. If we understand the openness to cultural translation as an added feature of cosmopolitanism, then Özdamar can further assume the status of cosmopolite. But she is also part of the Turkish diaspora in Germany, and one of the defining features of diasporic communities is a commitment to the restoration and/or maintenance of the memory of homelands. For this Turkish-German writer, Berlin's cityscape, which is not merely an agglomerate of asphalt and concrete and parks and monuments, but a palimpsest of images of Istanbul and Berlin, forms the backdrop for the diasporan's confrontation with the past and the lost home. In *Der Hof im Spiegel* [*The Courtyard in the Mirror*] (2001), a collection of Berlin and Istanbul stories, Özdamar's fascination with the histories and memories of both cities finds its expression in tales of her frequent visits to sites of remembrance – mosques, churches, libraries, ruins of former East Berlin, and, most significantly, cemeteries.

As she has indicated in many of her works, Özdamar saw Istanbul's cemeteries as the only peaceful sites in the city because the Turks were not in the habit of making cemetery visits – "Die Friedhöfe sind leer, es sind die einzigen ruhigen Orte in der Stadt" ["The cemeteries are empty, they are the only quiet places in the city"] – and the stillness of the dead amidst the soothing green of the cypress trees provided for her a space for reflection and the connection to departed and beloved lives.[9] The Arabic inscriptions on the gravestones have always fascinated Özdamar, as she makes clear in the story "Großvaterzunge" ["Grandfather Tongue"], where she expresses her lament for the loss of the Arabic script with the conversion of the Turkish alphabet to the Roman one. In the story in *Der Hof*, "Mein Berlin" ("My Berlin"), she tells of her frequent visits to Berlin's cemeteries that recall those of Istanbul. In Berlin, the communication she seeks is not with departed family members as in Istanbul, but with members of what she sees as her literary and intellectual family: Hegel, Heinrich Mann, and, most significantly Brecht. In a telling episode, during one of her visits to Brecht's grave, memories of her family and Istanbul overlap with the present moment as she recalls how her grandmother always planted the same flowers "KÜPELİ (mit Ohrringen)" ["FUSCIA (with earrings)"][10] that now cover Brecht's resting place. In the story "Mein Istanbul" ("My Istanbul"), in the same collection, she tells of visiting an Istanbul cemetery as a young girl with a poet who was copying down the inscriptions on the gravestones to use in his poems. He tells Emine, "Das sind die letzten Sätze der Menschen. Da gibt es keine Lügen" ["These are the last words of the people. There are no lies here"].[11] By Brecht's grave, she marks the words that are inscribed on the headstone, "Er hat Vorschläge gemacht, und sie wurden angenommen" ["He made recommendations, and they were accepted"].[12] Later she dreams of visiting Brecht's house, where he is lying on his bed, and tells his wife, the renowned actress Helene Weigel, that she wants to speak with him. Weigel tells her he is dead. Özdamar replies that he is not dead, just sleeping and asks his wife to give her something of his – his tie or his pillow cover – and Weigel gives her the pillow cover. In the same dream, she is suddenly transported to a moving ship and sees Turkish fascists following her, "Hinter mir standen Faschisten aus der Türkei" ["Behind me stood fascists from Turkey"].[13] Here the memories/dreams of her artistic life at Brecht's Berliner Ensemble in East Berlin and those of her persecution by the police in Turkey converge. In the same story, as she rides through the streets of Berlin, she reads the graffiti on the walls about the brutality of the German police, "Gott ist tot, die Henker nicht … Wir brauchen keinen Tränengas, wir haben genug Grund zum Heulen" ["God is dead, but not the executioners … We don't need tear gas, we have enough reason to cry"], and a resounding plea for remembering the forgotten, "Alles Vergessene schreit im Traum um Hilfe" ["All that is forgotten cries for help in dreams"].[14] Thus, by superimposing images/stories of Istanbul's geography and memories on Berlin's backdrop in *Der Hof im Spiegel*, Özdamar engages in a cross-cultural memory work and creates an interpretive model for understanding the algorithm of diaspora in the tale of two cities.

Los Angeles: Exile in Translation

While Berlin has become the chosen home mostly of writers and artists settled in the Turkish diaspora, the map of Los Angeles shows a far more variegated scale of settlements from around the globe. This is a dynamic and interactive map that represents the ebb and flow of arrivals and departures in and from this Janus-faced, real-and-imagined city of impoverished Mexican and Hispanic migrants, Asian and Middle Eastern immigrants, voluntary and involuntary exiles, post-Communist Russian billionaires, the largest Iranian exile community in the world – that has dubbed the city "Tehrangeles" – local and global celebrities, wannabe stars from far and wide, aspiring actors and musicians, expatriates, artists, and intellectuals fleeing oppressive regimes, multiply transplanted academic exiles, and more.

In the words of Kate Braverman, one of its best – although little-known – translators, Los Angeles is "this southern city which seems only peripherally and accidentally American." Once an outpost of Spain and a Mexican territory, "[t]his incomplete city which seems to have no recognizable past, no ground that could be called unassailably sacred," has understandably transformed into a site on which other pasts, memories, visions, and languages are inscribed. In its vastness and unboundedness, this city of "the voids, the unstitched borders, the empty corridors, the not yet deciphered," is the destination of eclectic and motley groups of displaced peoples.[15] The rooted infrastructure of multiple forms of displacement is reflected in two very different narratives of exilic experience – in Braverman's novel *Palm Latitudes*, where the city and the ethnic minority of its eastern barrios are the main protagonists; and in the archives of the German-Jewish novelist Lion Feuchtwanger, whose Villa Aurora in Pacific Palisades became the hub of a distinguished circle of expatriate and cosmopolitan writers and artists who fled Hitler's Germany in the 1930s.

Although Braverman – who was born in Philadelphia but raised in Los Angeles and considers herself a true citizen of Los Angeles – is not, strictly speaking, an exiled writer, she understands herself and her work as the product of the many "morphologies"[16] of displacement. Her sense of exclusion from this vast and impersonal city, as she describes it in her autobiographical *Frantic Transmissions to and from Los Angeles* (2006), lends her writing a profound insight into the lives of disenfranchised Angelenos,

> It [Los Angeles] was a city of subtle psychological apartheid, of them and us. We who actually lived here, and the others who might come if lured. Our dwellings were designed for transience. Apartments without dining rooms, as if anticipating a future where families disintegrated... It was an aggressive linearity designed for people who would be spending their decades in lines, identified by number, rather than name.[17]

Palm Latitudes could easily be mistaken as the novel of a Chicana writer in its profound understanding of the loss of one's language, its translation of Mexican pasts on the palimpsest that represents the hybrid formation of Los Angeles, and its still-enduring faith in the possibility of redemption in this City of Angels. Three Chicanas, transplanted from Mexico to the cultural inferno of Los Angeles's barrios, undergo physical and psychological dislocation, abandonment, and death. The gloom and doom of this cheerless plot is redeemed by the poetic prose that transforms even the squalid corners of the city into spaces that conceal an ineffable lure. Of the three women, Gloria Hernández, an apparently mute housewife and mother, is the most tragic casualty of forced displacement. The other two, Francisca Ramos, "La Puta de La Luna," a red-clad streetwalker who lives with the memories of her life in the Caribbean, and Marta Ortega, an old *curandera* (healer) type who endeavors to preserve traditional lore under the glaring sun of an alien culture, blend in with the city's other marginalized ethnic and racial groups. Through the character of Gloria, who appears merely stupid to her family and neighbors, Braverman shows how loss of language leads to muted rage and eventually to total madness. Many writers of exilic experience, such as Eva Hoffman, Maxine Hong Kingston, and W. G. Sebald, as well as psychiatrists treating displaced patients, have shown how exile from the protective home of one's language and the memories preserved in this language can trigger a dangerous fall into psychotic states. It is a philosophical truism that human reason resides in language, and when that language is no longer, then the light of reason goes out. Gloria remains mute throughout the story, but Braverman gives her an internal monologue that not only registers the acute physical pain of being expelled from one's language and identity but also reveals the descent of a highly intelligent mind into madness, as it loses language and thus the capacity to reason:

> I admit this I could not learn the English language... Perhaps it is inexplicable, but English cut at my eyes like barbed wire... English hurt my lips, the soft fibers of my tongue. When I repeated English phrases, my mouth embraced unnatural American objects, appliances, concrete, steel girders and electric lights in unnatural abundance and force... Spanish flows like the ocean, aware of cycle, waves, completion and return.[18]

It is clear from Gloria's silent monologue in metaphors – and the narrator's viewpoint – that Spanish represents an irretrievable time and space bathed in comforting silence and wrapped in nostalgia, whereas English is the embodiment of the urban plight and the jarring noises of Los Angeles. Gloria's silence mimics and evokes the comfort zone of her mother tongue, which, however, can no longer shield her against the violence inflicted on her voice by the external forces of a disorienting geography and against her descent into the dark abyss of rage and psychosis.

Palm Latitudes is a rare specimen of a narrative about the vicissitudes of exile in Los Angeles by an Angeleno. As such, it negotiates the insider's view with that of the outsider, for the insider has an empathetic understanding of the most abject citizen – the undocumented, marginalized migrant – but also, more importantly, she can translate across the gap of cultural differences and, like her character Marta Ortega, can connect viscerally with the destinies of the transplanted.

At the other end of the spectrum of Los Angeles narratives of exile is the work of refugees who fled Hitler's Germany during the Nazi reign. Arriving in Los Angeles when it was still predominantly a city of native-born white Americans, "[t]he cosmopolitan colonies of British expatriates and German (and Austrian) exiles made noteworthy contributions to the literary representation of Los Angeles, often placing the urban space of their new home in relation to the memory of their cultures of origin."[19] While the vertigo of separation from language thrusts the already disaffected migrant into stutter, if not total silence, Hitler's cosmopolitan exiles were established writers, artists, and musicians. Among them were such academics as Arendt, Bruno Bettelheim, Erich Fromm, Leo Löwenthal, and Herbert Marcuse, all of whom chose to remain in the United States after the war and, in different ways, revolutionized American academic and political discourse.[20]

The German-Jewish and anti-fascist refugees moved through various stations of exile in European countries as the Nazis expanded their power over the continent. Those who were able to secure passage across the Atlantic finally arrived in the safe harbor of New York City. While some of these exiles, including philosophers Arendt, her husband Heinrich Blüchner, and Fromm (who also taught at the National Autonomous University of Mexico during his exile), opted to remain in New York, many others, including Theodor Adorno and Max Horkheimer – who originally came to New York, but ended up writing their tour de force, *Dialectic of Enlightenment* (1944), in Los Angeles – were attracted to Southern California's Mediterranean-like climate and culture.[21] Away from the raging fascism that had enveloped Europe, some of the most prominent names of German letters – such as Brecht, Thomas Mann and his brother Heinrich Mann, Alfred Döblin, and Franz Werfel, along with composers Arnold Schönberg and Kurt Weill, and the film director Fritz Lang – established what came to be called a "New Weimar" or "Weimar on the Pacific" on the coastline of the greater Los Angeles area. The headquarters of this literary and artistic circle – the salon, where readings were held, work in progress discussed, and translation projects were initiated – was Villa Aurora, which Lion Feuchtwanger and his wife Marta were able to purchase some time after they arrived in Los Angeles. The villa, which was already a part of Los Angeles history as the "Los Angeles Times Demonstration House" at the end of the 1920s and a major showcase for modern high-tech living, became the hub of German-speaking writers who identified as cosmopolitans in the manner of their predecessors Johann Wolfgang von Goethe, Heinrich Heine, and Friedrich Nietzsche, who had self-defined and fashioned themselves not as Germans but as Europeans. For the German exiles in Los Angeles, cosmopolitanism designated a Europolitanism with a German accent but freed of nationalism. They considered themselves cosmopolitan because by the time of their exile, most of them were already internationally known writers and artists, were well educated and well traveled, bi- or multilingual, and, for the most part, were financially solvent. Their attitudes toward Los Angeles were mixed; while Thomas Mann professed his happiness with the clime and the geography, Brecht found the culture banal and vulgar and was eager to leave the first chance he had. In an ironic way, Kate Braverman echoes the same sentiments about the city that Brecht once expressed to his friends. Referring to Angelenos, Braverman writes, "We had no monuments or subways, no boulevards with bronze statues of poets, composers, or sages on horseback, no museums or artifacts with resonance, no recognizable areas sanctified by American systems of classification."[22] By the same token, the absence of such monuments to a romanticized past frees the city from both an unhealthy nostalgia and allegiance to the concept of hometown or home, which has become an unstable entity in an age of unprecedented movements the world over.

By the end of the war, almost every member of the Aurora literary circle had returned to Europe, but the Feuchtwangers lived in Los Angeles until the end of their lives. Thus, the trajectory of Feuchtwanger's exile went from the status of refugee (despite Arendt's claim, Hitler's exiles were refugees because they were persecuted Jews who actually sought refuge in other countries) to that of diasporan. While his books written in Los Angeles do not necessarily bear the stamp of his Southern California exile, they draw their narrative energy from his long personal history of flight from Nazi-occupied Europe and acute sense of exilic consciousness. Furthermore, in the final installment of his *Wartesaal* [Waiting Room] Trilogy (1930–40), *Die Geschwister Oppermann* (1933), Feuchtwanger offers one of the most compelling studies of the sociopsychological determinants of fascism, the mentality of its victims, and their resistance to leaving their country even in the face of certain death. Feuchtwanger was writing this book in 1933 while on a reading tour in France, and he decided not to return to Germany. He finished the book in six months; within the year it was translated into nine languages including English, in which it appeared as *The Oppermans: A Novel* (1934). Considered by some critics to be one of the greatest epic novels of German literature, *Die Geschwister Oppermann* foretells with uncanny precision the coming systematic persecution of German Jews.

Feuchtwanger's flight to Los Angeles was fraught with danger at every turn and replicated, to some extent, the experience of the fictional Oppermann brothers' multiple displacements over two continents. Once settled in the safe enclave of the city, Feuchtwanger put his resources at the service of other intellectual exiles who opposed fascism and thus helped bring the legacy of an enlightened humanism to bear on the culture of Los Angeles. Today, Villa Aurora is a Los Angeles cultural institution that promotes transnational artistic and literary ventures; it provides space, time, and income for fellows primarily living and working in Germany to pursue their projects in an idyllic setting, and it continues the humanistic legacy the exiles imported to their chosen city of refuge.[23] It is fitting that a number of German writers of non-German origin, including the Turkish-German Zafer Şenocak and the Iranian-German poet Said spent time at Aurora on generous fellowships.

Today, Feuchtwanger's oeuvre is enjoying a well-deserved renaissance, in part because of the academic and critical interest in exile and Holocaust studies. However, a major factor in the continuing success of Feuchtwanger's work lies in his mastery of language for the German reader and its trans-latability for others. He continued to write in German during his Los Angeles exile, but the impact of his works came in translation, although, like all writers who depend on translation, he felt that his craft was com-promised. In "The Working Problems of the Writer in Exile," an address delivered in October 1943 in California to a writers' congress sponsored by the Hollywood Writers' Mobilization and the University of California, Los Angeles, Feuchtwanger stated, "It is a strange experience to observe how the effect of our work does not emanate from the form in which we wrote it, but from a translation... [E]ven the best translation remains somehow foreign."[24] Although Feuchtwanger mourned the loss of "the aroma" and "the life" in "the translated word," a few paragraphs later, he conceded that the "foreign speech environment" enriches the writer's own idiom, "even the constant, enforced contact with a foreign language, which I loudly deplored a few paragraphs earlier, finally results in enrichment," for the author, who writes in the context of another's language, "almost automatically" and constantly checks his own against the foreign word, and upon finding a more "striking word" in the other language for what he wants to express, "sharpens, files and polishes the existent expression until it becomes some-thing new."[25] Feuchtwanger also indirectly credited the state of exile for transforming both the writer and the writer's product. "The new land in which we live affects the choice of our subjects and also affects the form," he admitted; "[t]he landscape which surrounds the writer changes the land-scape within him."[26] Here Feuchtwanger showed how the writer and the city stand in a dialectical relationship, each translating itself into the other's terms. The translatability of Feuchtwanger's prolific output of plays, novels, essays, and speeches lies in this reciprocity.

Translatability presupposes the primacy of certain universals, such as the search for connectedness, a common idiom, memory, and identity. The exile's work rests on these concerns that lend it relevance and a certain uni-versal appeal. Feuchtwanger and his fellow Los Angeles exiles succeeded in salvaging and smuggling into the city what was left of a humanistic leg-acy from a Europe in ruins. While transplanting this legacy onto the soil of the new metropolis, they changed the composition of that soil as well as that of their work. Although the greater part of Feuchtwanger's work in Californian exile focused on an often distant historical past and major figures of European cultural history, such as Goya and Rousseau, the events and personages of yesteryear were refracted through the experience of the émigrés writing in the vast urban landscape of Los Angeles. In *Goya oder Der arge Weg der Erkenntnis* [*Goya or The Wicked Way of Knowledge*] (1951), Feuchtwanger portrays Goya's appearance before the Inquisition in a manner that strongly evokes Bertolt Brecht and others before the House Committee on Un-American Activities in 1947. In "The Purpose of the Historical Novel" (1935), Feuchtwanger stated, "One topic that has deeply moved me as long as I can remember is the conflict between nationalism and internationalism in the heart of a single individual." Treating this contradiction in the form of a contemporary novel would let personal grudges and resentments overshadow the power of the story. Therefore, Feuchtwanger, who clearly personified the contest of nationalism and internationalism as a German and a cosmopolite, chose "to transplant this conflict into the soul of a man, the Jewish historian Flavius Josephus, who ... experienced it in the same way as so many do today, with the difference that he did so 1860 years ago."[27] However, Feuchtwanger's impressive literary output in Los Angeles was not confined to representing the city as a lens through which the past came to explain the present. One of his lesser-known works, the title story of *Venedig (Texas) und vierzehn andere Erzählungen* [*Venice (Texas) and Fourteen Other Stories*] (1946), does not interweave two (hi)stories but rather two geographies: Venice on the Adriatic and Venice on the Pacific. In a story with an ironic undercurrent typical of Heinrich Heine, one of his favorite authors and also a German Jew who lived and died in exile, Feuchtwanger presents a fictional account of the creation of the Angeleno Venice as a commercial venture. The historical facts surrounding the construction of the town – located a few miles south of Villa Aurora – are available in many publications, including Morrow Mayo's classic 1933 tome, *Los Angeles*. Feuchtwanger had read this book, which is still in the Feuchtwanger Memorial Library at the University of Southern California.[28]

Feuchtwanger's story incorporates some of Mayo's history in fictional form. Mayo observed how Los Angeles's vast physical space created a disconnected population, the very opposite of a close-knit community. In an effort of self- and cultural preservation, however, myriad groups of exiles and the German émigré writers had to forge close communities and circles. Mayo maintained that the newcomers who flocked to the city, almost all comparative strangers, came for entirely personal reasons; they were looking for Eldorado and for real estate. In Feuchtwanger's story, Venice on the Pacific becomes the new Eldorado. In one of the chapters of his book,

"Abbot Kinney's Dream," Mayo described the creation of the American Venice with its canals and imported gondolas and gondoliers and replicas of the Adriatic city. However, despite the many artists, writers, and singers invited to the American Venice to lend it artistic glitter and glamour, the city failed to attract visitors, was converted into an amusement park, and its canals were eventually filled. Feuchtwanger drew on the facts in Mayo's book but fused US history with his critique of both modern European and American civilizations. Entrepreneur Perry Knight, the fictional Kinney, falls in love with Gloria Desmond, who works in a travel agency that displays a poster, "Venice is waiting for you." The two marry, build the American Venice, but the marriage does not last, and both marry others. In the end, Perry Knight realizes that while both the Venice on the Pacific and the original on the Adriatic are enticing in their own right, the Venice on the poster is the most attractive of all. This short story, clearly inspired by the still-visible memory of a remnant of Los Angeles history, shows how the city, whether real or imaginary, and not the nation, becomes an object of desire and affiliation.

As a writer who was very conscious of how a German nationalism out of all proportion wrought havoc on millions of Europeans and who suffered through multiple migrations, Feuchtwanger embodied in his person and work the ideal of a cosmopolitanism free of all national bias. The telling quote from Nietzsche that serves as an epitaph to the second book, "Heute" ("Today"), of the *Geschwister Oppermann* stands as a testimony to Feuchtwanger's insight into the destructive potentiality of nationalism:

> Die Deutschen haben die kulturwidrigste Krankheit und Unvernuft, die es gibt, auf dem Gewissen, den Nationalismus, diese névrose national, an der Europa krank ist: sie haben Europa um seinen Sinn, seine Vernunft gebracht.

> [The Germans have on their conscience the most anticultural sickness and failure of reason that ever existed: nationalism, this national neurosis that afflicts Europe: they [the Germans] have deprived Europe of its sense and reason.][29]

The Metropolis in the Social Imaginary

Those who are banished from their homelands or driven away by threat of death and torture are rarely welcomed with open arms in the receiving country. For the many displaced writers of our time, the alternative to citizenship in a nation-state is citizenship in the metropolis, where different idioms, accents, colors, attire, and religious and cultural practices blend into the urban backdrop. Cities like New York, Berlin, Los Angeles, or Istanbul afford the writer anonymity and the freedom of the flâneur and the distanced observer. As sites of a multifaceted cosmopolitanism, they become a point of affiliation for both the noncitizen in exile and others who see themselves exiled within their own lands and societies. In "This, Here, Now: Imagining the Modern City," James Donald notes that "[c]ity life as a normative ideal acknowledges not only the necessary desire for the security of home, but also the inevitability of migration, change, and conflict, and so too the ethical need for an openness to unassimilated otherness."[30] The resistance to national myths and narratives of common culture allows the writer the latitude to move across not only temporal and geographical coordinates but also diverse linguistic and social communities.

In a speech delivered in 1996 at the International Parliament of Writers in Strasbourg, Jacques Derrida took up the question of "Cities of Refuge," which would offer migrants, refugees, and exiles a sanctuary. He reiterated the appeal previously made by this organization to institute "free cities," which are envisioned as self-determining and independent from the state and from one another, to the extent this is possible, and yet form alliances "according to laws of solidarity yet to be invented." The assignment of the writers would be the formulation of these laws that allow the cities to "reorient the politics of the state" and the "modalities of membership" in a way that joins a sovereign city as sanctuary to the state.[31] Here Derrida recalls Arendt's reference to the plight of a record number of refugees, who between the two world wars would not be granted any status recognized by international state laws, not even that of "stateless people."[32] Therefore, our present task as writers involves claiming for the city a new meaning and identity as a sovereign entity that would free it from the authority of the nation-state in matters of hospitality and sanctuary. The condition of the possibility of such cities presupposes its political realization. However, the political implementation of the idea reveals the contradictory logic of the cosmopolitan ideal. On the one hand, the principle of unconditional hospitality inherent in cosmopolitanism aspires to welcome all refugees; on the other hand, certain restrictions have to be imposed on rights of residence that Derrida, alluding to Kant's definition of cosmopolitanism, sees as dependent on treaties between nations.

I cite Derrida's essay, "Cosmopolitanism," not in expectation of, or hope for, the realization of such cities of refuge, but rather to show that the idea of a free city independent of state authority is part of the social imaginary of creative exiles who have sought sanctuary in the metropolis. While the creation of free cities in the world of *Realpolitik* is a near impossibility, those written out of home and history because of war, persecution, race, class, or gender keep alive the cosmopolitan ideal of the free city. This ideal is probably a destination one can never arrive at, like the idea of imaginary homelands, to which one can never return. However, for the many who have lost their footing in history and geography and whose multiple moves amounted to a fire, as the Turkish saying goes, the metropolis offers a niche where the memory of a lost home can be projected on the new cityscape; thus, Istanbul is superimposed on Berlin, Weimar on Los Angeles, Bombay on London, Frankfurt on New York, or Havana on Paris. Robin Cohen, an analyst of diaspora cultures, maintains that globalization has underscored the importance of the study of diasporas, which represent a historic opportunity for promoting tolerance and diversity in a world of continuous flows across borders.[33] Today most diaspora communities are concentrated in the major cities of the world. If the city also welcomes "the huddled masses yearning to breathe free" – in the words of Emma Lazarus's poem, "The New Colossus," inscribed on the lower pedestal of the Statue of Liberty in New York Harbor – then the cityscape of the globalized world becomes the canvas on which exiles of all creeds inscribe and paint their imaginary homelands.

NOTES

1 Karl Marx and Friedrich Engels, *The Communist Manifesto* (London: Verso, 2012), p. 38.
2 Hannah Arendt, "We Refugees," in Marc Robinson, ed., *Altogether Elsewhere: Writers on Exile* (San Diego: Harcourt, 1994), p. 110.
3 Bharati Mukherjee, "Imagining Homelands," in André Aciman, ed., *Letters of Transit: Reflections on Exile, Identity, and Loss* (New York: New Press, 1999), p. 69.
4 Ibid., pp. 71, 71, 73.
5 Juan Bruce-Novoa, *Retrospace: Collected Essays on Chicano Literature* (Houston: Arte Publico Press, 1990), pp. 57, 58.
6 Arjun Appadurai, *Modernity at Large: Cultural Dimensions of Globalization* (Minneapolis: University of Minnesota Press, 1996), pp. 164, 166.
7 Salman Rushdie, *Imaginary Homelands: Essays and Criticism, 1981–1991* (London: Penguin/Granta, 1991), p. 17.
8 Emine Sevgi Özdamar, *Mutterzunge* (1990); the text quoted is from *Mother Tongue*, trans. Craig Thomas (Toronto: Coach House Press, 1994), p. 52.
9 Özdamar, "Mein Istanbul," *Der Hof im Spiegel. Erzählungen* (Köln: Kiepenhauer & Witsch, 2001), p. 72.
10 Özdamar, "Mein Berlin," *Der Hof im Speigel*, p. 60.
11 Özdamar, "Mein Istanbul," p. 72.
12 Özdamar, "Mein Berlin," p. 60.
13 Ibid., p. 61.
14 Ibid., p. 58.
15 Kate Braverman, *Palm Latitudes* (New York: Penguin, 1988), p. 33.
16 Kate Braverman, *Frantic Transmissions to and from Los Angeles: An Accidental Memoir* (Saint Paul, MN: Graywolf Press, 2006), p. 17.
17 Ibid., p. 15.

18 Braverman, *Palm Latitudes*, p. 118.
19 Russell A. Berman, "British expatriates and German exiles in 1930s–1940s Los Angeles," in Kevin R. McNamara, ed., *The Cambridge Companion to the Literature of Los Angeles* (Cambridge: Cambridge University Press, 2010), p. 49.
20 These exiled German-Jewish scholars taught at major US universities and published their works in English. While Arendt and Fromm taught at a number of universities, Marcuse and Löwental chose to stay in the University of California system, at San Diego and Berkeley, respectively. Bettelheim taught at the University of Chicago. Marcuse achieved great fame during the Vietnam War years due to his critique of the war and the culture of capitalism; today, Hannah Arendt remains a much studied and referenced scholar of political philosophy.
21 The original German title is *Dialektik der Aufklärung: Philosophische Fragmente*. The first edition (1944) was published in a small mimeographed edition with the title *Philosophical Fragments*.
22 Braverman, *Frantic Transmissions*, p. 15.
23 Villa Aurora also administers a Feuchtwanger Fellowship, which is awarded to a writer from a country where freedom of expression is restricted, and a Berlin Fellowship, which sends a Los Angeles artist to Berlin.
24 Lion Feuchtwanger, "Working Problems of the Writer in Exile," in Robinson, ed., *Altogether Elsewhere*, p. 258.
25 Ibid., p. 259.
26 Ibid., p. 258.
27 From The Feuchtwanger Memorial Library page of University of Southern California Library web site, http://libguides.usc.edu/content.php?pid=31801&sid=592162.
28 For this reference, I am indebted to Harold von Hofe, "Feuchtwanger and America," in John M. Spalek, ed., *Lion Feuchtwanger: The Man, His Ideas, His Work* (Los Angeles: Hennessy & Ingalls, 1972), pp. 33–50.
29 Lion Feuchtwanger, *Die Geschwister Oppermann*, 10th ed. (Berlin: Aufbau, 2013), p. 124.
30 James Donald, "This, Here, Now: Imagining the Modern City," in Sallie Westwood and John Williams, eds., *Imagining Cities: Scripts, Signs, Memory* (London: Routledge, 1997), p. 200.
31 Jacques Derrida, *On Cosmopolitanism and Forgiveness*, trans. Mark Dooley and Michael Hughes (London: Routledge, 2001), p. 4
32 Ibid., p. 9.
33 Robin Cohen, *Global Diasporas: An Introduction* (London: UCL [University College London] Press, 1997), p. 176.

17

GREGORY WOODS

Gay and Lesbian Urbanity

The history of the modern subcultures of homosexuality offers a number of spectacular partnerships between cities and their gay inhabitants. Just to mention 1910s Harlem, 1920s Paris, 1930s Berlin, and 1950s New York in this context is to highlight a major presence of lesbian and gay artists in the development of modern culture. One can add more specific locations (Bloomsbury, Greenwich Village) and cultural movements: the Generation of '27 in Seville, the San Francisco Renaissance and its associations with the Beat generation, the New York School of Poets and its associations with Abstract Expressionism, and so on. One could trace the city's accommodation of same-sex desire back, through history and myth, from Haroun al-Raschid's Baghdad, through Renaissance Florence, to Martial's Rome and Socrates' Athens. One could even invoke the fate of the Cities of the Plain. But "the homosexual" as a type with a stable, lasting identity is a late nineteenth-century construction. Someone similar had been seen in the Whitmanian loafer and the Baudelairean flâneur, but the new type was largely based on subcultural behavior observed in European cities of the fin de siècle.

The city means abundance – of servicemen in Marcel Proust's wartime Paris, of black men in Federico García Lorca's New York, of sailors in Jean Genet's Brest, of proletarian youths in the Rome of Pier Paolo Pasolini and Sandro Penna. So many men, so little time... Specific locations, by virtue of the opportunities they offer for meeting, or even for actual sexual encounters, often acquire not only an erotic character but also one of high risk, since those who go there to meet each other may be laying themselves open to the dangers of arrest or homophobic attack. Parks, public lavatories, shopping arcades or markets with a particular reputation and, of course, gay bars and nightclubs repeatedly crop up in gay fiction as sites of significance, where important plot-driving events take place. Some such spaces are shared with the general populace or are predominantly gay only at night.

The initial anonymity of city life can have alienating effects; but for many lesbians and gay men, it provides some of the reassurance and protection of the closet. Indeed, anonymity may be the main attraction. It allows for the conditions of self-reinvention, whereby one escapes the prohibitions and inhibitions of family life.

The city novel in general and the gay novel in particular tends to start with an arrival – that of the wide-eyed, young provincial eager for new experiences but nervous of risk. Mikhail Kuzmin's novel *Wings* (1906) opens with a rail journey into St. Petersburg. His mother having died, Vanya Smurov is being transferred there by his uncle. The city begins to invade the train and Vanya's consciousness, first in the form of commuting travelers, and then in the view from the window: not the glamorous palaces Vanya has been expecting, but suburban kitchen gardens and cemeteries, which duly give way to a polluted cityscape of six-story tenements and wooden shacks. The bourgeois social environment of school and extended family that the youth enters is not as unprepossessing as this, but it is still a disappointment. However, the aesthete Larion Dmitriyevich Stroop, who befriends Vanya, sees a particular virtue in these apparently confining circumstances. He says to the youth, "You're in bad surroundings; but that may be for the best, as you're divested of the prejudices of any kind of traditional life, and you could become a perfectly modern man if you wanted."[1] In his allegiances to art and beauty, Stroop is pretty modern himself, and, knowing there is something odd about him, Vanya feels he should conceal from his uncle their chance meeting in the Summer Garden.

Where Mikhail Kuzmin invents an exotic, orientalist Alexandria in his verse cycle *Alexandrian Songs* (1906), Constantine Cavafy sees superimposed layers of cultures of homosexual desire, with the modern city of shopping, manual labor, bureaucracy, and cruising at the top. In his poems of modern Alexandrian life, strangers meet in cafés and go on meeting in the same or similar places; they become lovers in the private rooms above such places, presumably rented by the hour. Their hands meet across the merchandise in a shop; their eyes meet, in reflection, in the window of another shop. The plain are stopped in their tracks by the beautiful. Those with money rent the bodies of those without. For all the brevity of their physical collisions, and the sordidness of many of the locations in which they seize these clandestine moments together, their encounters often generate lasting beauty when transformed by those of them who are writers or artists, although it may not happen until many years later, when memories are fixed in the eternity of art. All of it is the product of the conditions of city life.

By the time Mark Doty comes to write his poem "Chanteuse," paying homage to Cavafy and using one of its phrases as the title of the collection in which it appears, *My Alexandria* (1993), the great Egyptian city has become a calm – one might almost say remote – state of mind. Doty's Alexandria is a cultural palimpsest whose most recent layer, the city of the present day, is of no interest to him. Doty's Cavafy's Alexandria can be taken anywhere, eternally present in the past. This context is also conjured up in Marilyn Hacker's love poem "Cities," in which the speaker says, from an obvious geographical distance, "The tree in the yard is heavy with snow, / the house is as still as a boat in morning, / and I taste Alexandria on your tongue."[2]

The title character of Oscar Wilde's *The Picture of Dorian Gray* (1891) leads the respectable, upper-class side of his life in West London, but when he yearns to experience the riskier, racier pleasures, he heads for the docklands of the East. It is here that he visits brothels and opium dens. To be sure, there are equivocal moments in the West End – for instance, a fruit seller in Covent Garden gives him cherries and refuses to take payment for them – and his intense friendships with Lord Henry Wotton and the artist Basil Hallward develop within the acceptable homosocial conventions of society clubs and residences. However, his implied secret life, which takes place at night and of which we see only brief glimpses – such as when he is observed brawling with foreign sailors in Whitechapel – takes place among the working-class and the transient, cosmopolitan underclasses of the great imperial port.

By stepping outside his class, the well-born homosexual encounters the physical heft of proletarian masculinity. He establishes multiple, transient contacts with such men without thereby subverting with misplaced loyalty the demands of family and dynasty. But, however easy his commercial transactions with them, he is always haunted by the possible power-reversal of blackmail or violence. The working-class man and his part of town are both a promise and a threat. In Proust, the Parisian *beau monde* is never hermetically sealed off from the rest of humanity. Its lower reaches are always permeable to upstarts; its great houses are staffed by the lower orders; and any aristocrat – or any male one, at least – may adopt a virtual cloak of invisibility, stepping out into the streets at night, incognito, and making his way to some discreet establishment like Jupien's brothel to purchase the splendors of working-class flesh. During the war, soldiers supplement their incomes by working in Jupien's place, whether in or out of uniform.

Of course, many novels about lesbian women are set in cities, too, and many about gay men are set in suburbs, small towns, villages, and the open countryside. But if we generalize about the male and female constructions of homosexual/gay identities that have come to prevail in western societies in the past century, and about the recognizable types and stereotypes that have most been used to represent them, we must acknowledge that gay male identity is more closely associated than its lesbian equivalent with cities and city life. Colette's Claudine learns a thing or two about lesbian courtship while she is attending her provincial school in *Claudine at School* (1900); but it is not until her father moves his family to Paris that she meets her first homosexual men, her beautiful cousin Marcel and his more experienced lover Charlie in *Claudine in Paris* (1901). Although Virginia Woolf's *Mrs. Dalloway* (1925) is so much a London novel, its main lesbian episode – Clarissa's memories of a period in her teens when she loved Sally Seton – takes place in the grounds and interior of a country house. In *Nightwood* (1936), Djuna Barnes tends to associate Matthew O'Connor, the cross-dressing, homosexual, fake gynecologist, with city life, but her lesbian characters, Nora and Robin, less so. (Conversely, in *Maurice* [begun in 1913, posthumously published in 1971], E. M. Forster could find no suitable happy ending for two male lovers in London, having to settle instead for sending them off into the implausible greenwood together.)

When Stephen Gordon, the central character of Radclyffe Hall's novel *The Well of Loneliness* (1928) goes to Paris, she finds – horror of horrors – a subculture of male and female inverts who seek comfort in each other's company. Her own origins are in the landed gentry: she grows up on a rural estate, following the country pursuits that might have been enjoyed by her father's son, if he had had one. Were she a man, she would simply carve out a life for herself following the example of her father and his. It is the Great War that takes her to France – as an ambulance driver – and the end of the war that takes her to Paris. For all her discomfort among the city's inverts, she reluctantly has to accept that her future lies in their subculture.

There is a similar ambivalence about the queer city in García Lorca's *Poet in New York* (1940). García Lorca had visited New York in 1927 and was bowled over by the glamorous modernity of Manhattan, a place throbbing with both creative and destructive energy. It gave him a distinctly erotic thrill. Like Walt Whitman, for whom the city was a hive of promiscuous comradeship, he was enthralled by the abundance of working men he saw there, and especially by so many black men. But he was evidently disturbed by the visibility of a specifically homosexual subculture. No enemy of camp in his own mannerisms and sense of humor, he seems to have found the commitment of stereotypically queer men to an openly defiant lifestyle perverse. As a consequence, in his "Ode to Walt Whitman" we are faced with a man-loving man sympathetic to a range of stigmatized sexualities nevertheless firing off a volley of homophobic epithets at camp men whose willed flamboyance tells him too much about himself.

In "The Tunnel," the infernal seventh section of his epic *The Bridge* (1930), Hart Crane descends into the underworld of the New York subway system and finds there, in a men's room, that love has been reduced to "A burnt match skating in a urinal."³ (The image is of casual sex in public spaces.) Regard it as you will – temple of desire, cesspit of vice – the public lavatory became a key symbolic feature of urban infrastructure in gay male literature, the space in which the anonymity enforced by social disapproval proved most beneficial – in the pleasurable opportunities it afforded – even in morally compromising circumstances associated with squalor and filth. Later in the century, Angus Wilson chose such a place for the moment of moral crisis at the heart of his first novel, *Hemlock and After* (1952). The liberalism of the book's central character, Bernard Sands, is severely tested and found wanting when he witnesses the arrest of a fellow homosexual for importuning in the men's lavatories in Leicester Square. Instead of seizing an opportunity to intervene, Bernard feels a surge of excitement at the look of terror in the other man's eyes. Wilson thereby associates Bernard with what he refers to as "the wielders of the knout and the rubber truncheon."⁴ A wonderful short story by Alfred Chester, "In Praise of Vespasian," published in his collection *Behold Goliath* (1964), follows Joaquin's quest for love from Spain to France, England, the United States, and back to France. The search involves his trailing an Algerian from pissoir to pissoir (or *vespasienne*) across Paris; passing notes between cubicles in an English cottage; through a realization, in a tearoom in New York (here called Sodom), that an affectation of indifference is probably the best expression of lust – until, on the verge of death by bowel cancer, he experiences a eucharistic moment of revelation at the feet of a gigantic laborer in another Parisian pissoir. Denis Belloc writes an autobiographical novel, *Neons* (1987) telling of a life of prostitution and petty crime in and around the public lavatories of Paris. Mutsuo Takahashi's long poem "Ode" (1971, revised 1980) stretches what might have been a narrowly realist representation of a sad individual pursuing a monotonously sordid lifestyle to a point at which, as a portrayal of desire whose satisfaction and disappointment desperation renders uncannily similar, the poem seems to have built up to a general relevance. Its public lavatories are no less recognizably universal than are the disembodied genitalia that haunt them.

By contrast with Crane's response to New York, the great Portuguese Modernist poet Fernando Pessoa, writing under his Whitman-influenced heteronym Alvaro de Campos, finds much to celebrate in the prolific sexual perversity of city life. In his "Triumphal Ode," when he mentions "The falsely feminine grace of sauntering homosexuals" he does so with self-evident approval. "(Ah, how I'd love to be the pander of all this!)," he adds, just three lines later. As the poem develops, the whole of the modern city is subsumed into an erotic vision united by the speaker's roving eye: "Ah, gazing is for me a sexual perversion!"⁵

The Berlin of Christopher Isherwood's *Goodbye to Berlin* (1939) provides something of the same perverse satisfaction for a narrator who sees all but participates in very little. Not until his post-Stonewall memoir *Christopher and His Kind* (1976) did Isherwood reveal not only his motive for having gone to Berlin in the first place, but also the atmospherics of his whole sojourn, in a single, striking sentence: "To Christopher, Berlin meant Boys."[6] John Henry Mackay's novel *The Hustler* (1926) had already given a much clearer picture of the lives of young male prostitutes operating from the Passage, a shopping arcade off Unter den Linden; but it was Isherwood's Berlin stories and their later manifestations – the Broadway plays *I Am a Camera* and *Cabaret* – that caught the imagination of non-Germans as having distilled the essence of interwar Berlin's "decadence," but without the potential offence of explicit detail.

In its reference to the myth of the city of Sodom (where Lot's wife was turned into a pillar of salt when she looked back at the city they were fleeing and witnessed its destruction), the title of Gore Vidal's novel *The City and the Pillar* (1948) refers to none of its specific urban locations (which include New York, Seattle, Los Angeles, and New Orleans). In Jim Willard's memory, all of them are Sodom by contrast with the pastoral glade in which he first made love with another boy; but so is male-male sex itself when experienced in anything less than innocent circumstances. In a similar mood, the opening page of John Rechy's *City of Night* (1963) proposes mapping out the whole of "America as one vast City of Night stretching gaudily from Times Square to Hollywood Boulevard ... America at night fusing its dark cities into the unmistakable shape of loneliness."[7]

New York took over from interwar Berlin as the world's most representative city of homosexuality. W. H. Auden's poem "September 1, 1939" was written in Dizzy's Club, a gay bar on West 52nd Street in New York, soon after his emigration to the United States just before the outbreak of the Second World War. It was here that Auden famously referred back to the decade in which he had made his name as "a low dishonest decade."[8] He used the New York bar scene again as his significant urban location for the broader discussion of human relations in his "Baroque eclogue," *The Age of Anxiety* (1948), which is initially set in a New York bar; its four main characters, Malin, Rosetta, Quant, and Emble, drift off into a pastoral dreamscape to work through the detailed implications of their desire for Emble (he being no less narcissistically enamored of himself than the others are).

New York's specific reputation, whether as a thriving haven for social and sexual diversity or as a sink of iniquity, tends to be centered on the traditional bohemianism of Greenwich Village. For the lesbian pulp novelist Ann Bannon, the women's bars of the Village are places that introduce woman-loving women to their identities as lesbians. Audre Lorde is more ambivalent about the lesbian scene in the Village in the 1950s in her memoir *Zami: A New Spelling of My Name* (1982), regarding it as both capable of providing something of the supportive atmosphere of an alternative family and yet, for non-white women like herself, as prone to racism as the broader society. The Greenwich Village of James Baldwin's *Another Country* (1963) is a much more complex place in which, for all its much-touted bohemianism, it is still difficult for a white man and a black woman to walk down the street together without attracting glances that range from the curious to the hostile. Yet it is also a place in which it is possible to begin to construct the many possibilities arising when people of different genders, ethnicities, backgrounds, and sexualities are brought together. But no matter how benevolent an environment the Village affords lovers of many types, nothing it offers can compare with the pastoral idyll Yves and Eric have been enjoying on a French beach. When Eric returns to New York and, in the novel's closing pages, Yves follows him there, the tone in which Baldwin presents their impending reunion is distinctly ominous.

When Molly Bolt, the central character of Rita Mae Brown's *Rubyfruit Jungle* (1973) arrives in New York – her roots are in rural Pennsylvania – she comes armed with the knowledge, found in "some trashy book," that Washington Square is the hub of Greenwich Village and the Village is the hub of the city's homosexual life. But she is disappointed to find that the Square is not teeming with the visibly homosexual people she has been hoping for. She spends her first night in a wrecked car with Calvin, a homeless man who just happens to be gay himself. He then shows her around the Village and takes her to her first lesbian bar, where she receives her first lesson in the fashion for the butch/femme division of gender roles among lesbian women. (The book is critical, as she is, of this supposed aping of heterosexual mores.) Calvin soon leaves to seek his fortune in San Francisco, but Molly decides to stay in what she calls "this ugly city."⁹

Novels of the gay liberation period – that is, between the Stonewall Riots of 1968 and the onset of the AIDS epidemic in the early 1980s – depict a Manhattan in the grip of a sexual frenzy that is both celebrated and deplored. The title of Michael Rumaker's novel *A Day and a Night at the Baths* (1979) accurately delineates its contents. Dedicated to the nine gay men who died in a fire at the Everard Baths on West 28th Street, Manhattan, on May 25, 1977, the novel overlays a dream of sexual freedom with an ominous nightmare of death by suicide, accident, or disease. Rumaker finds it difficult to celebrate the pleasures of the sexual carnival without acknowledging the skull beneath the skin. So immersed in New York's club scene are the central characters of Andrew Holleran's novel *Dancer from the Dance*

(1978) – over which looms a similarly ominous cloud – and so detached from its social context is their lifestyle, with its apparently limitless cycle of repetitive pleasures (sex and drugs and disco dancing), that when one of them uncharacteristically finds himself in a massive gay rights demonstration, marching to Central Park in "a sea of humanity," he is amazed to recognize virtually nobody from his own extensive social circle. Indeed, he concludes "there were tons of men in that city who weren't on the circuit, who didn't dance, [and who] didn't cruise."[10]

Larry Kramer's notorious novel *Faggots* (1978) opens with a sequence of invented statistics that are either merely plausible or startling, depending on the individual reader's point of view. "There are 2,556,596 faggots in the New York City area," the novel begins. The use of the insulting epithet here and as the book's title sets the tone for a narrative heavily critical of, yet luridly indulgent in, lifestyles of purely quantitative sexual pleasure rather than qualitative affectional connection. The opening passage continues: "The largest number, 983,919, live in Manhattan. 186,991 live in Queens, or just across the river. 181,236 live in Brooklyn and 180,009 live in the Bronx. 2,469 live on Staten Island."[11] The next occasion on which Kramer would grab the reader's attention with an arresting statistic would be March 7, 1983, when the *New York Native* would carry his article "1,112 and Counting" (referring to the number of deaths in the AIDS epidemic by that date) on its front page.[12] Kramer's play *The Normal Heart* (1985), an angry, autobiographical account of setting up Gay Men's Health Crisis in the face of the indifference and active obstruction of Mayor Ed Koch and the city authorities, was soon performed internationally on the apparent understanding that the specifics of the New York experience had not only emotional resonance but also direct political relevance elsewhere.

The extremes of the gay liberation period's sexual carnival in New York City – on the deserted and derelict wharves, in the Meatpacking District, in the bath houses, and the more notorious of the night clubs – and the beginnings of the epidemic – the soaring death statistics, the struggle to keep gay venues from being closed down, the violent antipathy of press and politicians – were so much written about that New York's exceptionality came to seem representative. Ever since, the localism of the Stonewall riots has been celebrated in cities around the world on Gay Pride Day.

As a genre, the celebratory narrative of sexual excess within a newly confident and burgeoning subculture metamorphoses into the AIDS novel of collective tragedies within the decline, fall, and rebirth of that same subculture. Quantity is significant in both: numbers of sexual contexts, numbers of deaths. Explicitly or not, the politics of one (the struggle for gay liberation) become those of the other (the allied struggles for humane treatment, for research funding, for accelerated drug approvals, for social acceptance, and against death itself). Like all tragedy, this later incarnation of the genre, when contrasted with the earlier, whether intertextually or within a single novel, is heavily freighted with dramatic irony. Edmund White's trilogy of autobiographical novels might be taken as representative of the arc of these social developments: from a provincial boyhood (*A Boy's Own Story*, 1982), through student life trying out both homosexuality and heterosexuality before a move to New York City and unequivocal homosexuality, even being present at the Stonewall riots (*The Beautiful Room is Empty*, 1988); then from the period of gay liberation to the gradual onset and remorseless denouement of the epidemic (*The Farewell Symphony*, 1997). Of course, it was not only gay New Yorkers for whom the epidemic was like a war zone. The Lebanese novelist Rabih Alameddine's *Koolaids: The Art of War* (1998) draws parallels between the civil war in Beirut in the 1980s and, in the subsequent decade, a San Francisco ravaged by AIDS.

At its best, the post-gay-liberationist city provides a communitarian spirit that British-born poet Thom Gunn and Armistead Maupin (whose *Tales of the City* series of novels began in 1978) find in San Francisco, and Sara Schulman discovers in New York. And yet, although the city is so often represented as a place where there is safety in numbers as well as choice, its streets and lots can be very dangerous places, even by day. In Alan Hollinghurst's *The Swimming-Pool Library* (1988), when Will Beckwith ventures into East London, unlike Dorian Gray who encountered exotic and illicit pleasures, he is queer-bashed by skinheads and his first edition of a Ronald Firbank novel is ruined. London life in Neil Bartlett's *Ready to Catch Him Should He Fall* (1990) is ruptured by regular outbreaks of homophobic violence, against which only the solidarity of the bar-based subculture is proof. Exploiting all the vulnerabilities of gay communities as well as all of their hard-won freedoms, a new subgenre of lesbian and gay crime fiction grew out of the post-Stonewall urban environment, usually with detectives who were themselves gay. Los Angeles alone hosts the detectives of Joseph Hansen (whose openly gay Dave Brandstetter solves crimes in twelve novels, starting with *Fadeout* in 1970), Katherine V. Forrest (whose lesbian detective Kate Delafield appears in eight novels, starting with *Amateur City* in 1984), and Michael Nava (whose Henry Rios first appears in *The Little Death* in 1986).

As European imperialism went into retreat, so too – if slowly – did the erotic Orientalism of western literatures, giving way to the fresh realism of native writers when their national cultures allowed them to speak of such scandalous matters. For several decades after the Second World War, for homosexual men the archetypal city of the Orient had been Tangier, notwithstanding the fact that it lies further to the west than all of the great European cities bar Lisbon. Apart from any other consideration, it was easy to get to, with minimal inconvenient travel beyond the bounds of Europe – a mere ferry crossing from Gibraltar. Versions of this compromised paradise for the seekers of sexual and narcotic freedoms appear in the fiction of such writers as Paul Bowles, William S. Burroughs, and Robin Maugham. Many years later, Tahar Ben Jelloun's novel *Leaving Tangier* (2006) reverses the pattern. Ben Jelloun objected to Bowles's habit of speaking on behalf, and in the voices, of illiterate Moroccan youths such as Ahmed Yacoubi, Larbi Layachi, and Mohammed Mrabet. His own work constitutes a major contribution in the speaking-back to the cultures of sexual colonialism.

In an effort to depict the reality and plurality of life in Cairo, Naguib Mahfouz daringly added homosexuality to the social mix, thereby stirring up a hostile response to his fiction from the beginning of his career. In *Midaq Alley* (1947), the café owner Kirsha uses his relative wealth to seduce a youth who works in a shop. In *Sugar Street* (1957), part three of the *Cairo Trilogy*, the intense friendship of Ridwan and Hilmi seems unexceptional until they solicit the influence of Abdurahim Pasha Isa, who is known to be homosexual. This association turns a private matter into something nameable and therefore at risk. But the main point, as far as concerns these novels, is to identify the variations of same-sex desire as contributing to the diverse living arrangements of the great metropolis.

Perhaps not surprisingly, cities around the world have comparable infrastructure to be taken advantage of by gay men subject to varying degrees of social anathema and legal sanction. The public park and the protective gay bar are recurrent in fiction. For Yuichi, the central character of Yukio Mishima's *Forbidden Colors* (1951), the open spaces of Tokyo offer up the most fruitful erotic possibilities. He meets the waiter Eichan in a park to whose sexual usefulness he has been alerted by an overheard conversation between two homosexual men, and he later meets seventeen-year-old Minoru at the zoo in Ueno Park. The two main locations of Pai Hsien-yung's novel *Crystal Boys* (1983), both in Taipei, are the New Park on Guanqian Street and the Cozy Nest, a gay bar on the bustling Lane 125 of Nanking East Road. The park is the stamping ground of a vibrant subculture – a loose, extended family – of rent boys, many of them banished from their families of origin and homeless.

As depicted in R. Raj Rao's novel *The Boyfriend* (2003), Bombay shows signs of the effects of globalization in its gay subcultures. The book's gay bar has the evocative name Testosterone; and the collective response of a group of camp gay men to the machinations of a blackmailing cop is given the name Operation Stonewall. For the reader, too, there is much that is cross-culturally identifiable. For instance, the book begins with a pickup in the men's lavatories at Bombay's Churchgate railway station. In Manil Suri's *The City of Devi* (2013), Jaz first meets Karun in a park near the Oval grounds in Bombay/Mumbai (both names are used). Karun is sitting on a bench between the children's slides and swings, oblivious of all the families around him, reading a book. When he looks up and notices Jaz's predatory gaze, he flees like a startled deer. Thus begins a long pursuit around the obstacles of Karun's internalized homophobia and through the increasingly apocalyptic landscape of a city devastated by pollution, religious strife, international terrorism, and war with Pakistan.

Benefiting from much historical scholarship in queer studies, recent writers have often followed a trend of associating their own present lives with those of lesbians and gay men in the past. Perhaps the most adventurous of these reimaginings has been the theatrical and fictional work of Neil Bartlett. In his book about Oscar Wilde, *Who Was That Man? A Present for Mr. Oscar Wilde* (1988), he is unable after living in London for many years to see the detail of the late-1980s city without imagining, beneath or behind them, the matching details of the same locations in the London of the 1890s. Typically, at one point, he asks himself, "How did the boys wear their hair in Soho a hundred years ago?"[13] Following much the same principle, Jonathan Kemp's *London Triptych* (2010) interleaves gay life stories set in the title city in the 1890s, the 1950s, and the 1990s. Across their various novels, Maureen Duffy and Sarah Waters have similarly mapped out and compared separate periods of lesbian life in London.

Meanwhile, city-based authors continue, like Theocritus in Alexandria, to turn from city to countryside when the pressures of urban living seem to overwhelm the possibilities of simple romance. This habit, whether nostalgic (a projection of adolescent memories) or idealistic (dreaming of rural escape) both undermines and strengthens the image of the city as an apt location for homosexual lives. This ambivalence is not unique to gay literature. Cities have often been thought of as better places in which to seek love than to settle down with it, places suited better to desire than to its fulfillment.

NOTES

1 Mikhail Kuzmin, *Wings*, trans. Hugh Aplin (London: Hesperus, 2007), p. 14.

2 Marilyn Hacker, "Cities," *First Cities: Collected Early Poems 1960–1979* (New York: Norton, 2003), p.28.

3 Hart Crane, *The Bridge*, in *The Complete Poems of Hart Crane*, ed. Marc Simon (New York: Liveright, 2001), p. 99.

4 Angus Wilson, *Hemlock and After* (Harmondsworth, UK: Penguin, 1992), p. 109.

5 Fernando Pessoa, *A Little Larger than the Entire Universe: Selected Poems*, trans. Richard Zenith (London: Penguin, 2006), pp. 155, 157.

6 Christopher Isherwood, *Christopher and His Kind, 1929–1939* (London: Eyre Methuen, 1977), p. 10.

7 John Rechy, *City of Night* (New York: Grove Press, 1963), p. 11.

8 W. H. Auden, "September 1, 1939," *Selected Poems: Expanded Edition*, ed. Edward Mendelson (New York: Vintage, 2007), p. 95.

9 Rita Mae Brown, *Rubyfruit Jungle* (London: Penguin, 1994), pp. 138, 151.

10 Andrew Holleran, *Dancer from the Dance* (London: Corgi, 1980), p. 243.

11 Larry Kramer, *Faggots* (London: Futura, 1980), p. 15.

12 Larry Kramer, *Reports from the Holocaust: The Making of an AIDS Activist* (New York: St. Martin's Press, 1989), pp. 33–51.

13 Neil Bartlett, *Who Was That Man? A Present for Mr. Oscar Wilde* (London: Penguin, 1993), p. 29.

18

KEVIN R. McNAMARA AND TIMOTHY GRAY

Some Versions of Urban Pastoral

The term *urban pastoral* might seem oxymoronic. *Pastoral* conjures fantasies of rural freedom: shepherds lounging in meadows piping on oaten flutes, as they often do in Theocritus' *Idylls* and Virgil's *Eclogues*, or professing undying love for their coy mistresses, a common pastime of early modern pastoral.[1] The word *country* derives from the Latin *contra*, meaning *against*, so we might assume that the country is in its very idea poised against the city, as it typically is in conventional pastoral. We might further assume that any collision of urban and pastoral must result in satire, and in the eighteenth century it did. John Gay's *Beggar's Opera* (1728) substitutes for the shepherds and coy mistresses of the courtly entertainment known as a pastoral marriage masque a cast of highwaymen, cutpurses, and bawds whose songs and speech burlesque the conventional figures and sentiments of love and marriage, and whose behavior satirizes the morals and manners of the upper classes. William Empson described it as "the pastoral method applied to Newgate," invoking the London prison that gave its name first to a series of pamphlets, the *Newgate Calendar*, then to a genre of novel, both of them devoted to the exploits of famous criminals.[2] Gay's friend Jonathan Swift likewise set the urban pastoral on a satiric path in his verse "Description of a City Shower" (1710) that brings neither burbling streams nor nourishment to fields and fauna. Instead, a flood tide of butchered livestock and drowned strays courses the swollen gutters of city streets.

Yet before *arcadian* came to mean rustic and simple, *Arcadia* named a historical region of Greece famed for its love of music and poetry, pursuits that kept it at peace until the Arcadian city-state of Cynaetha neglected them and fell into strife.[3] So, too, before *country* came to oppose *city* – in the sixteenth century, Raymond Williams said – it referred to "land spread out over against [*contra*] the observer," or a prospect.[4] Thus, what appears to be a necessary opposition between the pastoral and the urban is, in fact, the product of a particular history deeply invested with cultural and religious significance; it even informs the sociological romanticizing of organic community (*contra* instrumental society) that Stuart Culver discusses in Chapter 6.

Given that pastoral's "green world … is only metaphorically a place or space," Harry Berger, Jr., argued in a landmark 1965 essay, "it embodies a condition whose value should not remain fixed but should rather change according to the temporal processes of which it is a part."[5] One of the most significant changes, one crucial to the development of urban pastoral, was the shift in pastoral's focus from "the working countryman" to "the scientist or the tourist" in the eighteenth century.[6] In this change, the interplay between consciousness and environment became paramount; the aesthetic and psychological effects, and the moral lessons, of landscape were foregrounded. It is with this history in mind that Paul Alpers proposed that we understand the pastoral as a *mode* characterized by a set of "attitudes … about man's nature and situation" vis-à-vis the world, not as a genre defined by a set of conventions. As a mode, pastoral is sufficiently open to changing contexts that "it sometimes seems as if there are as many versions of pastoral as there are critics and scholars who write about it."[7] They share attitudes and poses taken over from ancient and early modern pastoral – desire for temporary withdrawal, communion with others, or immersion in, and imaginative transformation of, the life that surrounds us – and (along with pastorals from the eighteenth century onward) sensitivity to the aesthetic and affective properties of the landscape. In literature as in life, the art of urban pastoral inheres in ways of seeing that find or create within the city spaces or images conducive to pastoral moods. Perhaps the most concise example is the two lines of Ezra Pound's "In a Station of the Metro" (1913), which juxtapose, in order to identify, the faces of a crowd in the subway – that most mineral of landscapes – with the organic beauty of so many "[p]etals on a wet, black bough."[8]

Pastoral desires are most often suffused with an awareness of loss or sense of longing because the green world has always already vanished. Arcadia was no longer arcadian when Polybius wrote it into his *Histories*. The fate of all things arcadian is captured in a myth of historical progression expressed in Thomas Cole's cycle of paintings, *The Course of Empire* (1833–6). The five canvases depict a single fictional location – a Mediterranean harbor and its wooded shore – as it transitions from *The Savage State* through *The Arcadian or Pastoral State*, to *The Consummation of Empire*, and thence to *Destruction* before it finally reaches *Desolation*. The properly pastoral scene, second in the sequence, represents a balance between untrammeled nature and human community. As Cole correlated the cycle of history with the diurnal course of the sun, the pastoral flourishes when the pleasant light of mid-morning bathes "groups of peasants either pursuing their labours in the field, watching their flocks, or engaged in some simple amusement."[9] This balance cannot last, nor will the noontime glare of empire in which a resplendent city shines; it is a prelude to war and destruction. In the final canvas's dusk, foliage reclaims the broken columns, and the savage state returns.

In the hands of other artists, the world of ruins becomes the scene of a belated pastoral. Nearly two centuries before Cole, the French artist Claude Lorrain produced his *Pastoral Landscape with Ruined Temple* (1638) and *Landscape with Ruins, Pastoral Figures and Trees* (1643). So, too, poets filtered empire's remains through a pastoral gaze. The English poet John Dyer beheld in Rome "the rising sun / Flam[ing] on the ruins in the purer air / Tow'ring aloft upon the glittering plain." Wandering the city's seven hills, he saw ruins of pastoral as well: "vases boss'd, and huge inscriptive stones, / And intermingling vines, and figured nymphs, / Floras and Chloes of delicious mould / Cheering the darkness." The mood reaches its climax, appropriately, at "Maro's [Virgil's] humble tenement" on "th' Esquilian Mount," of which

> [a] low
> Plain wall remains; a little sun-gilt heap,
> Grotesque and wild: the gourd and olive brown
> Weave the light roof; the gourd and olive fan
> Their am'rous foliage, mingling with the vine,
> Who drops her purple clusters thro' the green.

Reclining there, Dyer imagined the poet engaged in easy conversation with Horace and "the ruler of the world; Happy Augustus!"[10] Back home, meanwhile, landscape architects erected "ruins" as visual features of country estates – some actually staffed with salaried, ornamental hermits. Each of these instances presents a dialectic of loss and recovery: the pastoral of ruins never pretends to innocence, is never free of history.

The aesthetic and psychological import of pastoral landscapes was formulated for the class of literate Londoners (most certainly including those scientists and tourists) by Joseph Addison. His essays on the pleasures of the imagination instruct us that

> [t]he Beauties of the most stately Garden or Palace lie in a narrow Compass, the Imagination immediately runs them over, and requires something else to gratifie her; but in the wide Fields of Nature the Sight wanders up and down without Confinement, and is fed with an infinite variety of Images, without any certain Stint or Number. For this Reason we always find the Poet in Love with a Country-Life, where Nature appears in the greatest Perfection, and furnishes out all those Scenes that are most apt to delight the Imagination.[11]

The English Romantic poets heeded Addison's prescriptive observation, William Wordsworth in particular. Yet he also memorably applied this gaze to the urban prospect in his sonnet "Composed upon Westminster Bridge, 3 September 1802." At daybreak, the imperial city's "Ships, towers, domes, theatres, and temples lie / Open unto the fields, and to the sky; / All bright and glittering in the smokeless air," as fixed boundaries between country and city melt away, and peaceful London's "mighty heart is lying still."[12] David Ferry proposed that "still" here means lifeless, that Wordsworth is in effect writing a pastoral of ruins and admiring the corpse of a city he elsewhere associated with the death of the soul.[13] However, the crepuscular city at peace, before or after the workaday din, was to be a frequent pastoral subject. More common than the sunrise city is the urban nocturne, whose lone ambler – author or painter – uses the "obscurity" produced by faint lighting to "reveal unsuspected formal and psychological depths in the urban landscape."[14] Painter James McNeill Whistler's London nocturnes of the 1870s and Edward Steichen's landmark photograph of New York's Flatiron Building in twilight (1904) achieve their effects in low light and the throng's absence. The less-well-known photographer William Fraser's *A Wet Night, Columbus Circle* (ca. 1897–8) turns Manhattan almost Venetian as flooded streets reflect light from distant buildings.

A century after Wordsworth, Georg Trakl cast far smaller, far less industrialized Salzburg as "The Beautiful City" (1913), rendering a scene filled with life but outside time. In the "sunlit silence" of a square, past and present, life and death, organic and mineral all merge: "pure images of death" peer from the churches toward which "[d]reamlike gentle nuns" hurry. Boys play by a fountain from which marble "[h]orses rise" while young girls look on, and from behind "the leafy frame of gardens" one hears fine women laughing and "young mothers singing."[15] This poem depicts the cyclical time of ritual and organic community rather than the mechanical time of modernity; its soft light might permeate any century. Proving that such atmospheric moments exist even in the density of twentieth-century Manhattan is James Schuyler's "February" (1960). The poem begins as a reminiscence of Italy, where Schuyler had been W. H. Auden's assistant, but the poet becomes distracted by the sunset-bathed facades of buildings outside his window and turns to close observation of the transient work of nature on the human-built landscape. The resulting work melds memory and sight, two times and two continents, into one figure of Italian sunlight playing on the water "by the temples" when

> One green wave moved in the violet sea
> like the UN Building on big evenings,
> green and wet
> while the sky turns violet,[16]

and many other colors – at least seven – that Schuyler describes as playing across the sunset skyline.

The great poet of the urban nocturne is Charles Baudelaire.[17] Realizing solitude amidst the pedestrian multitude of mid-nineteenth-century Paris, Baudelaire created an example emulated by many an urban stroller but rarely equaled. The searing vision of "The Swan" (1860), which Catherine Nesci discusses at length in Chapter 5, is a pastoral of ruins that recalls to memory the "field of hovels, the herd of rough-hewn cornice and chimney, the grass": the "old Paris" uprooted to build the imperial capital. Further images "flower" in the poet-speaker's memory, but they are all of a parched land: a swan escaped from a menagerie, its wings dragging the dust as it curses the heavens for rain, Andromache crying a river of tears as she mourns her exile from Troy and its Simois River, and "starved orphans dried like flowers." His "Morning Twilight" (1852) is dawn seen from the end of the night with the "man ... weary of writing, the woman of loving," the debauched, and the dying; it comes as "[s]hivering Aurora, in a garment of pink and green, rises slowly above the deserted Seine [and] gloomy Paris, rubbing its eyes, takes up its tools."[18] This city is but another exhausted laborer in a lyric that might be taken as a riposte to Wordsworth's rosy view of London, asleep at daybreak along the Thames. A half-century later, a different sort of ruin: The springtime sky above Parisian boulevards in Blaise Cendrars's *To the Heart of the World* (1919) has never been "as starry and leafy"; the "Milky Way ... swoon[s] ... and embrace[s]" the city, and a "water lily" graces "the Seine, it's the flowing moon" – a stark contrast with the Paris of "The Swan." Yet "Babylon and Thebaid are not deader, tonight, than the dead city of Paris," the poet-speaker laments of the wartime city. Condensing the pastoral of ruins into a single, striking image, the corpse-city that robs him of his past is "the cooled image of a plant / That reappears in its ashes."[19]

Walt Whitman's urban pastoral, contemporaneous with Baudelaire's, is far sunnier, a melding in full daylight of the natural and urban realms that Wordsworth could combine only while the city slept. Whereas Baudelaire sought "to extract *beauty* from *Evil*," the large-hearted speaker of "Crossing Brooklyn Ferry" (1856) seeks to absorb, and to be absorbed into, the living scene he beholds: "The impalpable sustenance of me from all things, at all hours of the day; / The simple, compact, well-join'd scheme – myself disintegrated, every one disintegrated, yet part of the scheme" that knits together fellow passengers, the floodtide below, the sun in the west, and the generations past and to come.[20]

William Carlos Williams recast the Whitmanian gaze in lyric snapshots of industrializing landscapes in New Jersey's suburban cities. In both the scrubby, late-winter landscape he foresees returning to vivid life in "Spring and All" (1923) and the foliage-free alleyway where the green glint of bottle-shards catches his eye in "Between Walls" (1938), the pastoral gaze roams beyond its customary frame. Williams' deeper engagements with history of the Great Falls of the Passaic River and Garret Mountain Reservation throughout his modern epic, *Paterson* (1946–58), contribute to an industrial pastoral that inventories the ecological and human cost of mastering nature to power a national manufactory. Flickers of ancient pastoral's survival are sighted on a Sunday afternoon among laboring families in the park:

> It is this air!
> the air of the Midi
> and the old cultures intoxicates them:
> present!

A woman "lifts one arm holding the cymbals, / of her thoughts, cocks her head / and dances! Raising her skirts," reminding the poem's protagonist of "the peon in the lost Eisenstein film":

> This is the old, the very old, old upon old,
> the undying: even to the minute gestures,
> the arm holding the cup, the wine
> spilling, stained by it:
> ...
> the female of it, facing the male, the satyr –
> (Priapus!)
> with that lonely implication, goatherd
> and goat, fertility, the attack, drunk,
> cleansed.

The music and dance, the satyr, and the goat all invoke Pan, the lusty god of the flocks whose name means "to pasture," and whose cult originated among shepherds in the hills of Arcadia. But the modern men cannot rise to the challenge; they are flaccid, defeated, "too damn lazy."[21] The scene leads to a conclusion voiced several times in Williams' poems, that the loss of "peasant traditions" among the American working class has unfitted them for life.[22]

Placing himself in the line of Whitman and Williams, Allen Ginsberg struggled with industrial pastoral. In "Sunflower Sutra" (1955), a dead but still standing sunflower in a rail yard figures a triumph of nature's endurance amidst an industrial wasteland, and a reminder of the vital nature within us. Yet as Terrence Diggory observes in his excellent analysis of Ginsberg's attempts in the mode, the poet faltered in his efforts to amalgamate the urban pastoral of Whitman and Williams with William Blake's dialectical pastoral in which "[t]he proper setting for [human] freedom is not in the garden, where the sunflower grows, but rather in the city," that is, in history. Ginsberg's difficulty is vividly captured by Diggory's juxtaposition of two passages from "Iron Horse" (1973), a poem in which Ginsberg's Williams-toned celebration of

> Brilliant green lights
> in factory transom windows,
> Beautiful!

is haunted by Blake-inflected anxiety:

> Why do I fear these lights?
> & smoking chimneys' Industry?
> Why see them less godly
> Than forest treetrunks
> & sunset orange moons?
> Why these cranes, less Edenly than Palmfronds?[23]

Arcadian longings, one suspects, are the root of the problem, the desire for "escape" to a world not ravaged by "time and flux and the intrusive reality of other minds."[24]

The visual pleasures of urban shepherds in Rome and New York who embrace the flux and flow of city life are the subject of poems by Pier Paolo Pasolini and Frank O'Hara, who cast themselves as peripatetic centers of cities whose streets are fields of desire. In Pasolini's *Roman Poems*, the poet-speaker finds a space that grants "The Privilege of Thinking" on a bus ride to the airport one "stupendous morning!" The bus passes "over the aqueduct banks," through a poor neighborhood, and then into "an outburst of sun on fields, grottos, caves / a natural baroque / with green laid on by a stingy Corot." The subject of this painterly pastoral is boys on horseback, riders and animals glistening in the sun; the horses' rumps are "delicious brown," the boys seemingly younger than the horses and unaware that "there's light / in the world around them." Headed one city evening "Toward the Caracalla Baths," Pasolini's poet-speaker encounters a man he imagines to be an actual shepherd, walking toward him "with bare chest, as if upon / his native Apennine slopes," out of a past of indeterminate "centuries smelling / of animals and holy ashes / from Berber countries," and "still warm with red sage, figs and olives."[25] The two poems exemplify divergent aspects of traditional pastoral attitudes – the desire for retreat and contemplation of the beauties of nature, and the casual meeting of shepherds in the "field" – here transposed to the city and more obviously laden with homoerotic desire.

"I can't even enjoy a blade of grass unless I know there's a subway handy, or a record store or some other sign that people do not totally *regret* life," the poet-speaker of O'Hara's "Meditations in an Emergency" (1954) cheekily protests after remarking that "all the greenery one needs" exists in New York and disavowing any "nostalgia for an innocent past of perverted acts in pastures."[26] In his urban milieu – buying gifts for weekend hosts in the Hamptons, cruising waterfront dives, or attending art gallery openings – O'Hara's studied ease suggests that high and low culture, cynicism, and naiveté are destined to coalesce in an urbane eclogue. Herbert Leibowitz cast O'Hara as "a Pan piping on city streets"; his friend John Ashbery recalled a poet who "juggle[d] the contradictory components of modern life into something like a livable space," accentuating a pastoral mood at once "lovely, corrupt, [and] wholesome."[27] In "A Step Away from Them" (1957), the poet-speaker ambles along the carnal streets of Manhattan

> where laborers feed their dirty
> glistening torsos sandwiches
> …
> 　　　　　　Then onto the
> avenue where skirts are flipping
> above heels and blow up over
> grates,

and through Times Square, where a group of Puerto Rican men make the afternoon "beautiful and warm." O'Hara might have been Pan, but an anecdote handed down from Plutarch says that Pan was not immortal. Death enters the poem when the mind flits from the men to a recollection of friends recently deceased, which gives the poem's title an overtone of foreboding – *et in arcadia ego* – then to a poster for the film *Bullfight* and a storage warehouse itself soon to be torn down, before it refocuses on "a glass of papaya juice" (further tropicalizing the city) that he will drink on the way "back to work."[28]

Nuyorican poet Victor Hernández Cruz moved from Puerto Rico to Manhattan and more thoroughly tropicalized his adopted city, as have other writers who have emigrated to the northern metropoles and rewritten them in the colors of their homelands. "A tropical wave has settled here," the poet-speaker announces in "Los New Yorks" (1973), "pulling the sun / With a rope"; the subway now runs to "Caguas" and the bus to "Aguas Buenas." "The Man Who Lived on the Last Floor" (1973), an elderly immigrant from Puerto Rico, casts mango seeds from the window of his sixth-floor apartment. They take root in the city and in the minds of men – in the head, in fact, of a passing policeman. In "RITMO 1" (1969), the poet-speaker and friends climb above the city on a summer night to

> rid[e] the roofs/look at the lights
> of palisades/the round circles in the black sky
> float all the way to the edge of the park,

all the while "quietly resting."[29] If the horizontal prospect is blocked in the cramped city, then vertical escape beckons, as The Drifters sang in their pop pastoral, "Up on the Roof" (1962).

Western travelers seeking a balance of nature and civilization they could not find at home have for centuries turned to warmer climes like "the Orient," usually projecting onto the landscape and indigenous customs at least as much as they derive from them. Mary Wortley Montagu, wife of the British Ambassador to the Sublime Porte in the early eighteenth century, found arcadian (indeed, even *Arcadian*) repose in Constantinople's Ottoman palaces, where

> galleries, which are numerous, and very large, are adorned with jars of flowers, and porcelain dishes of fruit of all sorts, so well done in plaster, and coloured in so lively a manner that it has an enchanting effect. The garden is suitable to the house, where arbours, fountains, and walks, are thrown together in agreeable confusion... 'Tis true their magnificence is of a very different taste from ours, and perhaps of a better. I am almost of the opinion that they have a right notion of life. They consume it in music, gardens, wine, and delicate eating while we are tormenting our brains with some scheme of politics... We die or grow old and decrepid before we can reap the fruit of our labors.[30]

As pastoral customarily has, this green world within the heart of empire functions as a critique of the urban world, even as Ottoman society as a whole is here imagined to be closer to that ideal than is "modernized" Britain. Near the end of the following century, French author and naval officer Pierre Loti recorded the pastoral beauty of Fez, even in winter, in his travel narrative, *Morocco* (1890):

> The old fanatical and somber town is bathed in the gold of all this sunlight; spread out at my feet, on a succession of hills and dales, it has taken on an aspect of unalterable and radiant peace; it looks almost smiling, almost pretty... A kind of ruddy radiance sleeps on the immobility of its ruins. And the air has suddenly become warm and tinged, giving an illusion of eternal summer.

Loti's depiction recalls Wordsworth's London in "Westminster Bridge," except that the ancient Moroccan city owes its beauty to ruined walls instead of polished domes, and one struggles to imagine a London whose women are so exoticized as to move with "[t]he air of startled gazelles."[31]

Writers native to "the Orient" engage this literary history of colonialism to repatriate such scenes. Two and a half centuries after Montagu, Ahmet Hamdi Tanpınar found the gardens and fountains on the grounds of

Istanbul's mosques, cemeteries, and palaces a portal from the westernizing, congested city of the Republican period to the Ottoman-era sites "where her heart is to be found," those works of "modest proportion" that present "the impression of having melted into the privacy of the city." Tanpınar's *Five Cities* (1946) devotes a chapter to the trees that "[a]ll travelers to Istanbul comment on… The Istanbuls of Lamartine, Gautier, and Lady Craven are full of trees and greenery, and a reader of Lamartine's '*Voyage en Orient*' [1843] often feels that the writer is describing a garden." Tanpınar called on these authors' testimonies to protest the sacrifice of public green space to development in mid-century Istanbul; reversing the direction of metaphoric transformation typical of urban pastoral, he lamented that "[t]he death of a tree is like the loss of a great work of architecture."[32]

Commenting on Tanpınar in a chapter on "The Melancholy of Ruins" in his own magisterial book on Istanbul, Orhan Pamuk argues that Tanpınar's citations of European travelers and descriptions of what he called "picturesque" and "paysage" Istanbul landscapes were part of a project to create for the Republican-period city a historical identity not dependent on its cosmopolitan landmarks.[33] This comment should not, however, be taken for an objection. Pamuk's own Istanbul is the city seen by western artists and writers, and filtered through Tanpınar and his contemporaries (notably the poet Yahya Kemal). That is to say, Pamuk's Istanbul is a city seen by melancholics: first the western travelers, who suffused the landscapes of an empire in decline with their own melancholy; then Tanpınar's generation, who enlisted that sentiment in a project to recover a historical identity; and now Pamuk himself, who argues that the melancholy – or *hüzün* – inherited from art, literature, and history, and woven into his own text and accompanying images, is a communal emotion that permeates and defines Istanbul.

Melancholy affected British writers at home, and as Raymond Williams shows us in *The Country and the City*, they frequently lamented the countryside's desecration and the physical, economic, and moral condition of Britain's industrial cities. Nor were they alone. Anxieties about the path of development produced the garden cities movement, a program of regional (city/countryside) planning first laid out in Sir Ebenezer Howard's *To-morrow: A Peaceful Path to Real Reform* (reissued four years later as *Garden Cities of To-morrow*) and the Scots botanist Patrick Geddes's *The Evolution of Cities* (1915); Geddes and his American disciple Lewis Mumford took the city's organic character rather more literally in their own work. Apprehension over the fate of the land is registered in E. M. Forster's *Howards End* (1910). Some of its characters regard urban railroad stations as portals to still-extant pastoral worlds. Mrs. Munt, for instance, imagines that "in Paddington, all Cornwall is latent and the remoter west;

down the inclines of Liverpool Street lie fenlands and the illimitable Broads; Scotland is through the pylons of Euston; Wessex behind the poised chaos of Waterloo." Yet when she travels toward Hilton in search of the country house at Howards End, she finds that the lay of the land has changed. She wonders if she is in "England or Suburbia?" – in a community with a history or a vague, traditionless extension of London.[34]

But on the June day that Clarissa Dalloway sets off to buy flowers for a dinner party, memory and the city excite a flurry of emotions, some rooted in the London present, others set at Bourton, the country estate where in the course of a years-ago summer Clarissa fell in love with Sally Seaton, Peter Walsh, and her future husband, the dependable if unexciting Richard. The present morning is "like the pulse of a perfect heart, life struck straight through the streets," Peter says to himself, but his own heart pains as he wanders those same London streets fighting the truth that he is no longer a lad. In *Mrs. Dalloway*, Virginia Woolf pits the empty, mechanical time of modernity kept by the leaden circles of Big Ben's chimes against experiential time and the eternal present of nature. The latter temporality is embodied by a musical voice "bubbling up without direction ... the voice of an ancient spring spouting from the earth." It belongs to a woman whose location "just opposite Regent Park Tube station" connects her to nature and the under-world. Flowing "[t]hrough all the ages," singing of love that endures even as "death's enormous sickle" harvests lives, the song sutures what clock time severs; it binds all who separately hear.[35] The novel thus triumphs over melancholy to prove that "urban experience, seen quite vividly in its abundant particularities, can provide the sense of invigoration, harmony with one's surroundings, and enrapturing aesthetic revelation that is traditionally associated with the green world of pastoral." For Clarissa, that sense she craves of connection to the world peaks in moments of "quasi-physical merging of self and scene" that comfort her with a quintessentially pastoral feeling that she can never truly vanish from the world.[36]

If children of the '60s left the city in search of that same deep feeling of connection to the land and other people, their own children reversed that exodus in pursuit of new pastoral dreams. In *Arcadia* (2012), Lauren Groff's novel about a rural intentional community, Brit, the protagonist, offers a theory of what lured his parents and why that desire can be sated in the city:

> it wasn't the country that was so beautiful about the whole Arcadian experi-
> ment, don't you see? It was the people, the interconnection, everyone relying
> on everyone else... [T]he same feeling exists now ... here, in the city, millions
> of people breathing the same air. This, here, now, is more utopia than utopia,
> more than your pretty little house out in the middle of the forest with only

woodchucks for neighbors… We've gone urban because we're all looking for what we lost… The closeness. The connection.[37]

These words, spoken out of a sense of imagined loss and a dream of recovery, betray the same romanticism that motivated his parents' return to nature. Yet the idealism would recreate the commune in "Occupy" encampments from New York's Zuccotti Park (the encampment of Occupy Wall Street in 2011–12) to Istanbul's Gezi Park (where protesters rallied to prevent the commercial development of an urban park in 2013). They also remind us that a pastoral attitude need not include real or imagined organic landscapes.

Brit's urban-pastoral dream starkly contrasts with the bleak realities of C. K. Williams' post-industrial urban pastorals – a falling-off even from the industrial pastoral of William Carlos Williams' *Paterson* – in which the "ruins" are human and live in neighborhoods that Brit's cohort might gentrify. In "From My Window" (1981), the poet-speaker recognizes two men, one wheelchair-bound, both drunk and "careening haphazardly" through a bleak Philadelphia streetscape. He then recalls an earlier moment when one of them

> went out to the lot and walked, paced
>   rather, almost ran, for how many hours.
> It was snowing, the city in that holy silence, the last we
>   have, when the storm takes hold,
> and he was making patterns that I at first thought were
>   circles, then realized made a figure eight,
> what must have been to him a perfect symmetry, but which,
>   from where I was, shivered, bent,
> and lay on its side: a warped, unclear infinity, slowly, as the
>   snow came faster, going out.
> Over and over again, his head lowered to the task, he
>   slogged the path he'd blazed,
> but the race was lost, his prints were filling faster than he
>   made them now, and I looked away,
> up across the skeletal trees to the tall center city buildings
>   some, though it was midnight,
> with all their offices still gleaming, their scarlet warning
>   beacons signaling erratically
> against the thickening flakes, their smoldering auras
>   softening portions of the dim, milky sky.
> In the morning, nothing: every trace of him effaced, all the
>   field pure white,
> its surface glittering, the dawn, glancing from its glaze,
>   oblique, relentless, unadorned.[38]

The remembered moment subtly resonates with Samuel Taylor Coleridge's meditative lyric, "Frost at Midnight" (1798), which also begins in a mood of deep isolation. Here, light from office towers replaces light from the stars and the moon and the man in the park Coleridge's son Hartley, who slept beside his father. This poem is certainly not assertively affirmative in the manner of "Frost at Midnight," in which translucent frost and icicles filled with moonlight invoke the poet's theology of the symbolic as the translucence of the eternal in the temporal, and Hartley's "gentle breathings, heard in this deep calm, / Fill up the interspersèd vacancies / And momentary pauses of the [poet-speaker's] thought."[39] "From My Window" is a political poem that inventories the urban condition: these are the lights of commerce – not God's creation and His promise – and the poet-speaker and his subject remain distant from, and anonymous to, each other. Yet it contains an unmistakable urban pastoral element in its handling of the winter landscape and its desire for communion with others. Absolution, such as it is, comes in the snow's erasure of the scene and the morrow's effacement of the memory, the untrammeled snow "glittering" in the dawn. Williams' poem offers none of the comforts of faith, but the empathetic viewer, the enveloping "holy silence," and the untrammeled snow to which they wake, all suggest something of a secular grace.

If Williams' concern is human connection within urban landscapes, others in the midst of the city are looking for a spot of repose whose pastoral *locus classicus* is probably Andrew Marvell's pastoral lyric, "The Garden" (1681). The African American poet Ed Roberson is a resolutely urban pastoralist who finds this treasured green world in a place of elemental unfussiness that is neither the American literary and political pastoral of a "New Hampshire nor Midwestern farm," nor the designer lifestyle of a "Hamptons garden," but a simple "street / pocket park," a product of 1960s-era urban development strategies for empty lots and interstitial spaces. In this green world removed from the noise of the city, but whose "simple quiet" is "definitely not the dead of no birds sing," the poet-speaker relaxes into what he calls the "bus stop posture in the interval / of nothing coming,"[40] thus weaving bucolic respite into the rhythm of city life.

The urban pastorals surveyed in this chapter exhibit a range of responses to the relation among the city, nature, and subjectivity, all of them informed by their historical and literary-historical moments. They show us that what Paul Alpers said about the multiplicity of pastoral modes is true of urban pastoral as well; its prospects are as broad as the ways of reflecting on, and reimagining, the human condition as it is expressed through, and in relation to, urban landscapes.

NOTES

1 Pastoral was not this one-dimensional, of course. Disruption and displacement are thematized in the first and ninth *Eclogues*, while early modern shepherds' literate and witty performances often conveyed coded expressions of personal ambition and commentary on court politics.

2 William Empson, *Some Versions of Pastoral* (Norfolk, CT: New Directions, 1960), p. 196.

3 Polybius, *The Histories*, trans. W. R. Paton, 6 vols., Loeb Classical Library (London: Heinemann, 1922), vol. 2, pp. 349–55.

4 Raymond Williams, *The Country and the City* (New York: Oxford University Press, 1973), p. 307.

5 Harry Berger, Jr., "The Renaissance Imagination: Second World and Green World," *Second World and Green World: Studies in Renaissance Fiction-Making* (Berkeley: University of California Press, 1990), p. 36.

6 Williams, *The Country and the City*, p. 20.

7 Paul Alpers, *What is Pastoral?* (Chicago: University of Chicago Press, 1996), pp. 50, 8.

8 Ezra Pound, "In a Station of the Metro," *Personae: The Shorter Poems of Ezra Pound*, rev. ed., ed. Lea Baechler and A. Walton Litz (New York: New Directions, 1990), p. 111.

9 John Hollander, "Landscape's Empire," in J. D. McClatchy, ed., *Poets on Painters: Essays on the Art of Painting by Twentieth-Century Poets* (Berkeley: University of California Press, 1988), pp. 355–6.

10 John Dyer, "The Ruins of Rome" (1741), *The Poems of John Dyer*, ed. Edward Thomas (London: T. Fisher Unwin, 1903), pp. 31, 32, 41.

11 *Spectator* 414 (June 25, 1712), Joseph Addison and Richard Steele, *The Spectator*, ed. Donald F. Bond, 5 vols. (Oxford: Clarendon Press, 1965), vol. 3, pp. 548–9.

12 William Wordsworth, "Composed upon Westminster Bridge, 3 September 1802," in *William Wordsworth*, ed. Stephen Gill (Oxford: Oxford University Press, 2010), p. 236.

13 David Ferry, *The Limits of Mortality* (Middletown, CT: Wesleyan University Press, 1959), p. 14. Wordsworth lamented "the increasing accumulation of men in cities" where life and labor "blunt the discriminating powers of the mind, and ... reduce it to a state of almost savage torpor," in his 1800 Preface to *Lyrical Ballads*. (William Wordsworth and Samuel Taylor Coleridge, *Lyrical Ballads*, ed. R. L. Brett and A. R. Jones [London: Routledge, 2005], p. 294.)

14 William Chapman Sharpe, *New York Nocturne: The City in Literature, Painting, and Photography, 1850–1950* (Princeton, NJ: Princeton University Press, 2008), p. 91.

15 Georg Trakl, "The Beautiful City," *Georg Trakl: Poems and Prose, a Bilingual Edition*, ed. and trans., Alexander Stillmark (Evanston, IL: Northwestern University Press, 2005), pp. 7–9.

16 James Schuyler, "February," *Collected Poems* (New York: Noonday, 1995), p. 4.

17 *Poèmes nocturnes* was Baudelaire's first working title for what became *Les Fleurs du mal*. (See Laure Katsaros, *New York-Paris: Whitman, Baudelaire, and the Hybrid City* [Ann Arbor: University of Michigan Press, 2012], p. 59.)

18 Charles Baudelaire, "The Swan," *The Flowers of Evil*, trans. Keith Waldrop (Middletown, CT: Wesleyan University Press, 2006), p. 116; "Morning Twilight," ibid., p. 135, translation modified by the authors.

19 Blaise Cendrars, section one of *To the Heart of the World*, in *The Complete Poems of Blaise Cendrars*, trans. Ron Padgett (Berkeley: University of California Press, 1992), p. 217.

20 Baudelaire, "Three Drafts of a Preface," *Flowers of Evil: A Selection*, ed. Marthiel and Jackson Mathews (New York: New Directions, 1955), p. xviii; Walt Whitman, "Crossing Brooklyn Ferry," *Leaves of Grass*, ed. Sculley Bradley and Harold W. Blodgett (New York: Norton, 1973), p. 160.

21 William Carlos Williams, *Paterson*, rev. ed., ed. Christopher MacGowan (New York: New Directions, 1992), pp. 57–8. Williams appears to commit the common error of conflating Priapus and Pan; Priapus's form is wholly human.

22 See, for example, "To Elsie" (1923), *The Collected Poems of William Carlos Williams*, 2 vols., ed. A. Walton Litz and Christopher MacGowan (New York: New Directions, 1986), vol. 1, p. 218.

23 Terrence Diggory, "Allen Ginsberg's Urban Pastoral," *College Literature* 27 (2000), 107, 115.

24 Berger, "Renaissance Imagination," p. 36, on the seductive danger of *all* green worlds.

25 Pier Paolo Pasolini, "The Privilege of Thinking," *Roman Poems*, trans. Lawrence Ferlinghetti and Francesca Valenti (San Francisco: City Lights, 2005), p. 27; "Toward the Caracalla Baths," ibid., pp. 35, 37.

26 Frank O'Hara, "Meditations in an Emergency," *The Collected Poems of Frank O'Hara*, ed. Donald Allen (Berkeley: University of California Press, 1995), p. 197.

27 Herbert Leibowitz, "A Pan Piping on City Streets: *The Collected Poems of Frank O'Hara*," in Jim Elledge, ed., *Frank O'Hara: To Be True to a City* (Ann Arbor: University of Michigan Press, 1990), p. 24; John Ashbery, Introduction, *Collected Poems of Frank O'Hara*, p. x.

28 O'Hara, "A Step Away from Them," *Collected Poems of Frank O'Hara*, pp. 257, 258, 258. "*Et in arcadia ego*," or "I, too, lived in Arcadia," is the legend that accompanies a skull in scores, if not hundreds, of Renaissance *memento mori* (remember that you will die) paintings.

29 Victor Hernández Cruz, "Los New Yorks," *Maraca: New and Selected Poems 1965–2000* (Minneapolis: Coffee House Press, 2001), pp. 52; "RITMO I," ibid., p. 46.

30 Mary Wortley Montagu, Letter to the Abbé Conti, 19 May 1718, *The Letters and Works*, 2 vols., ed. Lord Wharncliffe (London: Henry G. Bohn, 1861), vol. 1, pp. 369–70.

31 Pierre Loti, *Morocco* (London, T. W. Laurie, 1914), pp. 169, 205.

32 Ahmet Hamdi Tanpınar, "Three Sections from 'Istanbul' in *Beş Şehir (Five Cities)*," trans. Ruth Christie, *Texas Studies in Literature and Language* 54.4 (2012), 456, 461, 463,

33 Orhan Pamuk, *Istanbul: Memories and the City*, trans. Maureen Freely (New York: Vintage, 2006), p. 252.

34 E. M. Forster, *Howards End* (New York: Vintage, 1989), pp. 7, 12, 15.

35 Virginia Woolf, *Mrs. Dalloway* (San Diego: Harcourt, 1990), pp. 80–1.

36 Robert Alter, "Woolf: Urban Pastoral," *Imagined Cities: Urban Experience and the Language of the Novel* (New Haven, CT: Yale University Press, 2005), pp. 105, 112.

37 Lauren Groff, *Arcadia* (New York: Voice-Hyperion, 2012), p. 208.

38 C. K. Williams, "From My Window," *Collected Poems* (New York: Farrar, Straus, and Giroux, 2006), pp. 157, 158–9. Quoted by permission.

39 Samuel Taylor Coleridge, "Frost at Midnight," *The Complete Poems*, ed. William Keach (London: Penguin, 1997), p. 232.

40 Ed Roberson, "Urban Nature," *City Eclogue* (Berkeley, CA: Atelos, 2006), p. 83.

GUIDE TO FURTHER READING

Abraham, Julie. *Metropolitan Lovers: The Homosexuality of Cities*. Minneapolis: University of Minnesota Press, 2008.

Agathocleous, Tanya. *Urban Realism and the Metropolitan Imagination in the Nineteenth Century: Visible City, Invisible World*. Cambridge: Cambridge University Press, 2011.

Ahearn, Edward J. *Visionary Fictions, Apocalyptic Writing from Blake to the Modern Age*. New Haven, CT: Yale University Press, 1996.

Alter, Robert. *Imagined Cities: Urban Experience and the Language of the Novel*. New Haven, CT: Yale University Press, 2005.

Appelbaum, Robert. *Literature and Utopian Politics in Seventeenth-Century England*. Cambridge: Cambridge University Press, 2002.

Babelon, Jean Pierre. *Paris au XVIe siècle*. Paris: Diffusion Hachette, 1986.

Bagnall, R. S. "Alexandria: Library of Dreams." *Proceedings of the American Philosophical Society* 146 (2002), 348–62.

Banciu, Carmen-Francesca. *Berlin ist mein Paris*. Berlin: Rotbuch, 2007.

Barrows, Susanna. *Distorting Mirrors: Visions of the Crowd in Late Nineteenth-Century France*. New Haven, CT: Yale University Press, 1981.

Barta, Peter I. *Bely, Joyce, and Döblin: Peripatetics in the City Novel*. Gainesville: University Press of Florida, 1996.

Beaumont, Matthew, and Gregory Dart, eds. *Restless Cities*. London: Verso, 2010.

Benjamin, Walter. *The Arcades Project*. Ed. Rolf Tiedemann. Trans. Howard Eiland and Kevin McLaughlin. Cambridge, MA: Harvard University Press, 1999.

  Reflections: Essays, Aphorisms, Autobiographical Writing. Ed. Peter Demetz. Trans. Edmund Jephcott. New York: Schocken Books, 1986.

  The Writer of Modern Life: Essays on Baudelaire. Ed. Michael W. Jennings. Trans. Howard Eiland, Edmund Jephcott, Rodney Livingstone, and Harry Zohn. Cambridge, MA: Belknap-Harvard University Press, 2006.

Bennett, Michael, and David W. Teague. *The Nature of Cities: Ecocriticism and Urban Environments*. Tucson: University of Arizona Press, 1999.

Bentley, Nick. "Narratives of Cultural Space." *Contemporary British Fiction*. Edinburgh: Edinburgh University Press, 2008. Pp. 160–91.

Berman, Marshall. *All That Is Solid Melts Into Air: The Experience of Modernity*. New York: Penguin, 1982.

Bernstein, Carol. *The Celebration of Scandal: Toward the Sublime in Victorian Urban Fiction*. University Park: Pennsylvania State University Press, 1991.

Blanchard, Marc Eli. *In Search of the City: Engels, Baudelaire, Rimbaud*. Saratoga, NY: Amna Libri, 1985.

Bond, Erik. *Reading London: Urban Speculation and Imaginative Government in Eighteenth-Century London*. Columbus: Ohio State University Press, 2007.

Booker, M. Keith. *The Dystopian Impulse in Modern Literature: Fiction as Social Criticism*. Westport, CT: Greenwood, 1994.

Bowlby, Rachel. *Just Looking: Consumer Culture in Dreiser, Gisissing and Zola*. London: Methuen, 1985.

Boyer, M. Christine. *The City of Collective Memory*. Cambridge, MA: MIT Press, 1994.

  Dreaming the Rational City: The Myth of American City Planning. Cambridge, MA: MIT Press, 1986.

Brand, Dana M. *The Spectator and the City in Nineteenth Century American Literature*. New York: Cambridge University Press, 1991.

Brooker, Peter. *Modernity and Metropolis: Writing, Film and Urban Formations*. New York: Palgrave Macmillan, 2002.

  ed. *Modernism/Postmodernism*. London: Longman, 1988.

Burton, Richard D. E. *The Flaneur and His City: Patterns of Daily Life in Paris, 1815–1851*. Durham, UK: University of Durham Press, 1994.

Butterfield, Ardis, ed. *Chaucer and the City*. Cambridge: D. S. Brewer, 2006.

Calabi, Donatella, and Stephen Turk Christensen, eds. *Cities and Cultural Exchange in Europe, 1400–1700*. Vol. 2 of *Cultural Exchange in Early Modern Europe*. 4 vols. New York: Cambridge University Press, 2007.

Călinescu, Matei. *Five Faces of Modernity: Modernism, Avant-Garde, Decadence, Kitsch, Postmodernism*. Durham, NC: Duke University Press, 1987.

Caws, Mary Ann, ed. *City Images, Perspectives from Literature, Philosophy, and Film*. New York: Gordon and Breach, 1991.

Chaliand, Gérard, and Pierre Rageau. *The Penguin Atlas of Diasporas*. Trans. A. M. Barrett. New York: Viking, 1995.

Chambers, Iain. *Migrancy, Culture, Identity*. London: Routledge, 1994.

Chambers, Ross. "Baudelaire's Paris." In Rosemary Lloyd, ed. *The Cambridge Companion to Baudelaire*. Cambridge: Cambridge University Press, 2005. Pp. 101–16.

  Loiterature. Lincoln: University of Nebraska Press, 1999.

Chandler, James, and Kevin Gilmartin. *Romantic Metropolis: The Urban Scene of British Culture, 1780–1840*. Cambridge: Cambridge University Press, 1996.

Chauncey, George. *Gay New York: Gender, Urban Culture and the Making of the Gay Male World, 1890–1940*. New York: Basic, 1994.

Chevalier, Louis. *Classes laborieuses et classes dangereuses à Paris pendant la première moitié du XIXe siècle*. Paris: Pion, 1969.

Chisolm, Dianne. *Queer Constellations: Subcultural Space in the Wake of the City*. Minneapolis: University of Minnesota Press, 2005.

Coles, Robert, and Randy Testa. *Growing Up Poor: A Literary Anthology*. New York: New Press, 2002.

Connor, Steven. *Postmodernist Culture: An Introduction to Theories of the Contemporary*. Oxford: Blackwell, 1989.

Conrad, Peter. *The Art of the City: Views and Versions of New York*. New York: Oxford University Press, 1984.

Dart, Gregory. *Metropolitan Art and Literature, 1810–1840: Cockney Adventures*. Cambridge: Cambridge University Press, 2012.

——. ed. *Re-imagining the City*. Special issue of *Romanticism* 14.2 (2008), v–vi and 81–167.

Davis, Mike. *Planet of Slums*. New York: Verso, 2006.

de Certeau, Michel. *The Practice of Everyday Life*. Trans. Steven F. Rendall. Berkeley: University of California Press, 1984.

Debord, Guy. *The Society of the Spectacle*. Trans. Donald Nicholson-Smith. New York: Zone Books, 1994.

Den Tandt, Christophe. *The Urban Sublime in American Literary Naturalism*. Urbana: University of Illinois Press, 1998.

Dharwadker, Vinay. *Cosmopolitan Geographies: New Locations in Literature and Culture*. New York: Routledge, 2001.

Donald, James. *Imagining the Modern City*. London: Athlone Press, 1999.

Dougherty, Carol. *The Poetics of Colonization: From City to Text in Archaic Greece*. New York: Oxford University Press, 1993.

Dowling, Robert M. *Slumming in New York: From the Waterfront to Mythic Harlem*. Urbana: University of Illinois Press, 2007.

Drolet, Michael, ed. *The Postmodernism Reader: Foundational Texts*. London: Routledge, 1994.

Dubois, Jacques. *L'Assommoir de Zola. Société, discours, idéologie*. Paris: Larousse, 1973.

Dyos, Harold James, and Michael Wolff, eds. *The Victorian City: Images and Realities*. London: Routledge and Kegan Paul, 1973.

Eaton, Ruth. *Ideal Cities: Utopianism and the (Un)Built Environment*. New York: Thames & Hudson, 2002.

Edwards, Catharine. *Writing Rome: Textual Approaches to the City*. Cambridge: Cambridge University Press, 1996.

Elliot, Robert C. *The Shape of Utopia*: Oxford: Peter Lang, 2013.

Ellis, Markman. "Poetry and the City." In Christine Gerrard, ed. *The Blackwell Companion to Eighteenth-Century Poetry*. Oxford: Blackwell, 2006. Pp. 532–48.

Emperor, Jean-Yves. *Alexandria Rediscovered*. Trans. Margaret Maehler. London: British Museum Press, 1998.

Fanon, Frantz. *The Wretched of the Earth*. Trans. Constance Farrington. New York: Grove Press, 1963.

Feenberg, Andrew, and Jim Freedman. *When Poetry Ruled the Streets: The French Events of 1968*. Albany: State University New York Press, 2001.

Ferguson, Priscilla Parkhurst. *Paris as Revolution: Writing the Nineteenth-Century City*. Berkeley: University of California Press, 1994.

Fishman, Robert. *Urban Utopias of the Twentieth Century: Ebenezer Howard, Frank Lloyd Wright, Le Corbusier*. Cambridge, MA: MIT Press, 1982.

Flynn, Carol Houlihan. "Where the Wild Things Are: Guides to London's Transgressive Spaces." In Regina Hewitt and Pat Rogers, eds. *Orthodoxy and Heresy in Eighteenth-Century Society: Essays from the DeBartolo Conference*. Cranbury, NJ: Associated University Presses, 2002. Pp. 27–50.

Forderer, Christoph. *Die Großstadt im Roman. Berliner Großstadtdarstellungen zwischen Naturalismus und Moderne*. Wiesbaden: Deutscher Universitätsverlag, 1992.

Fordham, George. "Working class fiction across the century." In Robert L. Caserio, ed. *The Cambridge Companion to the Twentieth-Century English Novel*. Cambridge: Cambridge University Press, 2009.

Foucault, Michel. "Of Other Spaces." Trans. Jay Miskowiec. *Diacritics* 16 (1986), 22–7.

Gandal, Keith. *The Virtues of the Vicious: Jacob Riis, Stephen Crane, and the Spectacle of the Slum*. New York: Oxford University Press, 1997.

Ghent Urban Studies Team, ed. *The Urban Condition: Space, Community, and Self in the Contemporary Metropolis*. Rotterdam: 010 Publishers, 1999.

Giesecke, Annette Lucia. *The Epic City: Urbanism, Utopia, and the Garden in Ancient Greece and Rome*. Cambridge, MA: Harvard University Press, 2007.

Gilloch, Graeme. *Myth and Metropolis: Walter Benjamin and the City*. Cambridge: Polity Press, 1996.

Gleber, Anke. *The Art of Taking a Walk: Flanerie, Literature, and Film in Weimar Culture*. Princeton, NJ: Princeton University Press, 1999.

Gluck, Mary. "The Flâneur and the Aesthetic Appropriation of Urban Culture in Mid-19th-century Paris." *Theory, Culture & Society* 20.5 (2003), 53–80.

Popular Bohemia: Modernism and Urban Culture in Nineteenth-Century Paris. Cambridge, MA: Harvard University Press, 2005.

Graebner, Seth. *History's Place: Nostalgia and the City in French Algerian Literature*. Lanham, MD: Lexington Books, 2007.

Graña, César, and Marigay Graña. *On Bohemia: The Code of the Self-Exiled*. New Brunswick, NJ: Transaction, 1990.

Gray, Timothy. *Urban Pastoral: Natural Currents in the New York School*. Iowa City: University of Iowa Press, 2010.

Griffiths, Paul, and Mark S. R. Jenner, eds. *Londonopolis: Essays in the Social and Cultural History of Early Modern London*. Manchester, UK: University of Manchester Press, 2000.

Halbwachs, Maurice. *On Collective Memory*. Ed. and trans. Lewis A. Coser. Chicago: University of Chicago Press, 1992.

Hammond, Brean. "The City in Eighteenth-Century Poetry." In John Sitter, ed. *The Cambridge Companion to Eighteenth-Century Poetry*. Cambridge: Cambridge University Press, 2001. Pp. 83–108.

Harding, Desmond. *Writing the City: Urban Visions & Literary Modernism*. New York: Routledge, 2003.

Harkness, Deborah, and Jean Howard, eds. *The Great World of Early Modern London*. Special issue of *Huntington Library Quarterly* 71.1 (2008), 1–253.

Harris, W. V., and Giovanni Ruffini, eds. *Ancient Alexandria between Egypt and Greece*. Leiden: Brill, 2004.

Harvey, David. *The Condition of Postmodernity*, Oxford: Blackwell, 1990.

Paris, Capital of Modernity. New York: Routledge, 2003.

Haskell, Thomas. *The Emergence of Professional Social Science: The American Social Science Association and the Nineteenth Century Crisis of Authority*. Baltimore, MD: Johns Hopkins University Press, 1977.

Hatherley, Owen. *A New Kind of Bleak: Journeys through Urban Britain*. London: Verso, 2012.

Haywood, Ian. *Working-Class Fiction: From Chartism to Trainspotting*. Plymouth, UK: Nortcote House, 1997.

Heise, Thomas. *Urban Underworlds: A Geography of Twentieth-Century American Literature and Culture*. New Brunswick, NJ: Rutgers University Press, 2011.

Hell, Julia, and Andreas Schönle. *Ruins of Modernity*. Durham, NC: Duke University Press, 2010.

Herbert, Caroline, ed. *Postcolonial Cities: South Asia*. Special issue of *Moving Worlds: A Journal of Transcultural Writings* 31.2 (2013), 1–182.

Herring, Scott. *Queering the Underworld: Slumming, Literature, and the Undoing of Lesbian and Gay History*. Chicago: University of Chicago Press, 2007.

Highmore, Ben. *Cityscapes: Cultural Readings in the Material and Symbolic City*. New York: Palgrave Macmillan, 2005.

Hirst, Anthony, and Michael Silk, eds. *Alexandria: Real and Imagined*. Aldershot, UK: Ashgate, 2004.

Hoffman, Eva. *Lost in Translation: Life in a New Language*. New York: Dutton, 1989.

Holmes, Amanda. *City Fictions: Language, Body, and Spanish American Urban Space*. Lewisburg, PA: Bucknell University Press, 2007.

Holston, James. *Cities and Citizenship*. Durham, NC: Duke University Press, 1998.

Holstun, James. *A Rational Millennium: Puritan Utopias of Seventeenth-Century England and America*. Oxford: Oxford University Press, 1987.

Houlbrook, Matt. *Queer London: Perils and Pleasures in the Sexual Metropolis, 1918–1957*. Chicago: University of Chicago Press, 2005.

Howard, Jean. *Theatre of a City: The Places of London Comedy, 1598–1642*. Philadelphia: University of Pennsylvania Press, 2009.

Hughes, Jonathan, and Simon Sadler, eds. *Non-Plan: Essays on Freedom, Participation and Change in Modern Architecture and Urbanism*. Oxford: Architectural Press, 2000.

Hutcheon, Linda. *A Poetics of Postmodernism*. London: Routledge, 1988.

Huyssen, Andreas. *Present Pasts: Urban Palimpsests and the Politics of Memory*. Stanford, CA: Stanford University Press, 2006.

Jacobs, Jane M. *Edge of Empire: Postcolonialism and the City*. London: Routledge, 2002.

Jameson, Fredric. *Archaeologies of the Future: The Desire Called Utopia and Other Science Fictions*. London: Verso, 2005.

Postmodernism, or, The Cultural Logic of Late Capitalism. London: Verso, 1991.

Jencks, Charles. *Post-Modernism: The New Classicism in Art and Architecture*. London: Academy Editions, 1987.

The Story of Post-Modernism: Five Decades of the Ironic, Iconic and Critical in Architecture. London: Wiley, 2011.

Jenkyns, Richard. *The Legacy of Rome: A New Appraisal*. Oxford: Oxford University Press, 1992.

Jervis, John. *Exploring the Modern: Patterns of Western Culture and Civilization*. Oxford: Blackwell Publishers, 1998.

Kaiser, Charles. *The Gay Metropolis, 1940–1996*. London: Weidenfeld & Nicolson, 1998.

Katsaros, Laure. *New York-Paris: Whitman, Baudelaire, and the Hybrid City*. Ann Arbor: University of Michigan Press, 2012.

Keating, P. J. *The Working Classes in Victorian Fiction*. London: Routledge, 1971.

Klimasmith, Elizabeth. *At Home in the City: Urban Domesticity and the Modern Subject in American Literature and Culture, 1850–1930.* Lebanon, NH: University Press of New England, 2005.

Knapp, Jeffrey. *An Empire Nowhere: England, America and Literature from* Utopia *to* The Tempest. Berkeley: University of California Press, 1992.

Ladd, Brian. *The Ghosts of Berlin: Confronting German History in the Urban Landscape.* Chicago: University of Chicago Press, 1997.

Larmour, David H. J., and Diana Spencer, eds. *The Sites of Rome: Time, Space, Memory.* New York: Oxford University Press, 2007.

Latham, Rob. "The Urban Question in New Wave SF." In Mark Bould and China Miéville, eds. *Red Planets: Marxism and Science Fiction.* London: Pluto, 2009. Pp. 178–95.

Lauster, Martina. *Sketches of the Nineteenth Century: European Journalism and Its Physiologies, 1830–50.* New York: Palgrave Macmillan, 2007.

   "Walter Benjamin's Myth of the Flâneur." *Modern Language Review* 102 (2007), 139–56.

Le Corbusier (Charles-Édouard Jeanneret). *The City of Tomorrow and Its Planning.* Trans. Frederick Etchells. New York: Dover, 1987.

Lefebvre, Henry. *Critique of Everyday Life.* 2 vols. Trans. John Moore. London: Verso, 1991–2002.

LeGates, Richard T., and Frederic Stout, eds. *The City Reader.* 3rd ed. London: Routledge, 2003.

Lehan, Richard. *The City in Literature: An Intellectual and Cultural History.* Berkeley: University of California Press, 1998.

Leontis, Artemis. *Topographies of Hellenism: Mapping the Homeland.* Ithaca, NY: Cornell University Press, 1995.

Leroy, Claude. *Le Mythe de la passante: De Baudelaire à Mandiargues.* Paris: Presses Universitaires de France, 1999.

Leslie, Marina. *Renaissance Utopias and the Problem of History.* Ithaca, NY: Cornell University Press, 1998.

Levin, Joanna. *Bohemia in America, 1858–1920.* Stanford, CA: Stanford University Press, 2010.

Loraux, Nicole. *Born of the Earth: Myth and Politics in Athens.* Trans. Selina Stewart. Ithaca, NY: Cornell University Press, 2000.

   The Divided City: On Memory and Forgetting in Ancient Athens. Trans. Corinne Pache and Jeff Fort. New York: Zone Books, 2006.

   The Invention of Athens: the Funeral Oration in the Classical City. Trans. Alan Sheridan. Cambridge, MA: Harvard University Press, 1986.

Lorcin, Patricia. *Historicizing Colonial Nostalgia: European Women's Narratives of Algeria and Kenya, 1900–Present.* New York: Palgrave Macmillan, 2012.

Lynch, Kevin. *The Image of the City.* Cambridge, MA: MIT Press, 1960.

Machor, James L. *Pastoral Cities: Urban Ideals and the Symbolic Landscape of America.* Madison: University of Wisconsin Press, 1987.

Manley, Lawrence. *Literature and Culture in Early Modern London.* Cambridge: Cambridge University Press, 1995.

Manuel, Frank E., and Fritzie Manuel. *Utopian Thought in the Western World.* Cambridge, MA: Harvard University Press, 1979.

Marcus, Sharon. *Apartment Stories: City and Home in Nineteenth-Century Paris and London*. Berkeley: University of California Press, 1999.

Massey, Doreen. *Space, Place and Gender*, Cambridge: Polity Press, 1994.

Mayne, Alan. *The Imagined Slum: Newspaper Representation in Three Cities, 1870–1914*. Leicester, UK: Leicester University Press, 1993.

McCulloch, Fiona. *Cosmopolitanism in Contemporary British Fiction: Imagined Identities*. New York: Palgrave Macmillan, 2012.

McLeod, John. *Postcolonial London: Rewriting the Metropolis*. London: Routledge, 2004.

McNamara, Kevin R. *Urban Verbs: Arts and Discourses of American Cities*. Stanford, CA: Stanford University Press, 1996.

Mee, Jon. *Conversable Worlds: Literature, Contention, & Community, 1762–1830*. Oxford: Oxford University Press, 2011.

Mehrez, Samia. *The Literary Atlas of Cairo: One Hundred Years on the Streets of the City*. Oxford: Oxford University Press, 2011.

Merrim, Stephanie. *The Spectacular City: Mexico and Colonial Hispanic Literary Culture*. Austin: University of Texas Press, 2010.

Merritt, J. F., ed. *Imagining Early Modern London*. Cambridge: Cambridge University Press, 2000.

Miles, Malcolm. *Cities and Cultures*. London: Routledge, 2007.

Urban Avant-Gardes, London: Routledge, 2004.

Montandon, Alain. *Promenades nocturnes*. Paris: L'Harmattan, 2009.

Moylan, Tom. *Scraps of the Untainted Sky: Science Fiction, Utopia, Dystopia*. Boulder, CO: Westview Press, 2000.

Mumford, Lewis. *The City in History: Its Origins, Its Transformations, and Its Prospects*. New York: Harcourt, 1961.

Naaman, Mara. *Urban Space in Contemporary Egyptian Literature: Portraits of Cairo*. New York: Palgrave Macmillan, 2011.

Nesci, Catherine. *Le Flâneur et les flâneuses. Les femmes et la ville à l'époque romantique*. Grenoble: Université Stendhal, 2007.

Newman, Karen. *Cultural Capitals: Early Modern London and Paris*. Princeton, NJ: Princeton University Press, 2007.

Newmark, Kevin. "Who Needs Poetry? Baudelaire, Benjamin, and the Modernity of 'Le Cygne.'" *Comparative Literature* 63.3 (2011), 269–90.

Nuttall, Sarah, and Achille Mbembe, eds. *Johannesburg: The Elusive Metropolis*. Durham, NC: Duke University Press, 2008.

Nye, David E. *American Technological Sublime*. Cambridge, MA: MIT Press, 1994.

O'Byrne, Alison, ed. *London Scenes*. Special issue of *London Journal* 37.3 (2012), 149–251.

Ogborn, Miles. *Spaces of Modernity: London's Geographies, 1680–1780*. New York: Guildford Press, 1998.

O'Sullivan, Timothy M. *Walking in Roman Culture*. Cambridge: Cambridge University Press, 2011.

Parsons, Deborah L. "Flâneur or Flâneuse: Mythologies of Modernity." *New Formations* 38 (Summer 1999), 91–100.

Streetwalking the Metropolis: Women, the City, and Modernity. Oxford: Oxford University Press, 2000.

Pecora, Vincent. *Households of the Soul*. Baltimore, MD: Johns Hopkins University Press, 1997.

Peer, Larry H. *Romanticism and the City*. New York: Palgrave Macmillan, 2011.

Perl, Jed. *New Art City: Manhattan at Mid-Century*. New York: Knopf, 2005.

Perloff, Marjorie. *The Futurist Moment: Avant-Garde, Avant Guerre, and the Language of Rupture*. Chicago: University of Chicago Press, 1986.

Pillorget, René. *Paris sous les premiers Bourbons, 1594–1661*. Paris: Diffusion Hachette, 1988.

Pinder, David. *Visions of the City*. Edinburgh: Edinburgh University Press, 2005.

Pinkney, David. *Napoleon III and the Rebuilding of Paris*. Princeton, NJ: Princeton University Press, 1972.

Poovey, Mary. *Making a Social Body: British Cultural Form, 1830–1864*. Chicago: University of Chicago Press, 1995.

Porter, James I., ed. *Classical Pasts: The Classical Traditions of Greece and Rome*. Princeton, NJ: Princeton University Press, 2006.

Pradeau, Jean-François. *Plato and the City: A New Introduction to Plato's Political Thought*. Trans. Janet Lloyd. Exeter, UK: University of Exeter Press, 2002.

Prendergast, Christopher. *Paris and the Nineteenth Century*. Oxford: Blackwell, 1992.

Primorac, Ranka, ed. *African City Textualities*. Abingdon, UK: Routledge, 2010.

Rangel, Cecelia Enjuto. *Cities in Ruins: The Politics of Modern Poetics*. West Lafayette, IN: Purdue University Press, 2010.

Rice, Shelley. *Parisian Views*. Cambridge, MA: MIT Press, 1997.

Richards, David, ed. *Postcolonial Cities: Africa*. Special issue of *Moving Worlds* 5.1 (2005), 1–183.

Robins, Kevin. "Prisoners of the City: Whatever Could a Postmodern City Be?" In Erica Carter, James Donald, and Judith Squires, eds. *Space and Place: Theories of Identity and Location*. London: Lawrence & Wishart, 1993. Pp. 303–30.

Rosenau, Helen. *The Ideal City in its Architectural Evolution*. London: Routledge and Kegan Paul, 1959.

Ross, Kristin. *The Emergence of Social Space: Rimbaud and the Paris Commune*. London: Verso, 2008.

Rotella, Carlo. *October Cities: The Redevelopment of Urban Literature*. Berkeley: University of California Press, 1998.

Rowe, Colin, and Fred Koetter. *Collage City*. Cambridge, MA: MIT Press, 1983.

Sadler, Simon. *The Situationist City*. Cambridge, MA: MIT Press, 1999.

Said, Edward. *Culture and Imperialism*. New York: Knopf, 1993.

   Out of Place: A Memoir. New York: Knopf, 1999.

Sandhu, Sukhdev. *London Calling: How Black and Asian Writers Imagined a City*. London: Harper Collins, 2003.

Sanouillet, Michel. *Dada in Paris*. Rev. ed. Trans. Sharmila Ganguly. Cambridge, MA: MIT Press, 2012.

Sanyal, Debarati. *The Violence of Modernity: Baudelaire, Irony, and the Politics of Form*. Baltimore, MD: Johns Hopkins University Press, 2006.

Saxonhouse, Arlene W. *Fear of Diversity: The Birth of Political Science in Ancient Greek Thought*. Chicago: University of Chicago Press, 1992.

Schofield, Malcolm. *Saving the City: Philosopher-Kings and Other Classical Paradigms*. London: Routledge, 1999.

Scully, Stephen. *Homer and the Sacred City*. Ithaca, NY: Cornell University Press, 1990.

Sennett, Richard. *The Conscience of the Eye: The Design and Social Life of Cities*. New York: Knopf, 1990.

The Fall of Public Man. New York: Knopf, 1977.

Sennett, Richard, ed. *Classic Essays in the Culture of Cities*. Englewood Cliffs, NJ: Prentice Hall, 1969.

Seyhan, Azade. "From Istanbul to Berlin: Stations on the Road to a Transcultural/Translational Literature." *German Politics and Society* 23 (2005), 152–70.

Writing Outside the Nation. Princeton, NJ: Princeton University Press, 2001.

Sharpe, William C. *New York Nocturne: The City After Dark in Literature, Painting, and Photography, 1850–1950*. Princeton, NJ: Princeton University Press, 2008.

Unreal Cities: Urban Figurations in Wordsworth, Baudelaire, Whitman, Eliot, and Williams. Baltimore, MD: Johns Hopkins University Press, 1990.

Sharpe, William C., and Leonard Wallock, eds. *Visions of the Modern City: Essays in History, Art and Literature*. Baltimore, MD: Johns Hopkins University Press, 1987.

Shattuck, Roger. *The Banquet Years*. New York: Random House, 1955.

Smith, Karl Ashley. *Dickens and the Unreal City*. Houndmills, UK: Palgrave Macmillan, 2008.

Soja, Edward W. *Postmetropolis: Critical Studies of Cities and Regions*. Oxford: Blackwell, 2000.

Thirdspace: Journeys to Los Angeles and Other Real-and-Imagined Places. Oxford: Blackwell, 1996.

Spears, Monroe. *Dionysus and the City: Modernism in Twentieth-Century Poetry*. New York: Oxford University Press, 1970.

Starr, Deborah. *Remembering Cosmopolitan Egypt: Literature, Culture, and Empire*. Oxford: Routledge, 2009.

Stauth, Georg, and Bryan S. Turner. *Nietzsche's Dance: Resentment, Reciprocity and Resistance in Social Life*. Oxford: Basil Blackwell, 1985.

Stephens, Susan A. *Seeing Double: Intercultural Poetics in Ptolemaic Alexandria*. Berkeley: University of California Press, 2003.

Stierle, Karlheinz. "Baudelaire and the Tradition of the Tableau de Paris," *New Literary History* 11.2 (1980), 345–61.

Tabbi, Joseph. *The Postmodern Sublime: Technology and American Writing from Mailer to Cyberpunk*. Ithaca, NY: Cornell University Press, 1995.

Tafuri, Manfredo. *The Sphere and the Labyrinth: Avant-Gardes and Architecture from Piranesi to the 1970s*. Trans. Pellegrino d'Acierno and Robert Connolly. Cambridge, MA: MIT Press, 1990.

Tanner, Tony. *Venice Desired*. Oxford: Blackwell, 1992.

Terdiman, Richard. *Present Past: Modernity and the Memory Crisis*. Ithaca, NY: Cornell University Press, 1993.

Tester, Keith, ed. *The Flâneur*. London: Routledge, 1994.

Timms, Edward, and David Kelley. *Unreal City: Urban Experience in Modern European Literature and Art*. Manchester, UK: Manchester University Press, 1985.

Upstone, Sara. *Spatial Politics in the Postcolonial Novel*. Farnham, UK: Ashgate, 2009.

Vaillancourt, Daniel. *Les urbanités Parisiennes au XVIIe siècle: le livre du trottoir.* Farnham, Québec: Les Presses de l'Université Laval, 2009.

Vaillant, Alain. "Baudelaire, artiste moderne de la 'poésie-journal.'" In Guillaume Pinson and Maxime Prévost, eds. *Penser la littérature par la presse.* Special issue of *Études littéraires* 40.3 (2009), 43–60.

Vaneigem, Raoul. *The Revolution of Everyday Life.* 2d ed. Trans. Donald Nicholson-Smith. London: Rebel Books and Left Bank Press, 1994.

Varma, Rashmi. *The Postcolonial City and Its Subjects: London, Nairobi, Bombay.* London: Routledge, 2011.

Vasudevan, Ravi, et al. *Sarai Reader 02: The Cities of Everyday Life.* Delhi: Sarai, The New Media Initiative, 2002.

Versluys, Kristiaan. *The Poet in the City: Chapters in the Development of Urban Poetry in Europe and the United States, 1800–1930.* Tübingen: Gunter Narr Verlag, 1987.

Vrettos, Theodore. *Alexandria, City of the Western Mind.* New York: Free Press, 2001.

Walkowitz, Judith R. *City of Dreadful Delight: Narratives of Sexual Danger in Late-Victorian London.* Chicago: University of Chicago Press, 1992.

Wall, Cynthia. *The Literary and Cultural Spaces of Restoration London.* Cambridge: Cambridge University Press, 1998.

Walonen, Michael K. *Writing Tangier in the Postcolonial Transition: Space and Power in North African Literature.* Burlington, VT: Ashgate, 2011.

Wark, McKenzie. *The Beach Beneath the Street: The Everyday Life and Glorious Times of the Situationist International.* London: Verso, 2011.

Watson, Jini Kim. *The New Asian City: Three-Dimensional Fictions of Space and Urban Form.* Minneapolis: University of Minnesota Press, 2011.

Welch, Ellen R. "Cultural Capital: Paris, Cosmopolitanism, and the Novel in Jean de Préchac's L'Illustre Parisienne." *Journal for Early Modern Cultural Studies* 9.2 (2009), 1–24.

Whyte, William H. *City: Rediscovering the Center.* New York: Anchor-Doubleday, 1988.

Williams, Raymond. *The Country and the City.* New York: Oxford University Press, 1973.

Wilson, Elizabeth. *Bohemians: The Glamorous Outcasts.* London, I B Tauris, 2003.
Hallucinations: Life in the Post-Modern City. London: Hutchinson Radius, 1988.
"The Invisible Flâneur." *New Left Review* 191 (1992), 90–110.
The Sphinx in the City: Urban Life, the Control of Disorder, and Women. Berkeley: University of California Press, 1991.

Winkler, Michael, ed. *Deutsche Literatur im Exil 1933–1945. Texte und Dokumente.* Stuttgart: Reclam, 1977.

Wirth-Nesher, Hana. *City Codes: Reading the Modern Urban Novel.* Cambridge: Cambridge University Press, 1996.

Wolff, Janet. "The Invisible Flâneuse: Women and the Literature of Modernity." *Feminine Sentences: Essays on Women and Culture.* Berkeley: University of California Press, 1990. Pp. 34–50.

Wood, Paul, ed. *The Challenge of the Avant-Garde*. New Haven, CT: Yale University Press, 1999.

Woods, Gregory. *A History of Gay Literature: The Male Tradition*. New Haven, CT: Yale University Press, 1998.

"Queer London in Literature." *Changing English* 14.3 (2007), 257–70.

Cambridge Companions to...